MW00637837

FAITH ON TRIAL

FAITH ON TRIAL

*Mary Baker Eddy, Christian Science
and the First Amendment*

PLAIDSWEDE PUBLISHING
Concord, New Hampshire

Designed and composed in Fournier MT at Hobblebush Design Brookline, New Hampshire (www.hobblebush.com)

Printed in the United States of America

ISBN 978-0-9889176-8-2

Library of Congress Control Number: 2014948358

Published by:

P L A I D S W E D E   P U B L I S H I N G

P.O. Box 269 • Concord, New Hampshire 03302-0269

www.plaidswede.com

To the volunteers at the
New Hampshire Historical Society

CONTENTS

ACKNOWLEDGMENTS

The idea for this book came from my years as library director at the New Hampshire Historical Society, where much of the material for the book resides. As I became aware of the existence of the Chandler Papers, Streeter material, and Eddy's writings and biographies, I thought a book on the "next friends case" would be the perfect project for my retirement, almost like "low-hanging fruit." Once I got into the research, however, I realized the limitations of my own background in the antebellum period of U.S. history and the need to broaden my knowledge of religious history, the progressive era, and yellow journalism. Fortunately, help was available from many sources.

At the New Hampshire Historical Society, librarian Bill Copeley and my successor as library director, Sarah Hays, were always helpful. My colleagues at the society—Bill Dunlap, Joan Desmarais, Donna-Belle Garvin, Wes Balla, Anne Hamilton, and Del Delampan—also expressed interest and encouragement. Researching the subject brought me to the Mary Baker Eddy Library in Boston, where librarian Judy Huenneke guided me through the process of finding materials. Since many of Eddy's letters are copyrighted by the Mary Baker Eddy Collection, Sally Ulrich, copyright and trademark administrator, helped me attain the necessary permission. Curator Pamela Winstead assisted in the use of photographs found at the Mary Baker Eddy Library. Ralph Copper, a retired official of the First Church of Christ, Scientist, generously shared with me his extensive collection of materials. Mary Searles, librarian at the New Hampshire Law Library, also helped me locate materials.

My limited knowledge of Christian Science was greatly expanded by friendship with Christian Scientists Bill Treadwell and Patsy Watt. Patsy also read and critiqued the manuscript, as did William Upton, whose encyclopedic knowledge of New Hampshire history and legal history was invaluable. John Rule, who volunteers at the New Hampshire Historical Society, provided the digital photographs from the society's collection. In fact, this book is dedicated to the many volunteers who give of their time and expertise to the New Hampshire Historical Society and similar nonprofit organizations. It is only through the efforts of volunteers that such organizations are able to remain in existence as the volunteers provide for free work that otherwise would be expensive and prohibitive within the organizations' limited budgets. I am also grateful to the team at Plaidswede, particularly George Geers, the publisher, for his confidence in me and for his support. Martha Carlson-Bradley demonstrated patience and persistence in guiding me through the tedious editing process, and Sid Hall's expertise are on display in the book design and layout. While thanking all of these people for their assistance and advice, I wish to make it clear that any errors in the text or in interpretation are entirely my own.

PREFACE

I n the category "truth is stranger than fiction" is the case of *Eddy v. Frye*, argued before the Merrimack County Superior Court in Concord, New Hampshire, in 1907. Ostensibly, the case was about who should care for an eighty-five-year-old woman: her estranged son and adopted son, or the people who had surrounded her for years. But in reality, this was a heresy trial in civil court. The plaintiffs in the case were more concerned about discrediting the religious doctrine of the old woman, Mary Baker Eddy, and the religion she founded, Christian Science, than they were about caring for her in old age. In fact, the case was brought before the public by a great newspaper, litigated by a well-known progressive politician, and promoted by such famous Americans as Mark Twain, Willa Cather, and Joseph Pulitzer. The last heresy trial in the United States would test whether a new religious movement would be banned for teaching a reportedly dangerous doctrine, or whether the First Amendment to the U. S. Constitution truly protected the right of every American to believe and practice whatever religion they chose.

The fact that the trial took place in the sleepy capital city of Concord, New Hampshire, population less than twenty thousand, explains in part why it has received so little attention from historians in the years since the litigation ended in 1912. But in the years 1906 to 1912, every prominent American newspaper covered the story with front-page headlines and frequent editorials arguing one side of the case or the other. To Concord and New Hampshire, the case of Mary

Baker Eddy and her "next friends"—that is, plaintiffs who attempt to gain guardianship over an incompetent person—produced more media coverage than any other event in the state's history, including the nomination and election of Concord resident Franklin Pierce as president of the United States in 1852 and the tragedy of Christa McAuliffe, also from Concord, the first teacher in space, who died in the space shuttle *Challenger* disaster in January 1986.

In 1907, the only media were newspapers and magazines, and these were the days of a muckraking press and yellow journalism seeking out scandalous stories to titillate the American reader in order to sell copies. It was in this atmosphere that Concord resident Mary Baker Eddy and her religion were relentlessly probed and dissected, the press coverage ultimately leading to the bringing of what was called the "next friends case," which dragged the secluded founder of Christian Science before the public eye to determine her well-being and placed her religious views on trial in the courts and public opinion. In fact, litigation continued after Eddy's death, as the next friends contested her will.

Full disclosure requires me to state that I am not a Christian Scientist, and, in fact, have never been a particularly religious person, having become many years ago a lapsed Presbyterian who can best be described today as an agnostic. It is also important to state that I am not an attorney. Yet, in spite of these two handicaps, as a trained historian and author, I am attempting to tell the story of this important series of events because it has been over one hundred years since this litigation ended, and no one else has attempted to place the several next friends cases in their historical context.

One advantage I do have is knowledge of and access to the bulk of materials about the case, because of my former position as library director of the New Hampshire Historical Society. The society's library contains at least ten archival boxes of the letters and papers of William E. Chandler, senior attorney for the next friends, archives solely relating to this case and his role in it. Mary Baker Eddy's lead attorney, Frank S. Streeter, also left a box of materials about the case to the New Hampshire Historical Society, along with thirty-two albums of related newspaper clippings from around the nation. Other material resides at the Mary Baker Eddy Library in Boston and in the publications of the Longyear Museum outside of Boston. While biographers of Mary Baker Eddy have accessed this material and have written about the case in their books about Eddy, they were always focused on her life and not on the historical context of the next friends case. The reader will note that my perspective often seems to be from the plaintiffs' side of the case. The amount of evidence left by Chandler makes this perspective practically inevitable, but it is also fortuitous to have so much material relating to the motives of the plaintiffs, their activities and thoughts, and the role of the media in promoting the case. It is my hope that this study adds to a better understanding of what the United States and the American people were like a hundred years ago, of the important and changing role of the media in shaping public opinion, and of the nature of the progressives and the reforms promoted by them.

A Note on Textual Usages

Quotations from original sources are used throughout the narrative. No attempt is made to acknowledge or correct errors in the original sources. They are presented here exactly as they appear in the original. In most books about Christian Science, Mary Baker Eddy is referred to as "Mrs. Eddy." In keeping with current practice—except in quoted material—she is referred to here as "Eddy."

FAITH ON TRIAL

= 1 =

INTRODUCTION

The headline in the Sunday, October 28, 1906, *New York World* read, "Mrs. Mary Baker G. Eddy Dying; Footman and 'Dummy' Control Her." The lengthy exposé that followed went on to claim that the reclusive eighty-five-year-old founder and leader of the Church of Christ, Scientist, was dying of cancer and that another woman "impersonate[d] her in the Streets of Concord," New Hampshire, where the most famous woman in America had lived since 1889. According to the article, Eddy was under the control of her "Secretary-Footman" Calvin A. Frye, who, along with her "coterie," also controlled her fortune, estimated at $15 million, with an annual income of $1 million.[1]

Two reporters from the *World*, Slaght and Lithchild, had interviewed Eddy on October 15 at her home, Pleasant View, in Concord. They claimed that Eddy braced herself, "her hands on the edge of a heavy table," that she appeared "more dead than alive," and that she "was a skeleton, her hollow cheeks, thick with red paint, and the fleshless, hairless bones above the sunken eyes penciled in jet black." She appeared "pitifully emaciated," and "her weakness was pathetic." It was obvious to the reporters "that the unfortunate old woman had been doped and galvanized [with a battery] for the ordeal of identification." The reporters noted, "But it was equally clear that the utmost

3

stimulation could not keep the tortured woman upon her feet much longer." The reporters brought a neighbor of Eddy's with them to help identify her. The old woman greeted the neighbor, but he professed to be "astonished at her feebleness." The reporters stated, "She is a living corpse."[2]

The intrepid reporters also determined to prove that it was not the feeble Eddy who appeared each day to the residents of Concord on an afternoon carriage ride through the capital city. The reporters posted themselves along the usual route, and as the carriage passed by, one stepped to the right to look through the window. Immediately, the passenger in the carriage pulled a parasol over to block the view. At that moment the other reporter drove by in a carriage and had a clear view of the rider's face through the other window. The two men stated, "The woman in the Eddy carriage was younger than the aged founder of Christian Science by many years." They determined that the impersonator was Pamelia J. Leonard of Brooklyn, New York, a Christian Science reader who had been called to Pleasant View by Eddy several years before.[3]

More charges were made in the multipart article. Questions were raised about Eddy's wealth. According to the reporters, she had an annual income of $1 million, but no one knew where the money was. Supposedly, it was dispensed to various charities, but no record of these charities could be found. Finally, it was claimed that Eddy was under the care of a Boston physician, a cancer specialist. This was possibly the most damning charge of all, in that everyone knew that Christian Scientists disdained medical treatment, believing solely in the power of mental healing. If it could be proved that the founder and leader of the religion was receiving medical treatment from a worldly physician, what would it mean to the faithful who ascribed to the tenets of the religion? In all of their investigations, the *World*'s reporters had faced obstruction from the citizens of Concord, "this most conservative of New Hampshire cities," which was "absolutely dominated by the aged occupant of Pleasant View and her man Frye." To every question about Eddy, Concord citizens responded, "She is alive and hearty. You can see her every day in her carriage." According to the *World*, anyone who would tell the truth about Eddy was "sure to lose his job." Even the police claimed they would arrest anyone who "tried to take a picture of Mrs. Eddy's carriage."[4]

The fact that none of the charges made by the *World* were remotely true was of little concern to Joseph Pulitzer and the editors of the paper. In the age of yellow journalism, their one goal was to sell newspapers. With a daily circulation of over seven hundred thousand, the *World* had brought wealth and power to the paper and its owner through the sensationalism that characterized its contents. But attacking a little old lady living quietly in a remote corner of New England proved to be an abuse that would come to mark the beginning of the end of what Stephen J. Diner has called "the frenzy for journalistic revelations" that characterized the age of muckraking and yellow journalism. As the truth about Mary Baker G. Eddy was revealed over the next year, the public's tolerance for sensationalism "declined quickly after 1907," according to Diner, and the "public's interest in scandal seemed sated."[5]

Church leaders and the citizens of Concord came immediately to Eddy's defense. On the day the *World's* article appeared, Sunday, October 28, attempts were made to refute the "facts" contained in the story. Concord mayor and probate court judge Charles H. Corning recorded the day's events in his diary as "a remarkable & red marked day" in his life, commenting, "Yet I wonder if I appreciate the full meaning of it all." Bombarded all day with questions about Eddy from reporters investigating the "big scoop," Corning received a visit around 3:30 p.m. from H. Cornell Wilson, a member of the Christian Science Publication Committee, "with a request to go out to Pleasant View & see with [Corning's] own eyes the lady herself." Corning had never met Eddy, and a short time later Wilson returned "in a public hack" with Eddy's attorney Frank Streeter to escort Corning to Eddy's home. At Pleasant View, Corning asked to see Pamelia Leonard, whom the *World* accused of impersonating Eddy on her daily carriage ride.[6] Corning noted,

She sat near me so I had a good look. Her age may be 55 to 60, her hair is grey, her eyes very dark & here her physical similitude to Mrs. E. stops. Mrs. Leonard is well nourished, her figure filled out & her face is as different from th. of the woman she is said to personate, as a circle is different from a square. Her face & facial features are round while Mrs. Eddy's are long, peaked & lined.[7]

Corning was invited then to meet Eddy in the upstairs reception room, which he described as "a S. E. exposure well lighted with a balcony [with] easy access through the low windows." He wrote, "She rose and shook hands with us calling Streeter, General and addressing me as Judge Corning and incidentally remarking th. she & I had never met."[8] Corning continued, "Resuming her easy chair she said with emphasis, her eyes brightening & a slight color coming to her cheeks that the Lord was her refuge, that God wd. protect her & in Him she had always put her trust. If God is not our friend where is our friend, the finite God is our strength. While uttering these words she looked at S. & then at me."[9]

She went on to discuss the wedding gift she had sent to Streeter's daughter and a request from the state fair association. She sent for Calvin Frye to retrieve the documents about the fair and commented, "I have so much to do th. Mr. Frye might steal $100,000 without my knowing it but I'm sure he never will." After spending a half hour with Eddy, Corning recorded his final impressions.

She is 85 years old & she shows her years, face sharp, form slight, hands veined but warm in shaking hands, her wrinkles & age lines are prominent, she is naturally tremulous & I noticed a shaking of the head. She is slightly deaf & said so, her false teeth grate at times & her hands indicated age. But considering her years & her life's work & the work to be done daily I saw a woman who surprised me. . . . That she rides out daily I have no doubt. . . . She had returned from her drive & wore a beautiful grey waist embroidered and attractive & hanging from her

neck was a locket studded with diamonds or pearls. Her skirt was
black & had evidently been changed on her return.[10]

Streeter had Corning write "quickly what [he] had to say,"
which was immediately sent off to the press. Corning then went to
the Christian Science Church on State Street in Concord, where he
addressed a packed house. He noted hostility to the *World's* reporting: "The excitement is lively & non scientists [non–Christian
Scientists] are worked up over this contemptible performance." For
the next twenty minutes, Corning addressed the crowd about his visit
to Pleasant View "amid a hush such as [he had] never experienced."
Corning returned home with Streeter, who mentioned that he had
"made Mrs. Eddy's will and he had it in his safe." Corning wrote,
"[Streeter] slapped me on the knee as is his want now & then exclaim-
ing 'Charles, I thought of what she said about Fry's taking $100,000,
without her knowing it.'" Streeter went on to describe Frye's complete
loyalty to Eddy and to encourage Corning, as a probate court judge,
to turn to Frye for help "if a post mortem question arises." Corning
was not as impressed with Frye, writing, "[He] has shifty eyes, one of
those eyes that argue & suspect & supply what in others is known as
speech. I guess he is shrewd, self organized."[11]

The next day, October 29, 1906, newspapers all over the country
carried the statements of Corning, Streeter, Wilson, and others attesting to Eddy's mental and physical well-being. In Concord, the *Evening
Monitor* headline read "Cruel Falsehoods Promptly Refuted." The
Monitor's editorial lambasted "a certain section of the American press"
for publishing "grossly fantastic and entirely false statements concerning the personality of the Rev. Mary Baker Eddy, the Discoverer and
Founder of Christian Science." The *World* claimed its story was the
result of long investigation in Concord. The *Monitor* denied this possibility: "No honest investigator could have stayed here even so short
a time as a single day without learning from indisputable sources that
Mrs. Eddy is alive—and very keenly alive—to all that takes place
in the world, and that she is constantly alert and thoughtful to do

good to everybody, especially to the city of Concord." The editor of the *Monitor*, George Higgins Moses, added his personal testimony by writing that he had known Mrs. Eddy for ten years and had seen her "within a very short time."[12]

The *World* published all of the denials but emphasized that the many representatives of the press in Concord, including the Associated Press and reporters from New York, Boston, and New England, had been denied access to Eddy.[13] It was clear to those around Mary Baker Eddy that more needed to be done to completely refute the *World*'s story. Calvin Frye issued a statement to the *Monitor*, asserting that he was simply a paid employee of Eddy and noting, "[She] conducts her own affairs, financial and otherwise, to-day as she always has." Frye denied that she was "dominated or controlled by any sort of 'cabinet' or combination." He also claimed Eddy was in "her usual good health" and denied that Pamelia Leonard or anybody else had ever impersonated her on her daily drive. Leonard also issued a statement duly notarized, stating that she had never impersonated Eddy: "I have never stepped inside of her carriage and have never even looked inside of it." Leonard also stated "most emphatically" that Eddy was not suffering from any disease and that there was "not . . . any sort of galvanic battery" in the house.[14]

To Eddy's staff, it was apparent that the only way to counteract the story in the *World* was to make Eddy available to the press, at least in a limited way. The problem with this strategy was that she had met with the *World* reporters, Slaght and Lithchild, but they had entirely disregarded what they had learned about her from that interview. The interview had taken place on October 15 after, Slaght and Lithchild insisted, Joseph Pulitzer had sent them to Concord to determine if Eddy was alive or dead. After long interviews with Frye and others in Concord, the reporters still insisted that all they wanted to do was prove that Eddy was alive and well. They claimed it was not Pulitzer's purpose to use any material against Eddy other than to satisfy themselves that she was alive. With these assurances, Frye and Eddy's secretary, Lewis Strang, arranged for the reporters to meet

Eddy at Pleasant View at 3:00 p.m. that day, accompanied by one of
Eddy's neighbors, John Kent, for purposes of identification. Eddy
met the three men, standing the entire visit. Strang wrote that day,
"The little affair went through very nicely, and the men seemed thoroughly satisfied and quite impressed with our Leader's appearance."
After the visit, on the way down the stairs, Lithchild told Strang, "She
is certainly a well-preserved woman for her years," and Slaght also
expressed that "he was thoroughly satisfied" as to the soundness of
Eddy's physical and mental condition. The article that appeared in the
World less than two weeks later must have thoroughly shaken whatever confidence in the press remained at Pleasant View.[15]

Eddy's making herself more available to the press was not the
only effort to head off the negative article from the *World*. The editor of the *Concord Patriot*, Michael Meehan, a Roman Catholic, wrote
directly to Joseph Pulitzer, pleading with him "in a spirit of justice,
truth, square dealing" to squelch the "unqualifiedly false" statements
or insinuations that the reporters seemed determined to write. Meehan
knew Eddy, had "been in her home, in her study with her within a
few months" of the news story, and denied what the reporters seemed
determined to write. Meehan stated, "[They say] Mrs. Eddy is dead,
and that a mummy or a substitute, and not she, is in the carriage each
day . . . or [they] will say Mrs. Eddy is enfeebled and decrepid, and that
those brilliant faculties which in the past made her wonderful accom-
plishments possible have departed." Meehan went on to say that his
letter was in no way occasioned by any "zeal" on his part for Christian
Science but by his respect for Eddy and because the efforts of the
reporters were "unworthy of the *World*."[16] Pulitzer never responded
to Meehan's letter.

Having failed to prevent publication of the exposé, those surrounding Eddy decided to attempt to discredit the *World*'s story. They
arranged for the large number of reporters in Concord to see Eddy
at Pleasant View, on October 30, as she left for her daily carriage
ride. The brief, carefully orchestrated, interview would be conducted
by Sybil Wilbur of the *Boston Herald*, who had previously written

a laudatory piece on Eddy, based on personal interviews. Wilbur would ask Eddy four prearranged questions as Eddy descended the stairs on her way out the front door to her carriage.[17] The reporters in Concord—minus those from the *World*, who were not invited to attend—would be standing in the downstairs drawing room to observe the interview with Wilbur. The pressure of the moment and long years of abuse from the press seemed to strike the eighty-five-year-old, and her hands shook as she confronted the reporters. Wilbur dutifully asked the first question: "Are you in perfect bodily health?" Eddy responded, "Indeed I am." Wilbur asked, "Have you any other physician than God?" Eddy made a sweeping gesture: "No physician but God. His everlasting arms are around me, and that is enough." Wilbur then asked "Do you take a daily drive?" Eddy replied, "Yes," and with that Eddy turned away toward the carriage without waiting for the fourth prearranged question: "Does anyone besides yourself administer your property or attend to your business affairs?"[18] The interview failed in its intended purpose, as it was too short and too carefully orchestrated and as Eddy did, in fact, appear very frail and unsteady under intense scrutiny. The result was that reporters fell back on their preconceived ideas about Eddy and the *World* story in writing about the interview. The variety of responses that appeared in newspapers around country was delightfully summarized by Fleta Campbell Springer, who quoted from the different reports in her biography of Eddy.

> [Eddy] "bowed low and with ceremonial precision, reminding one of the entrance of a great diva before an audience made up of fashion and wealth"; "shaking and trembling, she tottered forward, clutching the curtains with palsied hands and paused swaying in the door"; "her eyes, large, dark and lustrous, sought out Mrs. O'Brien [Wilbur], whom she greeted with a smile"; "her faded lustrous eyes roamed vacantly in space above the heads of the crowd"; "her feebleness seemed only consistent with her great age"; "she stood before them shaking with palsy,

a physical wreck, tottering, pallid like a vision from beyond the grave"; "she stood before them erect and upright, nerved for the ordeal"; "she wore a black cloak"; "she wore a cape of white ermin.[19]

George H. Moses, editor of the Concord *Monitor,* was present for the interview. His impression was that Eddy had changed little since he last met with her, that "the passing years had left wonderfully slight traces upon her," and that she "smiled and bowed graciously to those before her." To Moses, her replies to Wilbur's questions were "clear and lucid." Edward N. Pearson, business manager of the Rumford Printing Company of Concord, who was also present, stated that he was not a Christian Scientist and was "without bias or prejudice in this matter." He reported that Eddy's "voice was clear and strong and her appearance was that of a woman in full possession of her faculties." Moses identified all of the people present for the interview, including six officials of the Christian Science Church; reporters from Hearst's *Boston American* and *New York American;* the *New York Times;* the *Boston Globe;* the *Boston Herald;* the *Boston Post;* the *Boston Journal;* the *Boston Traveller;* representatives of the Associated Press and the Publishers' Press; a stenographer, Mr. Pearson; and Moses of the *Monitor.*[20]

Those closest to Mary Baker Eddy realized that the interview had not gone as well as they had hoped. Confronted by at least eighteen people, the eighty-five-year-old woman was understandably taken aback upon entering the parlor on the east side of the ground floor at Pleasant View. Her secretary, Lewis Strang wrote, "The position was a very difficult one for our Leader, and although I told her to step right into the room and face the newspaper people there squarely, the mental blast seemed to beat her back momentarily when she reached the door, and so the effect was not quite so positive as we could have wished." At the last minute, Eddy had ordered that the door to the parlor be shut so that she was not seen descending the stairs. Strang, "as a newspaper man," believed this was a mistake, since she climbed the same stairs every day without assistance. Nevertheless, Strang wrote, "The matter is finished as far as we at Pleasant View are concerned."[21]

The public's appetite for news about Eddy had been whetted, however, and those who tried to protect her from the press were no longer in control of the situation. Mayor Corning recorded in his diary, "Reporters still cluster about the Eagle Hotel, interviewing, supposing & suspecting. It is a big spring of revenue for newspapers." To him, the interview at Pleasant View that was witnessed by the reporters was nothing less than "persecution."[22] But, he thought, the *World* was correct about one thing: "Legal action to ascertain the truth is practically assured."[23] Corning, a probate court judge, speculated about his good friend and Eddy's lawyer, Frank Streeter: "I can't help estimating the revenue Streeter will receive for his part in the excitement. $20,000 at least from first to last & the last scene will perhaps be played in the Supreme Court." Corning was right about the coming legal action, but he grossly underestimated how much his friend Streeter would earn from Eddy before the "last scene" had been played.[24]

꞊ 2 ꞊

MARY BAKER EDDY AND
CHRISTIAN SCIENCE

The most famous woman in America was also the most controversial. Mary Baker Eddy had done something unheard
of for a woman of that time: discovering and founding a new
religion and managing every aspect of its successful growth. Mark
Twain, a harsh critic of Eddy, called her "the most daring and masculine
and masterful woman that has appeared in the earth in centuries."[1] The
growth of the church in the years prior to 1906 was truly remarkable.
Eddy herself claimed as recently at 1898 to have over three hundred
thousand followers.[2] During the years of Eddy's residence at Pleasant
View, the church had expanded beyond the United States to Great
Britain, Canada, and Germany. Other evidence of the church's growth
included the new church buildings that had been erected in Concord,
New Hampshire; Portland, Oregon; Detroit, Atlanta; Toronto; Los
Angeles; Pittsburgh; Cleveland; Saint Louis; San Jose; Wilmington;
Duluth; New York, which had two buildings; and Chicago, which also
had two buildings. But nothing could match the new five-thousand-
seat "extension" to the Mother Church in Boston, dedicated on June
10, 1906, with some thirty thousand Christian Scientists in attendance,
although her "message" to the celebration challenged her followers
not to focus on the church edifice but to put God first in their lives.[3]

Eddy's absence from this occasion had prompted the newspaper investigations into her health. Nevertheless, the "magnificent temple" prompted the *Boston Globe* to comment, "One thing is certain: for a religion which has been organized only thirty years, and which erected its first church only twelve years ago, Christian Science has more fine church edifices to its credit in the same time than any other denomination in the world, and they are all paid for."[4]

Mary Baker, whom Mark Twain would later refer to as "the most interesting woman that ever lived, and the most extraordinary," was born in humble circumstances on a small farm in Bow, New Hampshire, on July 16, 1821.[5] She was the youngest of six children of Mark and Abigail Baker. Her father dominated the family through daily prayer and strict Calvinist theology. To Mark, sinners were totally depraved "and morally unable to do anything acceptable to God until they [were] renewed by the Holy Spirit."[6] Biographers critical of Mary have accused her father of trying to impress his convictions on his neighbors and of having an "ugly disposition" and a hot temper.[7] Mary's mother, in contrast, was "cheerful and hopeful," the "summer to Mark's winter."[8]

When Mary Baker was a child, her poor health prevented her from regular attendance at the local school. The nature of her frequent ailments is impossible to diagnose today, but her health was a constant source of concern to her family. According to the famous critical biography credited to Georgine Milmine but actually written by Willa Cather, who at the time was an editor for S. S. McClure, Mary was a very difficult child, suffering from "convulsive attacks of a hysterical nature." Due to her headstrong personality, she was permitted to skip school and "to throw off all restraint at home," with family rules being relaxed where she was concerned.[9] A more recent and balanced biography contends that young Mary was not suffering from hysteria, though neurasthenia (hysteria) was a common diagnosis for women at that time, ascribed to "too much leisure, too much education, too much dieting and too tight corseting, too many novels, too little work." This lack of work would not have been the case on the farm, where daily chores were expected, but it is possible that Mary had an eating disorder, anorexia, as a young woman. Whatever the source of her illness, it is safe to say that Mary was a sensitive young woman who probably used ill health to avoid unpleasant tasks and situations.[10]

Despite her poor health, Mary did love to read and was tutored by her older brother, Albert, eleven years her senior, whom she credited with instilling in her the love of learning.[11] Albert put himself through Dartmouth College and then studied law under Franklin Pierce in Hillsborough, New Hampshire, becoming Pierce's first law partner. Albert moved into the Pierce homestead to practice law and to care for Pierce's father, former governor Benjamin Pierce, in his old age, while congressman and later senator Franklin Pierce spent more time in Washington D.C., and, after his marriage, lived in Concord. Benjamin Pierce and Mark Baker knew each other and were connected through family marriage. Albert used his connection to the Pierce family to build a political career for himself as a radical Jacksonian Democrat. Albert served in the state legislature and had been nominated for the U.S. Congress when he died at age thirty-one of kidney failure in 1841. His sudden death was a devastating blow to young Mary, an impressionable teenager at the time, as Albert had set the standard for her achievement and intellect.[12]

With no sons remaining on the farm to help him, Mark Baker moved the family to Sanbornton Bridge (now Tilton), New Hampshire, in 1835. Mary, who had always battled with her father over religion, particularly by rejecting the concept of predestination, joined the local Congregational Church in 1838, despite her vocal disapproval of the belief in "foreordination." To Mary, it seemed inconceivable that God would not forgive man of his sins. She also objected to the long sermons and loud prayers typical of the Congregational Church.[13]

In December 1843, Mary Baker married George Washington Glover, eleven years her senior and a friend of her brother George. Glover was ambitious and energetic, as well as tall and handsome. Mary had become a tall, graceful, willowy, but delicate beauty with a witty mind. The couple moved immediately to the South, where

George had established a construction business. But George Glover died in June 1844 of yellow fever in Wilmington, North Carolina, leaving his young widow pregnant and destitute. The Wilmington Masons paid for her return to New Hampshire, where Mary was forced to move back home with her father and mother, to await the birth of her son, George Washington Glover II, which occurred on September 12, 1844.[14] Totally dependent on her family for support, Mary faced the coming years without the means or health needed to care for a child.

The years of her widowhood, 1844 to 1853, were a particular low point for Mary Baker Glover and her young son. Living with her parents, Mary was unable to achieve any sort of independence or self-sufficiency. She tried to write poems and short pieces, which were printed in local newspapers and *Godey's Lady's Book*, the preeminent periodical for women at that time. She also started a preschool in Sanbornton Bridge, but the school failed within a few months. Though she had a wonderful way with children, her refusal to employ corporal punishment on her young students, her lack of ability to play the piano or teach art, and the fact that she charged only twenty-five cents a week for tuition contributed to the failure of the school.[15] Her health deteriorated steadily during this period. She suffered from stomach and spinal problems, probably brought on by the enormous stress she was under as a young mother entirely dependent on her family for support. She became a controversial figure among the locals, who later reported that she fell into trances or apparent unconsciousness and became highly irritated by loud noises, and she was viewed as clairvoyant. Even a sympathetic biographer, Gillian Gill, concludes that Mary became a hysteric during these years, as she took to her bed for long periods of time and was unable to walk. Among her family, there were concerns for her life, though her ailments were likely psychological in nature.[16]

Her failure as a mother to her young son George would haunt her throughout her life and be used against her by her enemies. Her health made it difficult for her to care for the child, who as an infant stayed occasionally with Mahala Sanborn, a neighbor who had attended Mary

Glover at the child's birth. Young George even lost his home with the Bakers after his grandmother died in 1849 and his grandfather remarried almost immediately. As George became a boisterous, headstrong, loud child, Mark Baker refused to have him in the house with his new wife. Mary stayed, but in 1850 George was sent to live with Mahala Sanborn, who had married Russell Cheney and now lived in North Groton, some twenty-five miles from Sanbornton Bridge.[17] Mary later wrote of her devastation at being separated from her child and of her emotions at saying good-bye to the six-year-old George, but her critics would charge her with being a bad mother, in an age that accepted "pure, self-sacrificing motherhood as the highest value to which a woman can aspire." Mary had failed to play the role society assigned to her as a mother.[18]

Remarriage was the one avenue open to Mary to establish her own home and reunite with her son. In December 1852 she visited a dentist, Dr. Daniel Patterson, to have several teeth extracted. "A tall, well-built, handsome man with a long beard," Patterson began courting the widow. Daniel Patterson was a local dandy and a lady's man. What brought the two together is another of the controversies of Mary Baker Eddy's life. Patterson is viewed both as a good-natured, bumbling neophyte taken in by a devious hysteric and as a deceitful con man taking advantage of a desperate widow. Letters between the two show genuine affection, and they were married in December 1853. Dr. Patterson had promised to make a home for young George, but Patterson's dental practice apparently failed in Franklin, and the couple moved to North Groton in 1855, into a house mortgaged to Mary's sister, Martha Pillsbury. Mary remained in very poor health, and Patterson refused to take in the increasingly wild George, claiming Mary's health would not permit it. Patterson also fell behind in his mortgage payments because, he claimed, he was spending all his time taking care of his sick wife.[19]

It became clear to Mary Patterson and her family that Daniel Patterson "was more of a dandy and a talker than a worker, that he expected his wife's rich relatives to support them both, and that Mary's health became an alibi for his inactivity and financial ineptitude."[20] Moving closer to her son and the Cheneys did not improve things, as Patterson believed George had become unmanageable and was wrecking his mother's health and the Patterson marriage. When he married Mary, Daniel Patterson had filed papers to become George's legal guardian. In 1856, he apparently conspired with Mary's wealthy sister Abigail to help pay for a new home for the Cheney household, including George, on a small farm in Minnesota. The move was against Mary's and the boy's will, but he would not see his mother again until 1879. George always believed that Russell Cheney was receiving some kind of payment to become his legal guardian, and until George ran away from the Cheneys at age fifteen, he would be nothing more than a laborer on their small farm in Minnesota. It is now known that in 1859 Mary's father paid Russell Cheney two hundred dollars as compensation for the loss of George's farm labor. Mary and George knew nothing of these arrangements, but she suspected a plot or conspiracy by her relatives to move the troublesome boy as far away as possible so that she could not manage to follow him as she had to North Groton.[21]

Mary's life with Daniel Patterson went from bad to worse in the coming years. In 1860, despite her invalidism, she had to physically intervene to stop Patterson from being beaten with a shovel by two men to whom he owed money. Shortly after, her sister Martha reluctantly foreclosed on the Patterson home in North Groton, and Mary and her few belongings were unceremoniously moved by carriage to Rumney, New Hampshire. This was undoubtedly the low point in Mary's life. It became clear to her that her second marriage was not a solution to any of her problems. She would need to take control of her own life, and to do that, she would first have to find a solution to her debilitating health problems.[22]

In search of improved health, Mary practiced homeopathy for a time and experimented with placebos. She seemed to be moving toward a mental theory of disease. In 1862, after an unsuccessful visit to a hydrotherapy institute, Mary Patterson contacted Dr. Phineas P. Quimby of Portland, Maine. Quimby had established a prosperous medical practice by the use of mesmerism (hypnotism). He discovered that simple suggestion was enough to get control of a patient's mind and eliminate symptoms. Though he had no regular medical training, Quimby theorized that illness was error. Without using medicine or even hands-on manipulation, he would tell patients to correct the errors in their thinking about health. To Quimby, truth was the cure, and he radiated confidence and benevolence. Mary found immediate relief after she moved in to Quimby's institute in October 1862. She stayed for three months and left feeling completely cured, although she would suffer a relapse in the coming months. She returned to Quimby in December 1863 and stayed through the winter. A devoted convert to Quimby's method, Mary Patterson observed his cases and became his publicist. She often compared Quimby to Jesus Christ, though he denied any religious overtones to his practice.[23]

Mary Patterson accepted two important principles of Quimby's practice. The first is the concept of healing treatments from a distance, what Mary would refer to as Quimby's "angel treatments." The second feature that she accepted was Quimby's claim to "take on" his patient's pain. As Gill puts it, "Healing involved a transfer of energy from the healer to the patient that could leave the healer severely debilitated and even [lead to death]." Mary spent so much time with Quimby between 1863 and 1865 that she aroused the suspicion of Quimby's relatives and associates, who suspected her ambitions and feared that she was stealing Quimby's ideas. The family had no doubts about Mary's intelligence, and according to Bates and Dittemore, even Quimby feared "she lacked 'identity' or integrity." During this time, Mary Patterson continued to proselytize on Quimby's behalf, speaking in public at town halls to small audiences.[24]

Her health varied during these years, deteriorating at times of stress in her personal life. Although she continued to express affection for Daniel Patterson, they were apart for much of the time, as Mary lived with friends and Patterson was unable to establish a home for the two of them. The Civil War added to their separation. In early 1862, the governor of New Hampshire sent Patterson on a mission to deliver funds raised in New Hampshire to Union sympathizers in the South. In April, Patterson strayed from Union lines and was captured and sent to a prison camp in Richmond. He would escape in September 1862 and return to New England to try, unsuccessfully, to resume his dental practice.[25] Unexpectedly, Mary also heard from her son for the first time since he was taken to Minnesota in 1856. After running away from the Cheneys and working as a farm laborer, George Glover joined the Eighth Wisconsin Infantry Volunteers in 1861 at age seventeen. With the help of a friend, the illiterate George wrote to his mother in October of that year. Mary wept with joy at receiving the letter but was angered to learn that her fears about his upbringing were realized, in that George was incapable of writing for himself. She would remain in contact with her son and be concerned for his safety throughout the war, particularly after learning that George had been seriously wounded in the neck at the Battle of Corinth in October 1862. Following his recovery from the wound, George reenlisted and fought in the battles of Jackson, Vicksburg, Mechanicsburg, and Richmond. In July 1865, George was invalided out of the army, suffering from "consumption of the bowels." He made it to the Cheney home in Minnesota, where he slowly recovered.[26]

The turning point in Mary's life occurred on February 3, 1866. As with all important events in her life, this too is riddled with controversy. We know that on February 1 she suffered a fall on the ice in Lynn, Massachusetts, while visiting friends. The *Lynn Weekly Reporter* of February 3 reported the accident, stating that Mary Patterson was taken "in an insensible condition" to a nearby home and treated by a Dr. Alvin M. Cushing, who "found her injuries to be internal, and of a severe nature, inducing spasms and internal suffering." The next day Mary was moved, under Cushing's care and with the help of two hired men and a long sleigh, to her home with Daniel Patterson in nearby Swampscott. The doctor visited her several times over the weekend, and a minister was urgently called in. The next day, Sunday, February 3, Mary "asked for her Bible, sent everyone out of the room, and then

. . . getting out of bed unaided," she walked downstairs, to the amazement of her friends.[27]

In later years, Mary Baker Eddy gave various accounts of this self-healing and what it meant to her. According to one account, Cushing had predicted that she would not live for more than three days. Writing years later, Cushing denied making any such diagnosis, admitting only that Mary Patterson had suffered a concussion, was semihysterical, and complained of severe head and neck pain. He also denied that she had ever expressed to him that she had experienced a remarkable cure. His records show that he visited Mary Patterson six times between February 1 and February 5. She would later write about her immediate recovery: "[It] was like the falling apple that led me to the discovery how to be well myself, and how to make others so." If she experienced a sudden revelation at this time, it was not clear from her own letters. On February 14, she wrote to Julius Dresser, a close associate of Quimby, who had died in January, expressing her sorrow over the loss of this "much-loved friend" and hoping that Dresser would "step forward" and carry out Quimby's good work. In the letter, Mary Patterson recounts her fall on the ice and the fear that she would be left a "helpless cripple" but states that in two days she got out of bed "alone." She never states that she was well, however, and, in fact, asks Dresser's help with "the terrible spinal affection from which I have suffered so long and hopelessly."[28]

To those who were later critical of Eddy, these varying accounts of the event were "an exercise in deceit." Christian Scientists, in contrast, accept that the incident "was a moment of indescribable wonder and joy." As Eddy later explained, "That short experience included a glimpse of the great fact that I have since tried to make plain to others, namely, Life in and of Spirit; this Life being the sole reality of existence." Though she explained the event in different ways at various times in her life, the incident clearly meant something to Eddy. If nothing else, she had done, in Gill's words, "something brave and decisive." She would no longer be a victim but would take control not only of her own physical well-being but of her life. She would spend the next forty years trying to understand the meaning of the spiritual illumination she had experienced that day "alone with God and the Bible."[29]

It would be nine more years before Mary Baker Glover—after Daniel Patterson had left her for good in 1866 and they divorced in 1873, she no longer used Patterson as her surname—would publish the first of many editions of her book, *Science and Health with Key to the Scriptures*. For the rest of her life, she endeavored to understand and explain her "discovery" to the world, and in the process founded a new religion, Christian Science. What she had discovered was that God was the source of healing and health, that it was God's Spirit that was the only Truth and reality. Thus, the essential nature of reality, the metaphysical world, was God and Spirit. Conversely, the material world was "error" or sin and had no existence outside the mortal mind. Over time, Mary Baker G. Eddy concluded that God was only good and could not know evil, which existed only in the separate realm of mortal mind. Through Quimby, she knew of man's ability to hypnotize and dominate the mind of another through the power of suggestion or mesmerism. But true healing could be achieved not by one individual controlling the mind of another but only by each individual connecting to God and the Spirit. It was this need to tap into the divine strength, the religious intensity of her discovery, that separated Eddy from Quimby, though in the coming years his followers would charge that she had stolen his ideas and even copied his manuscripts and that she was only practicing mesmerism herself. What is clear is that she accepted from Quimby the idea of a strong mind controlling a weaker one, but she saw the tutor's or teacher's role as one of a person who had tapped into the Spirit world, helping the weaker individual connect with God. Quimby's was a mental technique, while Eddy's was, in Robert Peel's words, "a religious discipline, moral as well as metaphysical." To Eddy, "Life is Spirit."[30]

As Eddy began to attract followers and reach the public through her writing, two lines of attack on her teaching developed. Her views on Jesus Christ and Christianity prompted the opposition of religious leaders. To Eddy, God had sent Jesus to teach the reality that through God healing could occur, and according to the Bible, Jesus did heal the sick. Somehow over the centuries, Christianity had lost touch with this reality, and Eddy saw it as her charge to reteach it and reconnect man to God through the "science" of what Jesus had taught. What she called her discovery led her to several conclusions that threatened existing Christian denominations. First, she believed that death is simply a change and that there is no death to the divine idea that is man. According to Eddy, man is neither elected nor damned, and Christ's resurrection does not atone for man, but Christ's life offers a pattern of recognizing our oneness with God. Since God is all-knowing and all-good, prayer is irrational, if by prayer man tries to inform God of what is happening or asks him for what is desired. Audible prayer, particularly, is only public display and becomes a substitute for action. In the words of Eddy, such "hypocrisy is fatal to Christianity." Finally, her interpretation of the Bible ran counter to that of established churches. For example, she rejects the story of an angry God exiling Adam and Eve from the Garden of Eden, since this implies God's malice and unwillingness to allow man the opportunity to reform. To Eddy, this passage is the work of secondhand scribes who wrote "from the standpoint of matter attempting to define Spirit." Since God created woman after creating man, Eddy concludes, "The latter being last, [is] therefore the highest idea given of Him." In Eddy's opinion, there is more reason to call God feminine than masculine. Though no political activist or advocate for women's suffrage, Eddy does propound the metaphysical and theological notions of female equality. The growth of Christian Science prompted Reverend A. Lincoln Moore, pastor of the Riverside Baptist Church in New York City, to declare in 1906 that Christian Science was "unchristian, anti-Christian, anti-Biblical, Christless, Godless,—in brief, Pagan." He advised "uncompromising hostility" against it.[31]

This concept in particular, that God is the true reality or the true "science," prompted opposition from scientists and others who reflected the Enlightenment idea that by studying the world around us, using the empirical method of observation, experimentation, and reason, man can understand the universe that God had created. Particularly, the medical profession was threatened if illness was nothing more than "error" and that the only route to healing was through God and the Spirit. Eddy did teach "that modern medicine is both unnecessary and unproductive." Jesus had taught, in her words, that "soul held ultimate authority over body" and demonstrated this by showing that "matter had no power over" his curing the sick through what were wrongly termed, according to Eddy, miracles. Health was man's natural right from God. A medical war against Christian Science developed, as physicians attempted to attack Eddy's healing methods in the courts and state legislatures.[32] Everything about science and the progress of recent centuries was undermined if one believed, as Eddy taught, that matter does not exist or exists only through mortal mind. Thus, the more she wrote, the more followers she attracted, and the more her future church grew, the greater were the attacks on her.

Alone after her final separation from Patterson, Eddy spent the next years focused intently on her discovery and attempted to write what it meant. During one four-year period, she moved nine times, living in boarding houses and off the kindness of friends and converts. To many, she seemed like a snob who expected to be waited on despite her low circumstances, but to others her charisma attracted attention. She was always writing during these years and occasionally healing and winning converts, who tended to be Spiritualists. However one interprets her success at healing sickness, the primitive state of medical practice at the time meant that patients were usually better off letting nature take its course, particularly women, who always made up the majority of her followers. Eddy's frequent moves between 1866 and 1870 created another controversy after she became famous. Stories circulated that she had been thrown out of several homes for causing trouble. One story, later discredited, had her slashing a mattress and setting fire to her room after being asked to leave one home. Whatever the truth is about these years, stories about her vanity, callous and self-serving nature, and lack of truthfulness followed her forever.[33]

Mary Baker Glover aspired to be a teacher of healing rather than a healer. In 1870, she began taking on students, eventually developing a twelve-lecture course, for which she charged $300. Those who learned the healing method from her were also expected to pay her 10 percent of their earnings. Her best student and protégé during these years was young Richard Kennedy, who in 1870 signed a two-year contract with Eddy to pay her 50 percent of his earnings from healing. He established a very successful practice in Lynn, Massachusetts, but he soon broke away from Eddy rather than share his profitable practice with her. Kennedy's healing method involved touching the patient, something Eddy disapproved of, and he attracted an entirely female clientele with his erotic manipulation. The successful Kennedy began to disparage Eddy and her teaching, and for decades she considered him a real threat to her. Eddy believed that it was possible to read someone's mind from a distance and to exert purely mental control over another person without that person's knowledge or consent. She believed that Kennedy was threatening her with what she later termed "malicious animal magnetism," or M.A.M. Over time Eddy would modify her understanding of the harm produced by M.A.M. and conclude that there was divine protection from it, but her fear of it was real during these years.[34]

She soon had another protégé, Daniel Spofford, who became her most outstanding student and reliable helper. Spofford was instrumental in helping Eddy get out the first edition of *Science and Health* in 1875, as they overcame the many editing issues that Eddy blamed on Kennedy's use of M.A.M. on her publisher. Spofford was also a very popular teacher of Eddy's system and a practitioner of her healing method. But Spofford also had a checkered past, including a breakup with his wife, possible adultery, and an obvious infatuation with his older, but still attractive, mentor and teacher. He eventually broke away from Eddy in 1877, questioning her claim to what Peel calls "a unique spiritual mission." In turn, Spofford was expelled from the newly created Christian Science Association for immorality, and Eddy began ascribing to him the use of M.A.M. against her. The second, or "Ark," edition of *Science and Health* contained a lengthy diatribe against mesmerism, a diatribe that was clearly aimed at her perceived enemies, Kennedy and Spofford.[35]

Spofford may have contributed to his own downfall when he introduced Mary Baker Glover to one of his patients and students, Asa Gilbert Eddy. Eddy became one of Mary's students in 1876 and made an immediate impression on her as "calm, clear and strong, and so kind" when he helped her through one of her many attacks of illness. The two were married on January 1, 1877, to the surprise of everyone associated with the movement. Though Mr. Eddy's birth date is not known, he was at least a decade younger than his new wife, who was fifty-five years old. Brought up on a farm in Vermont, Mr. Eddy was a salesman for the Singer Sewing Machine Company at the time of his introduction to Christian Science. A mild, unmarried, small man in poor health in his midforties when the couple met, Mr. Eddy was often attacked by critics of Mary Baker Eddy for being eas-ily manipulated and controlled by her and was portrayed by some as an effeminate weakling. Though cautious and not very literate, Asa Gilbert Eddy proved very useful to his wife, working as hard as she did and never going against her wishes. He demonstrated both com-mitment and courage in the demanding role of consort to the founder of Christian Science.[36]

Mary Eddy's obsession with M.A.M. nearly proved her undoing at this time. She attributed every setback or failure of her movement to the mesmeric influence of her enemies, particularly Kennedy and Spofford. In this state of mind, she fell under the influence of one of her students, Edward J. Arens, who not only accepted her belief in malicious animal magnetism but advised her to fight back in the courts. Arens apparently convinced Mary Baker Eddy that he would take on this judicial activity and not only end the influence of her enemies upon her and Christian Science but also win back some of the money owed her by her former students. Little is known of Arens except that he was born in Germany, spoke with a thick German accent, and had no background or training in the law. Nevertheless, he began four lawsuits against Kennedy, Spofford, and two other former students for breach of contract. The first suit was successful, as the court determined that Kennedy owed Mary Baker Eddy over $750 for failure to pay her the $1,000 he had agreed to in 1870 for her instruction in healing. This amount was separate from the 50 percent of his healing fees that Kennedy had paid her during his two-year contract. The other cases were all dismissed by the court.[37]

With the failure of her suit against Spofford for breach of contract, Mary Baker Eddy convinced one of her students, Lucretia L. S. Brown, to file suit against Spofford, charging him with injuring her through mesmeric influence. According to the complaint, filed by Arens with the Supreme Judicial Court of Massachusetts, Spofford had "wrongfully, maliciously, and with intent to injure . . . by means of his said power and art" caused Brown "great suffering of body, severe spinal pains and neuralgia, and temporary suspension of the mind." Of all places, the suit was filed in Salem, inducing the newspapers to sensationalize the event as a modern accusation of witchcraft. At the preliminary hearing in May 1878, Mary Baker Eddy showed up with Arens and some twenty Christian Scientists as witnesses. Three days later, the judge dismissed the case, sustaining the demurrer of Spofford's attorney and stating it was not within the power of the court to control Spofford's mind.[38]

As if this case was not bizarre enough, an even more puzzling event occurred in October 1878, when Arens and Asa Gilbert Eddy were arrested on a charge of conspiring with James L. Sargent to kill or injure Daniel Spofford. Arens and Mr. Eddy were held in the Charles Street jail in Boston, with bail set at $3,000 each. The press seized on the case, calling it, if proven, one of the "blackest" crimes to take place in some time. At the preliminary hearing on November 7, the story was told by Sargent, a saloonkeeper, who stated that Arens had approached him, offering $300 to $400 to "lick" Spofford. Sargent stated that he met later with Arens and Mr. Eddy, who were operating under assumed names, and received $75 as up-front money to do the deed. Sargent admitted he was only trying to extort money from the defendants and had no intention of carrying out the crime. Instead, he reported it to a Boston police detective and then to Spofford himself. Spofford was clearly frightened, and Sargent advised him to leave town immediately. Spofford did so, moving into Sargent's sister's house of prostitution for two weeks without telling anyone, including his family, who reported him as missing. At first the press seemed to accept much of the story told by Sargent, but by January 1879, the case fizzled out as one witness recanted his testimony and Mr. Eddy and Arens were able to establish alibis for the night when the money supposedly changed hands. The court dismissed the case, the Boston police detective lost his job, and Sargent was later jailed on a morals charge. Undoubtedly, this was the lowest point in the early history of Christian Science, but the question has never been definitively answered as to what was going on with this case. Defenders of Mary Baker Eddy point to the fact that the $750 judgment against Richard Kennedy was overturned on appeal by a judge on November 8, 1878, the day after the preliminary hearing against Arens and Asa Gilbert Eddy. Could Kennedy, who worked in the same building as Spofford, have been behind the conspiracy in order to create such negative publicity against Christian Science and its leader as to influence the judge in the appeal? Interestingly, the whole plot fizzled as soon as Kennedy won his appeal. Opponents of Mary Baker Eddy believe that she was somehow behind the conspiracy, or, at least, that Arens was the perpetrator. For Mary Baker Eddy, the result of this period of litigation was nothing short of disastrous. Her movement became the subject of devastating newspaper coverage and ridicule, she had been defeated in court, and she was left with crippling legal debts.[39]

After this time, things began slowly to look up for Mary Baker Eddy and Christian Science. On August 23, 1879, the state of Massachusetts issued a charter for the Church of Christ (Scientist) with twenty-six members and with Eddy listed as president. At age

fifty-eight, she had founded a church. In November of that year, her
son, George Washington Glover II, arrived for a reunion with his
mother. They had not seen each other since 1856. In 1874, George had
married sixteen-year-old Ellen (Nellie) Bessant, who was probably
already pregnant with their first child, Edward Gershom Glover, who
would be called Gershom by the family. For several years, George,
who was excellent with horses, had been in the freighting business.
He soon moved his young family to the Black Hills of South Dakota,
where gold had been discovered, and began to work as a prospector
in and around Deadwood. His visit at this time was meant to rekindle
a relationship with his mother, but he also may have been seeking
financial help for his prospecting. He soon realized, however, that his
mother and new stepfather could not offer any financial assistance.
Mary Baker Eddy certainly noticed George's strong physical resem-
blance to his father, but otherwise, the two men had little in common.
The thirty-five-year-old George Glover was a true westerner, with a
full beard that only partly hid the large scar on his neck from his Civil
War wound. He dressed as a frontiersman, was completely lacking in
education and sophistication, and was functionally illiterate. During
his three months in Lynn, George did commit to Christian Science,
though his understanding of the religion is questionable. In true western fashion, he tried to help his mother, who convinced him of the
malicious mental attacks on her from Richard Kennedy. According to
George, he went to Kennedy's office and threatened him with a gun
if he did not stop attacking Mary Baker Eddy. Years later, Kennedy
denied that any such event ever occurred. In January 1880, a pathetic
letter from his wife called George back to his home in Lead, South
Dakota, reporting that the family was in such desperate straits that
there hadn't even been any Christmas presents for their three children.
Eddy kept in closer contact with her son and his family in the years
following his visit to Massachusetts.[40]

In January 1881, Eddy received another charter from the state, for
the Massachusetts Metaphysical College. Operating first out of her
parlor in Lynn and later in her home in Boston, the college trained

over a thousand students in her healing method. She taught most of
the classes and charged $300 for a twelve-session, later seven-session,
course. Students received a diploma proclaiming them members of
the Christian Science Association. In October 26, 1881, eight students
in Lynn resigned from the association, charging their "Teacher, Mrs.
Mary B. G. Eddy," of "frequent ebullitions of temper, love of money
and the appearance of hypocrisy." These were not unfamiliar charges
against her, as other defectors had made similar claims. Those who
remained in the association reconfirmed their support for Eddy by
expelling the eight and declaring her pastor of the church.[41]

Despite all these setbacks, the movement was growing and attract-
ing attention. The death of her third husband, Asa Gilbert Eddy, on
June 2, 1882, was one more blow to Eddy. Mr. Eddy had been a loyal
consort to his wife and a quiet, selfless worker, but his death aroused
one more controversy. Mary Baker Eddy loudly proclaimed to the
Boston Globe and the *Boston Post* that Asa Gilbert Eddy had been poisoned mentally. She insisted on an autopsy. The qualified physician
who performed the autopsy ruled the death was from natural causes
as a result of heart disease and took the extraordinary step of showing
Eddy her husband's heart to prove it to her. This did not convince
the founder of Christian Science, who blamed herself for not sav-
ing her husband from the power of malicious animal magnetism. To
Eddy, the guilty party was former student Edward J. Arens, another
of her defectors, who had recently published a book that was mostly
plagiarized from *Science and Health*. According to Eddy, Arens had
always been preoccupied with arsenic, and Asa Gilbert Eddy's death
was due to mental arsenic poisoning. While Asa Gilbert Eddy had
probably suffered with a rheumatic heart since childhood, and his six
years of unceasing labor on behalf of the movement may have led to
his death, his widow's grief at his passing was compounded by her
continuing obsession with malicious animal magnetism and her belief
that she could have interceded to protect him from it. She would soon
overcome her loss and determine to build on the legacy of Christian
Science, a legacy that their joint efforts had created.[42]

In 1883, Eddy began publishing and editing the *Christian Science Journal*. The eight-page monthly, with much of the early issues written by Eddy herself, was immensely important to the growth of the movement. Eddy encouraged local followers of her movement to hand out free copies and to persuade people to subscribe. The most effective part of each issue was the firsthand testimonials from people who had been healed by Christian Science practitioners. The letters from average citizens describing the extent of their illness and how much improvement they had experienced through Christian Science had an enormous impact, especially in remote areas of the country where people did not have access to modern medical care. The indictment of the medical profession was clear in each issue of the *Journal*.[43]

According to Eddy biographer Gillian Gill, while the "performance of healing—is the heart of Christian Science, writing is its brain." Eddy was constantly trying to clarify her theology through new editions of *Science and Health with Key to the Scriptures*. She saw herself as the "elucidator" of the scriptures, in that her science not only restored the healing practices recorded in the Gospels but revealed the divine truth that Jesus and his disciples had "demonstrated." Thus, she was showing the way to the eternal truths that had been hidden for centuries by the ecclesiastical dogma and institutionalism of modern Christianity. Between 1885 and 1891, she forged a working relationship with a theologically trained Bostonian and ex-Unitarian minister, James Henry Wiggin. Eddy knew that her syntax sometimes got in the way of her meaning, and she relied on Rev. Wiggin for help with the "general smoothing out" of her grammar and sentences. Although Wiggin attended her classes at the Massachusetts Metaphysical College, he never adopted Christian Science, and it is difficult to know if his more substantive comments on her work ever influenced the final manuscript. Nevertheless, when the sixteenth edition came out in 1886, Wiggin's influence was evident in the improved writing.[44] The marked improvement in the quality of the text of *Science and Health* has led critics of Eddy to conclude that Wiggin was her ghostwriter. Although Wiggin's connection with Eddy ended in 1891, his influence

remained in all future editions of *Science and Health*. According to
Mark Twain, "the immense contrast between the legitimate English
of Science and Health and the bastard English of Mrs. Eddy's miscellaneous work, and between the maturity of the one diction and the
juvenility of the other" proves that "she did not write Science and
Health."[45] The Milmine-Cather biography also credits Wiggin with
the improvement but adds that Wiggin "would have been the last man
in the world to claim any part in the real authorship of *Science and
Health*." In fact, Milmine (Cather) quotes extensively from a letter
written by Wiggin, in which he credits Eddy as "an awfully smart
woman, acute, shrewd, but not well read, nor in any way learned." He
goes on to conclude that "Mrs. Eddy [was] nobody's fool" and that she
had learned "one of the tricks of the trade" by making her theology
"open to various readings and meanings." Gill's more recent and balanced biography concludes that while Eddy was prone to inadequacies
and minor deceits, she was not guilty of plagiarism of either Quimby
or Wiggin.[46]

In spite of the rapid growth of Christian Science during the 1880s,
owing to the wide distribution of the *Journal* and the missionary zeal
of the graduates of the Massachusetts Metaphysical College, who
were encouraged to establish Christian Science institutes in various
locations, the sect was plagued by constant defections as the result of
small-minded quarrels and larger ideological issues. In 1888, thirty-six
members of the Boston church rebelled over the healing practices of
Eddy. The issue revolved around the first of several celebrated cases in
which a Christian Science practitioner was charged with manslaughter
after the death of a patient treated solely by the healer. The first case
involved Abby Corner, whose daughter had died in childbirth following mental treatment. While Corner was found not guilty, because
there was no way to prove that a "real" doctor could have saved the
patient, the defecting members of the Christian Science Association
insisted that Eddy should combine a mixture of standard and alternative healing in her new college course on obstetrics. While she continued to emphasize "demonstration," as the only method of childbirth,

Eddy was aware of the trend toward doctor-attended birth, and she began to advise her students that at the first sign of a problem, they should send immediately for a doctor.[47]

In 1882, following the death of her husband, Eddy had asked her son George to come and visit her. George had declined, stating that his wife would not allow him to make the long trip. But in 1887 George proposed a visit to his mother. The trip was prompted by a $10,000 legacy George had received from the estate of his aunt Abigail Tilton and the knowledge that his mother's movement was gaining in strength and that she was increasingly prosperous. He had a severe need for investment capital to carry out his mining ventures in South Dakota, and had a young family (a wife and three children) who had never met their grandmother. Eddy wrote back immediately, advising him not to come: "[I have] no room that I can let even a boarder into." She also commented, "I must have quiet in my house, and it will not be pleasant for you in Boston." She urged her son to stay away from her until her public labors had ceased and she had sent for him. She concluded that if George were to come after receiving her letter, he must have "no regard for [her] interest or feelings." George came any-way, accompanied by his wife and three young children. Eddy invited them to Thanksgiving dinner and later introduced them to the Boston church. There is no question, however, that Eddy was embarrassed by George and his family. She was appalled by their western ways and dress, the illiteracy of George and Nellie, and the children's lack of education. While she realized there wasn't much she could do for George and Nellie, she did hope to educate her grandchildren, and she frequently criticized the misspellings in the letters she received from them. She kept in closer touch with George in the years to come and increasingly offered money and opportunities for the education of his children. But Eddy and her son had little in common, and it was clear that while supportive of his mother, George was as interested in her money as in her affection.[48]

Three months with George and his family must have convinced Eddy that she would never be able to establish a true mother-son bond with the illiterate prospector. In recent years, she had also suffered the loss of her two last surviving siblings, and she was faced with defections from her church by longtime members to whom she had once been close. In a state of emotional turmoil and loneliness, she made one of the worst and most bizarre decisions of her life, adopting a son, Ebenezer J. Foster, M.D., a forty-one-year-old homeopath from Vermont who had been attracted to Christian Science after witnessing healings. He had arrived in Boston in 1887 and entered one of Eddy's classes. The stark contrast between the rough-hewn George and the charming and sophisticated Foster, almost the same age, may have played a role in her attraction to the latter. The official adoption in November 1888 must have been a shock to George in South Dakota, as he contemplated what the existence of a stepbrother, who took the last name of Foster Eddy, on the scene in Boston would mean to any future inheritance. Foster Eddy was fun, humorous, effusive in his praise, and affectionate to Eddy. She took him into her confidence and relied on him for help by assigning him to important positions in the Boston church, and in 1892 he became her publisher, the most lucrative position she could confer on any of her followers. Eddy was convinced of his sincerity and devotion, as he said all the right things about his commitment to Christian Science, but his laziness, inefficiency, and complacency in carrying out his duties caused increasing hostility toward the heir apparent among her hardworking followers. Eddy seemed to always forgive Foster Eddy, particularly for his profligacy with money, which she always provided him. She finally realized her mistake when he deceived her by taking on as his secretary and mistress a woman who had previously criticized Eddy in print. She ceased to think of him as her son and sent Foster Eddy packing in 1897 with a payoff of $15,000, though he legally remained her son and would reappear in 1907.[49]

More surprises were in store for Christian Scientists. In 1889, in a series of moves, Eddy first resigned as pastor of the Boston church. In June, she gave the *Christian Science Journal* to the National Christian Science Association, which she then adjourned for three years. That month she moved to Concord, New Hampshire. From Concord, she continued to dismantle her organization by dissolving the Christian Science Association in Boston, which was made up of her most faithful former students; she then closed the Massachusetts Metaphysical College, even though enrollment and applications were higher than ever. Finally, in December 1889, she dissolved the formal organization of the church. Clearly, at age sixty-eight, Eddy was exhausted by the unremitting toil associated with the growth of Christian Science, but she also had a remarkable organizational capacity, and during her nearly twenty years of residence in New Hampshire, she continued to direct the rapidly growing movement, vesting herself with the final authority on all matters. Eddy's reputation as the divinely inspired decision maker would prove the movement's most important asset. In fact, she relied on that reputation in order to take total control of all aspects of Christian Science. In 1894, at the dedication of the Mother Church building in Boston, she decreed that Christian Science services would no longer include a pastor and that only *Science and Health* was to be read at each service, with her name as the author being credited at the beginning and the end of each passage. A year later she commanded this of all Christian Science church services. No longer would there be any sermons by preachers. She created the *Manual of the Mother Church*, which was filled with bylaws that were to rule all future church activities. The bylaws, which were added to and deleted on a regular basis, gave her the power to excommunicate any member of the church, change any officer, and be the sole elucidator of the Bible and of *Science and Health*, a bylaw that could "neither be amended nor annulled, except by the consent of the Pastor Emeritus [Eddy]." The absurdities of the dictatorial edicts were exposed by Mark Twain in a series of articles in the *North American Review* and later republished in book form. Twain concluded, "A marvelous woman; with a hunger for power such as has never been seen in the world before. No thing, little or big, that contains any seed or suggestion of power escapes her avaricious eye; and when once she gets that eye on it, her remorseless grip follows." But in 1889, her decisions were viewed by many as a retirement and a move for more local control of each Christian Science church, and she did become increasingly inaccessible to anyone other than the members of her household and selected church officials. In 1890, she issued "Seven Rules" to be followed by all Christian Scientists, a list that declared she was not to "be consulted verbally, or through letters" on any matter of church government or "the treatment of the sick," although she professed to "love all mankind—and [to] work for their welfare."[50]

In June 1889, Eddy rented a house at 62 North State Street in Concord but was not satisfied with the run-down condition of the property or its close proximity to downtown. She remained in the rental property for nearly two years, but in the fall of 1891, while out on her daily carriage ride, she spotted a small farmhouse about one mile southwest of Main Street in Concord. She bought the property, with its expansive views of woodlands, meadows, and the hills of her childhood home in Bow, and after renovation to the property she moved in June 1892. She added bow windows and wide verandas and built a tower room with a balcony on the southeast corner, which commanded the best view of the hills and valley. She later bought more land, built a gardener's cottage, stables and outbuildings, and a large pond with a boathouse. The property became a working farm, producing vegetables and dairy products, and Eddy took a personal interest in what was planted each year. The beautifully manicured lawn and colorful flowers attracted the citizens of Concord annually as a rite of spring. Located on the south side of Pleasant Street, the property was named Pleasant View, and she would remain there, in splendid isolation, for the next fifteen and one-half years.[51]

Eddy described her own carefully regimented routine: her rising at six o'clock, dinner promptly at noon, a 2:00 p.m. carriage drive through town, and her retiring in the evening promptly at 9:00 p.m. She worked all day answering letters and meeting with church officials, who arrived by train from Boston, and with her household staff, which was recruited from Christian Science members and called to Pleasant View to spend a year or more serving "Mother." Heading the staff was

Calvin A. Frye, who had served Eddy since being called to Boston in 1882. Frye was a widower from Lawrence, Massachusetts, who had worked as a machinist. He became one of the most important figures in the history of Christian Science and the most mysterious. Described as "a small, inconspicuous, silent man," he "preferred to keep out of the limelight." Frye was mulish, antisocial, aloof, laconic, and lacking in charm and grace, and Eddy once described him as "the most disagreeable man that can be found." Yet he was scrupulously honest and devoted, and as she both seized dictatorial control over her movement and simultaneously retreated into seclusion, Frye became an object of resentment, to some appearing to be the man who controlled her, screened her visitors and mail, and served in all capacities: secretary, bookkeeper, even liveried footman. He would remain with Eddy until her death in 1910; always a workhorse, Frye became indispensable.[52]

Mary Baker Eddy quickly became the most celebrated citizen of Concord, New Hampshire. Because she was bothered by the rough roads on her daily carriage ride, she offered to pay the city to pave some of the streets in downtown Concord. She created a fund to provide shoes for needy boys and girls. In 1899, she invited the public to Pleasant View to see the house and gardens as a part of the state celebration of Old Home Week. In 1900 and 1901, she briefly attended the state fair, the grounds of which could be seen in the valley below Pleasant View. On both occasions, her carriage was driven around the track, to great applause from the large crowds, and she made a cash contribution each year to the state fair association. These rare appearances, other than her daily carriage ride, may have been orchestrated to counter the speculation that occasionally appeared in the press concerning her health. The *Concord Monitor* reported that "Mrs. Eddy appeared in the best of health and effectually proved to the 25,000 people who saw her the falsity of some reports . . . concerning her ill health." She also invited members of the Mother Church in Boston to visit her on occasion. The first of these visits occurred in June 1895. Other excursions from Boston to see Eddy occurred in 1897, 1900, 1901, and 1903, and in 1904 members came for the dedication of the

First Church of Christ, Scientist, in Concord, which she had paid for. In each case special trains brought throngs of well-dressed, well-behaved, middle-class church members from Boston to spend the day in Concord, where local restaurants, vendors, and other businesses welcomed the additional revenue. The size of the crowd grew with each invitation so that the 1903 visitation was estimated at ten thousand to twelve thousand people. Although Eddy never mingled with the visitors, speaking to them solely from the balcony of Pleasant View, the adulation and enthusiasm of her followers caused her concerns as she aged and thought about how her church would fare after she passed on. She wanted the church to be governed in the future according to the bylaws in the *Manual* and the theology found in *Science and Health*. With this in mind, she forbade any future visitations following the 1904 gathering at the church in downtown Concord.[53]

The relative seclusion of Concord did not diminish the challenges Mary Baker Eddy faced from within her own movement. The most serious of these was the case of Josephine C. Woodbury. Woodbury had been associated with Christian Science since 1879 and had become one of its best teachers and healers. She rose to prominence within the church through a combination of her intelligence, attractiveness, ambition, and effectiveness as a speaker, coupled with a strong sense of public relations and secured by a close relationship with Eddy. Woodbury drew a devoted following in Boston and later in Montreal, and in 1886 established her own Christian Science academy. Teaching a somewhat more emotional or sentimental brand of the religion, she attracted a mostly naïve, poorly educated group of spinsters and, as Gill puts it, "sad and dissatisfied young mothers" and their "cajoled, fascinated and entrapped" husbands and male relatives. While she preached sexual abstinence, she did not practice what she preached, and in 1890, though married, she found herself pregnant following a liaison in Montreal with Henry L. Putnam. She claimed that the illegitimate child was actually the result of "immaculate conception," christened him as the "Prince of Peace," and credited to Eddy's teaching that a repetition of the original virgin birth was possible to Christian

Science women of exceptional purity. Woodbury's Prince was thus the second Christ, immaculately conceived of the Holy Ghost, a revelation vouchsafed to Woodbury in *Science and Health*. She then demanded five- and ten-dollar tributes to her remarkable child from among her followers. The credulity of her naïve followers had finally reached its limits, however, and the *Boston Traveller* reported several lawsuits against her, suits charging, among other things, alienation of affection, a divorce case in which the husband had given all his earnings to support Prince, and a claim by several investors that Woodbury had pressured them to invest in her husband's dubious "air-engine" company. She sued the *Traveller* for criminal libel—and lost the case.[54]

For some unexplained reason, Eddy tolerated and protected Woodbury until 1896. Their correspondence shows that Woodbury was alternatively admitting her sins and begging forgiveness and attempting to charm Eddy with praise for her leadership and righteousness. Eddy even proposed Woodbury for membership in the Mother Church, but in 1896 she was finally expelled from Christian Science. Woodbury then turned her considerable talents against Eddy, working with Horatio Dresser, leader of the Quimby faction, on a two-part article titled "Eddyism Exposed," published in the Boston magazine *Arena* in 1899. Woodbury depicted her former idol "as a mercenary, hypocritical tyrant, and Christian Science as a cowed, craven, and cretinous group, wholly under the sway of their Leader, incapable of independent thought or moral conduct." Woodbury professed that Eddy terrorized the members of her church with injury through mesmerism if they crossed her. Eddy responded in her annual Communion Message of June 1899, which was read four times at the Mother Church. Using the Book of Revelation as her text, she denounced moral corruption as personified by "the Babylonish woman": "The Babylonish woman is fallen, and who should mourn over the widowhood of lust, of her that 'is become the habitation of devils, and the hold of every foul spirit, and a cage of every unclean . . . bird.'" There seems little doubt that Eddy was assigning to Woodbury the traits of the Babylonish woman, although Eddy never mentioned Woodbury in the message. On July

31, 1899, Woodbury brought a suit for libel against Eddy and related suits against six other Christian Science organizations and boards. The suits were filed in both Massachusetts and New Hampshire.[55]

Woodbury's lawyer, Frederick Peabody, filed an extraordinary declaration asking for $150,000 in damages and containing thirty-seven counts and fifteen thousand words of complaint against Eddy and Christian Science. Until the case was heard in 1901, the Woodbury-Peabody team would be the most pressing issue for Eddy and her church administration. Although Woodbury's activity and behavior seem bizarre today, Eddy feared that their exposure in court and in the press would bring ridicule on Christian Science and irredeemably hurt the movement. In fact, Peabody's motive was to discredit Christian Science and make a name for himself. Born in New York, Peabody had earned a law degree from Columbia, moved to Boston, and married into a prominent family. The marriage would prove an unhappy one, with Peabody bringing his wife to court three separate times on charges of desertion, as she left him to preserve her inheritance from his financial profligacy and deepening debt. Peabody's hatred and contempt for Christian Science would become the motivating factor in his life, and long after Woodbury disappeared from the scene, Peabody would continue to be the chief antagonist of Christian Science and the leading conduit of information and misinformation about Eddy.[56]

Most of his thirty-seven counts were indictments of Eddy, claiming that she believed she had been selected by God to start her religion, that she claimed to be the equal of Jesus Christ, that she believed that sickness, suffering, and death could be caused by mental effort, and that death and destruction would overtake all who opposed her. Peabody charged that Woodbury had been excommunicated without a hearing because of Eddy's jealousy and ill will. After filing the suit, Woodbury and Peabody continued to feed sensational stories to the press. In December 1899, Eddy's lawyers brought a contempt of court charge against Woodbury, who was found guilty, fined, and warned not to attempt to use the press to influence the proceedings in her libel suit. Eddy was very much involved in working with her attorneys, including Frank Streeter of Concord, throughout the preparation for the trial and occasionally redirected their efforts, based on her own instincts. The case finally came to trial at the end of May 1901. The judge summarily dismissed most of Peabody's thirty-seven counts, which, while they might have made interesting reading, were not illegal, as an attack on a religious leader for her teachings was seen by many Americans as a violation of freedom of religion and represented a line that no judge wanted to cross. By bringing such a broad-based indictment against a religion, Peabody had actually weakened his case for libel, and the judge quickly dismissed the suit. The suits against the other defendants were also soon dropped without coming to trial.[57]

Eddy was a decisive winner in court, but Peabody soon launched an aggressive crusade against her and Christian Science, with a vituperative lecture at Tremont Temple in Boston on August 1, 1901. The lecture was published as a pamphlet, *A Complete Exposé of Eddyism or Christian Science and the Plain Truth in Plain Terms Regarding Mary Baker G. Eddy,* which sold for twenty-five cents. Peabody claimed that Eddy was "a rank imposter" and that *Science and Health* was the product of "an insane mind, a degenerate mind" that perpetrated a "monstrous fraud upon the human race." His very public course attracted the attention of nearly everyone who had left or been forced out of Eddy's movement. Peabody was soon in contact with Richard Kennedy, Daniel Spofford, Ebenezer Foster Eddy, Horatio Dresser, and others. In turn, the information Peabody gathered from these sources would be passed along and influence the work of Georgine Milmine, Willa Cather, and Mark Twain. Peabody would also become an integral part of the legal proceedings that followed the *New York World* article in October 1906 and became known as the "next friends case."[58]

Based on scores of interviews with disaffected ex-Scientists, Peabody developed a persuasive case against Eddy, which is best summarized from the most recent scholarly biography of Mary Baker Eddy by Gillian Gill. According to Gill, Peabody attacked Eddy on nine counts: First, as a child she was a hysteric, prone to fits that manipulated others. Second, she had taken morphine to treat her

various ailments. Third, she had received almost no formal education, coming from a poor family, and was barely literate. Fourth, she
was a Spiritualist and had earned a living as a medium. Fifth, she had
taken all her ideas from Dr. P. P. Quimby, copying sections of his
unpublished work. Sixth, she was abnormally interested in sex and was
attracted to younger men. Seventh, she had almost no religious feeling
and was only motivated by money and power. Eighth, she was devoid
of all maternal feeling, having abandoned her only child. Ninth, her
religious doctrine had caused the deaths of thousands of innocent
children whose parents had treated them using only her method of
mental healing. All of these accusations would resurface in the press
or in court in the months following the article in the *New York World*.[59]

In spite of all the bitter attacks and attempts to discredit her, by
1906 Eddy had prevailed in establishing a new religion, which was
growing and flourishing around the world. Gill concludes that "truth
in Mrs. Eddy's case is often stranger than fiction" but that Eddy should
not be underestimated or ignored by history or by the feminist movement, for "what other woman in modern times has had this kind of
vision and this kind of power to implement it?" Gill asks, "What other
woman has established a religious movement of international stat-
ure? In what other religion or religious denomination is a woman's
message offered next to that of Jesus Christ?"[60] But Eddy faced one
more daunting challenge in her final years: a suit brought against her
by her son, adopted son, and other relatives, to control her and her
estate—and the accompanying enormous press coverage that invaded
the world of seclusion that she had tried to establish at Pleasant View.

= 3 =

CHANDLER AND STREETER

I n Lead, South Dakota, George Glover read an Associated Press
report of his mother's cancer and overall debility. He wrote immediately to Hermann Hering, first reader of the Christian Science
Church in Concord: "Will you be so kind as to give me the facts in
reference to the truth of this dispatch." Hering answered, enclosing
a copy of the *Concord Monitor*, saying, "You can rest assured that the
statements in the *Monitor* are correct. I have seen Mrs. Eddy several
times lately and can vouch for her good health and spirits."[1]

The *New York World* was determined to prove at least some of the
allegations made in the article of October 28, 1906. In November,
Samuel G. Blythe, business manager of the newspaper, contacted former U.S. senator William Eaton Chandler of New Hampshire to retain
him as counsel, informing him that the *World* "wanted a thorough
exploration of the facts with a view to suitable publicity in connection with the *World*'s function of telling all the news." Blythe specifically mentioned the charge that Eddy was being impersonated in her
daily rides. Chandler insisted on more information, and the *World*
sent reporter John W. Slaght to Chandler's home in Washington,
D.C. Before meeting with Slaght, Chandler wrote to Portsmouth,
New Hampshire, attorney John W. Kelley, who was recommended
by Blythe, asking Kelley to serve as cocounsel. Chandler laid out the

situation for Kelley: "If there is reason to believe that [Eddy] is practically imbecile and not having made a will while she was competent to do so, any property that she may possess or may leave belongs to her existing heirs, and unless she comes back to her senses and capacity she cannot make a will to give it to any one else." Chandler insisted that the first step was to find "genuine relatives of Mrs. Eddy who sincerely desire and have a right to take suitable steps." Those relatives also had a right to ascertain, with or without litigation, if her surroundings were "suitable and proper" and whether she was in "custody" of others. To Kelley, Chandler admitted, "The *World*'s interest is partly for sensational purposes but may be entirely legitimate."[2]

After meeting with Slaght on November 21 and 22, Chandler received confirmation that Kelley had agreed to act as cocounsel. Chandler then invited Kelley to Washington, D.C., for a meeting, concluding, "It is good business and preparation is going to be carefully made. Keep everything secret." Chandler and the *World* then sent Slaght to South Dakota to meet with George Glover.[3] It was a brilliant coup for the *World* to engage William Eaton Chandler as its lead attorney in the Eddy matter. Chandler was the most famous New Hampshire politician of his time and, along with Levi Woodbury and Franklin Pierce, one of the three most powerful politicians in New Hampshire history. Chandler was a recognizable name to many in the country at that time. But he was an enigmatic figure: a brilliant behind-the-scenes political operative for the Republican Party, an outspoken independent and progressive, and a consistent advocate for the powerless. That Chandler was all of these things makes it impossible to characterize his long political career in a few words.

Born in Concord, New Hampshire, on December 28, 1835, Chandler developed an early interest in the law, working as a sixteen-year-old in the offices of John H. George and Sidney Webster, close allies to Franklin Pierce. Chandler was assigned to collect legal fees owed to Pierce when he was running for president in 1852. Pierce had visited young Chandler when he was seriously ill in bed with a fever. Though Chandler became an outspoken Republican and abolitionist, he retained a soft spot for the kindly Pierce, later calling him the "gentlest and most joyous of men" and the "most gracious of the twelve Presidents with whom I was intimately associated."[4] Chandler received a bachelor of laws degree from Harvard in 1854 and returned to Concord, where he was appointed city solicitor and reporter of the supreme court. He married Ann Caroline Gilmore, the daughter of Joseph A. Gilmore, superintendent of the Concord Railroad and one of the richest men in the state. Chandler avoided military service during the Civil War but continued his steady rise within the Republican Party, becoming a member of the "drug-store clique," a political machine that dominated New Hampshire politics for decades. In 1863, he convinced his father-in-law to run for governor and secured his victory by helping create a third party of Union Democrats, to divide the popular vote and keep the favored Democratic candidate from receiving the necessary majority. Though polling six percentage points behind the Democrat, Joseph Gilmore was chosen governor by the state legislature. A year later, Gilmore won a second term, thanks to Chandler's complicated legislative and constitutional maneuvers that allowed soldiers at the front to vote. By a three-to-one majority, they supported Lincoln and Gilmore, helping to keep New Hampshire in the Republican column. Chandler considered this one of the two greatest achievements of his long political career.[5]

Chandler then moved to Washington, D.C., where he was appointed assistant secretary of the treasury by Andrew Johnson. Chandler resigned in disgust over Johnson's policies but remained in Washington, becoming a representative of the Union Pacific Railroad and a member of the Republican National Committee. His close friendship with Jay Cooke, banker and railroad magnate, helped fund Grant's campaign for the presidency in 1868. In 1871, Chandler's first wife died, leaving him with three young sons, Joseph, William, and Lloyd. In 1872, in his role on the National Committee, Chandler practically ran Grant's reelection campaign. He married Lucy Hale, the daughter of former senator John Parker Hale of New Hampshire, in 1874. Lucy Hale was once considered the belle of Washington. As a young girl, she had been courted by Oliver Wendell Holmes Jr., Robert Lincoln, and John Wilkes Booth. Chandler had once written her a love poem while he was a student at Harvard. Their only child, Jack, was born in 1885.[6]

Chandler always claimed that his greatest achievement in a long political career was securing the presidency for Rutherford B. Hayes in the disputed election of 1876. On election night, Chandler was the first to recognize that if the states of South Carolina, Florida, and Louisiana could be swung to the Republican column, Hayes would win the Electoral College by one vote. Chandler wired everyone he knew to prevent those states from confirming their results, then headed for Florida to personally supervise the effort. There is no question today that money changed hands, that genuine Democratic ballots were rejected, and that fraudulent Republican votes were counted in Florida. Chandler had mapped the strategy, directed the forces, and put the whole administration to work to swing South Carolina, Florida, and Louisiana into line. Historians have concurred that Chandler "was the brains as well as the force of the Hayes fight" and that "far more than any other man" Chandler was responsible for "this result." From this time on, Chandler was known as a corrupt politician who had stolen the election for Hayes, though Republicans recognized him as an intrepid political manager.[7] In 1884, Chandler managed James G. Blaine's unsuccessful campaign for the presidency, and recognizing the likelihood of a Democratic victory, he supported the third-party campaign of Benjamin "Beast" Butler of Massachusetts by funneling $5,000 a week of Republican money to Butler, to keep him in the race and divide the Democratic vote. This time Chandler failed, however, with Grover Cleveland winning the close election. Chandler was serving at the time as secretary of the navy in the Arthur administration. Though considered a corrupt "spoilsman" by Democrats, Chandler ran a clean department and had some success modernizing the navy.[8] Finally, in 1887, he was chosen by the New Hampshire legislature to fill an unexpired term in the U.S. Senate. He was reelected in 1889 and in 1895.

As a senator, Chandler struck a surprisingly independent course. He was adamant that the Republican Party had a responsibility to "the Negro," consistently supporting force bills that would secure African American voting in the South. In one impassioned speech in the Senate, Chandler stated, "A Republican can believe in tariff reduction or even free trade and yet properly adhere to the party, but he cannot fail to advocate the Fifteenth Amendment and all proper laws to supplement it and to enforce it and yet be a Republican. His only proper place is with the Negro-baiting Republican killing Democracy."[9] These efforts all failed, as neither party wanted to upset the truce that allowed southern whites to dominate blacks. Chandler also went against his party in advocating bimetallism, the coinage of both gold and silver, during the tumultuous 1896 election and after. In his later years in the Senate, his major crusade was against the corporate power of the railroads. He supported maximum rates and an end to free passes and other perks that the railroads freely dispensed to state and national legislators to win their support. His opposition to the political power of railroad corporations also led him to introduce a bill to ban all corporate contributions to political campaigns—the first national campaign-financing proposal.[10]

Chandler's outspoken hostility to the railroads cost him his Senate seat in 1901. Ever since the Boston & Maine had successfully consolidated all lines in the state, New Hampshire politics was dominated by its railroad machine. Anyone seeking a political career in the state between 1895 and 1906 had to win the support of the Boston & Maine. Though popular with the national press, Chandler had to run an uphill campaign for reelection. The *Boston Herald* admitted that Chandler was an "unscrupulous politician" but "his better traits offset the objections" to him. The *Boston Post* viewed the power of the Boston & Maine "with alarm," claiming that the railroad "by secret agencies and upon false pretexts" was striving to defeat Chandler. The *Washington Post* declared, "We cannot afford to lose Chandler." The newspaper seemed interested mainly in the entertainment value of his Senate career.

He is like the small boy who stirs up the animals in the cages for the pleasure of hearing them roar. When the senate lapses into dullness, Chandler launches a shaft of sarcasm, strikes the weak points of some fellow-senator's armor, incites an angry reply, and laughs at the disturbance which insues. He is the matador of the senatorial bull ring—the bear bater of the senatorial pit.

Chandler veneers his sarcasm with a crust of good nature which makes him irresistible. Nobody takes him seriously, not even the fiery [Ben] Tillman, whom he taunts with stinging jibe in public and admires in private. Under his most waspish sentences there is a laugh which robs them of their sting. He is keenly sarcastic because he cannot help it, and he has so many good qualities that everybody likes him.

If Chandler is retired into private life, the senate will be dull, indeed.[11]

Republican senators came out in support of Chandler, in spite of the independent course he had adopted, with Republican Senate leaders George Hoar, Nelson Aldrich, T. C. Platt, and others stating in the *Washington Post* that Chandler still retained the confidence of the Republican Party. But it was all in vain; the omnipotent Boston & Maine succeeded in defeating Chandler in the state legislature, replacing him with a cipher who would do the railroad's bidding.[12]

He was not out of a job for long, as President McKinley immediately appointed Chandler president of the Spanish Treaty Claims Commission. In this position, Chandler would preside over the dispensing of $65 million in some 542 claims made by American citizens against the Spanish government of Cuba, money that the United States had agreed to pay as part of the treaty ending the Spanish-American War. He was not out of the headlines for long either. On March 31, 1906, President Theodore Roosevelt called his good friend Chandler to the White House. The two met in private, Roosevelt apparently asking for Chandler's help in devising a strategy to get the Senate to approve granting to the Interstate Commerce Commission the power to set maximum freight rates for the railroads. This was the purpose of the Hepburn bill, which was languishing in Congress because, according to Roosevelt, the Republican leadership failed to push for the bill. Roosevelt asked Chandler to seek bipartisan support for the bill from his Democratic friends in the Senate. Chandler did so, winning support from an old friend, populist senator "Pitchfork Ben" Tillman of South Carolina. At some point, however, Roosevelt changed his mind, and the Republicans pushed the bill through Congress without bipartisan support. Chandler was furious that his deal with Tillman had not been honored by the president and called Roosevelt a "liar" in the press. Although Chandler considered himself a "radical progressive," he never forgave Roosevelt and would oppose him in the future within the Republican Party.[13]

By the time Chandler agreed to represent the *World* in the Eddy matter, he was seventy-one years old but in good health, and as an irascible self-promoter, he was not ready to be put out to pasture. A spare, thin man of about five feet eight inches in height, Chandler had sported a full beard for many years. Though born in Concord, he had a home in Washington, D.C., and another in rural Waterloo, New Hampshire, where he had remodeled an old farmhouse and enjoyed his daily walk and mountain climbing. He spent little time in Concord, though he had owned several businesses there, including the *Concord Monitor* newspaper and the Rumford Printing Company. By 1906, he had sold part interest in the newspaper to one of his sons, William D. Chandler, and to the editor, George H. Moses. A brilliant debater, with a quick mind, a strong independent streak, and a penchant for taking on causes that he could not win, Chandler was prepared to give his all to prove that Mary Baker Eddy was not in control of her life or her money.

In late November, *World* reporter John W. Slaght headed west to meet with Eddy's son, George Glover, armed with written instructions from Chandler. Based on his meetings with Slaght, Chandler determined that the issues to be investigated included whether Eddy was in the custody of strangers against her will, whether she was so "worn out in body, and mind" that she was incapable of managing her business or property affairs, and whether the "designing men" who controlled her were seeking to "wrongfully possess" her property or dispose of it contrary to her "deliberate intentions." Slaght was to try to convince her son of his duty "to solve the doubts; to correct wrong if it exist[ed] and to establish the right in every respect."[14] Slaght was to give Glover a letter from Chandler stating that the questions needed to be investigated "by no means any further as a mere newspaper enterprise but as questions involving doubts which from large and commendable motives all good citizens and especially all relatives of Mrs. Eddy should help to solve and settle."[15]

After meeting with Slaght, Glover agreed to participate, with the caveat that he "investigate for [him]self." He wrote, "Temporary lack of funds renders this impossible, but if my expenses are advanced I stand ready to go east at once to see my mother and judge of her condition and surroundings for myself." Glover insisted that his daughter, Mary, accompany him on the trip. If he determined that his mother was "enfeebled in mind and body" and "helpless in the power of Calvyn A. Frye and his associates," Glover would be glad to accept Chandler's legal counsel: "I will gladly avail myself of your legal services in the protection of her rights and my own. Furthermore I agree to confide the results of my investigation alone to you or to Mr. Slaght your accredited representative."[16] After returning to New York, Slaght wrote Chandler a detailed account of his visit with the Glovers. Slaght seemed genuinely touched by their poverty. Glover agreed to meet with Slaght only after the "pleadings" of Nellie Glover, who also "wept pitieously as they opened their hearts" to the reporter. Slaght stated that Glover was "in abject poverty," had received no financial assistance from his mother for the last six years, and had not heard directly from her in four years. His last meeting with his mother had been in 1892,[17] when Frye allowed him only twenty-five minutes alone with her. Glover's frequent letters to Eddy "remain unanswered." Glover was "literally penniless" from unsuccessful mining operations, and "the family [had] been close to actual starvation many times during the last year." Slaght reported, "Glover is intensely proud." But Slaght also wrote, "His real fear is that if by any chance his mother should be fairly sound in mind and not incompetent, as he firmly believes her to be, any action by him would lead to his certain disinheritance." After the meeting, Slaght still seemed unaware of Glover's illiteracy and questioned why his daughter needed to accompany him east: "Miss Glover could be of no service to us." The *World* was ready to send a check to meet all expenses of Glover's trip east.[18] It must have seemed strange to Slaght to meet such penniless people living in a beautiful, large, brick home. But Eddy had given a new house to her son in 1899. She had previously sent money but tired of funding his unsuccessful mining ventures. To Eddy, it seemed that her son was "always looking down into the earth, [as] she was looking up and away from it." The home in Lead was one of the most beautiful in the Black Hills, but Glover lacked the funds to maintain it or pay the taxes on it.[19]

Meanwhile, at the request of Chandler, his cocounsel, John W. Kelley, met in New York with the *World's* managing editor, Bradford Merrill. Kelley reported the meeting to Chandler, expressing some doubts about the *World's* commitment in the Eddy matter. Merrill sent Kelley to meet with the *World's* attorney, a Mr. Bowers, whose main purpose was to defend the paper's libel suits. Bowers "expressed contempt for any evidence or reports adduced by *World* reporters" but knew nothing about the facts in the Eddy matter, even questioning if there were any facts. He did state that if Chandler and Kelley found that the evidence looked reasonable and the *World* wanted to pursue the matter, "it would be done," but if there was no probable cause of action, "then no action would be begun, whatever the wishes of the *World* might be." Bowers did confirm that Slaght was "a competent man."[20] Kelley was one of the leading attorneys and citizens of Portsmouth, New Hampshire. A Republican and a Catholic, Kelley established a large and lucrative practice while also serving as city solicitor and county solicitor as well as a member of the board of education. Kelley was a Dartmouth College graduate and former varsity

football player who was thirty years Chandler's junior and who was at
the height of his profession at the time of the Eddy case. Besides having a "brilliant mind," Kelley "was a good fellow and a good friend."
His levelheadedness would serve the more volatile and headstrong
Chandler well throughout the Eddy litigation.[21]

After receiving Kelley's disturbing account of his visit to the *World*
in New York, Chandler immediately wrote to Bradford Merrill, seeking clarification. Chandler shared with Merrill Kelley's concerns that
Bowers "would advise against" any movement on behalf of Glover
and "against Eddy's custodians," that Bowers "distrusted" any "facts"
published in the *World* and would not base legal action on them, and
that Bowers feared there was a plan to proceed with litigation "without
thorough investigation." Chandler assured Merrill that he and Kelley
would "not be a party" to any legal proceedings without thorough
investigation, and Chandler knew that "Mr. [Joseph] Pulitzer would
not allow any such conduct." Chandler asked Merrill to define "the
relation of Mr. Bowers to the business" and asked that Pulitzer be
informed and "advise [Chandler and Kelley] of his wishes."[22]

Merrill's response was written two days later. Merrill assured
Chandler, "Mr. Bowers will not be asked to act in this case." Merrill also
stated, "We rely upon you absolutely to advise us as to the sufficiency
of the legal grounds for the case in equity after you shall have seen
Mr. Glover in person and after Mr. Slaght's further reports to you."
Merrill flattered Chandler: "You are doing a very unselfish and high-
minded thing—really a public service—in giving so much thought
without substantial compensation." To demonstrate the *World's* faith
in Chandler, Merrill enclosed a check for $500 to cover the expense of
bringing Glover east. Merrill added that the state of Pulitzer's health
made it impossible for the *World's* publisher to be consulted on the
matter, saying also, "But we make decisions and act on all public matters in his absence in accordance with his general policy and instructions." It is not clear what role Joseph Pulitzer played in the decision
to attack Eddy, but his hostility to Christian Science was well known.
He had once asserted, "There is a strong leaning toward the view that

the misguided religious people are hysterical women and weakminded men." According to biographer David Brian, "Pulitzer's attitude to all such movements was informed skepticism, and he encouraged the *World* to follow his lead."[23] The fact that Pulitzer was not involved in the Eddy decisions and could not be consulted in the day-to-day operations of the *World* should have been a red flag to Chandler, but subsequent events would show that this information barely registered with him.[24]

On Sunday, December 9, Chandler met all day in Washington with John W. Slaght, learning firsthand of his visit with the Glovers in South Dakota. The next day Chandler sent a lengthy letter to Glover. He focused entirely on the issue of Eddy's property and wealth and Glover's potential inheritance. To Chandler, the issue was that Eddy was probably "incapable of transacting business" and that she was surrounded and controlled by "strangers to her blood" who were engaged "in getting possession of her large property and illegally appropriating it to their own uses." Chandler concluded, "Something then it is clear should be done by somebody." He agreed with Glover's fear about receiving less in her will: "If you move Mrs. Eddy will be pushed on by her captors to anger against you." But Chandler tried to reassure Glover that if she was "incapable of doing any act," then she could not in the future either "disinherit [him] or make a future will in [his] favor." Chandler told Glover, "Judging from her treatment of you in the past . . . the probabilities are that she has left you but little." Chandler asserted that "by deeds and agreements and donations," Eddy had already "deprived herself of large values which otherwise" would have been her son's. Chandler concluded, therefore, that if Glover did "not move," he would "most probably . . . lose everything" because her assets were presently being "diverted from her," and it would be impossible to prove after her death that she was incapable of making decisions relating to the disposal of her property. Chandler went on to flatter Glover, expressing the understanding that Glover did not want to do anything to dishonor his mother or to take any step "which an affectionate and high-minded and honorable son should refrain from taking." But if Glover was concerned about any future "reproach" against him for acting, he should consider that Eddy's present situation was far worse "than any possible outcome of a full ascertainment and exhibition of the true and exact facts [could] possibly be." Chandler urged Glover to come east and predicted he would be "allowed a short interview [with his mother] carefully prepared for by Frye and peremptorily cut short" and would likely learn "no more about Mrs. Eddy's real soundness of mind" than Chandler and Kelley knew already. Chandler thus prepared Glover that he would learn nothing new from the visit but asked, "Why not go [to court] upon the evidence we now possess of her feebleness of body and mind and take our testimony and prove our case in the sight of the whole world?" Even if the *World* and its counsel were "mistaken," Chandler asserted, they could take satisfaction in going to court: "We shall have done our duty as faithful citizens and you will have done your duty as a considerate, devoted and courageous son." The letter made it clear that Chandler had decided to pursue a suit in equity based entirely on the erroneous facts provided by Slaght and the *World* and would not be swayed from this course even if Glover backed out after meeting with his mother. Chandler followed up this letter with another, reminding Glover "that the whole business [should] be kept secret until the exact steps in any movement [were] carefully decided upon and begun." Chandler expected Glover to come east within ten days and left it up to him to determine if his daughter must come with him. Slaght and Chandler may have finally understood that Glover needed Mary with him because of his illiteracy.[25]

The staff at Pleasant View was unaware of the activities of the *World* and William Chandler, focusing instead on the next challenge to Eddy and Christian Science from *McClure's Magazine*. As early as1904, a rumor reached Alfred Farlow of the Christian Science public relations staff in Boston that *McClure's* was planning a documented exposé on Eddy and Christian Science, similar to the muckraking articles the magazine had recently published against Standard Oil Company and U.S. Steel Corporation. Farlow was also aware that journalist Georgine Milmine Welles of upstate New York was the lead investigator of Eddy. "Miss Milmine," the name she used, had once been favorably disposed to Christian Science but had been turned against Eddy by Frederick Peabody, who led her to numerous sources critical of Eddy and Christian Science. *McClure's* was undergoing an upheaval of its own in June 1906, with the departure of staff writers Ray Stannard Baker, Ida M. Tarbell, and Lincoln Steffens, who were in a dispute with owner S. S. McClure. Christian Science officials believed the dispute concerned the decision about whether the magazine should go ahead with an attack on Eddy, with McClure determined to go on with the work. At around this time, Farlow and H. Cornell Wilson of the Committee on Publication visited the editorial offices of *McClure's* to meet with S. S. McClure. He sent them to his new managing editor, Witter Bynner, who assured them that he was not satisfied with Milmine's work and was having all of her facts checked by young journalist Mark Sullivan. Several months later Farlow and Wilson received similar assurances from Bynner's successor that *McClure's*, in Farlow's words, "had no intention of publishing an 'exposé' or an attack."[26]

Wilson was not fooled by the assurances from *McClure's*, expressing to Farlow that he believed church officials had only made the editorial staff more cautious and determined that every fact in the exposé would be verified by living witnesses. A letter from a Christian Scientist in Chicago confirmed that S. S. McClure had stated to a journalist in New York that the magazine was "going to start a crusade against Christian Science." The letter reported that the magazine staff would "take up every phase and development of Christian Science and do what they [could] to ridicule and destroy it."[27] It was knowledge of the upcoming *McClure's* series that prompted Joseph Pulitzer and the *New York World* to rush to print with its attack on Eddy, which appeared on October 28, 1906. Several days later, Mayor Charles Corning of Concord met with representatives of *McClure's* who were in town to determine the accuracy of the *World's* report. He was pleased to remember "the bright face & laughing black eyes of the person who spent an hour at [his] house in June, 1904," that is, Georgine Milmine, who visited Corning with her editor, Will Irwin. Corning took them to city hall, to check on "the exact sums contributed by Mrs. Eddy & her friends" toward the paving of streets in Concord. He found tickets for Milmine and Irwin for a lecture at the Concord City Auditorium that evening. Corning's reaction to the *McClure's* reporters was entirely different from his critical review of the newspaper reporters in town covering the "persecution" of Eddy. He said of Milmine and Irwin, "I enjoy meeting such persons and I lament my not falling in with them oftener than I do."[28]

The staff at Pleasant View was not fooled about the intentions of *McClure's* magazine. Lewis Strang was concerned about the magazine's investigation of the ownership of church property and how much of an inheritance a church could receive under Massachusetts law, which would become a major issue after Eddy's death. He suggested "the advisability of putting a committee of mental workers upon this McClure Magazine matter at once, and keeping them at work until the atmosphere [was] cleared and something [was] accomplished." The first installment of the fourteen-part series was to appear in the January 1907 issue and was to cover Eddy's childhood and family background. Willa Cather, who came to work for *McClure's* in 1906, was credited with rewriting much of Milmine's manuscript, which was published in book form in 1909.[29] After reviewing an advance copy of the first installment, the Pleasant View staff reacted with glee over an egregious error: the photograph of Eddy that accompanied the article was, in fact, not Eddy at all but a Sarah C. Chevaillier, the mother of a Christian Science student of Eddy's in 1885. If the magazine couldn't even get the photograph right, how much reliance could be placed on the "facts" in the article? Calvin Frye was the first to notice the photograph, writing to Farlow that "the picture published in McClure's Magazine" did not look as Eddy had "during the long period" that he had known her. Farlow answered, "That picture business is simply great and should make monkeys of the McClure people."[30]

On the day the first installment appeared, Alfred Farlow, who was in charge of public relations in Boston, wrote a long letter to

Eddy, explaining how her staff planned to combat the bad publicity. According to Farlow, "For about three years, the evil one has sought the publication of an accumulation of lies concerning our beloved Leader, which have been gathered at the suggestions of W [Woodbury], . . . Peabody, . . . and Dresser." He wrote, "The medium which has been chosen for the publication of this matter is McClure's Magazine. We have labored diligently by our prayers and otherwise to wipe all this out of existence by our understanding of the Allness of Divine Love." After *McClure's* announced the forthcoming series in its December issue, Eddy's followers "answered" through "almost every daily and weekly paper in the United States, England, Canada and Australia," which was necessary in Farlow's opinion because of the lengths *McClure's* had gone to in promoting its investigations: "I do not believe anything has ever been so widely advertised as their proposed series of articles." Farlow believed the pressures applied by Christian Scientists was getting to S. S. McClure, as much of his staff had resigned (including Baker, Tarbell, and Steffens): "Mr. McClure is at the present time almost a nervous wreck, which is probably due to the hypnotic pressure that he has been under, the gigantic determination to have him go on with this work." To guard against "the possibility of having things appear which might be offensive and provoke instead of destroy error," Farlow arranged to have Eddy's response appear in *Cosmopolitan* (with a circulation of seven hundred thousand) and "in all the Hearst papers," which, Farlow noted, had "a circulation of over five millions." William Randolph Hearst was known to be favorably disposed to Christian Science, particularly after his young son was cured of illness by a Christian Science healer. Farlow listed other periodicals that might be open to the Christian Science point of view. He concluded, "We certainly will need your wise counsel if anything new appears, as no one but yourself is in a position to know what is wise to say regarding yourself." The letter is important to consider because it shows the significance Christian Scientists attached to the *McClure's* series and how it had replaced the *World's* articles in importance in their minds. The letter also illustrates the manner in which

Eddy's officials addressed her, and her continuing predominance in the church's decision-making process.[31]

Unbeknownst to Eddy and her associates, Chandler was moving forward with his plans to litigate on behalf of the *World*. He sent Slaght to Boston to research the Christian Science organization, particularly all aspects of Eddy's financial assets, income, copyrights, and real estate. Chandler advised Slaght, "It is not intended to inquire far into what may be called *the religion*." But Chandler went on to state that if the system of healing was "fraudulent, and yet [went] forward with any connection therewith of her name it should be investigated whether it [brought] any money to her or not." Since healing was at the heart of Eddy's teaching, it is obvious from the outset that Chandler's approach was meant not only to secure an inheritance for Glover but also to discredit the religion, a fact that Chandler kept from Glover throughout the proceedings. Two weeks later Slaght reported back that he had "by hard digging" obtained the names of the men "in real control of Christian Science"—all of the committee members, financial and advertising agents, and "the men and women who direct[ed] the work of the cult 'healers' in every part of the world." He also reported a rumor that Frye and Eddy were "in reality man and wife" and planned to track that rumor to its source, Eddy's former publisher and one of her most violent opponents, William Nixon, who lived near Boston.[32]

Glover headed east on December 21, after writing a letter to his mother, requesting to meet with her. Receipt of Glover's letter may have been the first that Eddy and her associates realized that the primary threat to her and Christian Science was coming from that direction and not from *McClure's*. The sixty-two-year-old Glover, accompanied by his twenty-eight-year-old daughter and amanuensis Mary, reached Washington before Christmas and met all day on the twenty-sixth of December with Chandler. Slaght arrived from Boston the next day and joined the conference. On the twenty-eighth, Eddy sent Irving Tomlinson to Washington to see Glover and extend an invitation to meet Eddy at Pleasant View on January 2. Tomlinson was a former first reader of the Christian Science church in Concord, who still lived there and served Eddy in a variety of capacities.[33]

Chandler's plans were coming together. He wrote to cocounsel John W. Kelley, for the first time using the phrase "next friends" to describe the suit they were planning. "Next friends" are assigned by a court as guardian ad litem when an individual is proven unable to look after his or her own interests. These guardians are assigned most often to minor children, but occasionally to an older person who is not mentally competent. Such a suit would be filed in a court of equity, which, though covered by law, is also influenced by principles of ethics and fairness. At that time, Chandler seemed to believe that the next friend "must live within the jurisdiction of the court." Therefore, he was looking for "one or two N. H. citizens of character and respectability" to join Glover in the suit. Chandler's bias is evident from this statement: "Concord is so thoroughly besotted that I do not know that I could easily find a good man." Chandler hoped that Kelley might recommend someone from Portsmouth or elsewhere in Rockingham County. In a letter to Slaght, Chandler also demonstrated his bias against Eddy, when he instructed the reporter to prepare two lists of potential witnesses, "one of those who would be hostile and the other of those who would willingly tell the truth." It was clear that Chandler assumed everyone from Concord and all those who were hostile to the evidence gathered by Slaght and the *World* were wrong, despite the fact that these were the local leaders who knew Eddy personally and saw her on a regular basis and that they included the editor of Chandler's own newspaper, George H. Moses of the *Concord Evening Monitor*.[34]

Speaking to Kelley, Chandler tried to predict the strategy of the other side. He stated, "[They] will either rally and make a big fight immediately, trying to shake us off [before a suit is filed], or they will attempt delay and will demur to our bill." He noted that Eddy's lawyers could not demur until court was in session in Concord, which would not be until April 1907.[35] Eddy's legal strategy would be directed by Frank Sherwin Streeter, Eddy's counsel at various times from 1890 to 1912. Streeter had directed the defense in the libel suit

brought by Josephine Woodbury in New Hampshire in 1899. Streeter
was born in Vermont in 1853 and graduated from Dartmouth College
in 1874. After a brief period spent teaching in Iowa, he studied law
under Alonzo P. Carpenter in Bath, New Hampshire. Carpenter was
chief justice of the New Hampshire Supreme Court and one of the
most respected judicial minds in the state. In 1877, Streeter was admitted to the bar and also married Carpenter's daughter, Lillian.[36]

Streeter moved to Concord and began specializing in corporate
law. His most important client was the Boston & Maine Railroad, for
which he served as counsel for many years. Streeter also served in
the state legislature and on Republican state and national committees.
A former judge advocate general in New Hampshire, Streeter was
always referred to as "General," a courtesy title, "because it fitted the
man," according to Judge Frank Parker: "He was a general, skilled
in strategy and tactics. He had vision and diplomacy. He could plan
and command for others to execute. The plan once made, he had the
force to carry it out over whatever obstacles stood in the way, ruthless
perhaps at times of the consequences to others because of the importance, as it seemed to him, of the end aimed at." He even looked like
a general, according to journalist Bill Cunningham, who wrote that
Streeter "looked in the flesh like a portrait of Bismarck, with stern and
craglike features and wore a set of eyebrows that made the current
growths of [labor leader] John L. Lewis look like a bad case of falling
hair."[37] Streeter was serving at the time as a life member of the board of
trustees of Dartmouth College. He was a great joiner, being a Mason,
an Odd Fellow, president of the New Hampshire Historical Society,
a member of the state and national bar associations and numerous
social organizations, most significantly Concord's Wonolancet Club,
for which he served as president for over fifteen years. Streeter was
everything Chandler was not: a large bear of a man with a command-
ing presence, while Chandler was short, spare, and thin; a conservative
Republican closely aligned with the railroad machine, while Chandler
was of the progressive wing of the state party; intimately attached to
every political and social organization in the state, while Chandler

preferred his reputation to be that of an independent outsider who called things as he saw them. They had one thing in common, as both were Unitarians attending the same church in Concord. Unitarians reject the Trinity, believing that Jesus was a prophet and not God. Unitarians, also called Unitarian Universalists, oppose the concept of original sin or predestination, thus agreeing with Eddy on this point.

At the time the next friends suit was filed, Streeter had just resigned as counsel for the Boston & Maine. His resignation had been forced by the railroad's president, Frank M. Tuttle, and was the subject of much speculation in the press. Apparently, Streeter had angered Tuttle by using the railroad's political machine to push state legislation that would benefit his client in a personal injury case against a local railroad. Streeter was also accused of not forcefully backing the railroad's candidate in the recent gubernatorial election in New Hampshire, and there was speculation that his resignation was part of his strategy to win a seat in the U.S. Senate. Whatever the reasons for Streeter's resignation as the counsel for the Boston & Maine, Chandler claimed to have inside information, which he offered to share with the ace reporter for *Collier's* magazine, Mark Sullivan. Chandler may not have realized that Streeter's resignation only made him more available to serve Eddy.[38] As the New Year dawned, the players were in place for a monumental struggle over the life and property of Mary Baker Eddy and for popular opinion as to who was right in the matter and, most importantly, who was acting in the best interest of an eighty-five-year-old woman living in Concord, New Hampshire.

= 4 =

BOTH SIDES PREPARE FOR BATTLE

George Glover and his daughter Mary arrived by train from
Boston on Wednesday, January 2, 1907, for the meeting
with his mother, Mary Baker Eddy, at Pleasant View, just
over a mile west of the train depot in Concord, New Hampshire. The
train station in Depot Square was the largest in New England north of
Boston. Dominating downtown Concord were the station's Victorian
red brick exterior, iron train shed spanning six tracks, and ornate inte-
rior, featuring a two-story granite map of New Hampshire, which
loomed over one end of the central waiting room. New Hampshire
was a "railroad state," with the Boston & Maine controlling everything from the economy to politics and state government. The railroad
operated 2,280 miles of track in New England and employed nearly
fifteen hundred people in Concord alone. There were thirty-two passenger trains a day arriving at the depot, and through trains departing for Montreal and Portland, Maine. Horse-drawn wagons waited
outside the depot, to carry visitors to the Eagle or Phenix hotels or
to the State House, all of which were on Main Street, less than a half
mile from the train station.[1]

Later that day, with help from Mary Glover, George prepared a
lengthy report of the visit with his mother for his attorneys, William
E. Chandler and John W. Kelley. George and Mary arrived at Pleasant

View at 2:00 p.m. and waited for fourteen minutes. Mary heard a
"peculiar noise" over the parlor, and George speculated that it could
be a galvanic battery, the noise ceasing when the visitors were called
upstairs. They were ushered into Eddy's presence by Laura Sargent,
one of Eddy's longest-serving attendants. Eddy failed to acknowledge
their presence until Sargent addressed her a second time, at which
point Eddy pushed her papers aside and rose to her feet, greeting
George with a kiss. She also kissed Mary, stating, "I'm so glad to see
you both. Are you all well?" She commented that George looked thin-
ner than when she last saw him and remarked that Mary was now a
Christian Scientist: "All Christian Scientists are well. I hear you have
joined us."[2]

Eddy acknowledged that she was very busy writing a response to
the *McClure's* article for the press. She was particularly upset by what
the magazine had said about George's father, to which he responded,
"What, my father? What did they say about him?" Eddy answered,
"George, if ever there was a loving, tender husband, your father was
one." She went on to describe the magazine's abusive coverage of her
marriage to Daniel Patterson, at which point George moved to the
door to close it, reporting later, "I was under the impression that someone was hiding behind the door." As he closed the door, his mother
leaned back in her chair and closed her eyes as if, George wrote later,
she expected him to find someone behind the door and create a scene,
which she did not wish to witness. She went on describing the abuse
she suffered at the hands of *McClure's:* "People say I am dead, and
all such things and that it is only an imposter in my place. You know
me. I am your mother, George, am I not?" George then mentioned
several events of national news, including the recent San Francisco
earthquake, to judge his mother's alertness to the world around her.
She said she knew nothing about any of the events George mentioned,
for she was too busy to read the newspapers.[3]

Eddy then returned to the subject of Mary's conversion to
Christian Science, asking whom the young woman had studied with.
Mary denied that anyone taught her Christian Science, but Eddy

insisted it must have been a Mrs. McMann. When Mary again denied it, Eddy responded, "Why, Mary Glover, someone is lying. Didn't Mrs. McMann of your city teach you, Mary, and your family?" In his report about the visit, George stated that he then jumped into the conversation to say that no such lady lived in Lead, South Dakota, but his mother was determined to prove her point, reached for a bell cord, pressed a button, and "Mr. Strange" (Lewis Strang) entered the room. Strang responded that he knew the letter Eddy was referring to but that it did not state that McMann had taught the Glovers. Eddy insisted on seeing the letter. According to George, Strang then left the room to find the letter, "with a smile on his face as if he was making fun of mother." Eddy then began fumbling in the drawer of her desk in search of the letter. George noticed his mother looked fatigued and advised her not to look for the letter now, saying that she could find it later. Eddy then went on to explain that the will she had prepared years before was missing. She had a premonition one night and asked Frye to find the will. He looked for it and discovered it was missing. Eddy then immediately prepared another will, which was now in a safe place. George then asked her who the lawyer was who prepared the will, but Eddy appeared dazed and unable to recall the lawyer's name. George helped her by saying, "Was it General Streeter?" Eddy acknowledged that it was Streeter.[4]

Eddy went on to comment about Calvin Frye's honesty: "If Mr. Fry is not an honest man, I am not worth a penny in the world. I know he is honest for he has been tested by the bank." Eddy then told George a bizarre story about two men from Lead, who "wanted to get [Eddy] away and murder [her] for the will." George wondered how it was possible for someone to get into the house, and Eddy said, "Oh, yes, someone has been in and robbed the house, stole some of the furniture but I have it all back now. They came in through the window but I have the windows fixed so that no one can get in when the doors are fastened." She asked about George's sons and invited them to visit her at Pleasant View. A comment by George about her "fine driving team" led Eddy to tell another story, about two horses sent to her by a "Southern gentleman" and said to be valued at $4,000 each, though they turned out to be too aggressive and "could not be held by an ordinary man." She believed the horses were sent "for the purpose of doing her an injury." She spoke of what would have happened had she taken her carriage ride with them: "The horses would have run away, [broken] the carriage, and thrown me out. Then they would pick me up pretty near dead." George asked if she thought the man had sent the horses for the purpose of killing her, and Eddy responded, "You have it."[5]

Eddy asked George why he had come east, to which he responded that he was there on mining business. He mentioned a recent failed venture, and Eddy responded, "Oh, my son, you missed your calling. You will not make any money at mining." She then asked if George had seen the new church building in Boston, commenting that the dome was higher than the Bunker Hill Monument. George noticed his mother was tiring and began to end the interview, but Eddy invited him to spend the night in Concord at the Tomlinson home. George responded that he had business to conduct in Boston and was heading back there immediately. He promised to call again before heading back to South Dakota. Eddy reached out her hand and said, "Oh, you don't know how I love you, and I love all your family. You are my son and only child." She mentioned how very busy she was, kissed George "affectionately," and asked, "You will come and see me again, both of you, won't you?" George promised they would. As the visitors went downstairs, Mary looked back, and George recorded her impressions: "She says Mother was leaning over her hand. My mother looked up and her face was white. She looked as if she would collapse." On George and Mary's way out, Sargent acknowledged that the house had been robbed but that no papers had been taken.[6]

Although Glover and his daughter had been carefully prepared by Chandler, Kelley, and John Slaght to find evidence of Eddy's incompetence and decrepitude, her performance during the visit was another example of Eddy missing an opportunity to put minds at rest about her health. Her confused comments about McMann, the story about the lost will, her tale about the men from Lead who wanted to kill her, and her insistence that the gift horses were sent to do her harm, along with her inability to remember the name of her lawyer and her lack of knowledge of current events, all pointed to the conclusion that Glover and his attorneys wanted to make. Eddy was certainly distracted by her focus on rebutting the *McClure's* attack, but her staff and General Streeter had to have prepped her for the importance of the meeting with her son. Her failure to perform on this occasion could only lead to the threat of legal action continuing against her and Christian Science.

By prearrangement the Glovers had promised Chandler and Kelley that the Glovers would make no final decision about pursuing a lawsuit until after meeting with their lawyers, after the visit to Eddy. Kelley met them in Boston the day after the Glovers had visited Pleasant View. Their account of the visit "did not impress [Kelley] as producing very satisfactory results," but he did think the story of the lost will was "significant." Kelley understood that a legal standard of incapacity was higher than the occasional befuddlement and poor memory of an eighty-five-year-old woman as described by the Glovers. But he acknowledged to Chandler, "The Gs. were well satisfied of E's mental incapacity, but they seemed to lack the descriptive power to put it into words." Kelley sent them on to visit Chandler in Washington, D.C. The day after Kelley's meeting with the Glovers, Eddy's response to the *McClure's* article appeared in many newspapers around the country. Kelley wondered to Chandler whether Eddy really "writes these articles." [7]

Mary Baker Eddy had been reluctant at first to respond to the *McClure's* article. After first reading it, she stated to Alfred Farlow, "By thinking it or fearing it you strengthen it." But she was infuriated by the article: "Of all the history of lies ever written I belive this article is the most in excess." She also lashed out at her staff for not protecting her: "If you had more faith in me such stuff would not be circulated. It is the animal and material at war with the thoroughly spiritual."[8] She did begin preparing a response and was hard at work at it when George and Mary visited her on January 2, 1907.

In her widely circulated response, which appeared on January 5, she explained, "The attack on me and my late father and his family in McClure's Magazine, January, 1907, compels me as a dutiful child and the leader of Christian Science to speak." She corrected the Milmine article's depiction of her father by claiming he was "erect and robust," never used a walking cane, never used profanity, and was "a well-informed, intellectual man, cultivated in mind and manners." She objected to the description of her siblings as being poorly educated and working at menial jobs as adults. *McClure's* described Eddy in her youth as suffering from "hysteria mingled with bad temper." She insisted that this was not true and that her mother always referred to Mary Baker as the peacekeeper in the family. *McClure's* criticized Eddy for misappropriating the McNeil family crest and using it as her own. She explained how she had been given the crest by Fanny McNeil, daughter of General John McNeil, the brother-in-law of Franklin Pierce, and stated that Eddy was entitled to use it. Stories of Eddy's ill health, particularly stories that her father had spread straw on the road to keep passing wagons from disturbing her and that her husband Daniel Patterson had outfitted his wagon with "a couch or cradle" to allow her to ride in comfort, were all denied by Eddy. She also objected to Milmine's claim that she had been a medium who "dabbled in mesmerism" and that she had been especially interested in the Shakers as a young woman. Eddy also produced an affidavit stating that while the court granted her a divorce from Patterson "on the ground of desertion," it was really for adultery but that she had intervened to prevent Patterson from being arrested after running off with another man's wife. Eddy also responded to the implication that she was a bad mother, explaining that her son had been taken from her: "My little boy was not welcome in my father's house."[9]

The attempt to correct every misstatement of fact in the *McClure's* series proved too much for Eddy and her staff, however, and they abandoned the effort, ignoring all future installments of the Milmine-Cather series. A letter sent from Denver, Colorado, on January 7 turned Eddy's attention back to the more immediate threat of legal action from her son. James P. Wilson, a former business partner and attorney of George Glover, had read the *McClure's* article and wrote to warn Eddy: "I think I see breakers ahead." Wilson referred to the "many letters" from Eddy in George's "possession": "He has kept a copy of all letters written you, and has all your replies." Though Wilson did not state what use George might make of the letters, the implication was clear when Wilson wrote, "I need not tell you George has made mistakes." Wilson advised Eddy "to meet George and adjust all differences and . . . to get back many of [the] letters." Wilson, who was not a Christian Scientist, concluded, "Your work should not be interfered with and no misunderstanding *should arise in the future* over matters which you can adjust now."[10] Thus began a complicated dance, with Eddy trying to get her son to return all of her letters without explaining why, and with Glover and his attorneys delaying and avoiding doing so without letting on that they planned to file suit and might use the letters against her.

As soon as Eddy and her staff received the warning from Wilson, they set out to retrieve the letters from Glover. On January 11, 1907, she wrote to her son asking for their return: "Send *all* of them, be sure of that." Her reason for wanting the letters was vaguely stated as the result of "hypnotism" that was "acting on the minds of people to make them lie about [Eddy and her] family." She promised to send Glover and Mary "presents of *value*" in exchange for the letters. The next day she wrote her son again with a further explanation of her need for the letters: "*Counterfeit* letters have been circulated with my name signed to them—such letters as I never wrote nor would think of writing."[11] From the Elsmere Hotel in Washington, Glover, under careful guidance from Chandler, stalled her by stating, "I would only be too pleased to assist you in any way I can. I do not quite understand just what letters you refer to and want." Glover indicated that the letters were still in Lead and that he would be leaving for home "within ten days [or] a little more."[12] Eddy answered, "Send me every letter you have that has my name on it." She added, "I want to protect you from the hints as to holding letters against me or that would harm you or me to be seen by others." With each response Eddy's tone became more agitated, even desperate. She dispatched Irving Tomlinson, a member of her staff, to Lead, South Dakota, to retrieve the letters from Glover, promising again to "reward" him "with some presents."[13] Tomlinson arrived in Lead on January 24 only to discover that Glover and his daughter were still in the East and that Glover's wife, Nellie, claimed to know nothing about any letters. A few days earlier, Tomlinson sent Nellie a telegram asking her "to hold package until arrival here." Nellie wired Glover, asking, "What does it mean?" Glover wired back immediately, "Tomlinson means mischief. Know nothing and say nothing."[14]

Having realized her mistake in sending Tomlinson to Lead while Glover was still in Washington, D.C., Eddy wrote an angry letter to George: "Why did you deceive me as to the time when you would return to your home in South Dakota?" In fact, Glover had written her that he would not return to Lead for at least ten days, but Eddy, nevertheless, laid the blame on her son: "I pay this man for his trip and he has been waiting there since Jan. 24th to see you and to receive from you my letters." She continued, "Why do you treat your mother thus? Have I not helped you in need and out of need and is this my return from you?" She insisted on knowing when he would return to Lead, and "what . . . business" was keeping him "in Washington and New York." She also sent Alfred Farlow to Washington to meet with Glover, advising George, "Take his advice, and he will be honest."[15]

The presence of Eddy's representatives in Lead and in Washington, D.C., at the same time caused further complications for the Glovers and Chandler. To protect Nellie from Tomlinson, George Glover telegraphed his lawyer, Judge Granville G. Bennett, in Deadwood, South Dakota: "See wife immediately, learn facts assist if necessary. Watch emissary." Bennett had been Glover's lawyer for more than twenty years and was well known in the Black Hills. Born in Ohio but educated in Iowa, Bennett was admitted to the bar prior to serving in the Union army as an officer in two different Iowa regiments. After serving as an Iowa state representative and state senator, he moved to the

Dakota Territory in the 1870s. George Armstrong Custer's discovery of gold in the Black Hills brought Bennett to Deadwood to help bring law and order to the tough mining towns. Bennett was appointed to the territorial supreme court in 1875, and in this capacity he presided over a hearing on the murder of Wild Bill Hickok. In 1878 Bennett was elected as a Republican as a nonvoting delegate to the Forty-Sixth Congress, representing the Dakota Territory. After one term in Washington, D.C., he returned to Deadwood to practice law and serve as a judge of the probate court. Like Glover, only better educated and more sophisticated, Bennett was a true westerner, rubbing elbows in Deadwood with the likes of Calamity Jane, Ned Buntline, and others.[16]

On Sunday, January 27, the Glovers and Chandler met with Farlow at Chandler's house. They resumed their conference the next day, and to satisfy Farlow and further delay the matter of the letters, George Glover wired Nellie, "Deliver all desired packages to Tomlinson also desired affidavit covering the fact," while Chandler wired Judge Bennett: "Glover has sent telegram to wife to deliver letters not intending to have his order obeyed. See that wife tells emissary that she cannot give up letters on a telegraphic order." And to Nellie, George wired, "You will receive telegram signed with my name telling you to deliver all desired packages to Tomlinson. Pay no attention to it. I sent it to deceive friends of Tomlinson in this city. My reason is to puzzle Tomlinson and gain time." Nellie responded the same day: "Last dispatch received also wire from Chandler to Bennett instructions observed all well." In fact, the letters appear to have been in the East with the Glovers all along. On January 29, Chandler recorded in his diary, "Went with Glover to Safe Deposit & got letters for copying." Realizing the deception, Farlow tried pleading with Glover, claiming, "This business is purely between you and your mother." All Farlow was trying to do was "to fulfil [his] mission and be a faithful servant." He did not claim to know why Eddy wanted the letters: "I am only concerned to know that she wants them." Being rejected several more times and being unable to see Glover except in the presence of Chandler, Farlow finally left Washington on January

30, after receiving the following note from George: "Your continuous pressure upon me to get my mother's letters makes me suspicious that something is wrong. Besides I do not like your manner while cross-questioning and examining me." Chandler had a similar reaction to Farlow, wiring Bennett, "Farlow here importunate and offensive intercourse terminated."[17] The strange shell game was suspended at this point. Tomlinson left South Dakota, with Glover still in possession of his mother's letters, neither side knowing for certain what use was intended for the letters. The intense pressure applied by Eddy's representatives raised Glover's suspicions, however, and helped convince George to follow the advice of Chandler and Kelley regarding a lawsuit.

Bennett wrote a long letter to Chandler, describing the interaction between Nellie Glover and Tomlinson. Bennett assured Chandler that Nellie had not revealed to Tomlinson the location of the letters. Bennett told Chandler that after the final rejection, Tomlinson had left Nellie with the statement, "God [will] lead me and the truth will follow." Bennett noted, "He should have said, 'The devil will lead me and falsehood and mischief will follow.'" With Tomlinson gone, Bennett concluded that Nellie Glover would "not be troubled and tormented by this scoundrel any further."[18] Bennett had joined the Chandler legal team and received a $100 check as a retainer. He was an important addition, as he knew Glover and family better than any of the lawyers in the East and had represented George Glover in a number of lawsuits. In fact, Glover was very litigious and once claimed he had never lost a lawsuit. Due to his illiteracy, he may have assumed others were taking advantage of him in business dealings. Whatever the cause of his filing suit so often, Glover frequently reported his success in court to his mother, prompting a response from Eddy as far back as 1892: "I was amused at your proverbial success in lawsuits. I should think you would be the terror of the West in such matters."[19]

Bennett was the final addition to a legal team that now included Frederick Peabody of Boston and DeWitt Howe of Concord, New Hampshire. Peabody was first approached by John W. Slaght, who turned to Eddy's chief critic and tormenter for information about property owned by Eddy in the Boston area. Peabody had been obsessed with bringing down Eddy and Christian Science since serving as Josephine Woodbury's attorney. He provided Chandler with the information requested, but Peabody advised, "Mrs. Eddy's most valuable properties are her copyrights, and it would seem as if it might be safely assumed that they have been or will be assigned with the purpose of cutting off the son from any future ownership of them." Peabody sent Chandler a copy of Peabody's pamphlet "showing up" Eddy and would become an integral part of the team, writing frequently and at length from Boston. Although acknowledging "differences of opinion as to the woman's mental condition," Peabody had no doubt "that the old creature [was] entirely oblivious of the whole controversy." He relayed important information to Chandler about the individuals surrounding Eddy and their roles, and concluded, "Frye is the man who knows the *whole* story; and, as I suspect, although I have never been able to prove it, his interest will appear to be that of *husband* to Mrs. E."[20] Peabody would continue to provide Chandler with information and misinformation that led him to focus more on Peabody's perceived evils of Christian Science and to equate these with Eddy's mental condition.

Young DeWitt Howe was recommended to Chandler by John W. Kelley. With Chandler living most of the year in Washington, D.C., and at age seventy-one being less inclined to travel north, Kelley working out of Portsmouth, Peabody out of Boston, and Bennett out of South Dakota, it seemed important to have a local Concord attorney on the team, as any bill in equity would be filed and tried there. Kelley did not pick Howe because of any past connection, writing, "Everybody says he is a good lawyer. Personally I know nothing about him. The formation of his head I have observed at times, and it looks good for the purposes of this case."[21] Other than Peabody, whose desire to bring down Eddy and Christian Science had become a national crusade, Howe would prove to be the most persistent and nearly obsessive of Glover's attorneys. Unlike the others, however, as a young lawyer, Howe needed the legal fees that would result from a successful lawsuit. It is important to note that of the five lawyers who made up Chandler's team, none had ever met Eddy. This lack of first-hand knowledge would lead the Glover team farther from the truth and make them overconfident about their chances in court.

In addition to George Glover and his daughter Mary, Chandler included another party in his proposed suit: George Waldron Baker, the only nephew of Mary Baker Eddy. Baker, living in Bangor, Maine, had tried to communicate with his aunt through letters as far back as the 1880s. Most recently, in debt himself and caring for an aged mother and invalid wife, George Baker had tried to sell his aunt an heirloom watch once owned by her favorite brother, Albert. Convinced that she was not receiving his letters, Baker even enclosed a two-cent stamp, hoping for a reply. He finally "received a letter from an inmate of her house in Concord saying that the rules of the house prevented [such] letters . . . from being handed to her." Baker offered himself as a litigant, stating, "I am of the opinion that Mrs. Eddy is mentally and physically unable to properly care for her person and estate." Chandler had written to Slaght that he preferred Baker as a client, fearing that George Glover was unreliable and thinking that Baker "might be more faithful thereto" and, not being a direct heir, would be less objectionable to the press if they questioned that the case was really about money and not about Eddy's well-being. Chandler insisted that "B's name should not be mentioned to G," and it was not mentioned until after the case was filed.[22]

With his legal team and parties to a suit in place, and with a determination to pursue the matter as a next friends case in equity court in New Hampshire, Chandler, Kelley, Slaght met on Sunday, February 3, with Ralph Pulitzer—vice president of the *World* and Joseph Pulitzer's eldest son—and two other *World* executives, to inform them of the team's progress and plans.[23] The meeting took place at Ralph Pulitzer's New York home. Because Joseph Pulitzer was out of the country and physically unable to run the day-to-day operations of the newspaper, Ralph, along with the paper's business manager and financial manager, were serving as "a council of 3 to pass on the policies of the *World* during [Joseph's] absence." Ralph Pulitzer wrote, "The plan of procedure in the Eddy case as outlined on Sunday would not be a legitimate newspaper enterprise judged by the precedents which my father's many crusades have left us." In a handwritten letter to Chandler, Ralph Pulitzer stated that his father had "never himself employed litigation as a means to bring about any end for which he was editorially striving." Ralph promised to write his father "the facts in the case fully," stating, "If we are wrong in our judgment he will probably apprise us of it." Ralph concluded, "I am most sincerely sorry not to be able to see my way clear to entering this case as outlined. It is one with which I am individually in thorough sympathy."[24]

Chandler's lengthy response did not express any surprise at the decision of the *World* to decline participating in the suit. Chandler wrote that from the start he had never "contemplated" whether the "plan of procedure would or would not be a legitimate newspaper enterprise"; in fact, he had proceeded solely on the basis that there had been "a great wrong done, which could be proved and rectified by legal proceedings." But the withdrawal of the *World* at this point, he noted, "would do a great injury to persons who have been led by [the paper] through a false hope into an injurious and possibly fatal predicament." He asked Ralph Pulitzer to reconsider and to go forward with "a legal procedure brought in [Eddy's] name by her relatives and next friends" that was "intended to prove her unfitness to do business and to enforce the duty of those strangers to her blood who have surrounded her to give an account in court of their stewardship." To Chandler, the *World* had a duty to get at the "truth" in the matter. Personally, Chandler had other motives, stating, "I cannot throw it off!" He was committed to Glover and his daughter, who "were hopeless" until Chandler began to guide them: "I became *their* counsel as well as *yours* and their friend." Now, "relying wholly and implicitly on . . . fidelity and courage in pursuing a path" that Chandler's team had "marked out and [the Glovers] did not, but agreed to follow," George Glover and daughter Mary had "antagonized [their] opponents and cut loose from them." To "tell them to go back home, helpless, heart-broken" would leave them "feeling that they [had] been betrayed." Chandler wrote to Ralph Pulitzer, "You may feel that you can afford to send them there. I cannot." Chandler would do what he could to continue the case and believed Joseph Pulitzer would do the same. Chandler did request that the *World* pay for all expenses and "make a large contribution" to allow continuance of the case.[25]

Ralph Pulitzer responded with a formal letter: "The *World* will not consent to take any part in the litigation outlined in the case of Mrs. Mary B. G. Eddy, directly or indirectly." He explained that originally the *World*'s interest was to determine if Eddy "was virtually a prisoner" and "incapable even if advised." This "was an entirely proper field of public service for a newspaper," but at the February 3 meeting "it appeared that the proposed proceeding had taken the shape of a bill in equity, which [the *World*] understood to be practically a suit for property, a suit for which the *World* [could] have no part." The *World* also understood that upon Eddy's death, the newspaper "would aid in a contest of an unsatisfactory Will," which the representatives of the newspaper "instantly denied." Ralph Pulitzer enclosed a check for $5,000 in compensation for the work of Chandler and Kelley and for the expenses of the Glovers' in coming east.[26] Chandler accepted the $5,000 and agreed that "the World should be out of it" but appealed, nevertheless, to Joseph Pulitzer in Paris, enclosing copies of all correspondence. He asked Pulitzer for money: "My clients are destitute . . . and I also, alas, have none to spare for this duty."[27] Chandler never heard from Joseph Pulitzer but was committed to pursue the suit without the backing of the *World* because of the strong sympathy and fondness Chandler felt for the Glovers, and because of his overconfidence in the rightness of the cause.

Chandler and company had successfully kept their plans secret, but the conflict over Mary Baker Eddy's letters confirmed to the Eddy team that Glover's attorney was the famous former senator Chandler and that something of a legal nature was in the works. The Christian Scientists were determined to break up the Chandler-Glover team.

The best way to do that was to get Glover to go home to Lead, South Dakota, thousands of miles from Chandler, and to bribe Eddy's son with money. Irving Tomlinson saw firsthand the Glovers' poverty and also noticed that Glover's son-in-law, Warren S. Schell, lived in their home in Lead. Eddy wrote directly to Schell, expressing "utter astonishment" at the family's poverty and asking him to provide her with details about Glover's indebtedness and back taxes.[28] Schell had been married briefly to Evelyn Glover, the oldest daughter of George and Nellie. Evelyn was in poor health throughout her life. As far back as 1889, George had begged his mother to take on Evelyn's case, but Eddy refused, directing them instead to a local Christian Science healer. Eddy always blamed Evelyn's illness on malicious animal magnetism, writing to Glover in 1893, "It is nothing but *mesmerism* that has caused this state of her health." Eddy saw this maliciousness as directed at herself: "When [Evelyn] was in Boston she was regarded as somewhat like me, and that she would be a scholar, etc. This was enough for the result before named." A year earlier Eddy had rejected a proposal that Evelyn come to Boston to be educated under Eddy's direction, because of "the mesmerists . . . that caused dear Evelyn's sickness." Eddy wrote, "I am of the opinion it is not quite safe for those dear grandchildren to go there unless I am there too." Eddy was determined to educate the promising Evelyn and her less talented sister, however, and paid their way to study under a Christian Science teacher in Saint Joseph, Missouri. This experiment failed, the girls fleeing back to Lead and claiming the teacher had made improper advances and proposed marriage to Evelyn. Correspondence about the incident showed that Glover believed his daughters, and Eddy was torn between the insistence of the father and her trust in the Christian Science teacher, who denied everything. In 1902, Evelyn Glover married Warren Schell, but she died in 1904. Schell remained in Lead, was close to the Glovers, and was literate, which made him a likely target for Eddy's end run around the family. Schell provided the information Eddy wanted about Glover's finances but expressed surprise that his "Grandma" had written to him, as he had never heard from her before.[29]

Having received information provided by Schell, Eddy wired Glover in Washington: "Have sent money to National Bank Lead. Go home and you get benefit of it." She sent Glover another telegram a few days later: "I sent the money to you there because it is your duty to return there and support your family." Glover then received a letter from Josiah E. Fernald, Eddy's banker in Concord, stating that $125 a month was to be used by Glover only for the payment of his bills. At first, Glover was ready to accept Eddy's gift of money, explaining that he thought he could "use it" either for his "own benefit or [his] mother's protection," but on learning that the money was to be used only to pay his bills, he rejected it, stating further, "I do not believe the conditions are my mother's own desires." Fernald then more liberally defined the uses for the money, as payment "for taxes on Mr. Glover's home place, for clothing, for food and for fuel." On advice from Chandler, Glover continued to reject the money.[30] During the next few years, Chandler would consistently advise Glover not to accept any money offered by his mother, as the offers only proved that there was more money to be gotten if the team succeeded in its legal cases.

After more than two months in the East, most of it spent at the Hotel Elsmere in Washington, where they met sometimes twice a day with Chandler and on occasion with Slaght and Kelley, George Glover and his daughter Mary left for Lead on February 25, 1907. A bill in equity had been prepared, and all the details had been arranged for it to be filed in Concord, New Hampshire, on March 1, 1907. Chandler anticipated an "explosion" in the press when the suit was announced. He needed the Glovers to hold steadily to the course agreed to and would rely on Bennett in South Dakota to see to this, saying in a letter: "There will be tremendous pressure brought upon them to induce them to refrain from doing what is their duty both to Mr. Glover's mother and themselves; but they will, I think, stand firm." Chandler wrote that he had grown fond of George and Mary: "They are two people of high intelligence and great strength of character. Please tell Mrs. Glover that I so esteem them."[31]

In the winter of 1907, Harper and Brothers finally published Mark Twain's *Christian Science*. Originally, the book was to be published in 1903, but Harper's withdrew it. Now, with Christian Science and Eddy under attack and with public interest at its height, the book was released. It was a much-revised compilation of articles that Twain had written years before. In 1899, while living in Vienna, Twain wrote a humorous fictional article for *Cosmopolitan* about a hiker falling in the mountains in Germany, breaking every bone in his body and being cured by a Christian Science healer. This was followed in 1902–1903 by a more scathing critique of Eddy and Christian Science, in four parts in the *North American Review*. Unlike most of Eddy's critics, Twain accepts, in his book, the premise of mental healing, "No one doubts—certainly not I—that the mind exercises a powerful influence over the body." He proceeds to praise the religion.

> Remember its principal great offer: to rid the Race of pain and disease. Can it do so? In large measure, yes. How much of the pain and disease in the world is created by the imaginations of the sufferers, and then kept alive by those same imaginations? Four-fifths? Not anything short of that, I should think. Can Christian Science banish that four-fifths? I think so.[32]

Twain even acknowledges that the answer is spiritual and not material and that "the Christian Scientist has taken a force which has been lying idle in every member of the human race since time began." After reading Twain's articles in the *North American Review*, Eddy found "an undertone in it that is very complimentary to Christian Science." But Twain's acceptance of mental healing did not carry over to the founder of Christian Science. In Twain's view, Eddy was a power-hungry, money-mad entrepreneur who had created "trust" by assuming total control of every aspect of the religious organization. She claimed that

her religion was a revelation from God and that she was nothing short
of the equal of Jesus Christ. Her followers revered her, called her
"Mother," and made a shrine to her, the "Mother's Room," in the
Mother Church in Boston. According to Twain, Eddy reveled in the
adulation and had assumed absolute control over every local congre-
gation through her bylaws, which gave her the authority to appoint
or expel any member or reader in every local church, a "power that
exceed the Pope's." While rejecting the charge that Eddy stole her
ideas from Quimby, Twain accepts the claim that she did not write
Science and Health herself. After an analysis of all of her miscellaneous writing, he concludes, "It is not believable that the hand that
wrote those clumsy and affected sentences wrote the smooth English
of Science and Health."[33]

Twain was influenced by Frederick Peabody, who corresponded
with him, met him, and even introduced him to Josephine Woodbury.
While Twain did not go as far in attacking Eddy as Peabody wanted,
and while Twain professed to dislike Peabody, Twain did rely on the
"facts" provided by the Boston lawyer. Twain credited Eddy with
many "masculine" qualities—"devouring ambition," business acu-
men, selfishness, "extraordinary daring"—and her lack of femininity,
at least as Twain perceived it, was an underlying cause of his hostility
toward her. While Eddy had been successful in business and financial
management, Twain had been an abysmal failure, having declared
bankruptcy and relying on others to manage his finances. Twain's
ideal image of womanhood was his late wife, Livy, whose quiet faith-
fulness offered the support and understanding that his volatile personality required. Eddy, in contrast, had been married three times and had
given up her only son. Twain admired what she had accomplished but
disdained the manner in which it was done and the fact that it had been
accomplished by a woman. His ambivalence is clear in his statement
"It is thirteen hundred years since the world has produced any one
who could reach up to Mrs. Eddy's waistbelt."[34]

Like a general preparing to lead his troops on a military campaign,
Chandler planned every detail of the filing of the bill in equity, which

was to take place on Friday, March 1, 1907, in Concord. Because
DeWitt Howe was out of town tending to his dying mother, Chandler
assigned the duty to John W. Kelley. On that day, Kelley was to take
the train from Portsmouth to Concord, arriving in the afternoon. He
was "to drive from the railroad station directly to Pleasant View" and
hand the staff a letter from Glover to Eddy. Kelley was to keep the contents of the letter secret. Next, he was to proceed to the office of Martin
and Howe and sign the bill "George W. Baker by John W. Kelley his
Solicitor," which Martin was to sign for Howe. Kelley was to then
file the bill with the clerk of the superior court in Merrimack County
"late in the afternoon." Immediately after filing the bill, Kelley was to
give a copy to the Rumford Printing Company and have them print
additional copies. He was then to take a copy and hand it to Streeter
at his office, asking Eddy's attorney if he would "accept service" for
the ten defendants named in the bill. Only then was Kelley to take a
statement "prepared by direction of Mr. Glover showing the reasons
for his action" and give it to the Associated Press representative at the
office of the *Concord Monitor*. Kelley confirmed receipt of the instructions but informed Chandler that George W. Baker was coming from
Bangor, Maine, to sign the bill himself. Kelley also recommended having someone from Martin and Howe's office deliver Glover's letter at
Pleasant View, as "there may be a need of evidence of the service of
it some time, and if any of the attorneys serve it personally, it would
be embarrassing to testify."[35]

Glover's letter to his mother was a lengthy explanation of all of
his suspicions about "the persons to whom [she] had given [her] confidence" and his fears about her health. He went back as far as 1890
to describe a letter Eddy had written in which she "expressed a belief
that Malicious Animal Magnetism . . . was influencing" her son "into
hostility" toward her. He recalled his visit to his mother in 1903, when
he was allowed to see her for only one hour before being dismissed
by Calvin Frye. After expressing a desire to attend the dedication of
the Mother Church extension in Boston in 1905, he was informed that
she would be unable to see him if he came east. He was frustrated at

not being able to learn more about her health when the *World* article was published, so he traveled east with Mary and met his mother at Pleasant View on January 2. That visit had only confirmed his fears for her health, as "various notions" she expressed "seemed strange" to him, especially her claims that people had been trying to harm her, that her will had been stolen, and that she could not name her attorney, "Mr. Streeter." Next, Glover described her inexplicable effort to retrieve her letters, and particularly Eddy's own confusion in sending Tomlinson to Lead when she should have known that Glover was in Washington. He wrote, "You can imagine how strange such letters as these seem to me." If all of these letters had actually been written by his mother, he was astounded and concerned: "There is no end of my wonder and suspicion." Glover concluded that he had never meddled in his mother's affairs but felt "an evident duty" to intervene at this point rather than allow her "to be managed by cunning men" who Glover felt "sure [were] engaged in a scheme of private and public misrepresentation." While he did not specifically mention a lawsuit, the letter would serve as a complete explanation of his motive in being a party to a bill in equity.[36]

Eddy read her son's letter immediately but was confused by it. She showed the letter to her cousin, Henry M. Baker, who was visiting her at Pleasant View, commenting, "George could not write that letter, the letter was written by an educated man who was skilled in the use of language." She asked Baker, an attorney, what the letter meant. Baker reported, "I replied that the letter had such evident earmarks that unquestionably some hostile action was contemplated and that she would have to await whatever proceedings were intended." Eddy would have only a few hours to wait. The stage was set for the "explosion" that Chandler predicted would occur once the press learned of the lawsuit to be filed in Concord on March 1, 1907.[37]

꞊ 5 ꞊

THE BATTLE IS JOINED

On March 1, 1907, John W. Kelley carried out Chandler's plans as scheduled, filing the "Bill and Order, Mary Baker Glover Eddy v. Calvin A. Frye & A." with the clerk of the Superior Court of Merrimack County, New Hampshire, for the April term. The petition was brought by Eddy's "next friends George W. Glover, Mary Baker Glover and George W. Baker" against ten people, all officials of the Church of Christ, Scientist: Calvin A. Frye, Alfred Farlow, Irving C. Tomlinson, Ira O. Knapp, William B. Johnson, Stephen A. Chase, Joseph Armstrong, Edward A. Kimball, Hermann S. Hering, and Lewis C. Strang. Frye and Strang were Eddy's secretary and assistant secretary and lived in Concord, as did Tomlinson, a member of the church board of directors, and Hering, first reader of the church in Concord. Alfred Farlow was in charge of public relations for the church and lived in Massachusetts, as did Knapp, Johnson, Armstrong and Stephen A. Chase, who were all on the board of directors along with Kimball, who lived in Chicago.[1]

The petition charged that Eddy was eighty-six years old "and that her mind [was] and for a long time [had] been so impaired by the infirmities of age and otherwise as to render her . . . incapable of " managing her affairs and that she lacked the "prudence and discretion" to prevent others from controlling her or committing fraud or even to

understand "the present legal proceedings." The petition also asserted
several other points: Frye and Strang lived in her house and kept "her
carefully surrounded and secluded" and controlled all access to Mary
Baker Eddy. Her only child, George Glover, had been denied access
to his mother and had received letters explaining that her secretary
screened all her mail, and a brief meeting with his mother in January
"confirmed his fears and those of his daughter that his mother was
so feeble in body and mind as to be incapable of understanding the
condition of her property or of prudently managing her business."
George W. Baker, her only nephew, had also been denied access to
his aunt, even through letters, and he believed that she was "mentally
and physically unable to properly care for her person and estate and
that she [was] surrounded by designing persons . . . using her and her
condition for their own selfish ends." The petition also noted that
Eddy owned "extensive and valuable" property located mainly in New
Hampshire and Massachusetts, had "large sums of money as receipts
and expenditures as donations to her and as donations from her," and
that all of this business had "been done and [was] being done either
in her name by others or by her while unfitted for the transaction
thereof." The defendants were "engaged in a combination not only to
surround and seclude the person of the said Mary B. G. Eddy but also
while she [was] helpless in their hands and without intelligent volition
to take charge possession and control of all her property and business affairs and to manage the same solely according to their own will
and pleasure," and they had done this for so many years that she was
"not legally responsible" for the consequences of their actions. The
plaintiffs then listed her assets as including copyrights on her extensive publications and estimated the income from each. They listed the
Metaphysical College in Boston, which they claimed had trained some
4,000 healers at $300 tuition each: the plaintiffs reported that "3,333
practitioners" were "now advertising their power of healing." The
Mother Church in Boston, "with its extensive membership of 40,000,"
had "a large income." And her real estate transactions, including the

Concord church "edifice" and the Metaphysical College, had "all been controlled or received by the defendants" without a "complete or sufficient accounting from them." The plaintiffs concluded "therefor" that Mary Baker Eddy had "been possessed and controlled and her whole business conducted by the defendants without any sufficient intelligent expression of any wishes of hers and while she [had] been incapable of any complete volition concerning her property or business affairs." The plaintiffs "pray[ed]" that the "defendants be required to disclose" and account for all business transactions, and that if found "to have wrongfully received and held or disposed of any" of her property, "they be required to restore the same to her or be charged with the value thereof." The plaintiffs asked that the defendants be "enjoined" from engaging in any activity related to Eddy's business or property and that "a receiver or receivers be appointed to take possession of all the money and property of said Mary B. G. Eddy" and to "manage all her business affairs" and that "further relief" be provided "as to the court [might] seem requisite and just." The bill was signed by George W. Glover, Mary B. Glover, George W. Baker, and by the "Plaintiff's Solicitors," John W. Kelley, Martin and Howe, and William E. Chandler.[2]

After filing the bill at 4:45 p.m. with the clerk of the superior court, Kelley then found Eddy's attorney, Frank Streeter, at the Wonolancet Club. Streeter was upset about receiving a copy of the bill, asking Kelley why Chandler had not consulted with Streeter before filing. Streeter asked if "the matter could not be held up until he could have a consultation" with Chandler. Streeter informed Kelley, "The bringing of this action today is remarkable but you could have known nothing about that." He went on to say that Eddy was "perfectly competent, in fact—willful" and that he had "seen her three times within a week." Kelley next went to the *Monitor* office and delivered the papers to the representative of the Associated Press and caught the train back to Portsmouth at 6:13 p.m. When the train reached Nashua, Kelley was handed a telegram from Nathaniel E. Martin of Martin and Howe stating that a "very important" matter required Kelley's immediate return to Concord. Kelley arrived back at 9:00 p.m., and Martin told him, as Kelley recorded in a letter,

> Streeter called at my office just after you left and he looked as if he was going to have a shock. He said he wanted this suit held up & kept quiet until he could see Senator Chandler. He said Mrs. Eddy had just completed the execution of a trust in favor of Mr. Glover, he (Streeter) Tomlinson & one other being the trustees, giving Geo. & his wife the income for life & then the principal to the children equally at death of survivor of Geo. & wife. That Tomlinson had left Concord on the 5 P.M. train for Washington with a copy of the trust agreement to show George. I . . . asked him how much of a trust fund, he said 'large.' I said 'more than $100,000' he said 'yes.' I said 'why didn't you tell Kelley that.' He said 'I am so dazed I can't think quick enough. I should have.'

But the Associated Press reporter had sent the story out, and it "had got on the street" by the time Kelley received Martin's telegram. Streeter and Martin were both bombarded by calls from Boston reporters, and Streeter concluded that "it was no use trying to keep it still." Kelley was also informed by Martin that the trust agreement required that Glover not contest Eddy's will or he would forfeit all interest in the trust.[3] Tomlinson was recalled from his trip to Washington, and Kelley's busy day, and fruitless return to Concord, had ended.

The fact that Chandler insisted on secrecy prior to filing the bill in equity indicates that he was not primarily concerned with providing for the Glovers but was motivated as much by publicity and a desire to attack Christian Science. Had he been mainly concerned about the poverty of his clients, he would have consulted in advance with Streeter to determine if Eddy was willing to do anything for her son. The trust fund that Eddy had agreed to was for $125,000, more than $2 million in today's dollars, not an inconsiderable amount and one that Chandler might have increased for his client if the lawyer had negotiated with

Streeter, who wanted to avoid the negative publicity that would attach to a lawsuit, in order to protect Eddy's reputation and that of her church. But Chandler wanted the publicity and the "explosion" that he had predicted would follow the filing of the bill, and he got it. Every daily newspaper in the country had the story on the front page on March 2, and one could read the position of each paper by the way the story was covered. For example, the *Philadelphia Press* reprinted the entire *World* article from October 28, describing Eddy's debility and incompetence. The *Minneapolis Tribune*, in contrast, featured the denials by Christian Science "leaders" and recounted in detail Eddy's defiant carriage ride of March 2.

> Sitting erect and looking straight ahead, without leaning back against the cushions of her carriage for support, Mrs. Mary Baker Eddy yesterday took her usual daily drive through the streets of Concord, but whereas she is accustomed to ride about two and a half miles through the wide and beautiful thoroughfares of the city, the mother of the Christian Science cult, made a long detour, extending over about three miles in town and returning to her home, "Pleasant View." It seems to the citizens of the town, among whom Mrs. Eddy is greatly revered by all classes, that she had purposely extended her daily drive in answer to the sweeping charges circulated early in the day as to her physical and mental condition.

The *Tribune* concluded, "'Mother' Eddy looked a vigorous woman of 75 rather than borne down by the cares of 86 years augmented by responsibilities which few men would have withstood."[4]

In South Dakota, George Glover and family followed the news closely in the papers. Glover was sensitive to criticism that he was motivated only by money and did not really care about his mother's condition. An anonymous letter to Glover stated, "The spectacle of the old lady being dragged to the court will convulse the world with laughter. Such action on your part at her time of life will undoubtedly

kill her. . . . [But] the spectacle will be the greatest since the cruci-
fixion of Jesus." The letter enclosed many newspaper clippings that
quoted Frederick Peabody, whose national crusade against Eddy and
Christian Science was well known to Glover.[5] But Glover had not
been made aware by Chandler that Peabody was a member of his legal
team. When Glover questioned Peabody's involvement, Chandler
responded,

> You have had nothing to do with employing him. I took the
> responsibility of doing it because of the knowledge which he had
> of old matters and also because he had access to letters which
> were vital to our case showing that Mrs. Eddy in 1890 thought
> that M.A.M. was controlling you and therefore made up her
> mind to convey her property away from you and make a will
> hostile to you. We could not get on without that, therefore Mr.
> Peabody was employed by me.

Chandler tried to reassure Glover: "Mr. Peabody understands that
this fight is not in any sense the carrying out of his old fight. We are
not fighting Christian Science, we are not fighting Mrs. Eddy; we are
fighting in behalf of Mrs. Eddy against a gang."[6] Glover accepted
Chandler's explanation, proving again that while concerned about his
mother, his motivation was primarily financial.

Because Chandler understood Glover's immediate need for money,
the lawyer was concerned that news of the trust fund might weaken
Glover's resolve. On March 4, Chandler wired Glover, "Where there
is $1200 and $100,000 there is much more. Keep quiet and trust your
counsel." In a lengthy letter to Judge Granville Bennett, Chandler
speculated that the trust was irrevocable, even with the lawsuit pending. But Bennett advised that if Glover accepted the benefits of the
trust, it would be construed as "acquiescence" to the condition that he
not contest Eddy's will or any "deed of the donor." Both Chandler and
Bennett believed, however, that if Eddy was incompetent to deal with
her finances prior to March 1, then she certainly had also been "non

compos when she executed the deed" and that "it would be void." To get Glover to focus on continuing the lawsuit, Chandler explained this fact to him, concluding that Eddy was not competent to execute the trust and had not been competent to exclude him from any past will: "I believe that you are sure of the $100,000. I am very confident that by waiting you can obtain much more."[7] This was enough to keep Glover on board.

Glover's motive in filing the lawsuit was further attacked by James P. Wilson, his former lawyer and business partner, whose letter to Eddy had sparked the controversy over the possession of her letters to her son. In the *Denver Post*, Wilson charged that the suit was brought because of Glover's "burning desire to obtain money to open his mines in South Dakota," although Wilson did concede that Glover "honestly believe[d]" that "Frye and others" had Eddy "hypnotized" and were "going to get all of the property." According to Wilson, "Glover is prone to lawsuits. Our Dakota calendar was never considered complete unless his name was on the docket either as plaintiff or defendant." Wilson stated that Eddy was "perfectly sane," basing his conclusions on "the business letter she wrote" to him "on January 15," which was evidence of "a clear brain and steady hand." A copy of her signature from that letter was published with the article. Glover answered Wilson through Bennett, asserting that Wilson was in need of money, had asked Glover for a loan as recently as the spring of 1906, and was probably recruited by Tomlinson, on his trip west in January, to be "the paid tool and emissary of the conspirators surrounding" Mary Baker Eddy.[8]

Publicity about the lawsuit prompted two potential plaintiffs to come forward. Ebenezer J. Foster Eddy, Mary Baker Eddy's adopted son, emerged on March 4 with a letter to Laura Sargent, one of the residents of Pleasant View: "I want the dear little Mother and the older members of 'the household,' to know that I am not at all in sympathy with these diabolical actions against her." His effusive letter continued, "My constant prayer has been that none of you should have anything to meet through me for I am not a channel for error to any one. All channels are filled with Good." But the double-dealing Foster Eddy was immediately in touch with Chandler's team, which sent Slaght to meet him in Waterbury, Vermont, on March 6. Foster Eddy bore a grudge against those who had pushed him out of Eddy's good graces, but he claimed to Slaght that he "would not tolerate a spirit of revenge" but would act according to his belief in what "would be right and result in good to the world at large and especially to our beloved America." Foster Eddy told Slaght about private letters from Eddy contained in a rolltop desk in Boston and advised Slaght to retrieve the desk. Foster Eddy met with Chandler and company in Boston on March 8 and joined the lawsuit on March 11 on condition that it be "understood and agreed that no expenses shall be incurred by the said E. J. Foster Eddy for counsel fees or otherwise except such as may become a charge upon the estate of the plaintiff Mary B. G. Eddy." Chandler discovered that Foster Eddy was still Eddy's adopted son and was probably "a half heir to Mrs. Eddy's property."[9]

Fred W. Baker, of Epsom, New Hampshire—Eddy's second cousin, whose grandfather was the brother of Eddy's father, Mark Baker—also joined the lawsuit. He first contacted Chandler by letter on March 7, stating that years earlier Fred Baker had "a delightful visit" with Eddy but had recently been denied access to her by Frye, who had turned Baker away from Pleasant View, saying that he "could stand on Main Street at 3:00 p.m. and [watch] her carriage go by." Baker met Chandler and the team in Boston on March 9 and was added to the suit on March 11. Baker was described in the newspapers as about fifty years old and as an upholsterer who was living with his wife and two children on a small tract of farmland in the Gossville section of Epsom.[10]

The report of Foster Eddy's involvement was headline news throughout the nation, and Foster Eddy told a sensational story about how Frye and others had convinced Mary Baker Eddy that her adopted son was plotting to kill her. As a result of hearing about this "plot," according to Foster Eddy, his adoptive mother had reacted violently when he traveled from Boston to see her: "At the sight of me she sprang to her feet, shrieked for help and darted out of the room. I followed, thinking she had been seized by one of her mad attacks; but she fled, stumbling, falling, dragging herself along in terror. Through it all she never ceased to shriek 'Murder' at the top of her voice." Foster Eddy accused Frye of always being resentful of Foster Eddy's adoption and of initiating the story about the plot. Foster Eddy also reported Mary Baker Eddy's preoccupation with money when he served as Eddy's publisher and she insisted on new editions of *Science and Health*. When Foster Eddy advised against another edition, Eddy responded, "You must not talk that way, Ebenezer, the more new editions we print the more money we get." Behind the scenes at Pleasant View, Foster Eddy saw Mary Baker Eddy "rush around her room filling the house with her cries." He blamed her emotional turmoil on the pressures put on her by Frye and his colleagues, who were trying to destroy her faith in Foster Eddy. One night Foster Eddy found his mother "crouching under the bed clothes and clutching at her breast with both hands." He stated, "Morning dawned before I could quiet her." He acknowledged that his account books were audited and that he had "befriended" a woman and employed her in his office, decisions that resulted in "false reports" about their relationship. Finally, he had been so "tricked" by the Frye gang that, "utterly heartsick with the whole business" he decided he could not remain: "I left . . . , dropped the Eddy from my name and returned to my old home in Vermont." He never mentioned that Eddy had given him $15,000 to leave and told him never to contact her again.[11]

Throughout the spring of 1907, the *New York World* published one critical story after another about Eddy and Christian Science. If Slaght or Chandler received some new information in their investigations, it would appear in the *World* the next day. Chandler's team was investigating and gathering information throughout the months immediately following the filing of the bill. Chandler contacted an old friend in Concord, Henry Robinson, to assist with local research. Robinson, an attorney, had been postmaster of the city from 1890 to 1894 and again from 1898 to 1904, and he was mayor in 1895 and 1896. When

Chandler first contacted him, Chandler had to ask Robinson if he was working for the other side in the case, as Robinson had written laudatory pieces on Eddy in the past, one for an anniversary issue of the *Concord Patriot*, which had been reprinted in pamphlet form in 1903.[12] Robinson replied that he had offered his services to the other side, but said "[Streeter] is a little hoggish, you know, and I was 'left.'" Unlike any other member of Chandler's team, Robinson had met and interviewed Eddy several times and had corresponded with her frequently and recently. He informed Chandler that in all of his contact with her, she had never mentioned "animal magnetism, hypnotism, or anything of that sort." He wrote that Eddy was a "remarkable lady" and that his talks "with her impressed [him] much." Robinson had been assigned by Chandler to investigate the 1866 incident in which Eddy made her discovery of mental healing after a miraculous recovery from head and neck injuries following her fall on the ice in Lynn. *McClure's* most recent article included an interview with Dr. Alvin M. Cushing, who treated Eddy, an interview in which he denied her claim of a miraculous cure. In a letter written by Eddy to Robinson in 1903, she asked him not to include the incident in his piece for the *Patriot* because it was "too transcendental to be told to-day" and because narrating the story "now excite[d] the enemy to either a sneer or to wholly discard Christian Science."[13]

Robinson was successful in tracking down the story Eddy told her son about the horses being sent to harm her. The horses, named Tattersall and Exersall, were a gift from L. L. Temple of Texarkana, Arkansas, and were kept at Pleasant View for about a month in the spring of 1906. A newspaper story at the time indicated that the horses "shied at a dog," but Alfred Farlow, Eddy's press agent, denied that she had ever ridden behind them. Farlow did confirm that the horses "were too lively for the job." Robinson also had his pulse on public opinion in Concord about Eddy and the legal case. He informed Chandler that while "Mrs. Eddy herself [had] many personal and religious friends" in Concord, there was general hostility toward Frye and those who surrounded her: "Mrs. Eddy herself is very gracious, but many a writer,—including Miss Milmine—have gone away [from Pleasant View] nonplussed and aggrieved." Robinson explained "Nobody . . . is permitted—or has been for a long time—to see Mrs. Eddy, without Fryes's permission." Referring to Frye as "the boss," Robinson reported, "[If] he conceives a prejudice, the doors are closed." Robinson continued, "Frye & Co. are arbitrary, impolitic, undiplomatic." Yet, while many church officials were denied access to Eddy, "sometimes" she would see local Concord people who were not involved in Christian Science. Robinson concluded, "There was a shrewd policy in it." Robinson identified Streeter as part of this public relations campaign, as he was known to entertain at his club the "special newspaper correspondents who call on him." He had a way of "saying nothing" to them about the case but "sagaciously" imparting "what was being said on the street." In fact, Streeter had a surprise up his sleeve for the plaintiffs, which he would spring at the first hearing on the case on April 2, at the beginning of the term of the superior court. In his many interviews with Eddy, Robinson had taken along a stenographer. On leaving Pleasant View one day, he asked the stenographer "what she thought of Mrs. Eddy, and she remarked, 'if she is a fraud, she's a gilt edged one.'"[14]

Like a witch hunt, Chandler's investigations were focused only on negative information about Eddy. Chandler ignored Robinson's firsthand information. Instead, Chandler increasingly relied on less-reliable correspondents, including Emily and Robert Hannon of East Windsor Hill, Connecticut. The Hannons first wrote to George Glover in South Dakota, and he passed their correspondence along to Chandler. In rambling letters the Hannons told an elaborate story about Eddy being victimized by a power play taking place around her at Pleasant View. Her staff was divided over the succession to Eddy, with Frye being allied with Augusta Stetson, powerful leader of the church in New York City, and Cornell Wilson, Farlow, and others being opposed to Stetson's attempt to succeed Eddy. The Hannons claimed to have once been a part of Stetson's group in New York City, but upon learning of her plans, they broke away from her and had

continued their healing practice in Connecticut. They had not been
directly involved in church leadership since 1890. But according to
Emily Hannon, there was "a conspiracy on foot" because Stetson and
others held "a *secret* over Mrs. Eddy" that caused "her to *fail in Mind*."
With Frye's approval, Stetson had infiltrated Pleasant View with a
Mrs. Fitzpatrick, Stetson's agent in the scheme, who had convinced
Eddy that she was being victimized by malicious animal magnetism.
It is difficult to believe that Chandler would take this lunacy seriously,
but he visited the Hannons in Connecticut and bought their story so
completely that he wrote a lengthy letter to the *New York World* relaying the story in graphic detail.

> On the one side Jailer Wilson with his female assistants are per-
> secuting the feeble and helpless Mrs. Eddy with demands she
> shall not issue a decree making Augusta E. Stetson her succes-
> sor as the mother of the Church C.S. On the other side Jailer
> Calvin A. Frye and his female allies are worrying Mrs. Eddy
> with demands that she shall accept the Stetson argument and
> proclaim the new leadership of the Church C.S. This picture
> alone is sad enough; and is sending the aged and infirm prisoner,
> surely, even if slowly, toward earthly dissolution.

Chandler went on emotionally, "The days of witchcraft had no
fiercer horrors. Suicide has no greater inducements than Mrs. Eddy's
sad situation presents." He wrote, "All this would seem grotesque
and ludicrous were it not so inexpressibly saddening." Chandler
concluded, "What a spectacle!" The two sides were fighting for
control and tormenting "the leader whom they pretend to revere."[15]
Increasingly, Chandler was being led astray from the initial financial
concerns about Eddy's estate to a broader attack on Christian Science,
an attack based on the actions and teachings of its members and the
mental condition of its leader.

Chandler was further influenced by a so-called expert, Dr. Henry
Reed Hopkins, who was an alienist, or physician who specialized in

mental illness ("psychiatrist" by modern definition). Hopkins first wrote Chandler in early March, alerting him to an article Hopkins had written about the mental state of Eddy for a medical journal back in 1899. Hopkins recommended that Chandler employ a medical expert on his team. Hopkins practiced in Buffalo, New York, and was a prominent member of several New York state medical societies. He first charged that Eddy was a paranoiac, as evidenced by her claim in *Retrospection and Introspection* that her relatives had conspired to take her son away from her in the 1850s. At first, Chandler was cautious in accepting Hopkins's analysis, asserting, "Her religious delusions are only pertinent as they bear upon her fitness to do business." He recommended that Hopkins "originate a movement of physicians and surgeons to investigate Christian Science Healing and to expose and oppose it." And Chandler suggested a "similar movement on the part of ministers of the gospel of all denominations." But Hopkins persisted in suggesting that Chandler find a copy of Eddy's *Christ and Christmas*, which had been recalled after publication by the church because, Hopkins said, it "was too palpably insane for the public to see." Hopkins then recommended that Chandler investigate Eddy's family tree, on the grounds that insanity is hereditary. To Hopkins, any evidence of "epilepsy, of palsy, of eccentricity, of cancer, of consumption, of drunkenness, or of harlotry" among the women of the family were especially to be noted, because, in his opinion, "females transmit diseased propensities more often than men."[16]

Hopkins saw copies of Eddy's signature and concluded, "It is important evidence bearing directly upon the functional activity of her brain." He believed the deterioration of her handwriting was evidence "of Shaking Palsy-Paralysis Agitans now called Parkinsons Disease." He admitted that such a diagnosis "could not be made on hand writing alone" but claimed that Georgine Milmine told him Eddy had suffered from "paralysis agitans" for twenty-five years, and this had caused her to retire from public work in 1889. The "gang" that surrounded Eddy had covered up this fact ever since, which, if true, would be, Hopkins thought, "the joke of the Century." To Hopkins, a diagnosis of "shaking palsy" was evidence that Eddy was a lunatic. Chandler was buying into Hopkins's information, and the *New York World* and other newspapers sympathetic to the *World's* attack on Eddy published samples of her handwriting, showing its deterioration over the years and, most importantly, exposing what the papers claimed were forgeries of her signature uncovered by "the plaintiff's handwriting experts," who had analyzed more than one hundred of her letters. Excerpts from Hopkins's 1899 article "The Prognosis of Eddyism," which first appeared in the *American Medical Quarterly,* were published in newspapers friendly to Chandler's cause in the spring of 1907.[17] It is difficult to read Hopkins's letters today and not draw conclusions about the abysmal state of medical knowledge at the time, and the letters help us better understand why many Christian Scientists preferred mental treatment for disease. But Chandler was a believer in scientific progress, a product of the Enlightenment, and seemed to accept whatever was passed along to him as science.

Chandler was also in contact with William Nixon, a former close advisor to Eddy and head of her publishing society as recently as 1890. Nixon had letters from Eddy in which she refers to M.A.M. influencing her son to oppose her. To Chandler, this meant that any will of Eddy's that disinherited her son was likely prepared fifteen to twenty years earlier, and, therefore, the plaintiffs had to do more, according to Chandler, than show "evidence of her inability to do business for the last four or five years." In order to invalidate her deeds or wills, Chandler's legal team had to prove that she had been incapable of executing these documents twenty years earlier. To do this required exposing her "delusions," starting with her claims "that M.A.M. was making her son hostile to her." But where to stop in this investigation? If her belief in malicious animal magnetism was evidence of incapacity in 1890, then according to Chandler, she was also "deluded and unfit by reason of the delusion" in 1866, since her discovery and miracle cure were clearly a delusion. He admitted, "It is a bold and broad proposition that all Mrs. Eddy's delusions on religious subjects bear upon her fitness at all times in the past to such an extent or to make her incapable of conveying her property away from her son, natural and

adopted; but it is a sound proposal." Previously believing that Eddy
was a fraud, Chandler understood that "a villain may make a deed or
will." An insane person could not, however, and so Chandler decided,
"We will stand on the *honest delusion theory* until they attack it." He
understood, however, the consequences: "In spite of our purpose, not
only the gang but herself and the religion will suffer."[18]

Investigating Eddy's mental condition in the distant past put
Chandler in contact with many unreliable, unscrupulous, or unwilling witnesses. William Nixon, for one, was interested only in sell-
ing his letters to the highest bidder, who eventually turned out to
be S. S. McClure, who offered him $250. Nixon had asked Peabody
and Chandler for $1,000, but they had no money. A witness from
California, Luther Marston, had stories to share about Eddy's obsession with M.A.M. during his time as a student at the Metaphysical
College in the 1880s, but he refused to participate unless he was paid,
and it was too expensive for the impoverished legal team to bring him
east. Dr. Cushing was contacted after the *McClure's* article appeared,
but his son, a law professor at Columbia University, advised him not
to participate unless he received a summons from the court. George
Quimby, the son of Phineas Parkhurst Quimby, refused to get involved
or to let anyone see his father's manuscripts.[19]

Chandler's own financial interests interfered at one point. His
investigation of the Eddy book *Christ and Christmas* led him to the
publisher of the book, the Rumford Printing Company, of which
Chandler was part owner. Its business manager, Edward N. Pearson,
advised, "I hope you will not find it necessary to drag the Rumford
Printing Company into the controversy." In Pearson's view, Mary
Baker Eddy had "been a very generous customer of the Company . . .
during her entire residence in Concord, and certainly an officer and
stockholder in the Company ought not to be the person to use business
transactions of hers with the Company to her disadvantage."[20] Thus
Chandler's team was forced to rely more and more on Hopkins and
his secondhand diagnosis of insanity.

The pressures of the case began to wear on the seventy-one-year-
old Chandler. He had spent ten days in Boston in early March working

on the case with Slaght, Peabody, Kelley, and Howe. In turn, members
of his team traveled to his home in Washington, D.C., to continue their
work. For each day, his diary lists meetings and conferences about the
Eddy case. Finally, on March 24 he took to bed with a sleeping pill and
slept for eleven hours. On March 27 he visited a friend in the evening
and had his first drink ever of Coca-Cola. He awoke at midnight with
"violent heart action from Coca-Cola" and sent for a doctor, who
arrived at 2:00 a.m. and left at 3:00. The doctor returned later in the
morning and confirmed that "it was simply poison—affecting heart,
bowels & bladder." The doctor called again the next day, but Chandler
had recovered enough to visit his office. The bout with Coca-Cola
"poisoning"[21] was enough to convince Chandler that he must slow
down and rely more on the other members of his team. To Kelley, he
wrote, "I am growing old like Mrs. Eddy." Chandler continued, "Do
not rely too much on me. This is a big case. Think hard and let me
know when I must leave Washington." To Judge Bennett, Chandler
wrote, "I feel there is upon me too much responsibility and I wish others to share it with me."[22] Chandler and his team waited anxiously for
the opening of the superior court session on April 2, at which time the
defendants in the case had to answer to the charges brought in the suit.

Mary Baker Eddy was also feeling the pressure as the date for the
first court session approached. Though not a defendant in the case, she
was clearly allied with the defendants, who were all Christian Science
church officials, and not with the next friends, who claimed to be acting
on her behalf. Eddy's practice was to call church officials to Pleasant
View on short notice, requiring them to stay with her for a year or
more and to serve her in whatever menial capacity she chose. Now,
in late March, she directed one board member to come to Pleasant
View "to watch with [her] one or two weeks as the case may require."
The clear implication was to help her through the first sessions of the
superior court in Concord. She further explained, "This hour is going
to test Christian Science and the fate of our Cause and they must not
be found wanting." She wrote, "I see this clearly that the prosperity
of our Cause hangs in this balance."[23]

= 6 =

THE DEFENSE ANSWERS THE CHARGES

The long-awaited answer of the defendants to the charges of the next friends was filed in Merrimack County Superior Court at 2:35 p.m. on April 2, 1907. The answer proved the biggest surprise yet in the highly publicized case. Frank Streeter filed a motion reporting that on March 6, Mary Baker Eddy had conveyed all of her property to three trustees and that the trustees now asked to substitute for the next friends for the purpose of prosecuting the case. According to the trust deed executed by Mary Baker G. Eddy, the three trustees—Henry M. Baker, Archibald McLellan, and Josiah Fernald—had posted a bond of $500,000 as surety of their proper management of all of her assets; therefore, they should replace the next friends, who were simply volunteers purporting to act on her behalf, to recover any property alleged to have been diverted by the defendants. It was the duty of the trustees to preserve and protect the estate of Eddy, thus the motion to substitute the three trustees for the next friends named in the bill in equity. The implication, of course, was that if the court granted the motion to substitute the trustees for the plaintiffs, the trustees would soon determine that the defendants had not misappropriated any of Eddy's assets and withdraw the bill in equity.[1]

The three trustees were all highly respected, leading citizens of

New Hampshire. Henry Moore Baker was a cousin of Mary Baker Eddy. Baker, a former congressman, was a prominent businessman and lawyer who had long advised Eddy, although he was not a Christian Scientist. Josiah Fernald was Eddy's banker and the president of the National State Capital Bank of Concord. Archibald McLellan was editor of the *Christian Science Journal* and a member of the board of directors of the Mother Church. In the trust deed, Eddy conveyed to these three men "all [her] interest of every kind and description" to any "real estate, stocks, bonds, interests in copyrights, contracts, actions, and causes of action at law or in equity against any person." These trustees were given "full power" to care for and control all of her assets and to manage, invest, and reinvest all or any of her property and income. Eddy reserved for herself only her home, Pleasant View, and all the possessions on the premises; two houses in Boston, which she was to either occupy or rent; and a small income from the trust to maintain her lifestyle. The trust was to terminate upon Eddy's death, with all of her assets passing to the executor of her will.[2]

It is important to note that Streeter was Eddy's attorney and that Eddy was not a defendant in the case, though she was nominally a plaintiff, if an unwilling one. Streeter's motion made it clear, if there was any doubt, which side Eddy was on. In fact, the defendant's attorney, New Hampshire Attorney General Edwin G. Eastman, did not file an answer to the charges made against the defendants, only filing in the court as their counsel, which was all that was required on this occasion. Clearly, Streeter and Eastman had developed this strategy together and, in fact, would work together as cocounsel to Eddy: Eastman soon withdrew as the defendants' attorney and joined with Streeter in what would prove to be the major thrust of the case, contesting the charge that Eddy was incapacitated and incapable of executing any trust deeds or a will, at the time of the current hearing and in the past.[3]

Edwin Gamage Eastman served as New Hampshire attorney general from 1892 to 1912. He was in the same class at Dartmouth as Frank Streeter, and along with Streeter read law with Alonzo P. Carpenter, future chief justice of the New Hampshire Supreme Court.

Eastman was very much involved in Republican state politics, serving at one time in the state assembly and as a state senator before moving to Concord and becoming the state's attorney general. He was frequently mentioned as a potential candidate for governor. But Eastman developed a large and lucrative law practice in Concord and had a reputation as a "cool, clear-headed and sagacious" attorney with "no trait of the demagogue in his make-up." Eastman had always worked closely with Streeter, even though they had never been in partnership. As attorney general, Eastman had been in court with Streeter on many railroad cases as well as cases on criminal matters. As did Streeter, Eastman had become a wealthy man, owning a 750-acre farm in his hometown of Grantham, a farm noted for its prized Ayrshire cattle and well-kept apple orchards.[4]

Eddy's decision to place all her assets in the hands of trustees was made on her own, against the advice of her attorney. Sometime in February she had made the decision, in biblical terms, to render unto Caesar the things that were Caesar's, and once the decision was made, she could not be dissuaded. In fact, Streeter had hinted to John W. Kelley, when they met on March 1, that Streeter had seen Eddy several times in recent weeks and that she was not only competent but "willful." Streeter understood that any move Eddy made to divest herself of her wealth would be seen by the opposition as an admission that she was no longer competent to make financial decisions. Therefore, to prove that she was both competent and in charge, on March 6, the day set aside for the signing of the trust deed, Eddy insisted on reading the entire document orally to her staff and church officials, who gathered at Pleasant View for the ceremony. Those present then signed statements testifying to what had occurred, and the trustees carried off all of her financial documents to Fernald's bank, where they were checked and verified in full view of witnesses. Of course, except for those closest to Eddy, this was all kept secret from the outside world and especially from Chandler's team and the next friends until the surprise announcement of April 2.[5]

Lawyers for the next friends who were present in court that

day—Kelley, Martin, and Howe—would not discuss the surprise move with the press until they could confer with senior counsel, William E. Chandler. Later that day, Chandler declared that the new trust for Eddy's property was "a trick contrived by her jailors" to avoid a possible receivership and that the defendants had "used her delusions and incompetency to serve their own selfish ends." The two sides differed as to how the court would proceed. Eddy's side believed the court would uphold the trusteeship and replace the next friends with her new trustees, while Chandler's team predicted the trusteeship could not stand until the matter of Eddy's competency had been established. The establishment of the trust deed in no way affected the main issue in the whole case: Eddy's competence to make such decisions. Henry M. Baker, one of Eddy's new trustees, declared in the press that the laws of New Hampshire provided that a trust established by an individual who was supposedly insane or incompetent was not void until or unless the mental incapacity was later proven, and since there was no examination of Eddy, he contemplated the trust would remain in effect.[6]

To address the question of Eddy's competence, the Chandler team proposed to Frank Streeter that each side select "three competent gentleman" and that at a mutually convenient time, all six would visit Eddy; at this visit only those six would be allowed to "talk with her," though six other persons (presumably three attorneys apiece for each side) would also "be permitted to be present." The prospect of twelve men invading Eddy's privacy to examine her was too much for Streeter, who rejected the proposal along with Chandler's request to be shown a copy of the trust established earlier for George Glover. Streeter replied that he declined to show the plaintiffs "such deeds" because the bill in equity was "inconsistent with their being entitled as beneficiaries under the trust deed."[7]

Through the newspapers, George Glover learned of the surprise move of the defendants. He declared the "substitution of duly appointed trustees as plaintiffs in place of the 'next friends,' a very cunning move" made for "the purpose of dismissing the suit at the very earliest opportunity." Glover understood that if the new trustees were substituted for the next friends, his mother's safety would be "destroyed." He also understood that if she were capable of executing the trust deed after the suit in equity was filed, then she also was capable of looking after her own finances and so had "no occasion for doing it" at all. Granville Bennett concurred with Glover's thinking and went a step further, calling the move "a legal anomaly, if not an absurdity, for which [he had] never seen a precedent or authority." He believed, as did Chandler, that creation of the trust deed at this time was "an admission of the allegation" of the bill on which the legal team's "right of action rest[ed], i.e. her incompetency to manage and control her property and business," and that Eddy felt "impelled to place the same in the hands of trustees." Bennett recommended that Chandler file a supplemental bill "bringing the three trustees into the suit as defendants." Chandler did exactly that on April 6. If the judge granted Chandler's motion, there would be thirteen defendants to the suit in equity.[8]

To Bennett, Chandler advised that the plaintiffs be patient. Much had been accomplished, as their suit had forced "the other side to admit Mrs. Eddy's incompetency and put her in the hands of three trustees instead of twenty self-constituted guardians." He declared the move to substitute the three trustees for the plaintiffs "ludicrous" and said that it would be "abortive," but it had served a purpose: "The property now is in safe hands." Thus the plaintiffs had time "to investigate the past in order to see whether" Eddy had been "capable of making her wills and codicils." Chandler proposed going back "to the noises she heard in childhood" and reviewing her ideas "down to her belief in the miracle of 1866." He would investigate her belief in M.A.M., particularly the poisoning death of Asa Gilbert Eddy "by malicious suggestion," in order to show that she was incapable of doing business throughout her life. Chandler understood the consequences of his approach: "The howl will immediately be made that we are meddling with religion and that these ideas of hers are only religious notions like those entertained by many other founders of religious sects." But he had a good answer for this charge: the laws of business say that only persons in their right mind are allowed to do business, while "religious fanatics and crazy people" may start religions. Chandler was not claiming fraud on Eddy's part, "only delusions honestly entertained." The religion built on delusions would suffer, however, and this might bring the other side to the table, to negotiate a settlement before too much damage was done to Eddy's reputation and to Christian Science. But for the moment, Chandler noted, "The gang is not yet sufficiently frightened to make overtures."[9]

In a lengthy editorial, Michael Meehan of the *Concord Patriot* attacked Chandler, claiming that the suit in equity was not brought by Eddy's relatives but that they were being used by the *New York World* for the purpose of bolstering its sensationalism. To the *Patriot*, Glover and company were innocent dupes, well-meaning in their intention but tricked by Chandler and the *World* into a mean-spirited suit designed to harm Eddy and Christian Science, not to help or protect her. The paper analyzed all the stories published in the *World* since the suit was initiated on March 1, to show that the *World* had inside information coming from Chandler and that the newspaper was still directing the course of the lawsuit. Chandler responded through the *Concord Monitor*, of which he was still part owner. He reproduced the letters sent to Glover that offered him the "legal opportunity" to lend his name to the suit and denied that the *World* was behind the lawsuit. He admitted only that the *World* had initially contacted him about the matter. The *World* had admitted that Glover could neither read nor write, yet in his reply to the *Patriot* editorial, Chandler offered Glover's letter to his mother of February 25 as evidence of the well-intentioned motive behind the bill in equity. The *Patriot* implied that Chandler had written the letter for his client, who could not have written it on his own. In the small, competitive world of New Hampshire's capital city, the Eddy case became a contentious issue between the two daily newspapers. The *Patriot* seized the opportunity to defend Eddy and lambast the other side in editorial after editorial, while the *Monitor*, edited by George H. Moses, who was sympathetic to Eddy, held its tongue because Chandler and his son, William D. Chandler, were part owners of the *Monitor*.[10]

On April 15, the three trustees of Eddy's estate, Henry M. Baker, Archibald McLellan and Josiah E. Fernald, answered the "supplemental bill," which proposed to name them as defendants along with the original ten Church officials. The trustees requested "a speedy hearing" on their motion to be substituted as plaintiffs in place of the next friends and insisted on an investigation to determine whether the lawsuit was being "brought in good faith by the so-called 'next friends,'" whether the case was really about protecting Eddy's property, and whether the proceedings were brought "by other undisclosed persons [that is, the *World*], not friends but enemies of Mrs. Eddy." In answer to each of the charges made in the original petition, the trustees stated that Eddy had never been surrounded or secluded by any of the defendants, that she was competent to create the trust deed, and that except for Frye, none of the ten defendants had any knowledge "of said deed until several weeks after its execution." They further stated that "the allegations by said 'next friends' of the grantor's [Eddy's] incompetency to make such deed and contract" were "immaterial." The three trustees concluded that they held "no relation to the ten defendants" that would prevent them from properly managing Eddy's trust estate.[11]

Although subsequent developments had made it almost an anticlimax, the original ten defendants to the bill in equity filed their answers to the charges on April 17. The four defendants living in New Hampshire—Calvin A. Frye, Irving C. Tomlinson, Hermann S. Hering, and Lewis C. Strang—answered identically, denying that Eddy was incompetent and that they had kept her "surrounded and secluded." As to the mismanagement of her property, each defendant responded, "The defendant does not admit the same, but demands proof thereof." They each concluded "that the said bill of complaint" was "not brought by the so-called 'next friends' . . . for the purpose of protecting [Mary Baker Eddy's] person and property; but . . . the same was begun without the consent and contrary to the wishes" of Eddy and was "now being promoted and carried on by persons . . . hostile to [Eddy] and the religious principles of which she [was] the discoverer, founder and exponent, for the purpose of annoying her and attempting to bring herself and the said principles into disrepute, and thereby to hinder and retard her said work." The other defendants—Alfred Farlow, William B. Johnson, Ira O. Knapp, Stephen A. Chase, and Edward A. Kimball—lived in Massachusetts or Illinois and filed their defense in Massachusetts that same day. Each filed an identical answer to the charges, though it was somewhat differently worded than that of the New Hampshire defendants. The out-of-state defendants were even more direct in attacking the next friends, claiming that "certain evil-minded persons not related in any way" to Eddy were "furnishing money for the prosecution of said bill of complaint for their own purposes and to advance their own selfish interest." What is most revealing about the defendants' answers is that nine of the ten, excluding Frye, claimed to have never had any involvement or knowledge of Eddy's finances or property. This fact was first revealed by Streeter on March 2 in his reply to the filing of the bill in equity and reflects badly on the research done by Slaght and Peabody in determining the workings of the church and the relationship of these officials to Eddy.[12]

Two days after the defendants filed their answers, around 3:00 a.m. on April 19, Mary E. Tomlinson of Concord, New Hampshire, jumped to her death from a fourth-floor window of the Parker House in downtown Boston. Mary Tomlinson had been second reader of the Christian Science church in Concord and was the sister of Irving C. Tomlinson, one of the defendants in the next friends suit, former first reader of the Concord church and the close advisor to Eddy, who had sent him to South Dakota to retrieve her letters from George Glover. Mary Tomlinson was well known in Concord, entertaining visiting Christian Scientists in her home and playing an important role in the dedication ceremonies of the new church in Concord in July 1904. The local press reported she had hosted visiting Christian Scientists from Chicago very recently and was not known to be suffering from any mental trouble. By coincidence, William Chandler was staying at the same hotel, one floor below Tomlinson at the time of the tragedy. He heard a noise at the time but learned only later that day what had happened. Chandler immediately assigned Peabody to investigate to determine if her death was in any way related to the case.[13]

The thirty-five-year-old Tomlinson had left Concord by train on the eighteenth, arriving in Boston around 10:00 a.m. She went immediately to the home of Ida Berkman, a Christian Science healer, seeking medical attention. Berkman, recognizing a mental condition, sent Tomlinson to a city hospital. The hospital sent for her friend Edward F. Woods, a Christian Scientist, who tried to get Tomlinson to go to his home. She refused but finally agreed to go with Woods to the Parker House, where she was registered in room 311. (Chandler was in room 236.) Woods sent for the patient's two brothers, who arrived at the hotel with a nurse around 8:30 p.m. The hotel clerk advised that a doctor be called, but the men explained that they were Christian Scientists and did not want a doctor. The men registered in an adjoining room to Mary Tomlinson and kept a close watch on her until around 3:00 a.m., when she somehow managed to lock the door between their rooms. The brothers rushed into the hall to get into her room but had previously locked that door from the inside to prevent her from escaping. They returned to their own room and burst through the door, only to find the window open and the room empty. Peabody interviewed the hotel manager, who stated that Mary Tomlinson was brought back to her room unconscious; Irving Tomlinson then asked for a doctor, expressing regret at not having called for one earlier. According to the hotel manager, Mary's condition had "knocked all the Christian Science out of him [Tomlinson]." Mary Tomlinson's brothers had expressed to the manager earlier in the evening that she had suffered such "anxiety" attacks before and that perhaps her uneasiness over the litigation was the cause of this recurrence. The doctor apparently reported the same conversation with the brothers, but said that he disagreed with them, stating that "*the condition* would have come about regardless of the excitement occasioned by the suit." Peabody said to Chandler, "[It was] a singular coincidence that the woman should have sought *your* hotel and that you should have been so close together that you actually heard the brothers hammering at her door. How little you realized its significance and how oblivious of the mangled creature on the stone of the street."[14] Chandler was still suspicious, however, concluding, "Whether Miss Tomlinson was driven crazy by her knowledge of the stupendous fraud that is being practiced we shall never know. The brother said she had been worried about this suit—and then [he] sat in his room and let her jump out of the window of the next room. Why did he not heal her before she went to bed? Why did he not have a doctor until she was dying?"[15]

The Tomlinson incident would prove to be only a temporary distraction, however, as Chandler was on his way to Concord at the call of his cocounsel. A meeting had taken place between Frank Streeter, DeWitt Howe, and Judge Robert N. Chamberlin of the superior court, to determine how to proceed on the motion of Eddy's trustees to intervene by substituting for the next friends. Chamberlin was fifty years old and had been a superior court judge since 1904. Previously, he had established a law practice in Berlin, New Hampshire, which he represented in the state legislature. In 1892, he was chosen Speaker of the Lower House prior to becoming a municipal court judge. As were all other participants in the case, Chamberlin was a power in the state Republican Party. The judge set May 13 as the date for a hearing on the motion, and Chandler was called from his home in Washington, D.C., to help his team prepare their answer to the motion of the trustees. Over the next few weeks, he spent much of his time at the Eagle Hotel in Concord, meeting with Martin, Howe, and Kelley, as well as visiting Streeter in his office to discuss the case. He also traveled with Kelley to Vermont to meet with Ebenezer Foster Eddy and spent time with next friends Fred Baker and George W. Baker and with Slaght, who joined the team in Concord. Chandler also kept Granville Bennett and George Glover informed, asking for their signatures on the answer to the motion prepared by the team. Chandler also wrote a curiously flirtatious letter to Mary Glover, complimenting her on a photograph in the newspapers and asking if she "had any offers of

marriage on account of the publicity" that she had received. He complimented her on her "character and cheerfulness" and advised her
to read Longfellow. It was important to keep the Glovers committed,
patient, and satisfied as the case dragged on.[16]

Chandler continued to try his case in the press. Whatever information about Eddy's past was discovered through the investigations
of Slaght, Peabody, and the Hannons or through the recollections of
Ebenezer Foster Eddy appeared immediately in friendly newspapers.
The Spofford and Woodbury cases were repeated in all their detail,
along with "proof " that many of Eddy's recent letters were forgeries,
as indicated by her deteriorating handwriting. There were also lengthy
explanations of her belief in malicious animal magnetism and of the
"indescribable torture" she manifested from her many "delusions."
The supposed attempt by Augusta Stetson, in league with Calvin Frye,
to be recognized as Eddy's successor also made the headlines at this
time. Streeter's team, in contrast, knowing firsthand Eddy's relative
health and mental condition, remained silent, believing they had the
law on their side.[17]

In early May, Chandler was called back to Washington, D.C.,
and Chamberlin postponed the date for the next court hearing on the
Eddy v. Frye bill of equity to Monday, May 20. At that time, arguments would be heard on the petition of Eddy's three trustees, Baker,
McLellan, and Fernald, to replace the plaintiffs in the suit. In preparation for hearing the arguments on the motion, Streeter filed two
affidavits, the first from Fred N. Ladd, one of Eddy's secretaries and
a banker in Concord, attesting to the events of March 6, when Eddy
officially signed the trust deed turning all of her property over to the
trustees. Ladd confirmed that Eddy read the deed aloud to church officials and that she stated she understood the document before signing it.
The total amount turned over to the trustees was $778,776 in bonds, a
promissory note of $50,000, and three savings books totaling $8,614.64.
The value of real estate holdings was not included in this accounting.
The second affidavit was made by Harvey N. Chase, an accountant
from Boston, who audited all of Frye's accounts and verified Ladd's

figures. Chase certified the total amount of Eddy's estate at $871,861. He concluded that from 1899 to the present, the books and accounts kept by Frye accurately reflected the actual receipts and disbursements of Eddy's accounts, although Chase also noted,

> Minor clerical errors are evident, and . . . in two cases coupons of $50 were omitted from the cash book, although deposited to Mrs. Eddy's account in the bank. Other clerical errors appear upon these cash books, but, taken altogether, the balance of errors is in Mr. Frye's favor. From the examination thus far made it appears that the balance due from the trustees to Mr. Frye amounts to $677.41. From our entire examination of these books we have been necessarily convinced that Mr. Frye was an honest agent for Mrs. Eddy, although mathematically a poor accountant.[18]

On May 20, the courthouse was packed for the 11:00 a.m. hearing. Besides the attorneys for both sides, the three trustees, and seven of the ten original defendants, there were three tables filled with newspaper reporters, and six stenographers. Every remaining seat was occupied, mainly with Christian Scientists, mostly women, all of whom were named by the local newspaper. The only person missing was Judge Chamberlin, who had become ill on his way to Concord. Mayor Charles Corning wrote in his diary of the vast crowd of Christian Scientists at the courthouse: "But M.A.M. or as Mrs. Eddy terms it 'Malicious Animal Magnetism' got in its work by laying out Judge Chamberlin and thus postponing the case. Chamberlin is at Margaret Pillsbury [the local hospital] with severe indigestion which is slow to depart." The case was postponed until Thursday, May 23. The tension was getting to Eddy, who regularly called the Pleasant View staff together for spiritual instruction. On May 22 her usual Christian charity was taxed, as she told the staff that "she had always forgiven her enemies etc [but] that she could not see the justice of God in this law suit of her 'next friends.'" She recovered her equanimity quickly, however, and called her staff members back to her room "and told [them] not to say she had said this . . . and opened the Bible to Luke 10–22." Her coachman, August Mann, was brought to tears one day during the suit when Eddy, alighting from her coach, said to him, "It is very hard." To Eddy, the case was like a "leaden weight."[19]

The courtroom at the Merrimack County courthouse on North Main Street in Concord was packed again on Thursday, May 23, for the hearing on the motion to substitute the three trustees for the next friends. Judge Chamberlin arrived on schedule at 11:00 a.m., "looking a little the worse for his illness," but immediately laid out the guidelines for the hearing. He explained that arguments should be confined strictly to the question of intervention of the trustees for the plaintiffs and should not concern the central question of Eddy's capacity to make decisions. Eddy's attorney, Frank Streeter, then began his argument in favor of the motion. Streeter spoke from just after 11:00 a.m. until a recess was called at 12:30, then began again at 2:00 p.m., and concluded at 4:30. He reminded the court that the suit was brought without Eddy's knowledge and against her wishes. She had created a genuine, legal trust turning over all of her property to the three trustees. To Streeter, the issue of Eddy's capacity to make a valid trust had to be decided first. Judge Chamberlin asked why. Streeter replied that next friends' actions could be brought only when the person in question was incapacitated. If Eddy was of sound mind, then the next friends had no standing in court. He cited case law attesting to this fact, concluding that it was entirely at the discretion of the court to decide whether a next friends suit should be allowed to proceed. According to a federal court decision, next friends had to proceed at their own risk and be prepared to "defend and vindicate the necessity" of the proceeding at any time they were called upon. Streeter was calling on them now. John W. Kelley then responded for the next friends, saying that Streeter had filed no motion or answer to this effect. Streeter answered that Eddy was not incompetent, and the next friends were required to show that she was incompetent at the outset. Judge Chamberlin asked, "How?" Streeter replied, "The law presumes all persons to be of sound mind, and if adults, capable of managing their

own affairs." Streeter added that Chandler had not asked for guardianship of Eddy, only for receivers to secure her property. Thus the
implication was that Eddy was competent to place her property in the
hands of the trustees. Streeter went on to charge that the suit was not
instituted in good faith but was brought for the purpose of bringing
Mary Baker Eddy and the religion she founded into disrepute. The
suit was not brought in Eddy's best interest, he asserted, and the court
should investigate that fact. The court had no jurisdiction to resolve
a religious controversy. Streeter concluded that the only question for
the court to decide was whether the trust deed was made for benefit of
Eddy and whether she was competent or incompetent.[20]

Streeter presented an affidavit written by Eddy, which explained
why her relatives found it difficult to see her. According to notes taken
at the hearing, "she had often been asked to see persons whom she
desired to see but was obliged to decline solely" for one reason: she
said, "I find that I cannot 'serve two masters'—I cannot be a Christian
Scientist except I leave all for Christ." In other words, as Streeter
explained, she could not devote herself to her religion "without keeping herself more or less in seclusion." Streeter concluded that if the
deed turning all of her property over to trustees "was for her benefit,
then her competency [was] not inquirable by this court."[21]

The hearing resumed at 10:00 a.m. the next morning, with fewer
people in attendance. DeWitt C. Howe spoke for the plaintiffs, arguing against the motion to substitute the trustees for the next friends.
Howe reminded the court that Streeter had been asked the previous
day how Eddy's competency was to be determined, but he had never
answered the question. Howe proceeded to answer it for him: it was to
let the three new trustees determine the question of her competency.
Of course, Howe noted, the attorneys for the defendants would prefer
to have the trustees become the plaintiffs in the case: "They would
choose . . . a sham battle in preference to a real one." The only question to be decided by this hearing was the legal right of the trustees to
be substituted for the plaintiffs in *Eddy v. Frye*. To Howe, Streeter had
substituted a false issue: do the trustees "believe this case unfounded?"

Howe asserted that the very presence of the defendants, Frye, Farlow, Knapp, Strang, and Hering, in the courtroom was evidence that they hoped to see the case turned over to the trustees, because they all thought alike, and Eddy thought as they did—after all, she did establish them as her trustees. In fact, "She thinks as Frye does, and she will think as Frye does so long as she and he stay at Pleasant View together." Howe then imposed a religious argument: Suppose that all those trustees and defendants upon cross-examination believed that Eddy could make an apple tree bloom in midwinter. Would this impact their credulity? That lack of credulity was the reason the next friends asked for a receivership, which was what the trustees and defendants feared. Howe charged that the act of imposing Eddy's signature on a trust deed, with Frye standing over her shoulder, was nothing short of contempt of court. Despite the $500,000 bond, there was no liability, and the trustees could be as careless as they pleased. The trust deed Eddy signed could just as easily be revoked, with Eddy's estate drifting back into Frye's hands, exactly where it was prior to the execution of the trust deed on March 6. If, as the next friends contended, Eddy was completely under the influence of Frye, then the trust deed was, in fact, Frye's creation, and if the trustees were permitted to substitute for the next friends, it would be the same as if Frye had become both plaintiff and defendant in the same case, a legal absurdity. Howe asserted, "It is preposterous to bring in a man as plaintiff who should be a defendant." Howe stated that according to Streeter's testimony, the trustees had prejudged the motives of the next friends and determined that they were not in Eddy's best interest. Howe concluded, "[The trustees] all say there is nothing to this suit. Give us a chance, gentleman, to show whether there is anything to this suit or not; that is all we ask."[22]

Mayor Corning, who was watching the case closely from the sidelines, concluded that based on Judge Chamberlin's demeanor, "one might predict the undoing of the trustees." Corning wrote in his diary, "Howe made a strong, clear & learned argument completely demolishing Streeter's attempt of yesterday. Everyone speaks in high terms of Howe's address."[23]

Chandler provided the only fireworks in the hearing, when he spoke for the first time following Howe's remarks on Friday afternoon. The press reported that "sensations were abundant" in Chandler's argument, which "provided all that had been expected in the way of interest, entertainment and excitement." Chandler admitted a reluctance to speak at all, praising the effort of his colleague Howe, but Streeter's argument had defied the judge's instruction to speak only to the motion to substitute the trustees for the next friends: in Chandler's opinion, Streeter had covered "the whole ground in this case, past, present and to come." But everyone knew, Chandler said, that Streeter was "a law unto himself in this state," so he was allowed to argue that Eddy was competent and to question the motives of the next friends. Chandler tried to answer to both points, contending that Eddy's competency had been a public question for many years and that an affidavit signed by her supporting the substitution of the trustees should not be credited, since "the alleged incompetent person [might] deny incompetency."[24]

Chandler's main argument was to defend the motives of George Glover in bringing the suit. Chandler explained how Glover had been separated from his mother at an early age, had toiled as a farm laborer and been denied an education by his guardians, had fought for his country and been wounded in the Civil War, and had worked hard to establish a living for his wife and family under strained circumstances. Yet he still cared deeply for his mother and had tried in recent years to determine her well-being, writing prior to the suit to Hermann Hering and inquiring about newspaper reports of her poor health. Glover came east to see for himself, met with his mother, and later wrote her a long letter explaining his concerns, which Chandler advised the judge to read. But Glover and his daughter Mary, "a most intelligent and amiable young lady," had been viciously attacked with charges that they were "tools in the hands of somebody else." Streeter had no business bringing this up at this hearing. Despite a lack of education, Glover was "a brighter man than either General [Henry M.] Baker or General Streeter naturally."[25]

Chandler said, "I wish George Glover were here in this courtroom to listen to these proceedings.

"Why isn't he here?" asked Streeter.

"Because we haven't the money to get him here," snapped Chandler.

"You have," said Streeter.

Chandler glared at Streeter, saying, "I can take the lie from Mr. Streeter. I am used to having it from higher persons than he." Chandler was referring to his recent controversy with President Roosevelt.[26]

This exchange made headlines around the nation, headlines like "Streeter Passes Lie to Chandler," which in the vernacular of the times was the same as accusing Chandler of lying. But it was what Chandler said next that had greater implications for the future of the case. Chandler claimed that the suit did not "aver" that Mary Baker Eddy was incompetent from the infirmities of age alone, nor that she was incompetent only when she was induced by Frye to make the trust deed, but rather that she had been incompetent "in mind and body" for a long time, from "the infirmities of age and otherwise." Chandler went on to explain that the term "otherwise" meant he intended to show that Eddy had been incompetent "many years into the past" and that this was not due solely to infirmities of the body, but also to infirmities of the mind. Her "grievous delusions" unfitted her to properly manage her property. There is no question that Chandler was referring to religious delusions, stating at one point that Eddy had sent Farlow to Washington to get Glover "to certify that while he was on the battlefield, about to be placed upon a stretcher, a Christian Scientist came up to him, and [Glover] jumped up and ran off cured." But, Chandler pointed out, Glover still suffered from his neck wound. Chandler admitted, "We may not win in this suit." But he did expect ultimate vindication, because "under the peculiar protection of George W. Glover and the other 'next friends,'" Eddy was protected legally and yet being left alone while the defendants were inflicting "torture upon this woman in order to make her do with her property what they want[ed] her to do with it." The continuing hostility between Chandler and Streeter was evidenced by this exchange: Chandler said, "Every case in the books that the Senator (I mean counsel) can find—I forget he is not yet senator." Streeter replied, "You mean not a has-been, but a-going to be." Chandler said, "Don't mortify me by reminding me of past glories." Judge Chamberlin interrupted, saying, "Proceed."[27]

Streeter concluded for the trustees, claiming that if substituted for the next friends, they would do their duty "whether it [lead] them to follow in Mr. Chandler's footsteps or not." Judge Chamberlin asked, "Is there any escape from a trial by jury upon this main question of competency?" Streeter offered that "the court [should] go and sit down and talk with Mrs. Eddy" and find out whether she was competent: "[If] Mrs. Eddy is all right these next friends are all wrong." Chamberlin signaled his ruling by asking Streeter, "What possible harm would it be in trying it in the ordinary way [to] determine the fact that they are all wrong and she is right?" Streeter replied that the harm was in putting a "lady 86 years old to a trial, unless there [was] some foundation for it." The hearing closed at 6:00 p.m. on Friday, May 24, with Judge Chamberlin promising a ruling on the motion within a week. On June 5, Chamberlin denied the motion to substitute the three trustees for the next friends, thus allowing the suit to continue. He later explained that the execution of the trust deed by Eddy granting power of attorney to the trustees did not entitle them to substitute for the next friends.[28]

Although it would seem that her lawyers would have prepared her for this decision, Eddy was, nevertheless, very upset by it. In a letter to Streeter she pleaded,

> If you let this case remain as it now is could the 'next friends' take possession of my person? If they could not then is it not better to let this suit stand *as it is*? I fear if you press it they will get Judge C. (in his weakness) to decide it against me and give my person to my enemies (called 'next friends') and they will take me away from my real friends, Students, and thus *get rid* of me by such means, then fight over my last will.

In a postscript she added, "I read in the enemy's mind their purpose now is to *kill me*. . . . O do not let me be put in Glover's hands
I can stand anything better *than this*." She sent a copy of the letter to
someone identified only as "N.B.," adding "I beg you to consider
that m.a.m. is hard at work on dear, good Gen. Streeter and he may
not know what this last move he is thinking to make—may cost me."
Eddy continued, "O do not let them take me away from my students.
Be sure as to this."[29]

Streeter responded immediately: "I can positively say to you that
you are just as safe and secure in your   own house as Mrs. Streeter is
in hers; no next friends can go there to trouble you. I wish you would
dismiss any thought of such a thing from your mind, because there is
no occasion for it." Streeter reminded Eddy that Judge Chamberlin
had done nothing to interfere with the trust deed and that her property was "secure and safe." He also assured Eddy, "You will not be
expected, at any time or in any event, to be in court." Any occasion
requiring her statement would be conducted at her house. Streeter
offered further assurance: "Your household will in no way be interfered with; your friends who are there will remain there so long as you
wish and no longer; you are mistress of your house with precisely the
same power and authority that every lady in New Hampshire has over
her household." One of her three trustees who was also an attorney,
Archibald McLellan, confirmed Streeter's analysis, telling Eddy, "I
fully concur in what he has said and assure you that you need have no
fear of any personal annoyance from those who are persecuting you
in this suit."[30]

Judge Chamberlin's denial of the motion to substitute the three
trustees for the next friends now turned the attention of both sides
to the upcoming trial of Eddy's competence. On the same day the
judge issued his decision, DeWitt Howe ran into Frank Streeter at
the courthouse, and the two met with Chamberlin informally to discuss how to proceed with the case. Howe reported the conversation
to Chandler, stating that the judge recommended "a regular judicial
trial of the question of capacity" at the earliest possible date but said

that the question should be tried before a master rather than a jury. (A master is an officer of the court assigned by a judge to hear and report on matters referred to him.) To Howe, the conversation became "acrimonious" when Streeter launched into an attack on Chandler and Peabody, claiming they were tools of the *World* and that the real purpose of the suit was to attack Christian Science. Streeter also objected to any use of alienists in whatever testimony was obtained from Eddy. Howe reported that the "gabfest" of June 5 was not a hearing but that Chamberlin scheduled one for June 10 to determine when the trial should take place.[31]

To Kelley, Chandler expressed frustration that Howe, Streeter, and Chamberlin had met to discuss important aspects of the case without Chandler and Kelley. Chandler was so exasperated by events in Concord, he said, "I cannot stand it & feel inclined to give up in despair." He expressed the opinion that Streeter was taking advantage of Chandler's absence and pressuring the judge into making a decision to "have a rush trial [rather than] a reasonable and proper trial." The plaintiffs needed time to take depositions from all the people they had identified in Eddy's past, like Cushing, who could testify to her mental state. Chandler insisted that Howe file a motion for a jury trial at the June 10 hearing and inform the judge that Chandler was not prepared to argue any other motion at that time and that the plaintiffs be given enough time to gather depositions.[32]

At the June 10 hearing, Judge Chamberlin ruled that the first question to be determined in the suit was the competency of Eddy and that her competency would be determined after an inquiry by a master, not by a jury trial. He promised to name the master within a few days. Chamberlin's ruling came after a lengthy statement by Streeter attacking, once again, the motives of the next friends and claiming that the suit was brought by a newspaper, not to benefit Eddy but to discredit the religion. Streeter's statement supported several motions he filed that asked the "chancellor" (Judge Chamberlin) to protect Eddy's rights by discharging the next friends and suspending the proceedings until the questions of the motives of the next friends could be investigated. After Chamberlin's ruling that a quick trial be conducted of Eddy's competency by a master, not a jury, Streeter suspended his motions. Howe and Kelley were present for the plaintiffs, with Howe expressing Chandler's desire for a jury trial of Eddy's competency but agreeing not to file a motion to this effect after the judge's decision to send the matter to a master.[33]

Though not present for the hearing, Frederick Peabody later read in the transcript that Streeter, in support of his allegations about the motives of the next friends, had charged Peabody with "boasting" in public that he would "drag [Eddy] down from her pedestal" and that any testimony taken in the form of depositions would be given immediately to the newspapers in advance of the trial. Peabody wrote to Howe, denying that he ever "made this alleged boast." Peabody also asserted, "from the time of my retainer in the case, some weeks before the bill was filed, to to-day, I have not said to any newspaper man anything derogatory of Mrs. Eddy or Christian Science." He called Streeter's statement "deliberate lies" and asked that his own letter be shown to Judge Chamberlin.[34] Peabody's long national campaign against Eddy and Christian Science made his membership on the Chandler team a public relations liability.

Further cracks in the Chandler case came from one of the next friends, Fred W. Baker, whose alcoholism became a potential scandal in Concord. While still in Concord for the earlier hearing, Chandler wrote in his diary that he "saw Fred W. Baker who [was] blundering." Soon after Chandler returned to Washington, Baker was apparently picked up by the authorities in Concord for some type of rowdy behavior and was to be forced into the state hospital. Howe intervened, placing Baker in the private Margaret Pillsbury Hospital, where he was "straightened out and shipped . . . back home." Baker then wrote a letter to Howe, offering to withdraw as a plaintiff from the case. Interestingly, Howe wrote that Chandler's son, William D., would "have the weekly allowance forwarded to F.W.B.'s wife this week," indicating that some financial incentive was being provided to the next friends from one of Chandler's local enterprises, possibly the

Concord Monitor. Chandler accepted Baker's withdrawal and indicated to Howe that the main thing was that "all the heirs [were] in," since Baker was only a distant cousin to Eddy and not in line for any inheritance. The local press seemed unaware of the circumstances of Baker's withdrawal and editorialized that it was proof of the weakness of the plaintiff's case. To Baker, Chandler was much more solicitous, declaring his "sincere friendship" and his hope that Baker would become "a good citizen and a faithful member of [his] family." Chandler told him, "You have friends who will help you reasonably but the great work of overcoming any habit and of being a whole man must be done by you." After Baker's withdrawal from the case, a reporter from the *Boston American* contacted him, asking why he had withdrawn. Baker reported to Chandler that he had denied receiving any money to withdraw and that he still supported the next friends and "gave Frye a roast." He promised Chandler, "I shall *never* do again what I have done I don't know what made me do as I did I can't understand it. I am in a hard place just [now] my wife and girl are sick and myself no work but the thing will end some time."[35] Whatever his original motive in bringing the suit, Chandler had become genuinely concerned for the well-being of the next friends, with the possible exception of Ebenezer Foster Eddy, whose obsequiousness grated on him.

The judge's earlier decision to deny Streeter's motion to substitute the trustees for the next friends raised alarm among Christian Scientists, who understood now that a major public challenge to the religion was in the offing. Frye wrote to Streeter and offered unneeded advice that the next friends intended to investigate Eddy's past and claim that she had been incompetent for years: "Her views and acts may appear eccentric to those who *do not understand* her doctrine but to those who do—and many highly intellectual people do—her teachings are logical and divinely natural, and to such people her teachings are no proof of an unbalanced mind, but on the contrary of an unusually well balanced mind."[36]

Christian Scientists in Concord for the June 10 hearing were suspicious that there was collusion between the plaintiffs' attorneys and the judge. In two separate letters to Alfred Farlow, Eddy's public relations expert, William R. Brown, and John V. Dittemore wrote about a luncheon they attended at the Eagle Hotel at 1:00 p.m. on June 10, only minutes after Judge Chamberlin had adjourned the hearing. Dittemore, Brown, and their wives were seated at a table with Irving C. Tomlinson when the judge came in and was seated at the same large table and was soon joined by Kelley and Howe, as if the meeting was "a prearranged affair." Brown and Dittemore each overheard Howe comment to the judge that Streeter would not have been allowed to speak at such length before a less liberal judge, to which they all laughed. Chamberlin reportedly said, "Oh! well I had to let him go on and make his speech or his clients would have discharged him. He (Streeter) had to make it to hold his clients." Brown and Dittemore reported, "More laughter." Chamberlin then mentioned a letter sent to him by a Christian Scientist, remarking that the writer was "crazy" but "that they [Christian Scientists] were all crazy," at which the three laughed again. The judge soon left the table, with Kelley commenting to Howe, "Well he is 'on'—they (the Christian Scientists and General Streeter) can't fool your Uncle Henry (Judge Chamberlin)." Both Brown and Dittemore reported that remarks about Streeter were made in a "joking and sarcastic manner," that profanity was used by Kelley and Howe, who made a great effort to "flatter Judge Chamberlin," and that it appeared the judge and Kelley and Howe "all had the same ultimate object in mind." After the judge left the table, Kelley said to Howe, "Well, our work together until ten o'clock last night was all for nothing. Instead of having something tangible to meet this morning we were only up against a puff ball."[37]

With a trial of Eddy's competency now a certainty, Streeter, Alfred Farlow, and Eddy decided to launch their own media campaign to improve Eddy's image and convince the public of her mental well-being. On June 8, Arthur Brisbane of *Cosmopolitan* magazine was invited for a one-hour interview with Eddy at Pleasant View, Streeter being present throughout. Though Brisbane's article would not appear in *Cosmopolitan* until the August issue, this interview with Eddy was covered in the newspapers. Brisbane wrote his editor that Eddy was well able to take care of herself, that she was mistress of her household, and that the effort to deprive her of her freedom of action was "stupid and vicious." Chandler was alerted by the editor of the *World*, John J. Spurgeon, that Brisbane "found that the old lady [was] mentally sound and competent to care for herself and fortune." Spurgeon did write that Brisbane was not an objective reporter, since he had "very strong leanings towards Christian Science," though Brisbane claimed to have "no interest whatever in Christian Science." When the article did appear, Brisbane described Pleasant View as a modest New England home, called Eddy a "beautiful and venerable woman," and declared that her "mind on all points brought out was perfectly clear, and her answers were instantaneous." When asked about the reasons why the next friends brought the suit, Eddy replied: "Greed of gold, young man. They are not interested in me, I am sorry to say, but in my money, and in the desire to control that. They say they want to help me. They never tried to help me when I was working hard years ago and when help would have been so welcome." Brisbane went on at lengths, decrying his belief that the suit was as an intolerant attack on religious freedom, that any success of the effort "would be shameful, a degradation to all womanhood and old age." The charge that Eddy was "a victim of hallucinations" was equivalent to deciding "that fixed religious belief is a hallucination."[38]

Another interview with Eddy was conducted on June 15, by Edwin J. Park of the *Boston Globe*. Park wrote that after meeting and talking with Eddy, "the thought that she was not fully competent mentally would have been the last one that ever would have entered [his] mind." Park reported that when he arrived in her study, Eddy was reading a book without glasses. He asked her questions mostly about her son, George Glover, to which Eddy replied, "You mean the 'next friends' alias 'next enemies,' do you not?" Eddy related the story of how she had lost physical custody of her son, claiming that when George was "eight years old" she had "determined to leave [her] father's house to pursue [her] literary work. Eddy continued, "I selected as the woman best calculated to care for the child [Mahala Sanborn Cheney,] who had been our nurse and whom I knew to be a good girl, kind and tender, and who I knew would take good care of my boy." This somewhat fanciful and self-serving story went on to describe how the Cheneys cared for the boy but denied him access to his mother, claiming Eddy was dead. She later learned the truth and asked George to come to her, "but he preferred the Black Hills." Nevertheless, she had bought him a house in Lead, calling it "a better house than the one I live in," and had sent him money "from time to time." To Chandler, the Park interview was "a ramble" and was "disconnected." He remarked on Eddy's "pitiable effort" to explain "why she abandoned her boy, five years old!"[39]

Another interview was granted at this time to William E. Curtis of the *Chicago Record-Herald*. The article was headlined "Mrs. Eddy, Marvel in Mental Activity," and Curtis raved about her "vitality" and "perfect health." He claimed to have no difficulty securing an interview and concluded, "Mrs. Eddy is very sane, very responsible, very competent." Chandler knew Curtis and asked him about the interview, learning that Eddy and Curtis had talked mostly about China and that Michael Meehan of the *Concord Patriot* was also present at Pleasant View. Chandler noted that Curtis was a distant relative of Eddy's but did not mention that during the interview with her. In yet another interview, *Philadelphia North American* reporter Leigh Mitchell Hodges asked Eddy, "What do you feel will be the result of the present controversy?" She replied, "Why some good must come out of it, of course. Hard as it is to bear, it cannot but cause truth to stand out more clearly in the end."[40] By this time Chandler had to question his assumption that Eddy was mentally incompetent, or at least that she was no more incompetent now than she had been all along. Thus he recognized the need to go further back into her life to prove that she had been insane and subject to hallucinations or delusions for decades.

Besides a media blitz, Streeter had another ace up his sleeve. He had never informed Glover or his attorneys of the contents of the trust

fund of $125,000 established for Glover and family. To try one last time
to separate Glover from the case, Streeter, on June 19, sent a copy of
the trust deed to Glover, claiming that the trustees were concerned
about the education of Glover's youngest sons, George and Andrew,
and believed that the trust should go into effect "with out delay, and
that they should receive the benefit of the trust funds in promoting
their education beginning with the next school year." Putting the
trust into effect would allow the Glovers time to determine if the boys
should stay in Lead for their education "or go to some good school
in the East." Streeter assured Glover that his mother had "a strong
desire" to care for her son and his family. Streeter may have thought
that Glover was in a vulnerable position at the time, as he was far
removed from Chandler's influence and Bennett was out of town and
could not advise him. But the wily, litigiously attuned Glover did not
fall for the ruse, wiring Streeter immediately that he would not accept
the deed. In fact, after reading it, Glover informed Chandler that it
was "the most humiliating . . . transaction of business" that Glover
had ever seen. According to the deed, the education of the two boys
was to be under the supervision of Irving C. Tomlinson, and young
George was to receive a college education, but Andrew's education
was only to go through high school. Why Eddy had made this distinction is not known, but Glover was angered by it, especially by the role
of Tomlinson in directing the education of the boys. Glover was also
to receive only $1,500 a year from the trust. He wrote Chandler, "My
mother in her right mind would never [sign] an instrument that places
her son and grandchildren in the degraded position that the copy of the
Trust Deed does." Streeter's intention to trick Glover into accepting
the trust, thus ending the suit, is clear in the fact that Streeter did not
send Chandler a copy of the trust until a week later.[41]

Glover also reported to Chandler that a visitor, Eva Thompson,
had arrived in Lead, carrying a letter from his mother. Thompson
was a Christian Scientist from Burlington, Iowa, and was a friend to
the Glovers, especially to Mary. On a visit to the East, Thompson met
on June 16 with Eddy, who gave her a brief letter to carry to George.

I love you, my only child. Why do you allow yourself to be used to bring this great grief and trouble on your own aged mother!

As ever affectionately,

Mary B. G. Eddy

Thompson stayed in Lead for two weeks, writing in her reminiscences that George Glover was being influenced by a "young man from New York" who she claimed was "a regular detective and agent of Mrs. Eddy's enemies." Thompson, in turn, tried to cure Glover and family of the "mental malpractice" they were under, and left only after assurances from Glover that he was departing soon for the East and would "end the suit." Glover informed Chandler of the letter from his mother and stated that this was the first he had heard from her in months and that the handwritten letter showed "great feebleness and a wonderful weakness of mind."[42] Glover likely told Thompson what she wanted to hear in order to get her to leave Lead, as there is no evidence in any of his correspondence with Chandler of his wavering at all in his determination to carry on the suit. Glover did inform Chandler of the suspicious man from New York who was in Lead for three months and who told Glover he represented potential investors in Glover's mine. Glover suspected the man was a spy for the other side. Chandler objected vigorously to Streeter about communicating directly with Glover without going through his attorney. Streeter explained that he had sent Glover the trust deed only after meeting with Eva Thompson for an hour and a half one day and learning from her about the lack of plans and means to educate the two boys. Streeter promised to not contact Glover again.[43] Both sides in the case waited anxiously for Judge Chamberlin's announcement of a master appointed to investigate, determine, and report on the competency of Mary Baker Eddy.

A MASTER TAKES CHARGE OF THE CASE

On June 27, 1907, Judge Robert Chamberlin announced the appointment of Judge Edgar Aldrich as master to determine the competency of Mary Baker Eddy. Chamberlin instructed the master to complete his work and file his report by September 30. Aldrich was to hear all pertinent evidence submitted either by deposition or orally that related to Eddy's competence on March 1, 1907, "and for such period of time before that date as to the master may seem reasonable." How far prior to March 1, 1907, the plaintiffs would be allowed to submit evidence would turn out to be the critical decision of the master, but for now both sides expressed approval of Chamberlin's selection of Judge Aldrich.[1]

Edgar Aldrich was one of the highest-ranking and most respected jurists in New Hampshire. Appointed by President Benjamin Harrison in 1891 to the federal bench as district judge for New Hampshire, Aldrich had served with distinction, operating out of his office in Boston. Another leading Republican involved with the Eddy case, Aldrich was born in Pittsburg, New Hampshire, in the far north country of the state, but had moved to Littleton to practice law. He had served in the state legislature, being elected Speaker of the House during his tenure. Aldrich was a graduate of the University of Michigan Law School and had received honorary degrees from Dartmouth

College and the University of Michigan. At the state Constitutional Convention of 1902, he was the author and chief proponent of the so-called trust and monopoly amendment to the state constitution, an amendment intended to check "the enormous growth of the trust evil." In 1905, he had spoken before the state legislature in favor of a bill to create a public monument to Franklin Pierce, a long-time cause of William Chandler, who had once worked with Pierce. The Republican-dominated legislature had long opposed any memorial to the only president from New Hampshire, a Democrat who had opposed the Civil War. But Chandler, who knew Pierce personally, believed the state was remiss in not recognizing the only native son to reach the White House. Aldrich's views on both trusts and a Pierce memorial placed him in the reform-minded, progressive wing of his party, and his appointment as master greatly pleased the plaintiffs in the case. John W. Kelley expressed this to Judge Granville Bennett in South Dakota: "Judge Aldrich, the master appointed to determine this question of competency is an exceedingly able jurist and strong minded man between whom and Senator Chandler there has always existed a strong bond of personal friendship; and between whom and Mr. Streeter there has existed for several years such a spirit of hostility that we were somewhat in fear Mr. Streeter would protest him, this he has not yet done." In fact, Frank Streeter also expressed "much satisfaction" at the selection of Aldrich and declared to H. Cornell Wilson, Eddy's current secretary, "I think he is a perfectly fair man."[2]

Aldrich refused to accept the appointment unless Chamberlin appointed two comasters "of high standing in respect to mental conditions." Chamberlin agreed with Aldrich and appointed as comasters Dr. George F. Jelly of Boston and Dr. G. Alden Blumer of Providence, Rhode Island, both alienists. Blumer declined to accept the appointment, at which point Chamberlin selected seventy-four-year-old attorney and former congressman Hosea W. Parker of Claremont, New Hampshire as the third comaster.[3]

The naming of alienists as comasters in the case came as an unpleasant surprise to Christian Science officials, who met in Concord with

Streeter to plan strategy. Even before knowing the successor to Blumer, Streeter filed a bill of exceptions with Judge Chamberlin, charging that the naming of alienists from outside New Hampshire was unconstitutional. Streeter also indicated that alienists were unsuitable because of bias or preconceived opinions about Eddy and Christian Science. Among the motions filed by Streeter was one objecting to the court's failure to rule previously on the charge that the motives of the next friends were not what they stated—that is, to help and protect Eddy—but rather to discredit her and her religion. Streeter asked the judge to suspend the next friends from pursuing the case until their motives could be investigated. Streeter reserved the right to take these matters to the state supreme court if necessary. He also wanted the judge to limit the taking of depositions in the case. This was a major goal of the plaintiffs, who were anxious to get on the record the testimony of some of Eddy's former associates who would testify to her belief in M.A.M., her so-called delusions about the miracle cure in 1866, and the many other controversial events in her life. In fact, depositions were scheduled to be taken on July 9 in Concord, with church officials Calvin Frye, H. Cornell Wilson, and Laura Sargent among the first to testify, only to be postponed at the last minute when Chamberlin agreed to a hearing on all the motions, to take place on July 25. Chandler had also filed a motion with the judge to have the expenses of the plaintiffs in prosecuting the case paid out of Eddy's estate and asked the judge to waive a bond required of the plaintiffs because of their poverty.[4]

In the meantime, Chandler had moved from Washington to his summer home in Waterloo, New Hampshire, and began focusing on Eddy's taxes to the city of Concord. His investigation showed that Eddy had underpaid during recent years, mostly by not declaring her entire income but only the value of her house and its contents. Chandler placed the blame on Frye, who had signed her tax bills for the past five years, which proved, Chandler thought, that "she was imbecile and that her advisers were faithless if not dishonest." He claimed she should have paid between $10,000 and $16,000 per year rather than the $5,000 average that she had paid under Frye's calculations. The

local press covered the tax questions in detail. In correspondence with
Dr. Henry Reed Hopkins, Chandler explored the medical treatment
provided by Christian Scientists, concluding, "They seem to think
that because they call themselves religionists and religious healers and
discard all knowledge of medicine and anatomy, physiology, hygiene
and therapeutics, they are entitled whenever questions arise in court
to be exempt from all the rules of evidence and rules of treatment in
the law which apply to all the rest of the christian and heathen world."
Chandler promised to find money to bring Hopkins to Concord for the
trial. Hopkins agreed to waive his honorarium if his expenses could be
paid. To Hopkins, the case needed to be tried "for the larger court—
the World." Chandler also promised Granville Bennett that Chandler
would come up with the $500 needed to bring George Glover and
daughter Mary east for the trial.[5]

Willa Cather, who was the main author of the *McClure's* series
on Eddy's life that would later be published in book form under the
authorship of Georgine Milmine, contacted Chandler, asking for
permission to travel to South Dakota for an in-depth interview with
Glover. She promised to "submit to [Chandler] proofs of the article"
in advance of publication: "I shall ask you to cut out any statement
of Mr. Glover's which might be detrimental to his interests." Cather
promised that the interview with Glover about his relationship with
his mother and the current litigation would not appear until the final
installment of the series, in the February 1908 issue of *McClure's*. The
interview never took place, as Glover was in the East by the time
Cather was ready to travel to her home in Nebraska.[6]

The Chandler team had been trying the case before public opinion
from the start but were losing on this front, largely because of the
efforts of Streeter, Alfred Farlow, and Eddy to allow her to be interviewed by prominent journalists who attested to her intelligence and
good health. Chandler admitted to Hopkins that the expected interview with Eddy by the masters might not prove his team's contention.

> She may possibly be braced up by stimulants so that she may
> appear to be capable of taking care of her property. Then they

will say that no matter about her delusions which are a matter of religion. Yet the evidence is going to be so strong of her craze about M.A.M. that I do not believe it can be rejected as immaterial . . . [because] the delusions affected her feeling towards them [her son and adopted son] and made her a prey to strangers to her who hated Glover and Foster Eddy.[7]

In mid-July Streeter announced that the state attorney general, Edwin G. Eastman, had officially become cocounsel for Eddy, moving over from representing defendants Frye, Tomlinson, Hering, and Strang. Streeter and Eastman had worked closely on the case from the start, and with the focus of the masters on Eddy's competency and not on the actions of the defendants, it made sense for Eastman to join Streeter's team in preparing Eddy's case.[8]

When the Streeter-Farlow-Eddy publicity machine permitted journalists to meet with Eddy, the members of Eddy's team anticipated positive stories in the press, and they got it. *Chicago Record–Herald* reporter William E. Curtis wrote, "I did not see the slightest sign of the 'senile debility,' 'mental infirmity' or 'physical incapacity' which has been alleged as the basis of the suit to deprive her of the care of her property." Curtis spent less than one half hour interviewing Eddy, but he spent several days in Concord and may have contributed to Eddy's public defense by his analysis of the reasons behind the suit. In his "Letters from New Hampshire," Curtis recognized that the main problem was Calvin Frye.

> [He] is not at all popular in Concord. He is reserved and taciturn, never speaks to any one unless he is spoken to and evidently does not care to make friends. Although he has lived in Concord for twenty-one years he has never been on terms of intimacy with any person, but everybody admits he is absolutely loyal and devoted to Mrs. Eddy and that he has been honest and shrewd in the management of her business affairs. The only criticisms are provided by his morose disposition and tactlessness.

Curtis reported, "Public sympathy is almost unanimously with Mrs. Eddy. She is highly respected in the entire community, almost without exception. . . . The editors of the two daily papers both testified to me of her high character and extraordinary ability."[9]

The plaintiffs expected Judge Aldrich to conduct the hearing before the masters like a trial. Aldrich proposed starting the judicial proceedings on July 26, the day after Judge Chamberlin disposed of the many motions filed by Streeter and Chandler. But Chandler and Howe appealed to Aldrich to delay the hearing to allow the plaintiffs to prepare their case, as they had not begun to take depositions, because they were preparing for the hearing before Chamberlin scheduled for July 25. Aldrich still scheduled the hearing before the masters for 11:00 a.m. on July 26 but determined that the issue of taking depositions would be decided then, when everyone got together for the first time.[10]

At the hearing before Judge Chamberlin on July 25, Chandler opened the argument, stating that the plaintiffs were financially unable to meet the requirement for a bond to cover the costs of the proceedings before the master. Chandler asked the judge to suspend the rule in this case and also asked him to set aside a certain sum from Eddy's trust fund for the purposes of meeting the expenses of the suit. Streeter then argued for his previously filed exceptions. He explained the defense team's concerns that Dr. Jelly was not a resident of New Hampshire and that alienists could not judge Eddy because of their built-in bias against Christian Science. Streeter also presented once again his belief that the motives of the next friends in bringing the suit should be investigated prior to any hearing about Eddy's competence. Streeter also excepted to the judge's previous decision to not allow Eddy's three trustees to replace the next friends as plaintiffs in the case. The Chandler and Streeter teams argued vociferously over the powers of the masters in the case, with Judge Chamberlin asking the defendants if they agreed to "be bound by the findings of the masters." Kelley wanted assurance that if the masters found Mary Baker Eddy incompetent, the plaintiffs would not have to go over the question of competency again when the court later proceeded to try the defendants for misappropriation of her property. The issue of the taking of depositions was also argued, with Streeter stating there was no legal justification for the taking of depositions, as the masters were ready to begin the hearing, and Chandler claiming that the plaintiffs had the broad statutory right to take depositions and that he would not consent to be limited in this right, which was ultimately about "finding and perpetuating truth." Following what Chandler described in his diary as "quite a debate," Chamberlin ruled against all of the motions, including the motion to replace Jelly, the motion to limit the taking of depositions, the motion made once again to replace the next friends with the trustees as plaintiffs, and Chandler's motion for an allowance from Eddy's estate to conduct the case for the plaintiffs, though Chamberlin did say he might reconsider this decision if Eddy were found incompetent. The judge did postpone a decision "for further consideration" on Chandler's motion to suspend the rule requiring the plaintiffs to furnish a bond for court costs. Chandler seemed satisfied with the results of the hearing, and, in fact, the press also thought the next friends were "winners" based on the judge's decisions.[11]

The next day the masters met for the first time with the attorneys for both sides. Judge Aldrich asked for any "suggestions counsel [might] have to make with reference to this case." Chandler spoke up first, stating that the next friends would have liked more time to prepare their case, as "the burden of proof [rested] upon them." But Aldrich asserted that the masters did not have the authority to extend the deadline of September 30 to file their report with Judge Chamberlin. Streeter remarked that the sole question for consideration by the masters was Eddy's competence on March 1, 1907, to care for her property. At age eighty-seven she was "entitled to a speedy hearing." The charges should never have been brought , he said, "unless the men who made them were prepared to go on." To Streeter, "the very foundation of the suit" was "pure, bold fiction." Judge Aldrich reminded Streeter that the only question of the day was when a hearing should take place. Aldrich proposed a private conference with counsel to set a date for the hearing, but even in private the

contentious attorneys could not agree on a date. At the end of the
day, Aldrich handed down his orders, stating that Judge Chamberlin
"contemplate[d] a speedy hearing" but that "reasonable time should
be accorded to the plaintiffs." To Aldrich, there was no need to delay
because of the taking of depositions in Concord, as those witnesses
could appear in person, but he did think it was reasonable to delay
so that the plaintiffs had the "opportunity to take depositions outside
of the jurisdiction," that is, in Boston. He concluded, "This hearing
is therefore postponed until Tuesday, August 13, at 11:30 o'clock."[12]

On July 29, the controversy over the taking of depositions became
a media circus. Magistrate Edmund Cook had issued summonses to
Calvin Frye, H. Cornell Wilson, and Laura Sargent, all residents at
Pleasant View, to testify before him at 11:00 a.m. At that time, Frye
and Sargent failed to show and only Wilson arrived, accompanied
by his attorney, Frank Streeter. After Magistrate Cook duly swore in
the witness, Streeter objected to the taking of the deposition, claiming that the masters had ruled that no depositions were to be taken in
Concord and that the granting of a delay in the hearing until August
13 was made by the masters solely to expedite the taking of depositions outside of the jurisdiction of the court. Magistrate Cook, who
was simply a justice of the peace assigned by the court, asked Streeter
what Judge Chamberlin had ordered regarding depositions. Streeter
answered that Chamberlin had stated that the plaintiffs had a statutory right to take depositions but that that the masters would have
absolute control over the trial. Kelley then handed the magistrate an
order signed by Chamberlin on July 25 stating, "The motion to limit
the taking of depositions so far as it is a matter of discretion is denied."
Kelley asked Cook to charge Wilson, along with Frye and Sargent,
with contempt of court for failure to comply with the summons. Kelley
stated that the masters had no right under their commission to limit the
taking of depositions, and in fact, they could not legally do so even if
they wanted to. Kelley advised Cook to proceed with the deposition; it
would be up to the masters to decide if they wanted to use it. Streeter
responded at length that he had asked the masters for an immediate

hearing, but to accommodate the taking of depositions outside of Concord, they had agreed to postpone the hearing until August 13. The masters specifically stated that the delay was not for the taking of depositions in Concord, where witnesses could appear in person at the hearing before the masters. The long argument was followed by Cook's stating, "I do not see any reason why the deposition should not proceed . . . as [the plaintiffs] had the right common to all parties to take depositions in view of the fact that there is no restraining order from any court." Wilson's deposition began, but he responded to each question asked by Kelley by saying, "For the reason stated by my counsel and by his evidence I decline to give my deposition at this time." Attorney General Eastman then spoke up for the defense, asking for a delay until the masters could rule on the taking of depositions. Cook agreed that it would be helpful to him if the counsel for both sides could get together and communicate with the masters on the issue. Cook ordered a recess until 2:15 p.m.[13]

At this point, the acrimony between Chandler and Streeter reached new heights. Streeter invited Chandler to his office to telephone Judge Aldrich at his home in Littleton, New Hampshire. After getting Aldrich on the line, Chandler claimed that he couldn't hear Aldrich. Streeter then remained on another line, to translate to Chandler what Judge Aldrich was saying about the taking of depositions, but unbeknownst to Chandler, Streeter had a stenographer on a third line who was taking down a transcript of the phone call. Aldrich advised that he did not think the statutory right to take depositions existed during the trial that had begun on July 26, when the masters first met with the counsel for both sides. He confirmed that in suspending the trial, he was attempting only to accommodate the taking of depositions outside of the jurisdiction and that he "would not have entertained the idea of granting the delay for the purpose of taking depositions of Concord witnesses." Aldrich advised Chandler that it would be far "more favorable" to have the local witnesses present in court so that they could be cross-examined. But in this Aldrich was only making a suggestion, not an order. To Streeter's recommendation that the masters reconvene in Concord the next day to rule on the question, Aldrich declined, saying, "It would be personally very disagreeable for me. I want to get a little rest." He also did not know if he could convene the board of masters on such short notice. Chandler declared he was "very sorry" not to accept Aldrich's oral advice, but his duty to his clients required him "to act on Judge Chamberlin's written order" of July 25, which denied the motion to limit the taking of depositions. Aldrich understood, recalling that Chamberlin had said "that this case should be tried before the Masters by depositions and other evidence." Chandler concluded that what Aldrich had issued on July 26 was not an order: "It was advice for us to consider." Aldrich remarked, "I have not made an order." But he also stated that he was not advising Chandler, only reiterating his own understanding of the situation. Chandler replied that his "understanding of the situation" was "what [was] in writing." Streeter again asked if the masters could get together, to which Aldrich again replied, "I don't think so." Aldrich stated, "Your remedy . . . is to apply to Judge Chamberlin." Streeter understood that Chamberlin had "gone into the woods somewhere" on vacation. In response to Streeter's prompting, Aldrich restated his understanding of the situation: "It is perfectly clear. The trial was postponed against your [Streeter's] wishes, and I suppose for the accommodation of the other side to prepare their case—not for the purpose of taking Concord depositions." Chandler finally asked if this then would "blot out Judge Chamberlin's order," to which Aldrich replied, "I don't understand any such thing."[14]

The confusing phone conversation left Magistrate Cook with little recourse but to postpone until August 6 the taking of local depositions until Judge Chamberlin could be reached for his decision on the matter. But the controversy over the phone conversation flared when Streeter presented Cook with a transcript of the call, stating that Streeter had had the transcript made "to make sure of it being correctly reported." Chandler insisted, "Gen. Streeter buncoed me." Streeter replied. "You poor lamb." Chandler continued,

> I was buncoed by his sending me word that Judge Aldrich
> wanted to talk to me. Mr. Streeter asked me to come to his office
> to have that conversation. I fell into his trap. I ought to have
> known better than put myself in the clutches of Gen. Streeter,
> but I did not. I supposed he was not lost to every sense of honor
> that prevails among gentleman. Mr. Streeter admitted me to one
> room in the den of thieves and put me on the telephone. He went
> into the other room, where he could carry on a conversation,
> and put a shorthand writer in still another room with another
> instrument, and never told either myself or Judge Aldrich what
> he was doing. It was manifestly a dishonorable transaction and
> is so regarded among gentleman.[15]

Streeter claimed that he had told Chandler that the call was
being transcribed.

"No, sir," Chandler said.

"Then you and I can't agree," replied Streeter.

"I say it is a lie!" Chandler shouted, his face white with anger.

"I didn't intend to use that word, but if you repeat that statement
I shall tell you it is a lie."

Streeter said, "I can't say as you can that I have had such distinguished men in the country use that term. You have the advantage of
me. More distinguished men have called you that."

Chandler responded, "I don't think the President of the United
States would notice you under any circumstances." This latest flare-up
between Streeter and Chandler made headlines around the nation.[16]

Mayor Corning, an interested but not neutral observer, wrote in his
diary, "Chandler and Streeter are calling one another liars and bunko
steerers over the question of taking depositions in the Eddy case."
According to Corning,

> the odoriferous Jack Kelly [John Kelley] of Portsmouth
> demanded Cornell Wilson's instant commitment to jail for

contempt. At this point black corpuscles began working. For
two days Streeter has beat off all attempts on jailing Wilson.
The controversy among the rival attorneys is getting bitter and
bloodthirsty for really it is a half political duel between Bill
[William Chandler] and Streeter. Neither deserves further public confidence yet both try to persuade themselves that they are
indispensable to the party.[17]

Corning's insight into the political ramifications of the contest
between Streeter and Chandler is significant, as each represented a different wing of the dominant Republican Party in the state. Chandler,
the progressive, and Streeter, the conservative, had been competing
politically for years, especially when Streeter represented the Boston
and Maine Railroad as attorney and Chandler was trying to get legislation passed to restrict the political power of railroad corporations.
In the small world of New Hampshire, the fact that the two political
rivals should be lead attorneys in a lawsuit of such national interest is
not all that surprising, but the complication of their political rivalry
undoubtedly made their personal interactions more contentious when
they were representing their clients and made it less likely that either
would give in, regardless of the evidence in the case.

As both sides waited for Judge Chamberlin's ruling on the matter
of taking local depositions, Frederick Peabody proceeded to depose
witnesses in Boston. During the first days of August, Peabody successfully deposed Dr. Rufus Noyes, who had been a professor at the
Metaphysical College in the 1880s and had performed the autopsy on
Asa Gilbert Eddy; William G. Nixon, once Eddy's publisher, who had
become one of the church leader's most violent opponents and owned
many letters written by Eddy; and current church officials Alfred
Farlow and Archibald McLellan. Streeter came down from Concord
to sit in on the Farlow and McLellan depositions, with Peabody reporting that Streeter was "amazingly decent." Within days, Peabody proceeded to depose Arthur Buswell, a student at the college in the early
1880s, and Daniel Spofford, while Luther Marston—another former

college student now living in California—was apparently deposed there. Horace Wentworth told the story of Eddy's attempt to wreck and burn his mother's boarding house when asked to leave it way back in 1870, a story denied by other members of the Wentworth family. Dr. A. M. Cushing was too ill to appear, but Chandler expressed his pleasure at the work Peabody was doing in Boston. Peabody was also in contact with Willa Cather, who lent some early editions of *Science and Health* to the attorneys for the next friends. Chandler appreciated the loan of the earlier editions, stating that he had been using for his research an 1893 edition, which was now "mutilated" from overuse. Peabody also arranged for two Boston-area alienists to appear as witnesses for the plaintiffs, if called. Drs. George T. Tuttle and Henry R. Stedman, partners whose office was on Beacon Street, agreed to appear if paid $100 each per day. Chandler, lacking funds to pay for expert witnesses, unsuccessfully appealed once again to Ralph Pulitzer for money to prosecute the case.[18]

Judge Chamberlin was finally heard from on August 6. He ruled, "[The] plf's [plaintiffs] have the right to take depositions of witnesses in or out of the state if they can do so without interfering with the hearing before the Masters." Chamberlin's pique at Streeter was obvious in the judge's written statement: "I thought I disposed of deft's [defendant's] motion to limit the taking of depositions at the hearing [on July 25], and I now consider that I did so." The ruling did not help the plaintiffs, however, as Kelley tried to summon Calvin Frye to appear before Magistrate Cook in Concord on August 8. Once again, Streeter and Frye did not appear. This time, Streeter's representative explained that the court had previously ruled that depositions could not be taken in two places at once, and since depositions were progressing in Boston, Frye could not be deposed in Concord that day. Cook agreed, and even Kelley stated personally that he had "no desire to try to take depositions in two places at the same time." Kelley also remarked that the plaintiffs had enough material in Boston to go on for three weeks, or longer, so Cook once again postponed Frye's deposition in Concord.[19]

Chamberlin's ruling did arouse the emotions of Eddy, however, who wrote to Streeter how she had been "misinformed" that Chandler would be prevented from taking depositions: "Now I see that hypnotism inaugurated it to draw you into the field of Peabody and Kennedy and Woodbury where old plots were enacted." She viewed Chamberlin as her enemy, writing, "You thought he was our best friend in the beginning. That proved abortive. Is he not now defeating your other assurance that no depositions should be taken?" In a draft of the letter at the Mary Baker Eddy Library in Boston, Eddy crossed out the following line: "It would seem as if plot after plot is being carried out to worry my life out of me for the next and final threat to be carried out relative to a will." Though she may have not sent this final line to Streeter, it expressed her honest sentiments and concerns about what would happen to her will after her death.[20]

Eddy was undoubtedly frustrated by the nearly six months of legal proceedings since the suit was filed on March 1, but it was the plaintiffs who were beginning to have doubts about their chances of success at the trial before the masters, which was scheduled to begin on August 13. In letters to Judge Bennett in South Dakota, Chandler speculated about the possibility of a settlement. Bennett was all for it, as he had firsthand knowledge of Glover's poverty and need of money. Based on interviews with Glover and family, however, Bennett reported their resolve to carry on the lawsuit. Under no circumstances would Glover accept the $125,000 trust fund with Tomlinson listed as a trustee. Glover also insisted that any settlement must provide equally for the education of the two younger sons; that the older children, Gershom and Mary, each receive $500 per year; and that Glover's annual allotment be increased from $1,500 to $2,000, which must also be guaranteed to continue to his wife on his decease. Bennett did not believe Glover's conditions were likely to be accepted by Eddy's attorneys.[21]

George Glover, accompanied by his daughter Mary, arrived in Waterloo on August 5 to prepare for the trial. Chandler registered them at "Mrs. Thompson's boarding house on the hill in nearby Sutton," New Hampshire. On the way to Chandler's home, Glover had passed through Boston and Concord, speaking with journalists, who reported him more convinced than ever "of the justice and necessity of the suit." According to one Boston newspaper, Glover arrived in the East "heavily armed and ready at an instant's notice to defend his life at the point of a revolver, if need be." Glover told the *Boston Post* that he was under constant surveillance throughout his trip and that the presence of spies caused him to begin carrying arms. Chandler confirmed in the *Post* that "spies have dogged his [Glover's] footsteps for the past several weeks."[22]

Over the next week, Chandler met daily with his team in Concord or at his summer home in Waterloo. Dr. Henry Reed Hopkins arrived from Buffalo and stayed at the Eagle Hotel in Concord, where he was joined by Dr. Ebenezer Foster Eddy. The forgotten man among the next friends, George W. Baker of Bangor, Maine, wrote Chandler a long letter, asking to be updated on the case and wondering if he would need to travel to Concord to testify. Chandler responded politely with assurances that "everything" was "going well," but he did not expect to call Baker as a witness. But everything was not going well for the plaintiffs. At a meeting on the piazza at Chandler's Waterloo home, DeWitt Howe recommended dropping the suit entirely. Chandler and Kelley, supported by Glover and Foster Eddy, determined, "We must go on." But Kelley concluded that this position was taken only at the insistence of George Glover. Kelley was afraid that the plaintiffs might "not be afforded legal reasonable opportunity" by the masters, at which point the team would "consider" dropping the case. In the meantime, Kelley offered Chandler detailed advice as to how to prepare his opening statement before the masters on August 13. The backlog of depositions still to be taken in Boston and in Concord required Chandler to state that "more time would be necessary" to adequately present their case. Kelley stated, "Remember your opening is very very very important, is the very very very great thing in this case." He urged Chandler to "ruminate—think—all leisurely." Chandler should make his delivery on Tuesday "deliberate, steady, imperturbable." Kelley advised him, "Do not hurry." Kelley also said,

"Permit no interruptions—use no sarcasm in rejoinders. [Be] earnest, but not impetuous. Dignified always." Chandler needed to explain to the masters,

> At times Mrs. E. is in a period of religious exaltation. She is an external atmosphere or stature high above the earth and heeds not at all earthly or material affairs. At other times she is in perdition or purgatory, in a stratum far below. Every man's hand is against her, every malicious & powerfully militant mind is aimed at her. She sees ten gun barrels all concentred on her, she is helpless, in despair, she is alone but for Frye, she must lean for support, she leans on him Frye, who helps create the very situation that makes her need his help & in this condition she is equally unable to attend to earthly matters.[23]

The Streeter-Eddy public relations campaign continued right up to the date of the trial. At first, the defense team had allowed Eddy to be interviewed by journalists, who were all charmed by her and convinced of her alertness and intelligence. In the month before the trial, Streeter had her examined by alienists to provide expert testimony. In mid-July, Dr. Edward French, a noted alienist who was superintendent of the Massachusetts Hospital for the Insane in Medfield, Massachusetts, examined Eddy. He found her concentration and mental application to be good, and her memory excellent. He asked her many questions and even had her write a letter "which was well expressed, logical in construction, and coherent both in language and ideas." He found Eddy above the average in intelligence and directness, and concluded, "She is mentally capable and competent to manage her own affairs of whatever nature."[24]

On the eve of the trial, August 12, 1907, the nation's most well-known alienist was given an extended interview with Mary Baker Eddy. Dr. Allan McLane Hamilton was the grandson of Alexander Hamilton and Louis McLane, former secretary of the treasury and minister to England. At age fifty-eight, Allan Hamilton had over thirty-five years of medical practice and had examined the mental condition of presidential assassins Charles Guiteau and Leon Czolgosz. Hamilton had recently testified in the famous murder trial of Harry K. Thaw and had also testified against Christian Science in a New York case. His hostility to Christian Science was well known and was probably a factor in Streeter's determination to consult with him on Eddy's condition. Prior to meeting with Eddy, Dr. Hamilton read over one hundred letters written by her and determined "there [was] no mental defect indicated," although much anxiety was indicated over certain subjects. He visited Eddy at 2:00 p.m. on August 12 and found her "dignified, though cordial, and possessed [of] a certain sense of humor which [led] her to perpetrate a joke about the so-called 'next friends,' to whom she referred as 'nexters.'" He concluded, "I found nothing the matter with her." She conversed at length about her relations with her son, and the trust deed she had established for his family. Hamilton made a special point to address the question of her belief in malicious animal magnetism (M.A.M.).

> The allegations concerning Mrs. Eddy's belief in 'malicious animal magnetism' are ridiculous. I am convinced that the words are only used synonymously with 'malign influence,' 'malignant' or 'mendacious animal magnetism' and is therefore a *facon parler*, as the French say. She certainly had been subject to sufficient annoyance to entertain the fear that she is to be subjected to further disturbance.

Hamilton went on to explain,

> Mrs. Eddy has no insane delusions, and in print and elsewhere simply enunciates the conventional part of her creed which she and eight hundred thousand believe in. No matter how improbable or unacceptable it may prove to be to the community generally, it is no more remarkable than others that have been before or that exist to-day, and her alleged delusion regarding mesmerism,

the non-existence of matter, and the power of healing, form an integral part of very many religious beliefs.[25]

Hamilton had correctly placed Eddy's belief in M.A.M. within the context of the tenets of Christian Science and, therefore, within the scope of the First Amendment, a presumption that Chandler and company consistently ignored, to their ultimate discredit. Hamilton's complete report of the Eddy interview did not appear in the *New York Times* until August 25, after the next friends case had been dismissed, but immediately the press reported his visit to Pleasant View and his general impressions of Eddy. To the *Times* reporter, Hamilton admitted that he had arrived at Pleasant View in "a decidedly prejudiced state of mind" but that the half hour he spent with Eddy produced a "a complete revulsion of feeling."[26]

What did Mary Baker Eddy mean by "malicious animal magnetism"? Was it, as Chandler charged, a crude belief in black magic, and evidence of insanity, or was it, as Dr. Hamilton surmised, merely her pet phrase to describe all the opposition she had experienced over the years? The answer is more complicated and depends on what period of her life one is referring to. We know that Eddy believed it was possible not only to read someone's mind but to exert purely mental control over the mind of another without that person's consent or knowledge. This belief led to an obsession with M.A.M. that was poisoning her life during the 1870s and early 1880s, as she projected malicious mental influence on her enemies and struggled in seeking God's help to rise above their mental control. Because of the frequent defections from within her movement, M.A.M. became a code word for the spying and sabotage activities of her rivals, and malicious animal magnetism was a frequent topic of her teaching at the Metaphysical College. But, as with all aspects of her religious doctrine as reflected in the many editions of *Science and Health*, her understanding of M.A.M. evolved over the years. While she always accepted that "mental malpractice" of one mind controlling another was injurious if practiced for a "wicked purpose," she came to accept that the real power of evil was one's belief in it. Protection against evil affects came from an omnipotent God, whose opposition to mental attacks offered a sure defense. By the time she settled at Pleasant View, M.A.M. had become "anything that pulls thought down from its spiritual elevation"; she stopped mentioning M.A.M. in her teaching and the "taking up" of enemies had become a thing of the past. As Robert Peel notes, by 1907 M.A.M. had become, Eddy's "name for the conscious enmity, as contrasted with the unconscious resistance, of materialism to spirituality." In this sense, Eddy viewed the next friends suit as a conflict between the material world and the spiritual world, another serious challenge to all that she stood for and was trying to teach through Christian Science.[27]

= 8 =

THE TRIAL BEGINS

The trial before the masters began in Concord on Tuesday, August 13, 1907, at 11:30 a.m. A sketch of the courtroom in the *New York World* shows the three masters—Judge Edgar Aldrich in the middle, flanked by attorney Hosea W. Parker and alienist Dr. George F. Jelly—seated on a raised platform with the witness chair to their left. Before them were seated the attorneys for both sides at two separate tables. The next friends, George W. Glover and Mary Baker Glover, were present, along with alienist Dr. Henry R. Hopkins of Buffalo. Counsel for the next friends included William E. Chandler, John W. Kelley, DeWitt C. Howe, and Frederick Peabody. Mary Baker Eddy was represented by Frank S. Streeter and his partner, Allen Hollis, with Edwin G. Eastman. The defendants present included Irving C. Tomlinson, Hermann W. Hering, and Alfred Farlow, who were represented by their attorneys, Oliver E. Branch of Manchester, New Hampshire, and William A. Morse of Boston. The trustees of Eddy's estate—Henry M. Baker, Josiah E. Fernald, and Archibald McLellan—were also in the courtroom. An official transcript of the hearing was the responsibility of the court stenographer, a Mr. Rogers, but he was assisted by two stenographers and three typewriter operators working in relay to provide a daily report to the masters and counsel, and a local shorthand expert, W. M.

Haggett, who made a verbatim copy of the proceedings for the newspaper reporters, who included, on the first day, Slaght of the *World*,
Ford and Robinson of the *Boston Herald* (who were accompanied by
sketch artist Hayden Jones), Park of the *Boston Globe*, Richardson of
the *Boston Transcript*, Decker of the *Boston Journal*, Mulcahey of the
Boston Post, Clark of the *Boston American*, Keeler of the *New York Sun*,
and Hill of the *Manchester Union*, in addition to the representatives
of the local newspapers, the *Concord Monitor* and the *Concord Patriot*,
and the press associations. The press was placed at tables to the right
of the masters, along the left wall of the courtroom. The remaining
seats at the back of the courtroom were occupied by spectators, most
of them women and Christian Scientists.[1]

The jury box was empty, for this was not a true trial; instead, it was
a hearing before masters who would issue a report to Judge Robert
Chamberlin of the superior court. The one and only question to be
considered by the masters was Mary Baker Eddy's competence to
execute the trust deed on March 6, the day she transferred all of her
property to the three trustees. But both sides and the masters called it
a "trial," and it was to be conducted as such: each side would present
evidence and witnesses who could be cross-examined, expert testimony was permitted, and most importantly, all expected that at least
one face-to-face interview with Eddy would take place. In fact, though
the masters would submit a report to Judge Chamberlin for a final
decision, all participants in the hearing before the masters and the press
expected the hearing to be definitive.

Chandler began his three-hour opening statement at 11:35 a.m. He
declared that the suit was brought in good faith by relatives concerned
about Eddy because of the "mystery" that surrounded Pleasant View.
Originally, "kind friends" had assisted with the bringing of the suit
"but this [had] ceased." The suit demanded an accounting of Eddy's
property, which the plaintiffs believed had been mismanaged as a
result of Eddy's incompetence, and which, in fact, had been misap-
propriated. It was an unusual case, Chandler said, but well within the

MRS. MARY BAKER G. EDDY DYING; FOOTMAN AND "DUMMY" CONTROL HER

Founder of X Science Suffering from Cancer and Nearing Her End, Is Immured at Pleasant View, While Another Woman Impersonates Her in the Streets of Concord.

MRS. LEONARD, BROOKLYN HEALER, IN FALSE ROLE.

Drives Out Daily in Closed Carriage with Calvin A. Frye, Secretary-Footman, Who Is the Supreme Power at the Eddy Home — Founder Estimated to Have Accumulated a Fortune of $15,000,000, and to Have an Income of $1,000,000 a Year, but Members of Her Coterie Say She Has Spent It All in Charity, Though No Records of Large Gifts Can Be Found.

New York World, *October 28, 1906*

I

Portrait of Mary Baker Eddy by John Nelson Marble, 1916

Mary Baker Eddy, circa. 1906

III

The Fairgrounds with Pleasant View in the middle background

The Fairgrounds with Pleasant View in the right background

Eddy, Frye, and August Mann in her carriage

Mary Baker Eddy on her balcony addressing a crowd (circa. 1903)

Calvin A. Frye

*William Eaton
Chandler at the
time of the trial*

*US Senator William
Eaton Chandler*

Frank Sherwin Streeter

George Washington Glover II

Ebenezer J. Foster Eddy

John W. Kelley

DeWitt C. Howe

Frederick Peabody

Mary Baker Glover

George W. Glover III and
Andrew Glover

Robert N. Chamberlin

*Federal Court Judge
Edgar Aldrich*

Henry M. Baker

Edwin G. Eastman, NH
Attorney General and
Streeter Cocounsel

George H. Moses, Editor Concord Monitor *and future US senator*

well-established principles of equity. One object of the bill in equity had been attained, in that a large part of Eddy's property had been taken out of her hands by "a board of three upright but rather venturesome citizens," an "act" that Chandler "consider[ed] a contempt of court." But, this having been done, it remained to establish the fact of incompetence, to determine if any further protection was necessary, and to determine if the defendants were "guilty of maltreatment of Mrs. Eddy." Chandler then spoke about an amendment to the bill, which would further amplify Judge Chamberlin's term "otherwise" in the original bill. At this point Streeter interrupted to say that his side had printed a complete record of the case, which would be furnished to the masters and counsel. Chandler, as instructed earlier by Kelley, objected to Streeter's interruption of his argument. Chandler continued, saying that the amendment had been disallowed by the court, which placed the plaintiffs under a disadvantage. In fact, Chandler asserted, this was just the latest of many disadvantages encountered by the next friends. They had been denied a hearing on the matter of Streeter's "innumerable" aspersions to the press about the motives of the next friends. "We ought to have been allowed to defend ourselves," Chandler said. Streeter, despite representing millions of dollars, had served notice that the plaintiffs were required to "furnish a bond" for the costs of the case, but they were unable to do so. The plaintiffs had asked for "an allowance from Mrs. Eddy's large property to enable [the team] to properly prepare and present this case," but the court refused. Instead of the trusteeship established by Eddy, there should have been a receivership supervised by the court. Chandler stated, "The low state of our finances has been a constant disadvantage to us in our fight against the organized healers of the country." He continued, "[Another] disadvantage is the denial of our motion for a jury trial." In addition, "the opposing counsel [had] placed upon the record an objection to the constitution of this tribunal because of Dr. Jelly's non-residence." This objection would allow the other side "to take the matter to the supreme court and possibly make [the next friends] try the issue twice." Chandler also noted, "We have been denied access to witnesses on our side." And Chandler stated that the plaintiffs were prevented from taking depositions in New Hampshire.[2]

Chandler then stated that the plaintiffs had twice, on March 28 and July 6, asked Streeter to help them "secure access to Mrs. Eddy" but had "received no answer." Streeter interrupted again: "You secured an answer to your other letter [March 28] in the meantime, didn't you?" Chandler again complained about the interruptions, stating that they made him "timid," which reportedly produced "smiles" throughout the court room. Continuing to present the disadvantages encountered by the plaintiffs, Chandler professed,

> I will not go into the telephonic methods employed in convincing the magistrate before us. I am behind the times, I know. I don't understand these modern methods of writing letters to the judge when he is not on the bench; of taking down private conversation over the telephone by shorthand writers. But the fact remains that we have been prevented from examining witnesses. And if there ever was a case in which such advance examination was necessary it is this case, this conspiracy case, in which practically all the evidence is in the hands of the other side.

Judge Aldrich now interrupted to state that the masters "regarded this suit, not as an adversary suit, but, as a friendly suit, even though it [had] not been conducted in an entirely friendly manner." As to the telephone episode, the judge admitted that he did not know that "the conversation was being taken down." At this point, Judge Aldrich's chair collapsed, sprawling him at an awkward angle and necessitating a short interruption while a new chair was brought in. Chandler soon resumed with the ninth disadvantage in his list: "too short a time to prepare the case." Aldrich interrupted again, to remind Chandler that since this was a friendly case and since there was no adversary party to the proceeding, that statutory right to take depositions did "not apply in this case." Chandler continued his opening statement:

Whether it is a friendly suit or a bitter contest, it is of vast importance and we ought not to have been called up to meet the issue
within a fortnight. We have met with defeat everywhere in New
Hampshire in our efforts to obtain evidence. In Massachusetts
we have done better, but taken as a whole I am obliged to say
we find we ought not to be obliged to bear the burden of these
disadvantages. Nevertheless, we feel that our case is so strong
that we are willing to go on.[3]

At this point a recess was called. At 2:40 p.m. Chandler continued his opening statement. He complained that one defendant,
Joseph Armstrong, who was responsible for Eddy's financial matters
in Boston, had been absent from the depositions. His testimony was
important in determining Eddy's competency on or about March 1,
when the bill in equity was filed. In a move that proved Eddy's incompetence, Chandler asserted, only five days later all of her property
was placed in the hands of trustees. More evidence of her incompetence was evasion of taxes in Concord, which "she would never have
made had she been in her right mind," the evasion being done by the
"gentleman" (Calvin Frye) who controlled her. Chandler proceeded
to read from the statement of the auditor, Harvey N. Chase, to show
that Eddy's estate included one million dollars in interest-bearing
securities but that all she had paid taxes on was $19,275, the value of
her real estate, horses, cows, and vehicles. Only in 1906 was interest
income of $35,000 added to that amount. Frye swore to the correctness
of the tax forms, though he left numerous sections blank. But even
though "the tax laws of this state" had "not been rigidly enforced,"
Chandler asserted, this evasion was not justifiable: it was "a piece of
gross deception and wickedness on the part of Calvin Frye." Chandler
continued, "Truth, truth, truth is the very burden of Mrs. Eddy's life.
She dwells upon it constantly in her writings. She could not have been
fit to transact her own business when this fraud was perpetrated in her
name upon the city of Concord."[4]

To Chandler, this tax issue and the creation of the trust was enough to prove her incompetency, but the next friends also had to go into "the details of the delusions under which Mrs. Eddy [was] suffering." First, in the book *Science and Health*, Eddy showed that she was suffering from "a fundamental delusion of the non-existence and non-reality of the physical universe, organic and inorganic." Chandler continued, "All her delusions are built upon this one." Chandler then made his second point: "She possesses the delusion of the supernatural nature of the science which she calls her own and of its super-natural revelation to her." His third point was her delusion "concerning the diseases of mankind, their cure and prevention." Fourth, she was deluded about the relations of Christian Science to philosophy and Christianity. The fifth delusion concerned the nature and existence of malicious animal magnetism: "This involves persecution and diabolism. It embraces a large part of her mental life and greatly influences her personal comfort and business relations." Sixth was her delusion that malicious animal magnetism was related to the causing and curing of disease, and to the idea that "mental suggestion" was "capable of producing death." The seventh delusion that Chandler mentioned was that malicious animal magnetism was involved in the "perpetration of crime." These delusions had, Chandler said, "already brought her to the very verge of senile dementia." They had produced in her "the delusion of grandeur and greatness in one moment, and the delusion on the other hand of persecution, of fear, in the next moment." According to Chandler, Eddy believed that she was "God's mouthpiece" and commanded her followers to believe this. Malicious animal magnetism was the most pernicious of delusions, Chandler asserted, as it was "a belief that malpractitioners, sons of the devil, can by fixing their mind on a person and wishing him evil produce poison in his veins, stop the beating of his heart, put him to death." Chandler explained that Eddy thought her friends could exert a counter mental influence in her behalf. This could all be done without a word being spoken. For example, when she was putting out a new edition of *Science and Health*, Eddy believed that "the diabolical workers [tried] to prevent her by malicious animal magnetism." She believed Richard Kennedy was guilty of M.A.M., a person Chandler described as "a man as innocent as any of us here." Chandler concluded his opening statement by painting a word picture of life at Pleasant View: "Mrs. Eddy alone with her delusions . . . living in a state of terror, controlled by Calvin Frye, aided by Cornell Wilson and backed up by Hermann Hering, [was] the victim of a senile dementia which is to all intents and purposes insanity."[5]

Following Chandler's opening statement, the first witness was called. John H. Quimby, tax assessor of Ward Seven in Concord, produced the inventories of Eddy's property from 1901 through 1906, with those from 1902 to 1906 signed by Calvin Frye. A discussion occurred between the judge and counsel about Concord witnesses, with Streeter promising to have local witnesses present whenever they were needed. Kelley then stated that the plaintiffs wanted to see defendant Joseph Armstrong of Boston the next day, along with all of Eddy's financial books and papers. Streeter offered to produce the documents but not the books, as Eddy's business affairs should not be "spread over the country in the present situation of the case." The second witness, George H. Moses, editor of the *Concord Monitor,* then took the stand and was examined by Chandler. Moses produced a bundle of letters from Eddy and began to read from the first of them. In the letter, Eddy apologized for typographical errors, claiming they were "the result of a cause which 'we both know.'" Moses stated that he understood that the "cause referred to was evil mental influence." Streeter objected to this, at which point Judge Aldrich began a general discussion of the type of evidence to be introduced. Aldrich stated, "At some time we should like to know if we are to have an opportunity to examine Mrs. Eddy herself on this matter." Streeter replied that Eddy did not have "sufficient physical strength to come" before the court "and stand the stress of an examination," but she would be glad to confer with the masters at any time. Chandler objected to the idea of a conference between the masters and Eddy, to which Streeter responded that what he meant to say was to propose a visit to Pleasant View by the masters and one counsel from each side. Judge Aldrich agreed with this idea, and Streeter suggested that the visit be made at

2:00 p.m. the next day, Wednesday, August 14. Chandler said he was
not ready to go to Pleasant View at that time, to which Judge Aldrich
proposed "a friendly conference between counsel" to determine the
time of the visit. At 4:50 p.m., court was adjourned for the day, to
resume at 9:30 a.m. on Wednesday.[6]

The next morning Chandler withdrew Moses as a witness, to offer
a proposal for an examination of Eddy. In his memoirs, written in
the 1940s, the future U.S. senator George H. Moses wrote that he
had assumed he was still technically on the witness stand, since he
had never been informed that he was dismissed. However, the official
court transcript shows that Chandler did withdraw Moses as a witness.
Chandler made a six-part proposal for examining Eddy, including that
the first visit be preliminary only, that Chandler should have the right
to examine Eddy, that Glover and his daughter be present along with
a court stenographer, that there be at least five other examinations of
Eddy following the preliminary one, and that if the masters concluded
that Eddy "physically" could not "sustain" such examinations, counsel
for the next friends be afforded an opportunity to have her examined
by "persons of their selection." If the preliminary visit revealed that
Eddy was "unable mentally" to sustain further examinations, the masters "should announce that the plaintiffs have established a prima facie
case." Finally, Chandler proposed that all examinations should be at
varying times of the day, without notice, and that no other members
of the household should be present. Streeter reminded the court of
the preliminary question to be settled, the competency of Mary Baker
Eddy to manage her business affairs. During the first day, there was
"not a syllable of a suggestion that Mrs. Eddy's business affairs had not
been managed properly." Streeter remarked, "Counsel on the other
side have misconceived the purpose of this hearing. This is not as we
understand, a trial or an examination of the soundness of any particular religion." Streeter went on about the "suggestions of delusion,
which simply" indicated that Eddy believed "in some things that Mr.
Chandler and others" did not. Streeter continued, "Unless those are
in some way connected with her transaction of . . . business affairs

they are absolutely incompetent." If someone believed something that seemed "very likely to many of the world ill-founded," Streeter pointed out, but if that belief had no relation to the management of her business, then under the law it was "not only immaterial but . . . incompetent."[7]

Chandler stated that he did not believe "that a person can entertain, not a solitary delusion, not an occasional delusion, a delusion that occasionally manages itself, a simple delusion,—perhaps all of us entertain on some subjects." He continued, "That isn't our case. It is that this woman has been possessed, for all these past years, of systematized delusion that make a part of her life. Therefore, they are unfitting her for doing any kind of business. As a result, Chandler asserted, the inquiry cannot be limited to simple questions like "Do you know what property you have got?" and "Is it taken care of as you want it taken care of?" The court must ascertain "whether by reason of this condition existing during all these years she . . . had fair treatment from the persons who . . . surrounded her, controlled her and manipulated her through the agency of Calvin A. Frye." At this point Judge Aldrich admonished the press, "We want to be indulgent with the newspaper reporters, but I noticed yesterday, and again this morning, there is an undertone of conversation carried on that is disturbing to the counsel. I wish everybody would refrain from that. Proceed, Mr. Chandler." The counsel for the next friends then "very earnestly" objected to the "formal and momentary inspection" of Eddy that was proposed by Streeter.[8]

Eastman entered the debate, stating, "If Mrs. Eddy is competent to manage her business affairs, then they [the next friends] have no standing in court." To Eastman, the best evidence of Eddy's ability to manage her affairs was whether they were well managed. If they had been mismanaged, then the next friends must go further to show that the mismanagement was due "to these delusions" the plaintiffs were talking about. Any person, Eastman noted, "may entertain the wildest notions," but "if they manage their business affairs, then that delusion has nothing to do with it." The fact that someone entertained "certain notions" about religious subjects did not mean that they were not competent to do business. Eastman noted,

> They talk about malicious animal magnetism. You know and I know and everybody knows that people entertain religious notions, very good people too. They believe that they are influenced by the devil, more or less. It is not an uncommon thing at some religious meetings to hear very good men get up and say they have been tempted by the devil during the week and they made great efforts to ward off the devil and his influences, but you are not going to say that if they conduct their business properly—I may not believe the devil has had anything to do with it, you may not, but they believe it, and so long as they are competent to do their business and take care of their property, why, nobody can interfere with them because they entertain these notions.[9]

Chandler then charged that Eastman had put "the cart before the horse." Eastman's point was "contrary to Judge Chamberlin's directions," which were to exclude the question of an accounting and "to find out whether [Eddy] was competent to do business." Chandler stated, "You cannot tell whether her affairs have been properly managed by her and Calvin A. Frye until you find out whether she has had these delusions and what the extent of them is." Eastman responded, "The Court has jurisdiction only where property rights are in danger." Therefore, it did "not jeopardize anybody's rights . . . to determine that question first, as to how this property [had] been managed." If it had not been "well managed," then it would be "open to inquiry."[10]

Judge Aldrich tried to reign in the discussion, which had gotten off the point of determining what kind of examination was to be made of Eddy. He did try to answer both points, however, by stating. "This hearing is not for the purpose of disestablishing the Christian Science faith. . . . Neither is this hearing had for the purpose of laying any foundation for an accounting." The masters had no plans to go into anything in connection with the business except to show whether "Mrs. Eddy was in actual control of her estate or not." The judge went on to say evidence would be presented, "but how far it would be useful to go back" was "something that should not be determined" in the hearing, "but it should be determined upon reasonable lines, of course." This question of how far back in time the next friends would be allowed to go in presenting their evidence of Eddy's delusions was at the heart of their case, as they wished to go back to her childhood or at least to her miraculous cure and discovery in 1866. Judge Aldrich stated that it made no difference whether a delusion was religious but only whether it "might operate upon the mind of Mrs. Eddy in her present condition of health and strength." Aldrich summarized Chandler's view that there were two types of delusions operating on Eddy, one in which "some occult force" prejudiced her against her relatives, which operated upon her property management. The other delusion was that "certain individuals were operating against her in respect to her property interests, her workings and writings." It was "competent" to go into this "because it [showed] a frame of mind which might make it possible that the delusion would operate unfavorably and prejudicial to the contingent rights of relatives." As to an examination of Eddy, Aldrich concluded that the presence of the next friends would not be beneficial and that they had no constitutional right to be present; even counsel did not. Aldrich asked the counsel to get together to decide on a time. Kelley spoke up that counsel had already agreed "that 2:00 o'clock [on that] afternoon would be a suitable time for a preliminary visit" and that Streeter and Chandler alone would be present, representing counsel. It was to be left up to the masters, depending on Eddy's condition, to determine the "scope of the inquiry." At this point Aldrich announced that they were not adjourning the hearing or taking a recess: "The hearing is going on, but going on at another place."[11]

The much-anticipated interview with Mary Baker Eddy took place at Pleasant View at 2:00 p.m. on Wednesday, August 14, 1907. Newspaper photographers were present as Frank Streeter picked up the visitors at ten minutes before two in his "motor car" at the Eagle Hotel on Main Street in Concord, directly across from the State House, and drove them the mile and a half to Eddy's home on Pleasant Street. A grainy photograph of the group in Streeter's automobile graced the front page of newspapers the next day, showing Streeter behind the wheel and Judge Aldrich in the front seat. Chandler, Parker, and Jelly were in the rear seat, and the court stenographer and Streeter's chauffeur in the third, or "pullman," seat. The *Monitor* stated, "A flock of newspaper men in carriages followed the automobile."[12]

At Pleasant View Laura Sargent escorted the visitors to Eddy's second-floor study. Judge Aldrich began, "Mrs. Eddy, the gentleman here wish to have an interview with you, and we desire to make this call as comfortable as possible for you, and we want you to let us know if we weary you."[13]

Eddy responded, "I am very glad to see you, and thank you for the suggestion."

Aldrich began the questioning: "What was your native town?"

"Bow, in New Hampshire. My father's farm lies on the banks of the Merrimac. He did much of his haying in Concord, but it was Bow the house was."

Aldrich asked, "How long have you lived in Concord?"

Eddy responded, "About 20 years; between 18 and 20 this time. At this time, do you mean?"

"Yes, the last time," Aldrich replied.

"Since I came here, after my marriage and residence in Boston."

Aldrich said, "Well, the gentleman present want to ask you some questions."

"And I beg pardon, my only difficulty is a slight deafness," Eddy said. " I can see to read common pica, but I don't hear distinctly without some difficulty."

"I do not think I speak very distinctly," Aldrich said.

Eddy said, "I hear you."

"Mr. Chandler says I do not," Aldrich replied.

Eddy said, "I hear you. I don't feel that at all."

Aldrich stated, "We all want to make this interview as pleasant for you as possible [Eddy interrupted here, saying, "Thank you very much."]—and to have regard at all time to your comfort and convenience, and if you feel at all fatigued we want to have you say so at any time."

Eddy asked, "What?"

"If you feel fatigued," Aldrich said, "we want to have you speak of it and let us know."

Eddy said, "Thank you. I can work hours at my work, day and night, without fatigue when it is in this line of thought, but when I go to worldliness I am sometimes fatigued by it, and yet, these things are indispensable and I regard them as sacred."

The pleasantries dispensed with, the masters began to ask more specific questions. Judge Aldrich asked several questions about Pleasant View, including how many acres there were. Eddy did not know this, however, and the Judge responded, "That is something that women do not always carry in their minds." She did state that she still attended to the property and made suggestions as to construction, including the installation of a "little pond" with a boat and boathouse. Dr. Jelly wanted confirmation that this work had "been done under [her] direction," to which Eddy responded, "You can ask my foreman, August Mann, he resides in the cottage." Parker then asked if she raised fruit on the property. Eddy said, "Yes, sir," and offered that all of the trees, except the Normandy pines, had been planted at her direction, even though she had been told that some would not grow in Concord. Her response had been "Try it and see if it will succeed," and every one grew.[14]

The questions then turned to her interest in local Concord affairs, including money that she had given for public improvements. Eddy responded,

> I have [given], with great pleasure. When I came here they had no State fair grounds, and very little pavement. A one horse car moved once an hour. They have two horses now hourly—there

was very little done in Concord compared with what I anticipated when I came. It seemed to be going out, and I admire the
apparent vigor and flourishing condition of this dear city now.
I had a great desire to build up my native place—am I talking
too much?

She went on, "They asked me in Boston to remain. Jordan &
Marsh, White, and other firms requested me earnestly not to leave the
city and they said to me, 'Haven't we helped you accumulate money
since you have been here?' and I replied, 'Haven't I helped you?' and
they said, 'Yes, you have, and that is why we want to have you stay.'
Then I said, 'I want to go home and help my native State a little.'" Jelly
and Parker then asked several questions about her move to Concord
and Pleasant View, and Eddy forgot, at first, that she had lived for
a time on State Street: "I had forgotten that." Aldrich returned the
questioning to her support of the paving of Concord streets. Eddy
stated she had given "$10,000 at one time" to pave Main Street and
State Street and that the idea, in her words, "was mine." She also spoke
of donations by her students, but they "left the decision" to her. She
then turned to the subject of the building of the Concord Christian
Science Church, which "cost over $200,000," which was "one-half of
[her] property" at the time.[15]

Judge Aldrich then turned to the subject of Eddy's investments. He
asked whether she thought life insurance was a good investment, to
which Eddy responded, "I don't put it into life insurance, never. God
insures my life." Aldrich pressed her further about life insurance, but
Eddy reiterated, "I respect the life insurance; I think it is very valuable to many, but I haven't any need of it." Aldrich then asked what
she thought a good investment would be. Eddy again misunderstood,
saying, "Trust in God. God is life. God is infinite. Therefore, if we
are the image and the likeness of Infinity, we have no beginning and
no end, and are His image and likeness, that is my life insurance."
Aldrich replied, "I do not think you quite caught my idea." He pressed
her further about "a sound investment of money that comes from life

insurance, or anything else." Eddy again failed to understand the question, responding, "For this property?" Parker finally interrupted to clarify, "How would you invest it, he means?" Eddy stated, "[I would] invest it in the hands, at my age, of trustees that I could vouch for from my knowledge." She then went on to discuss the growth of her church and the demands on her time concluding, "Which shall I do, carry on this business that belongs to property, or shall I serve God?" She answered her own question: "I said—and it came to me from the Bible—'Choose ye this day whom ye will serve. Ye cannot serve God and Mammon.'" So she chose to give her property: "[I gave] $913,000 to the trusteeship, to others for the benefit of my son—no, not for the benefit of my son, but—no, $913,000 trusteeship for myself, for myself. For my son I gave $125,000 into trusteeship for himself and his family." Aldrich asked where the idea for a trusteeship originated. Eddy replied, "Utterly with myself. It came to me in an hour in this room, and I think the first one that I named it to was Laura Sargent, and I said to her: 'Don't speak of it, but I feel impressed that it is my duty.'" Eddy confirmed that the idea first came to her in February 1907.[16]

Aldrich said that he had still "not quite made [himself] understood." He continued, "For instance, without regard to your trusteeship now, if you had a hundred thousand dollars to invest to-day, . . . what kind of investments would you consider sound, Municipal bonds, or Government bonds, or bank stock, or what?" Eddy answered, "I prefer Government bonds. . . . I haven't entered into stocks." When asked why, she responded, "Because I didn't think it was safe for me. I didn't want the trouble of it, that was all." She mentioned once following the advice of a student and investing $10,000 in western land only to lose the money: "I never got caught again. I always selected my own investments." She was pressed as to how she selected her investments before turning her money over to trustees. She replied, "I had books that gave definitely the population of the States, and their money values, and I consult those and when I see they are large enough in population and valuation to warrant an investment I make it." When asked why she made population the standard for investing, Eddy responded, "Because I think they can sustain their debts, of course, and pay them, can't they?" When pushed further, she again fell back on her trustees: "I don't take these things into consideration." But Jelly persisted in asking what she would invest in, and Eddy responded, "Municipalities, I should think." She said she preferred investing in the East rather than the West.[17]

Dr. Jelly then turned the discussion to Christian Science: "Are you willing to tell us something about the development of your special religion?" Eddy again had trouble hearing the question, saying, "If you will sit nearer I can tell you more distinctly. That is why I dread a Court room, because I can't hear distinctly." But, when the question was repeated, she answered, "I would love to do it." She began, "I was an invalid born in belief, I was always having doctors," but was questioned about the meaning of "born in belief," to which she responded, "I mean born according to human nature, born not of God, but of the Flesh." She continued, "I was an invalid from my birth." She was unable to describe her symptoms, however, beyond saying, "I was weak and a dyspeptic." She continued, "My father employed M.D.'s of the highest character, and they were estimable men, and they would say, 'Don't doctor your child, she has got too much brains for her body, keep her outdoors, keep her in exercise and keep her away from school all you can and don't give her much medicine.'" She went on to describe treatment by a homeopath, Dr. Morrill, who "healed cases that other M.D.'s did not" and said that she got well under his treatment so that she decided to study homeopathy. She stated she cured a case that a doctor could not, and began to "think something about what it was that cured." She began to suspect the effectiveness of drugs and sent some to a chemist in Boston, a Dr. Charles T. Jackson, whom Dr. Jelly knew personally and who claimed there was nothing in the medicine except "common table salt." So Eddy decided to give some of the medicine to a patient, who recovered quickly. Eddy then took away the medicine, and the patient soon complained of symptoms.

Eddy then administered a placebo, "a single pellet" of sugar, and the patient "gained again just the same." Eddy commented, "There was my first discovery of the Science of Mind. That was a falling apple to me." She determined "that mind governs the whole question." She then turned to "spiritualists who were claiming to be mediums" but "found it was humbug and hypocrisy, and . . . pronounced it so." At this point, the masters stepped out of the room to confer. When they returned, Dr. Jelly stated, "I will not trouble you to go into that any further just now."[18]

Hosea Parker then took over the questioning, saying, "I want to talk about every day affairs, may I?" He asked if she traveled much. Eddy responded, "No, I haven't," but when told that Parker lived in Claremont on the Connecticut River, she claimed to know it was a beautiful town. When asked to describe her carriage drives, Eddy stated that she was out every day from "half an hour to an hour" and that it was "a pleasant recreation": "It keeps me away from my desk and I get rested." But she allowed that she never went out of town, even to Boston, although she "could." She said, "But I should not wish to undertake it because I have so much resting upon me here to do." She described her daily work routine, which consisted of rising at 6:00 a.m. and going to bed at 9:00 p.m. and working the full day except for three hours of breakfast, lunch, and supper (she said, "We have no dinners here, and have not had for many years"), and going on her daily drive. Asked about letter writing, Eddy proclaimed that she either wrote letters herself or dictated them. Her staff "never" wrote letters on her behalf, except "through dictation." Eddy continued, "Then I look them over and see if they are right." When pressed, she stated that she even looked over letters about her property affairs although admitting "unless I don't know when they write." Again, she reminded the masters, "I am answering you there about my action before I constituted the trusteeship." When Parker stated that she had placed a "large responsibility" on the trustees, she responded, "Yes, Mr. Fernald here is the superintendent of the Old Folks Home, so he is a good man to take care of me, isn't he?" She also spoke confidently of her cousin, Henry Baker, and Archibald McLellan, saying about him, "A better man we do not need to have."[19]

Returning the discussion to her daily activities, Eddy stated that she enjoyed reading and was fond of music: "I have got an artificial singer up here in my house. You know what I mean by that. I will have them show it to you in the vestibule in the house." She rang a bell for an attendant, who responded promptly. Eddy then asked to see Frye, who came quickly and explained that the "artificial singer" was, in fact, "a graphaphone." Judge Aldrich resumed the questioning, stating that his own mother was eighty-seven years old. Eddy said, "And tell her God bless her, and that she is not a day older for her 87 years, if she is growing in grace." Eddy elaborated,

> She is rising higher. Decay does not belong to matter so much as to mind, does it? We don't lose our faculties through matter so much as mind, do we? Now, my thought is, that if we keep our mind fixed on Truth, God and Life and Love, He will advance us in our years to a higher understanding and change our hope into faith, and our faith into spiritual understanding, and our words into works, and our ultimate into the fruition of entering into the Kingdom. That is my thought."[20]

At this point the masters excused themselves. Eddy offered, "Pardon my mistakes, if I have made any." She said to the stenographer, "Thank you. We have kept you very busy. Thank you for your services." After listening to the "graphaphone" in the vestibule, Judge Aldrich was informed that Eddy wanted to see the board of masters again, as she had thought of something she had omitted. Returning to her study, the masters heard Eddy state that she had not finished "with regard to the footsteps to Christian Science." Judge Aldrich interrupted to say that the masters had left the room previously to discuss the issue of questioning her about the religion: "In certain quarters it is suggested that this investigation is an attack on your doctrines, and we did not want to have it appear that we were requiring you to make any statements about it." Eddy responded, "Not at all. I shall regard it as a great favor if you will condescend to hear that." Eddy then launched into an eloquent summary of her "discovery."

> When I came to the point that it was mind that did the healing, then I wanted to know what mind that was. Was it the mind which was in Christ Jesus, or was it the human mind and human will? Then I went to investigating spiritualism and mesmerism and hypnotism to see if I could find out, and I didn't find God there, therefore I turned to God in prayer and said, 'Just guide me, guide me to that mind which is in Christ,' and I took the Bible and opened it to the words, 'Now, go write it in a book.' I can show you where it is in the Bible. I then commenced writing my consciousness of what I had seen, and I found that human will was the cause of disease instead of its cure, that hypnotism or mesmerism or human concepts did not heal, they were the origin of disease instead of its cure, and that the Divine mind was the healer, and then I found it through Scripture—through the Scripture—'He healed all our diseases. Go into the field, preach the gospel, heal the sick,' and I felt there was my line of labor, and that God did the healing, and I could no more heal a person through mortal mind or will power than I could heal them by cutting off their heads, and I could not heal them by it, for I don't know how to use will power to hurt the sick, and I don't know how to do it. When they began to talk mesmerism first, I began to doubt it, and I said to a facetious student, 'Hanover Smith, you go into the other room and see if I can sit down and tell lies enough to make you suffer.' He went into the other room and I commenced what they said to make folks sick, and I did my best talking it, and he came in and I said, 'Hanover, do you feel mean?' He said, 'I never felt better in my life than I do now, I feel better than when I went in, I feel rested.' A Christian Scientist can no more make a person sick than they can be a sinner and

be a Christian Scientist. They can no more make them suffer or
injure them in any way, they have not the power to do it. All the
power that they have comes from on High. We have no other
power and not faith in any other power. Now I am finished. I
thank you for your kindness and attention very much.

The party then left Pleasant View, returning to the courtroom to
resume the hearing. On the way, Streeter reported that his side was
satisfied with the results of the interview. Chandler also expressed
satisfaction, while reminding the reporters that Eddy's delusions were
not touched upon in the interview.[21]

While the local Concord newspapers simply reprinted the interview in its entirety without comment, most newspapers around the
nation reported the interview as a vindication of Eddy's competency.
The *Boston American* was typical: "Badly worsted by the convincing
showing by Mrs. Mary Baker Eddy in her long preliminary examination by the Masters at her home Pleasant View, counsel for the 'next
friends' have begun a savage attack on Christian Science as a faith." It
seemed clear to most that Mary Baker Eddy had succeeded in proving
herself before the court and the nation. In fact, a member of Eddy's
staff reportedly overheard Chandler stating "She was as sharp as a
steel trap." The exception to the positive reports of the interview came
from the *New York World*, which editorialized unscrupulously that
the masters "found Mrs. Eddy paralyzed and emaciated, yet strangely
nerved for the ordeal of examination." Though no reporter was present, this did not stop the *World* from stating, "Throughout the long
fateful hour she took no step or made no movement that she did not
clearly indicate pitiable physical weakness. The parchment-like skin
was drawn tight upon her almost fleshless face, but the light-blue eyes
shone with strange brightness from their deep hollows." The *World*
even found a way to explain away Eddy's remarks: "For the first thirty
minutes of the session Mrs. Eddy answered every question clearly
and slowly in a high inflectionless voice, suggesting the recitation of a
well-learned lesson." To the *World*, her explanation of the discovery
of Christian Science was a shock to the listeners: "While the Masters

and lawyers sat in surprised silence the aged woman told of her God-given powers to heal the sick and of her miraculous appointment to the great work. Out of her own mouth within the space of ten minutes she had covered the whole ground of alleged delusion charged by the 'Next Friends.'" The *World* managed to make the playing of the "graphaphone" a suspicious event: "A weird melody travelled through the house and out to the waiting group in the roadway. To them it sounded like the muffled shriek of a human voice, and the report spread that Mrs. Eddy had collapsed in a fit." The *World* read much into the lack of any statement from the participants in the interview, reporting, "The face of every man in the party was grave. Senator Chandler's bearded visage looked ashen gray. While Lawyer Streeter's was sickly white. It was clear that these men had passed a memorably distasteful hour and had heard and seen unpleasant things." The *World* did acknowledge that the majority of Concord citizens "expected the result of that visit would be the instant collapse of the 'Next Friends' suit," but the newspaper's interpretation of events seemed vindicated by the fact that "the three masters hurried straight to the court-house from Pleasant View and reopened the trial."[22]

The trial resumed at 3:48 p.m., with Kelley introducing the deposition of Arthur T. Buswell of Barton, Vermont. Kelley read the deposition, which had been taken in Boston several weeks earlier. In it, Buswell spoke of his relationship with Eddy from 1879 to 1884 and of her obsession with malicious animal magnetism during his years at the Metaphysical College. After reading the deposition, Kelley began to question Buswell. Immediately, Streeter objected, on the grounds that Buswell's last knowledge of Eddy was twenty-three years before and was too remote. Judge Aldrich inquired if the entire examination of Buswell was about "something that occurred, or ended twenty-three years ago." Aldrich then asked to see the deposition. The judge then launched into a statement of his understanding of what kind of evidence was to be allowed.

> We are under the impression that this, presented in this broad
> way is not within the ruling or within the suggestion of this

morning which in effect was a suggestion that Mrs. Eddy at the
present time or at a time not remote from the first of March was
under a particular delusion in respect to the 'next friends' or in
respect to forces operating upon her mind . . . to prejudice her in
her present condition. . . . Now, this deposition which confronts
us seems to present questions of whether, speaking broadly, it
is relevant or open to the plaintiff to show that she practiced a
system of Christian Science twenty-three years ago; . . . I haven't
ruled on that question or intimated what that ruling will be.

Aldrich stated he was ready to hear arguments on the matter. Howe
spoke for the plaintiffs, stating it was proper procedure "for the party
who objects to be heard first." Streeter explained his objection on three
grounds: that the testimony was "too remote to prove any issue in
the case"; that Buswell's testimony, which contained his version of
Eddy's religious beliefs between 1879 and 1884, could not "have any
bearing upon her capacity to manage her property March 1, 1907";
and that there was "not a word of testimony in the deposition" relating to Eddy's belief that her son and daughter were prejudiced against
her. Howe defended the testimony: "Calling insane delusions a religious belief will not alter the fact that they are insane delusions. . . .
The testimony contained in the deposition does not show a religious
belief; it shows an insane delusion." Howe also stated that "the insane
condition of [Eddy's] mind" led to her prejudice against her son and
granddaughter. Aldrich asked Howe to be more specific as to how this
testimony was material. Howe stated, "Our position is that this is a
case of general insanity; that we show that condition of insanity back
a good many years ago."[23]
    Judge Aldrich claimed that Howe's position was much more broad
than that of Chandler in his opening statement, which Aldrich summarized: "[While] Eddy was capable in many respects, she is subject to
particular delusions, and those particular delusions are of the character
that operate on her mind with respect to management of her property,
and a character which may result in the disinheritance of the natural

heirs." Aldrich asked Howe, "Now, you put it upon the ground of general insanity, do you say?" Howe agreed: "I never put it anywhere else." In fact, Howe expected to go "as far back as 1866" to prove general insanity. Dr. Jelly asked what Howe meant by "general insanity." For a legal definition of insanity, Howe quoted from two cases, *Taylor v. Trich* in Pennsylvania and *In re Beach* in New York.

> General insanity is where the insane beliefs have so unsettled the judgment as to leave the party under the influence of a delusion that has usurped the place of reason and control the will. In such case the question is whether the peculiar views of the alleged incompetent have so impressed her mind as to become as it were so incorporated in her mental constitution as to control her judgment in regard to her business and property.

Referring to the New York case, Howe added, "It is not the abstract belief in spiritualism that raises the presumption of incompetency, but the fact that a person has surrendered his will to the control of such influences rather than to the exercise of sound judgment." Howe then distinguished general insanity from partial insanity by stating, "Partial insanity is a disturbance of some particular point not involving the mind at any other point." To Howe, limiting the scope of the inquiry could be done only in cases of partial insanity, as general insanity "once established . . . will continue, and does continue," requiring one to go back in time to establish general insanity. It was important "to show the permanency of the disease" to distinguish it "from a partial mental disorder."[24]

Aldrich accepted that Howe's question must be "met and ruled upon." It was a question whether to accept "in the broad sense" that Eddy's doctrine with respect to Christian Science was "relevant and competent evidence tending to show insanity" or to limit the inquiry to evidence "showing a delusion which in her present condition . . . might operate to control her mind and put it into channels where it ought not to go." Aldrich gave a tentative conclusion: "Our impressions are rather against your general proposition." But he agreed to hear more before making a ruling. Chandler now joined the discussion, questioning whether what Eddy was teaching twenty-three years ago was a religion and whether it was "a religious question because it has the name 'Christian' put upon it." To Chandler, her "various notions together" were "systematized delusions" that had "reached senile dementia." Chandler was not as familiar with the concept of general insanity as Howe was but concluded that the counsel for the next friends must be allowed "to argue and argue fully": "Before you [Aldrich] decide, we wish to argue that no limit of time as to the reception of testimony shall be fixed." Aldrich agreed not to rule on the question until all parties had been heard, but he raised another question for the plaintiffs: if Eddy now held the same views as she held twenty-three years ago, "why [was] it practically important to go back so far?" Kelley spoke to this question, stating that someone of Eddy's age could have a decaying memory, which would distort her recollection of important beliefs or events in the past.[25]

Streeter proceeded to summarize the question to be decided by the masters: "The proposition is put up plainly now without reserve, that the Christian Science religion as taught by Mrs. Eddy twenty-three years ago indicates that the teachings of Christian Science religion twenty-three years ago was by an insane person, and the five hundred thousand or a million followers of her since are all insane, and we are prepared to meet the question." Kelley objected: "[Streeter] misstates our position entirely." Streeter went on,

> I understand that it is charged that these teachings of Mrs. Eddy twenty-three years ago were delusions, and more than twenty-three years ago. My brother Howe goes back forty years ago to 1866, forty-one years ago, and charges her with general insanity from that date of forty-one years ago and God knows it would be a mighty good thing for Mr. Howe and myself, and almost every-body in this room, if we could have had the same amount

of insanity during the last forty years and accomplished what she
has done, laying aside the spiritual side, even with the financial.

    Streeter and Chandler indicated a willingness to proceed with the
question, but Howe wanted more time to prepare with the other attorneys for the next friends. Judge Aldrich agreed and adjourned the
hearing until 9:30 a.m. on Thursday, August 15.[26]

    It had been a rough day for the plaintiffs. Eddy had conducted
herself well in the face-to-face interview with the masters. While she
had admitted partial deafness and failed to understand some of their
questions, she demonstrated basic understanding of her finances and
investment strategy and was eloquent in speaking of the foundation
of her religious beliefs. Her recent interviews with journalists and
alienists had prepared Chandler and company for the likelihood that
she would perform well in the interview. As a result, the plaintiffs
were ready to turn to evidence of her long-term mental deficiency,
found in all of the depositions they had taken in Boston, most of which
went way back to the discovery of her religion in 1866 through its
turbulent period of growth. Streeter promptly challenged this type of
evidence as too remote, and the masters adjourned the hearing to the
next day, when they would rule whether to limit the type of evidence
introduced by the plaintiffs. Chandler, Kelley, Howe, Peabody, and
Hopkins would have a long-night meeting to prepare their argument
to not limit the evidence in the case, knowing that the decision of the
masters on this question would determine the fate of the next friends.

= 9 =

THE TRIAL: DAYS THREE AND FOUR

Thursday, August 15, did not begin well for the next friends, particularly for Dr. Henry R. Hopkins, their expert alienist. In his hometown of Buffalo, New York, Hopkins was known to take an early morning run each day for health reasons. Unfortunately, jogging was unknown in Concord, New Hampshire, where Hopkins was staying on South Spring Street, at the home of William D. Chandler, son of former senator Chandler, after moving from the Eagle Hotel to save money for the plaintiffs. The *Concord Patriot* describes the scene: "When the birds were singing their mating to their Maker, and the rising sun was gilding the tree-tops this morning, a man of light build and somewhat nimble motion, without any hat, coat, collar, neck-tie or socks was detected speeding down Fruit street at a gait that well nigh baffled pursuit." Neighbors Critchett and Kilburn observed the man and came to the conclusion that an inmate of the State Hospital for the Insane, the grounds of which bordered Fruit Street, "had escaped, and was getting beyond the reach of the authorities with all possible haste." Critchett and Kilburn telephoned the hospital, which sent an attendant to capture the escapee. As Dr. Hopkins was running back down Fruit Street, unaware of the hospital attendant in hot pursuit, Critchett and Kilburn sprang into action, jumping into the runner's path and detaining him until the attendant could catch up. The *Buffalo Sunday Courier* picked up the story: "The attendant stepped up to the morning sprinter and tearing open his shirt front displayed to the gaze of the crowd his manly chest. The manly breast, however, bore none of the mysterious symbols with which the State Asylum decorates its inmates and the attendant was forced to the conclusion that somebody had made a mistake." Hopkins then explained who he was, what he was doing in town, and why he was out running that morning. No arrest was made and no police report filed. In its satirical story, the *Concord Patriot* promised Dr. Hopkins the free run of the city for as long as he was in town, then concluded with a direct reference to the next friends case: "The incident compels the conclusion that Concord is not sufficiently cosmopolitan and does not make sufficient allowances for the vagaries and mental irregularities and health-giving delusions of men who come to us from the outside world, from such centres of thought as Buffalo, New York."[1]

No one commented at the time about the fact that the state of New Hampshire tattooed a number—much like the identification number of Jewish concentration camp inmates in Nazi Germany only thirty years in the future—onto the chests of the inmates at the state mental hospital.

Hopkins was in place when court resumed at 9:40 a.m. DeWitt Howe opened for the plaintiffs, arguing against any limitation on time in the presentation of evidence of Eddy's "general insanity" and citing court cases that defined the term. Judge Aldrich interrupted to remind Howe that the masters were only going to determine Eddy's competency to manage property on March 1, not her general insanity or religious delusions, which were "irrelevant" unless proof was shown of their connection to her ability to make business decisions. Howe promised to show that "a condition of insanity influenc[ed] every action of her life" and that Eddy was "not governed by will, reason, a judgment, but by insane delusions, which [had] taken possession of her and . . . influenced her since 1866, in her relations to her children and otherwise." Howe went on to say that Christian Science is not a religion, at which Aldrich interrupted: "Who has the right to say that? They have churches and hold religious services, with many attendants." Howe explained that the Supreme Court had ruled that Mormonism was not a religion; neither was "Millerism and other doctrines." Judge Aldrich then quoted the Constitution, noting that every citizen has the "inalienable right" to his own religious beliefs, and asked if the masters had "any more right to decide against Christian Science as a religion than against Catholicism or Spiritualism." Howe declared that Christian Science was "a system of medicine, not a religion" and explained that Eddy's delusion "distort[ed] her every action." As an example, he stated, "The belief that there is no such thing as pain is a delusion, an insane delusion, from which the mind cannot be freed." Judge Aldrich asked what particular elements of Christian Science showed delusion, to which Howe gave the example of Eddy's belief that in 1866 "she was miraculously and suddenly cured from an injury which, as a matter of fact, yielded only to constant and long-continued medical treatment." The judge asked, "But who has the right to say that the religious belief of a million people is an insane delusion? Has not the Constitution recognized the wisdom of not attempting to so differentiate?" Howe responded that the Constitution did not intend "to recognize insane delusions as religion"; if so, every criminal claiming they were victims of "religious mania" would be freed.[2]

Aldrich asked if it was possible to prove that prayer did not cure disease. He went on to tell the story of a minister who preached the doctrine of prayer but "told his flock it was no use to pray for rain to stop while the wind was in the east." Aldrich then asked, "How many Christian Scientists are there?" Howe looked to Frederick Peabody, who responded that there were forty thousand, which brought gasps of astonishment from the audience, which was made up mostly of Christian Scientists. Frank Streeter corrected the record by claiming there were five hundred thousand to one million. Howe proceeded to state that it was necessary for the plaintiffs to go back to Eddy's first supporters—Richard Kennedy, Daniel Spofford, Edward J. Arens, Clara Choate, and Arthur Buswell—to show how Eddy's delusions impacted her feelings toward them. Aldrich asked if it was possible to connect these "isolated cases of prejudice with Eddy's feelings toward George W. Glover." Howe responded in the affirmative. Aldrich concluded that the prime question was, "Shall Christian Science bodily go in or stay out of this hearing?" He stated, "If Mrs. Eddy has a particular belief as to some sort of force operating upon her son to prejudice him against her, it is competent [relevant] to discuss that belief. But it will be a waste of time to bring in all of Mrs. Eddy's writings and sermons for 40 years and discuss them." Howe responded, "A diseased brain is less likely than a well brain to do business properly, and each added degree of debility increases the likelihood that the business will not be managed properly."[3]

Streeter's objection to the acceptance into evidence of Arthur Buswell's deposition describing Eddy's belief in malicious animal magnetism from 1879 to 1883 had prompted the discussion about how far back the plaintiffs would be allowed to go in presenting evidence of Eddy's incompetence. Aldrich now allowed Kelley to resume reading Buswell's deposition, but Streeter again objected when a question was read regarding M.A.M. Streeter remarked that there was no suggestion in the deposition of any business act by Eddy. Judge Aldrich asked about Eddy's copyrights, with Streeter answering that they were now held by the trustees, though Eddy had held them for many years. Chandler spoke up: "That is what we want to find out about." Streeter then stated that Chandler had admitted that the suit was intended as "an investigation of the Christian Science doctrine," which Chandler quickly denied. Streeter criticized the next friends for attempting to break "Eddy's will in advance" by attacking her ability to turn over her property to trustees. Streeter stated, "Her property is in the hands of trustees, where it will stay and where it is safe."[4]

Aldrich responded, "If the question was whether Mrs. Eddy's property is now in good hands, we could have determined it long ago. But, the question is her competency on March 1."

"If she had the competency to make that trust deed this suit is at an end, Judge Chamberlin said so." said Streeter.

"Not in his commission to us," answered Aldrich.

"That is our misfortune," replied Streeter, who returned to his objection to the Buswell deposition and the fact that Eddy's views then were "not the views she now" held or taught and that there was nothing in the deposition relating to her son or his daughter: "No connection can possibly be made between this doctrine of malicious animal magnetism and Mrs. Eddy's son and her granddaughter. It is her present attitude toward these relatives which should be presented." Hosea Parker asked if it would be "wise . . . to dictate the manner of procedure to counsel." Streeter answered it would be "just" for the masters to ask counsel for the next friends "how they expect[ed] to connect his doctrine with Mrs. Eddy's next of kin." Streeter stated, "It is unjust to Mrs. Eddy to have Mrs. Eddy's views of 1879 paraded in the press as her views of today." He continued, "If this testimony as to delusions is admitted piecemeal, that will finally get in which has been ruled out as a whole. It is not for this tribunal to determine the relations between Mrs. Eddy and her son, or to guess what the result of those relations will be in her will." At this point, recess was called at 1:00 p.m., with the hearing to resume at 2:30 p.m.[5]

Before court resumed, a long conference was held between Chandler, Streeter, and the masters, with a stenographer present. During the conference, Streeter suggested that if the issues of Kennedy, Spofford, and Arens were to be introduced by the plaintiffs, there would have to be a trial on each to determine whether they were telling the truth about Eddy. Chandler commented on Streeter's claim that Eddy's ideas in 1878 were not the same as her ideas at the time of the hearing, stating that he disagreed and that her ideas had not changed. He spoke of Eddy's letter of 1890 claiming George Glover was influenced by M.A.M. to break her will, after which she transferred her copyrights to her adopted son, Dr. Ebenezer Foster Eddy. She later transferred the copyrights to Calvin A. Frye, Edward A. Kimball, and others, and these retransfers were all due to her belief in malicious animal magnetism. Aldrich thought the discussion was unduly broadening again. But Chandler insisted that the entire Buswell deposition be admitted, as Eddy mentioned to him the "red dragon" that controlled her mind. Chandler believed the next friends had done nothing "which next friends without expectation of heritage might not have done." Aldrich reiterated his position "to keep the matter of inheritance out of this trial entirely." Finally, the hearing resumed at 3:15, when Aldrich issued the following ruling.

> I desire to say in making a brief ruling upon the question that has been under discussion, that we appreciate that it is a delicate question under the Constitution, and that we can only give it such consideration as comes up on a trial under progress. We make the ruling upon such impressions as we have and we understand that it is subject to exception, and we fully understand that it will operate to limit somewhat the scope contended for on the other side. It is this.
>
> We are all of the opinion that evidence tending to show that Mrs. Eddy is in a delusory mental condition in respect to forces operating upon her relatives and 'next friends,' and through them upon her business, if of a character to show mental impairment and to influence her in business affairs, is admissible. This is limited to alleged delusions which reasonably connect themselves with Mrs. Eddy's mental condition with respect to the management of property affairs. The majority of the board think that as these alleged delusions relate to conditions of mental prejudice, that going back to 1890 is not remote.

Streeter immediately excepted to the ruling. Kelley then began reading the Buswell deposition, but Judge Aldrich ruled he should not go on, as the evidence was too remote in time. Chandler stated that it was necessary for his side to prove what malicious animal magnetism was by presenting these depositions or else by introducing all of Eddy's writings. Aldrich said no to this, as Chandler must confine himself "to the influence exerted upon Mrs. Eddy by some delusion." Kelley reminded the court that since 1892 Eddy had been living in seclusion, "making it impossible to secure witnesses as to her condition

who [were] not defendants in this action." Therefore, the plaintiffs had
to go back in time to prove their case. Aldrich stated that his ruling not
to go earlier that 1890 would stand, and Kelley then excepted.[6]

Kelley tried to introduce several letters from William Nixon,
Eddy's publisher in 1890. As they related to business, Aldrich allowed
them in as evidence. One letter from Eddy criticized Nixon's management of Christian Science publications, bad management that was due
to "the abuse of mental practice." In another letter to Nixon, Eddy
threatened to "rip up all her business relations" and referred to "the
curse in this platform of [Augusta] Stetson's." Another letter charged
that "action external" was influencing Nixon. The most important
letter was written on September 22, 1890, and was reproduced in its
entirety in the official transcript of the trial. In this letter Eddy states,
"I see this morning the purpose of the enemy! It is to break my will
at my decease. . . . My son in South Dakota is a victor at law and M.
A. M. will influence him to break my will." Eddy ordered Nixon to
find the best copyright lawyer to determine if she could "assign" the
copyright "to someone who would hold it if [her] will was broken and
never name this party in [the] will or name it to whom it is assigned
whichever would make it legal." She continued, "So . . . if the will
is broken the assignment [of copyright] would be valid." In a postscript Eddy added, "The Boston lawyers whom I have employed are
demoralized by M.A.M. Note this." This letter was followed by one of
September 28, 1890, in which Eddy stated she had changed her mind
about reassigning the copyright. The court was then adjourned from
5:10 p.m. until 9:30 Friday morning.[7]

The residents of Pleasant View were kept informed of the progress
of the trial by the many Christian Scientists who attended each day.
John Salchow, one of Eddy's most senior and loyal staff members,
sent his wife to the courthouse. She reported that "Mary Glover and
E. J. Foster Eddy would sit there and laugh and snicker at everything
said against Mrs. Eddy." When court resumed on Friday, August 16,
Streeter announced that Calvin A. Frye was present and ready to
testify if called by counsel for the next friends. Kelley stated that he

didn't have "the slightest idea now" when or if Frye would be called to the stand, to which Streeter replied that he would have Frye remain until 10:30 a.m. in case. At 10:30 Streeter interrupted Kelley again to state that the defense was sending Frye back to Pleasant View but that he could return within fifteen to twenty minutes if called. Kelley responded with sarcasm, "I hope he will eat a hearty dinner."[8]

The full impact of the ruling of the masters to limit testimony since 1890 was felt by the plaintiffs on Friday, as Kelley repeatedly attempted to submit and read depositions taken in Boston by former associates of Eddy dating back as far as 1867. At first, Kelley continued introducing the letters of William Nixon from 1890 and later. In a letter dated November 3, 1890, Eddy wrote to Nixon, "Say nothing to [H. Cornell] Wilson of our arrangement. He is sensitive over having anyone out of the printing examine the proofs of his printing. This is M. A. M. and it governs [editor James Henry] Wiggin as it has done once before to prevent the publishing of my work." On January 1, 1891, she again wrote Nixon, urging him to "push with all [his] ability the publication" of *Science and Health*, which "the *enemy* [was] holding back." A conflict arose between Streeter and Kelley over a fragment of Eddy's writing, which was identified only as "94." Kelley offered to have Peabody read the fragment, and Streeter remarked that he had no objection but that Peabody's name "should be entered as . . . counsel in the case," as Peabody had "been acting as counsel and . . . should appear on record." Peabody proceeded to read from "94": "You have no power to make anybody sick or do any harm. Truth is the master of error and you know you are utterly powerless to beat Truth. This you do know and have no faith that you can. Every time you argue a lie you destroy effect of the lie for the lie kills itself. The lie and the liar are one and are self destroyed." Peabody then offered to read two lines that had been crossed out on the back of "94." Streeter wondered if Peabody had crossed out the lines, which prompted a reply from Chandler to defend Peabody. Streeter, "Do you propose to go to trial on that question?" Chandler, "Yes, if you wish to. All the side issues you want to try, if the Masters will allow us to." He went on to explain that Foster Eddy had given him the paper, which had remained in Chandler's possession ever since, and that the "lines were drawn through it when it was given" to Chandler. Peabody then read the two lines, "You have no power to do evil. You can't make some folks sick and then heal others. If you try to make sickness it stops healing. You can't help . . ." The fragment ended there with no punctuation.[9]

Kelley then attempted to reintroduce the Buswell deposition, claiming that it was important evidence in proving Eddy's insanity, in showing her delusions that existed then and that "now exist[ed] in intensified form." Streeter objected, stating that the masters had already ruled against such remote testimony. Aldrich ruled, "The deposition is excluded on the ground that it is remote in point of time. . . . Also on the ground that so far as it relates to the peculiar force known as malicious animal magnetism, it has not connected itself with the 'next friends' or property management of Mrs. Eddy." Kelley went on to introduce the deposition of Dr. Rufus K. Noyes, who had performed the autopsy on Asa Gilbert Eddy in 1882. Kelly stated, "[The deposition] tends to show this belief of M. A. M. in Mrs. Eddy to such an intensified form that she believes that her husband died of arsenic mentally administered and had this autopsy by a doctor of her selection in order to determine that fact." Again, Aldrich ruled the deposition out because it was too remote in time, commenting also on the contentious atmosphere in the courtroom: "I always notice that Friday morning is an unfortunate day in the week. Counsel get tired and treat unimportant matters as something important." Kelley then tried and failed to introduce the deposition of Henry C. Dunnells, who had been involved in the infamous Salem trial, but Streeter objected again that Dunnells had not seen Eddy since 1879. Streeter charged that Kelley was trying "to offer [depositions] piecemeal and get a statement before the Court, not for use in this Court, but for general public uses." Kelley denied "doing this for the purpose of publication, or for any other purpose, except getting [his] exception regularly noted on the record." Aldrich tried to explain to Streeter that he had no choice but to entertain Kelley's attempt to introduce each deposition: "If we were sitting here as judges rather than as Masters of course it would be a different kind of a trial in many respects. We are required, I believe, under the Commission, to report all the evidence and to state all the exceptions, and that would perhaps include reporting evidence which was offered in the shape of depositions and excluded, perhaps." Streeter answered that the "practical result" of this practice was to evade the ruling of the masters regarding testimony prior to 1890. Aldrich replied, "Now we are sitting here as Masters—not as judges—and we are a tribunal with very limited powers." He commented that it was the counsel that was making this "friendly investigation" difficult, concluding, "We don't seem to be making much progress this morning."[10]

Kelley proceeded to offer the depositions of Catharine Isabel Platt, who knew Mary Baker Eddy from 1867 to 1870, and the deposition of Lucretia L. S. Brown, plaintiff in the Salem trial who had granted power of attorney to "Mary B. G. Eddy to appear in court to manage and prosecute the same for [Brown]." These were also excluded by the masters.[11]

Kelley then offered two motions for the masters to consider and rule on before the end of the day. The first proposed a series of visits by alienists to examine Eddy at her home if she was unable to come to court. The motion included a request that the next friends—George Glover, his daughter Mary, and Ebenezer Foster Eddy—be allowed to attend the visits along with all counsel for the next friends. The second motion would require Joseph Armstrong and the other defendants to present in court "all books, contracts and other writings . . . which relate in anywise to the financial transactions and business affairs of Mrs. Eddy from the year 1890 to [the present]." Armstrong's attorney, W. A. Morse, spoke up, explaining that Armstrong, Eddy's publisher, had been "unable to give his deposition in Boston," that he was prepared to present all of the letters Eddy wrote to Armstrong, but that bringing all of the books was an inconvenience, as they were large and heavy to transport. Streeter responded that he did not think the "details of the business affairs . . . of Mrs. Eddy ought to be exhibited generally." But after Aldrich suggested having counsel for the next friends examine the books in Boston over the weekend, Streeter changed his tune, saying, "Instead of turning anybody loose in the private personal books of Mrs. Eddy or Mrs. Eddy's publishers, . . . the evidence ought to be brought here." Morse relented, saying, "I will bring the books," and Kelley expressed satisfaction that all the books from 1896 to date would be presented when court resumed on Tuesday.[12]

Kelley then resumed the tedious business of introducing as evidence letters written by Eddy to her adopted son, Foster Eddy, since 1890. The letters tended to document the deterioration of their relationship, as indicated by her opening greetings over time, from "*Dearest* Mama's *darling*" in the early letters to "Dear Doctor" in her last letter to her son. In one, she wrote, "Those persons named are utterly incapable of handling the Red Dragon. They can command serpents but not the last species." On March 17, 1897, Eddy wrote, "You conceal from me all you should tell—and which I would save you from doing—and then when you get into difficulty come to me for help. . . . But you were governed by hypnotism to work against me and yourself and take me as your authority for so doing." This was written after the Christian Science church in Philadelphia had dismissed Foster Eddy as first reader: "The Church has written me a loving letter with regrets (?) that they had to do by you as they did." Finally, on October 28, 1900, their relationship had ended, but Eddy's letter to Foster Eddy makes it appear that he was done in by others, not by her:

> I have longed for time enough to say to you that I acted not in your dismissal from the Mother Church. I only assented in order to chose the least of two evils viz your case coming before the church from a branch church and the charge being criminal according to law or simply to drop your name and reject the other charge. . . . May you realize that mother has done the best for you that she knew, even if she is not understood yet she is faithful. You are better to be removed from M. A. M. in Boston.[13]

After the noon recess, the hearing resumed at 2:10. Kelley proceeded to introduce into evidence letters written by Eddy to her son, George Glover. The first letter was ruled out by the masters, as it was written in 1889. Kelley succeeded in reading into the record a letter from August 12, 1892, in which Eddy wrote about the education of George's daughters, Evelyn and Mary. Eddy wrote that she had decided not to bring the girls east because of "mental malpractioners in Boston, alias the mesmerists, that caused dear Evelyn's sickness." She wrote, "I am of the opinion it is not quite safe for those dear grandchildren to go there unless I am there too." She did request that George send the girls to a boarding school, "where they [could] have the opportunity to be in the company of educated people." Kelley then introduced a letter written by Eddy on August 16, 1893, in which she advised her grandchildren to read all of her works. She expressed particular concern for Evelyn, who was reportedly too ill to attend school: "It is nothing but *mesmerism* that has caused this state of her health. When she was in Boston she was regarded as somewhat like me, and that she would be a scholar etc. This was enough for the result before named." Next, Kelley read the letter from April 27, 1898, in which Eddy lamented the false reports of her "dying, [or being] wholly decriped and useless, etc." She wrote of her fame in leading three hundred thousand people, and being complimented by "Lords and Ladies, Earls, Princes, and Marquis and Marchioness from abroad." Nevertheless, she also wrote, "I am *alone* in the world, more lone than a solitary star." This is the letter in which Eddy wrote of her beautiful home but reminded George that it was "simply a house and a beautiful landscape" and that her "help" were not "companions and scarcely fit to be [her] *help*." She wrote of her adopted son and her hope that he would take "Mr. Frye's place" as her "bookkeeper," but Foster Eddy had proved a disappointment, as "his books could not be audited they were so incorrect." She described Frye as "the most disagreeable man that [could] be found" but said that at least he was honest. To Eddy, the "severest wound of all" was the lack of education of her "kin." She stated that if George were educated "to-day [he] could, would, be made President of the U.S." She also wrote, "Mary's letters to me are so misspelled that I blush to read them." She did conclude that she was proud of George even though he mispronounced his words, because he displayed "good manners" and because she loved him. In a postscript she spoke of her finances, which had been audited by "Mr. Ladd" and shown to be "all right," even though Frye had not set things down in a "coherent" or an "orderly way." In a letter of August 21, 1900, Eddy denied George's request for money, stating, "I have given you in money and land and houses over $20,000 and now I have resolved to throw away no more money on you or your family and receive in return for it only disrespect, ingratitude, and new requests for more money." She advised George not to send future letters to her by express, as all her letters were read first by her "secretary." If George broke "this rule," Eddy would "return that letter . . . unopened." Eddy's letter was typewritten, but in a handwritten conclusion she writes, "Never let any one address me mentally for it will injure them and I shall know who does it and not be influenced by any person in my work for God and man."[14]

A dispute arose over the next letter that Kelley tried to introduce. The letter of February 25, 1907, supposedly written by Glover to his mother, was objected to by Streeter as not having been written by George but by Chandler. The letter should not be admitted, Streeter asserted, until George Glover took the stand as a witness. Streeter charged that the letter was written "for the purposes of publication, and for the purposes of making evidence" for the next friends. If the letter expressed George Glover's views, Streeter said that Glover "should state these views before the Masters and not with the man who wrote the letter sitting right [there] in the presence of the Masters [and] under-taking to put in a letter expressing views, and not being examined." Judge Aldrich seemed to agree, stating that the letter was "inadmissible" because it was "the production of a party in interest who offer[ed] it, putting in proof his own statement." But the judge went on to say that the letter "need not be read" and that he would decide later if it should be accepted as evidence.[15]

Judge Aldrich then took up the motions presented by plaintiffs earlier in the day. The motion to require Joseph Armstrong to produce all books and papers relating to Eddy's business affairs in Boston had already been agreed to by counsel and required no ruling by the masters. The other motion, to require Eddy to undergo examination by alienists, produced a heated exchange. Aldrich first stated that the presence of an alienist, Dr. Jelly, on the board of masters did not preclude "the rights of the parties one way or the other in respect to proofs." Streeter then interrupted with an impassioned plea that Eddy was a "lady" who had "some fundamental rights," particularly "that a citizen . . . charged with being an incompetent" was "not obliged to open his house to the 'next friends,'. . . not obliged to have doctors or alienists or other people sent to the house." Streeter did not believe the masters had "any power" that allowed them "to submit this aged lady to that examination of experts." He had hoped that after having met with Eddy, the masters "would not advise [her] to submit to the examination of any experts that she did not choose to have come to see her." Judge Aldrich asked if anyone knew any case law in New Hampshire "upon that point." Streeter responded that to his knowledge there had never been a case like it. Chandler then made a strong declaration of the rights of the next friends. The request for alienists to examine Eddy was "a reasonable thing to do," and he did not expect such an objection to it. According to Chandler, "if these two sons thought it best to go and get her and bring her into court, they could do it." Chandler said of Streeter, "[He] forgets what this case is. It is a case to determine whether she has that mental capacity to decide such questions for herself." Chandler asserted that the court could not allow Frye, Streeter, Baker, and the trustees to exclude Eddy's relatives from their fundamental right to send experts to Pleasant View. The counsel for next friends had written Streeter twice, on March 28 and July 6, asking for access to Eddy, and had received no answer; if the next friends' "fundamental rights were to be carried out, habeas corpus would bring her [to the courtroom]." Based on the fact that Eddy went out riding an hour before the masters visited her on Wednesday, there appeared

to be no "reason why she should not come" to the "court room and
. . . make her own statement."[16]

Judge Aldrich interrupted Chandler to comment that "in the public
eye" at least "something had been established," in that Eddy's very
existence and the fact that she did ride each day had been proven:
"So we have accomplished something." Chandler proceeded to state,
"I think she should come here, I think we should go there, I think
these considerate interviews should be had." In Chandler's opinion,
the masters should have had more interviews with Eddy; if they had,
"that might [have obviated] the necessity of having examination by
alienists." But Judge Chamberlin had directed "that the case was to be
tried according to the regular and orderly methods of judicial procedure," except that he established "this preliminary inquiry." Chandler
said of the next friends and their counsel, "[We have been placed at]
marked disadvantages from which the other side has not at all tried to
relieve us . . . and now wishes to add another burden, and that is that
we shall not have alienists go there unless . . . their names are first submitted to Mrs. Eddy." Chandler asserted that Eddy was incompetent
to make the decision and would be controlled by Frye and Streeter,
just as "four days after this suit began she . . . signed a paper in which
she undertook to appoint some 'next friends' in the place of George
Glover, Mary B. Glover and Dr. Foster Eddy."[17]

Howe spoke next: "The law of New Hampshire appears to be
settled on that point." Offering from Streeter's own "Summary of
Positions," Howe asserted, "The filing of this bill ipso facto places Mrs.
Eddy's person and property under the protection of the chancellor
[Judge Chamberlin]." Thus "the question of examination of [Eddy] by
alienists" was entirely up to the court. Kelley then offered the names of
two alienists, Dr. Henry R. Stedman and Dr. George T. Tuttle of the
McLean Asylum in Massachusetts, who were selected by the plaintiffs
to examine Eddy. For the defense, Edwin Eastman addressed Howe's
interpretation of the statement relating to the court's protection of
Eddy's "person and property." Eastman stated, "That does not mean
that the chancellor is to ignore all the rights that a citizen has at all.

It simply means that the chancellor will see that the rights of a party are duly protected." He also stated, "[If Eddy was] competent to take charge of her affairs on the first day of March, [we] have no right to be here at all, and that is the end of this case." He also warned that if the ideas of Chandler and company prevailed, "any person might get up and say, 'Here is Mr. Smith,' or 'Mr. Jones,' he is an old man and needs protection, I will go to work and institute proceedings as 'next friend' and have that question determined. He has no rights at all if he is bound to submit himself to an examination of alienists, and experts, and anybody that comes along." Eastman concluded the consequences if that idea prevailed: "We are all in danger."[18]

Judge Aldrich tried to "reiterate the idea that this suit [was], at least in theory, a friendly suit" and promised to treat Eddy "as [he] would the case of any party . . . under the limitations which natural conditions under ordinary circumstances impose upon humanity in general at 87." He then went on to say, "Mr. Chandler [should] name two alienists who may go at such times as the Masters and counsel go, who may observe Mrs. Eddy's physical and mental appearance under examination by the Masters and counsel, and make tests for themselves in the presence and under the direction of Mr. Chandler, in the presence of the Masters." Chandler agreed to that arrangement, and Streeter stated, "To me personally,—that is a good solution." But Streeter wanted to confer with Eddy before agreeing to it. Aldrich accepted Streeter's request, saying, "if you feel that you want time." Aldrich then adjourned the hearing until 10:30 a.m. Tuesday, August 20.[19]

Chandler and company would have a lot of work to do over the weekend to try and salvage their case. By deciding that testimony about events in Eddy's life prior to 1890 was too remote to determine her competency to manage her affairs on March 1, 1907, the masters had ruled out much of the plaintiffs' evidence dating back to Eddy's discovery in 1866. The plaintiffs' assertion that the religious "delusions" of Eddy were the best evidence of her lunacy had been rejected by the masters, who were reluctant to engage in any kind of exploration of religion, which to them was a delicate constitutional problem, except as her "delusions" could be shown to directly impact her business decisions. The plaintiffs had, thus far, been unable to make a direct connection between the two or to undermine in any way Mary Baker Eddy's reputation as a sagacious and hardheaded business woman. The plaintiffs had introduced many of Eddy's letters to her son, George Glover, and adopted son, Ebenezer Foster Eddy, but these revealed more about Glover's constant need for money and his inability to take advantage of his mother's strong desire to educate her grandchildren and Foster Eddy's ineptness at each task assigned to him by his adopted mother than they did about Eddy's belief in M. A. M. and its impact on her decision making.

Eddy was kept informed of what was happening in court each day by Alfred Farlow. He tried to reassure her on Friday evening that the decision of the masters to allow her to be examined by alienists was not to be feared: "I am of the candid opinion that the Masters do not intend to have you annoyed nor allow that this proceeding shall have any weight in the case but that it has been suggested as a means of removing the last excuse and preventing the so-called 'next friends' from demanding further privileges." According to Farlow, the masters had to act as they did to conduct the case as Judge Chamberlin directed, so as not to be "rejected by him." Farlow stated, "Judge Chamberlin did not manifest the degree of consideration for you which I hoped he would." Farlow reported to Eddy that her side had made much progress over the past two days: "Much of their [the plaintiff's] stuff was presented and disposed of," he said, and the letters that were admitted "all made [her] stalwart Christian character and business capacity stand out like a monument." Farlow predicted, "The hearing will close by Wednesday or Thursday." He concluded, "I beseech you not to be in the slightest moved by this prospective interview. It will be conducted very conservatively and in a very dignified manner and no opportunity for any indignities will be allowed by these three gentleman."[20]

The *New York World* viewed the "suggestion" of the masters to

permit alienists to examine Mary Baker Eddy as a major victory for
the plaintiffs: "It was the first official assurance that no special consideration was to be shown toward Mrs. Eddy." But other newspapers
around the nation simply reported the facts of the day's events without
editorial comment, indicating that increasingly the press was no longer
anticipating sensational news to come from the courtroom and was
prepared for the inevitable end to the case.[21]

= 10 =

CASE DISMISSED

Chandler anticipated spending the weekend of August 17–19 at his home in Waterloo preparing to continue the case of *Eddy v. Frye*. He invited Frederick Peabody to stay with him and on Saturday morning wrote letters to DeWitt Howe in Concord and to John Kelley in Portsmouth. Each attorney had been assigned a different role in the case: Howe to present evidence of mental incompetence and insanity, and Kelley to investigate financial indiscretions and mismanagement. Chandler's letters advised each as to how to pursue their part of the case. To Howe, Chandler wrote that he expected the other side to offer witnesses to attest to Mary Baker Eddy's mental and physical well-being. Chandler advised Howe to object to any conclusions by the witnesses who would not be competent to "sum up by an opinion as to business capacity." Chandler advised Kelly to ignore the trust deed of March 6 and consider only whether Eddy's property was safe on March 1 and whether "she was solely at the mercy of Frye and Co. if they chose to steal from her." Chandler promised each colleague that he intended to work on the case all day and would write them again that evening, but he never did.[1]

Chandler also wrote another letter to Ralph Pulitzer. Chandler stated that he hadn't expected the *World* to change its position in reference to supporting the case, but he wrote, "[I hope you can] help

me out personally if I get badly in debt beyond my means to pay."
Chandler had already spent around $2,000 of his own money on the
case and was faced with the prospect of reimbursing two alienists at
$100 each per day to examine Eddy. He stated, "Such expenses become
large quickly." He informed Pulitzer that the next friends' legal team
were "getting on well" in spite of the limitations imposed by the
masters. In Chandler's opinion, the visit with Eddy "showed mental
activity on ordinary subjects, but [she introduced] her crazy notions,
although the Masters in their plan for a first interview tried to prevent
her." He continued, "To me she showed symptoms of delusions abun-
dantly vindicating my opening statement." Chandler also asked Ralph
Pulitzer to pass the letter along to his father, saying, "My personal
relations with him were always pleasant—although 'long ago.'"[2]

That same day Chandler dispatched Dr. Henry Hopkins to
Massachusetts and Rhode Island to investigate the suicide of Mary
Tomlinson by interviewing the persons who were attending to her
at the time. Chandler had always suspected that her death had some-
thing to do with the case of *Eddy v. Frye*, possibly relating to Mary
Tomlinson's discovery of nefarious activity by the defendants, particularly her brother Irving. Hopkins wrote the next day of his interviews
with a Dr. Payne and Miss Telfair, the nurse who had been with Mary
Tomlinson at the Parker House that night, April 18. Telfair reported
that Mary Tomlinson was quite pleased to see her brother Rev. Vincent
Tomlinson, who had rushed to her that evening from his home in
Rhode Island, arriving at the hotel around 9:00 p.m. Vincent was not
a Christian Scientist, and when Irving Tomlinson arrived at the hotel
from Concord at 11:00 p.m. and took charge of Mary's care, Vincent
"showed plainly that he was not pleased" and was dismissed by Irving,
as was Nurse Telfair. It was Irving who left Mary alone in the room,
but it was Telfair and Vincent who heard the window open and who
broke into the room to find it empty and Mary on the ground four
floors below. On Monday, Hopkins interviewed Vincent Tomlinson
at his home in Wakefield, Rhode Island. He told a similar story of
arriving at the hotel to find his sister alternating between periods of

lucidity and insanity. Hopkins reported, "During one of these lucid and quiet moments she told [Vincent] that she had become cured of her belief in Mrs. Eddy and that she could never believe the system again and never undertake to teach or practice the peculiar method of healing." Vincent asked her why she had changed her attitude toward Eddy, to which Mary replied "that Mrs. E. was quite wrought up over the Next Friends suit or the Next Enemies, as she termed them, and had asked her, Miss M.T. to treat the next friends effectively and finally to the end that the suit should stop there and now." This request had opened Mary's eyes that Eddy was making "such a criminal request," and Vincent stated he was convinced that "the sad state of mind of [Mary] was due in part or in whole by the shock and shame and regret of hearing Mrs. E. make such a request." Vincent invited Mary to leave Concord and live with him. According to Hopkins, Vincent "said [that Hopkins] was at liberty to report the matter" to Chandler, and Vincent appeared willing to testify "upon the insanity of Mrs. E. and its results."[3]

After Hopkins left, however, Vincent Tomlinson had a change of heart about testifying. He wrote Chandler, "I have long felt that Christian Science is unsound as a philosophy, and unsafe in its practical workings. My personal feeling is, that my sister was a victim of it." But, since she was clearly irrational on that occasion, Vincent "came to the conclusion that anything she said to [him] that evening would have no weight as evidence." He was confirmed in this opinion by an alienist he had consulted, who indicated the "worthlessness, as evidence, of such talk under such conditions." Because his sister "arraigned" Christian Science "bitterly" on that occasion "but on no other occasion," Vincent concluded, "Both myself and my departed sister might be entirely eliminated from [the case]." Though investigating Mary Tomlinson's death had been unlikely to provide much evidence, Tomlinson's letter effectively closed off one more avenue by which the plaintiffs might explore Mary Baker Eddy's mental condition.[4]

On Sunday, Chandler sent checks as a retainer to Drs. Stedman and Tuttle, advising them that they could be called "as rapidly as possible after Monday." Chandler expressed his view that Eddy was "a very cunning lunatic" and that she had probably been "stimulated into a state of high exaltation" prior to the interview with the masters on August 14. Dr. Stedman returned the checks, stating that no retainer was necessary: "We should prefer to have our remuneration when our work is done." He also indicated that at least four interviews with Eddy would be necessary. Stedman hoped that the alienists would be permitted to examine Eddy in private, as " the task of getting at her line of thought, delusions, etc. [would be] exceedingly difficult if not impossible to accomplish" with so many people present, as prescribed by the masters' recent ruling.[5]

Although he had promised to work all weekend on the case, Chandler attended his youngest son's town baseball game in the company of Frederick Peabody on Saturday afternoon, hiked a nearby mountain with George Glover and Mary Glover on Sunday, and entertained guests not associated with the case both days. Chandler may have begun to realize the hopelessness of proceeding with the case, and the personal expense he was incurring by bringing alienists from Boston for four or more examinations of Eddy. Chandler may have been among the last persons to realize the ultimate result of the case. Around the nation, editorials were appearing in newspapers, decrying the attack on an eighty-seven-year-old woman. The *New York Journal* was particularly effective in criticizing the *World:* "It would be interesting to know just what satisfaction newspapers find in their persistent persecution of a very old woman." The *Journal* stated that the case was offensive in three ways: "They attack a woman, they attack old age and they attack religion. Those three things should be respected." The editorial noted the irony that the leading newspapers attacking Eddy—the *World* and the *New York Times*—were "both owned by Jews." Based on the fact that Jews had "suffered outrageously and bravely for centuries on account of their religious belief," the editorial said, "a Jew should be the last man to encourage, much less to begin, attacks upon the religion of another." The *Journal* concluded that the Jewish editors did not speak for "the people of Jewish blood in America": "The Jews came to this country to escape from the very persecution, from the false accusations, that the *World* and the *Times* now make against Mrs. Eddy and her followers." With public opinion so put off by the relentless prosecution of the case, what could possibly be gained by continuing it?[6]

On Monday, Chandler traveled back to Concord for meetings with Kelley and Howe. The two attorneys had met the previous day with Streeter in Exeter, New Hampshire. It was clear that the plaintiffs were seeking a graceful means of ending the suit. Kelley met two or three times on Monday with Streeter, Foster Eddy arrived and met with the attorneys, and in the evening Kelley and Chandler had a meeting with Streeter and Hollis. Later in the evening Hopkins returned from meeting with Tomlinson in Rhode Island. Streeter preserved a copy of the suggestions made by Kelley and Chandler on Monday evening. Chandler proposed that when the hearing resumed on Tuesday, he would tell the masters that the next friends were filing a motion to dismiss the case and ask Judge Chamberlin to grant the motion. Streeter would state his disapproval and state that if he had the power, he would go forward with the hearing to reach a decision on Eddy's competence, but recognizing the rights of the plaintiffs, he would not ask for a finding in the case and accept the dismissal of the bill in equity. Chandler and Streeter would then each state their reasons for their positions. The attorneys agreed to meet again at 9:00 a.m. on Tuesday, the twentieth, at which time Streeter informed Chandler and Kelley that he could not consent to any understanding "which would 'put any strings' on the counsel of Mrs. Eddy in any way." If Chandler proposed a motion to dismiss the case, Streeter would "take such positions as the interests of Mrs. Eddy might seem to require," regardless what was proposed at the conference on Monday evening.[7] Streeter then informed Eddy that the case was nearing an end and asked for her instructions. She wrote back, "I hereby declare for two points to be stated and *decided* namely, *my competence* when I had my trustees appointed; also the *speedy close* of this prosecution, alias persecution, by my 'next friends,' alias enemies."[8]

With negotiations stalled, Chandler and company had no choice but to resume the hearing on Tuesday, August 20. The decision having been made to dismiss the case, however, the fifth day of the hearing was devoid of important revelations. Kelley began by asking if Joseph Armstrong had filed the books and documents from Boston relating to Eddy's financial operations. Streeter stated that they were all in Concord, but he refused to allow the plaintiffs to see them, because this was his, the defense's, evidence, which the defense team would present when they were ready. Kelley insisted on access to the books as the only way to determine if Eddy's business had been misman- aged. Judge Aldrich was taken aback by the disagreement, as he had thought that counsel had made an arrangement on the matter; if not, the masters would have to consult with Judge Chamberlin to rule on the question. Aldrich did not want to delay the trial now to seek a ruling from Chamberlin. Streeter did agree to the suggestion made the previous week concerning the visit of the two alienists to examine Eddy, but Chandler again protested the masters' decision that only one counsel for each side would attend the examination and that the next friends would also be excluded. Aldrich again reminded Chandler that this decision about an examination of Eddy was "a tentative sugges- tion to which [Chandler had] acceded promptly and meritoriously." Aldrich restated his position that the next friends did not have "any fundamental right to be present."[9]

Kelley then reverted to the discussion of Eddy's finances, request- ing a complete list of all her securities. Streeter again objected and stated that these were all in the hands of her counsel. He also said, "We preferred to put that in in our own case." Judge Aldrich inter- rupted to state that Kelley could call Eddy's trustees to the stand for that information and did not have to seek it from Streeter. Kelley then called Henry M. Baker as a witness, but when Streeter objected to the first question asked of Baker—about Eddy's securities—Kelley immediately excused Baker from the stand. Streeter then tried to cross-examine Baker, asking him questions about his past relation- ship with Eddy. Kelley objected that Streeter did not have the right to cross-examine Baker, as Judge Aldrich had only allowed Baker to be a witness to answer one question about Eddy's securities. Aldrich agreed that Streeter should not cross-examine Baker "under the circumstances." Aldrich was clearly getting frustrated by the constant arguing among counsel: "It would surprise a good many people to see how much of this record . . . is discussion, and how little relates to proof." Streeter responded that the plaintiffs should "put in some testimony, . . . if they have got any." Aldrich admonished Streeter: "I hardly think that remark is called for."[10]

Aldrich reminded the plaintiffs, "Eddy's business holdings are of no consequence; we are not conducting a hearing with reference to them." Kelley stated that the list of securities laid "the foundation" for the plaintiff's claim that Eddy was incompetent. Aldrich replied, "You should lay the foundation first." Aldrich continued, "There are a thousand reasons why the Courts should not pry into people's business unless it is necessary to help out on some controversy." Kelley then proceeded to read into evidence the entire correspondence between Mary Baker Eddy and George Glover relating to his visit to Eddy in January and her attempts to retrieve all of her letters written to her son. Aldrich questioned "how this connect[ed] itself with the business side of the situation," to which Chandler responded, "It all connects itself with the business situation on the theory of explaining what Malicious Animal Magnetism was and is in Mrs. Eddy's mind." Chandler asserted, "[M.A.M.] is a part of Mrs. Eddy's whole life, and we have shown that she believes that it has taken possession of her, will take possession of her son, George Glover, and lead him to break her will." Chandler continued to try to push the idea of Eddy's insanity as evident in her belief in M. A. M., and he now used information acquired by Hopkins from his interview with Vincent Tomlinson about his sister's apparent rejection of Eddy because of her attempt to harm her next friends by mental means. Chandler stated, "If a mental practitioner is trying to put poison into the veins of a person whose life he wants to take, the Science worker endeavoring to protect that person undertakes to put poison into the veins of the mental practitioner and destroy him." According to Chandler, Eddy's writings were full of this idea, from her first edition of *Science and Health* in 1875 to 1907. To Chandler, the idea was "grotesque," it was a delusion, it was insanity, and it was "destructive of the rational sentiments of any human being." Again, Aldrich ruled much of this evidence out, stating, "So far as it tends to safe-guard souls we think it is sacred enough not to be gone into, but so far as her Science tends to establish or dis-establish the case as to property and business management it can be gone into."[11]

Chandler continued to struggle against the masters' ruling regarding evidence prior to 1890. To establish "delusion," he needed to go back to Eddy's writings to prove that it impacted every decision of her life and made her incapable of conducting business. To Chandler, Eddy's belief in M. A. M. made her believe that her son, George, was stopping "the publication of her books" and that M.A.M. "drove Dr. Foster Eddy out of her household." But the masters' ruling would make it impossible for the court to "decide this question unless" the judge gave the plaintiffs "the privilege of showing what the damned thing is." Chandler tried to introduce one undated letter, claiming it was written in 1890, but Streeter objected that it was written earlier than that. Since the letter belonged to Dr. Foster Eddy, Chandler called him to the stand to testify that the letter was written in 1890. Judge Aldrich agreed, based on Foster Eddy's testimony, to allow the letter to be read into evidence. In the letter Eddy instructed her students about "Poison," saying that it could be employed by mesmerists mentally to kill people. If, when healers treated patients, "symptoms puzzle[d]" the healers and they had "tried the ordinary arguments . . . and the power of Spirit to heal them but without success," Eddy gave this advice: "Then treat your patient against the effects of this malicious argument, knowing as you ought . . . that God made all and it was good hence there is no poison and your patient does not suffer from it and is not poisoned." At this point, Judge Aldrich adjourned the hearing until 2:30 p.m.[12]

During the recess, Kelley and Chandler met in an anteroom with

Streeter and Edwin Eastman; then Eastman and Chandler met with the
masters in their room at the courthouse. Eastman's involvement was
probably an attempt to intervene between the hostile personalities of
Streeter and Chandler, to promote some kind of understanding about
dismissing the case. It apparently worked, as the meeting with the
masters during the recess was undoubtedly to inform them of the decision to dismiss. When court resumed after 3:00 p.m., Chandler stated
that his side needed time to arrange for the visit of the alienists and
to look into the books and papers of Joseph Armstrong, which were
now in possession of the masters. Chandler asked for an adjournment.
Aldrich agreed, with the hearing to resume at 9:30 a.m. on Wednesday,
August 21. Chandler returned that evening to Waterloo with Foster
Eddy and Peabody.[13]

The negotiations between the two sides were noticed by the reporters in Concord who were covering the case. The Monday-evening
meeting between Streeter and Hollis on the one side and Chandler,
Kelley, and Howe on the other were widely reported. There was also
speculation that the suit in equity would end without any compromise,
as Eddy's lawyers had "all along declared they would not compromise
the case." The Boston Globe reported, "It is believed they stand firmly
on that proposition now."[14] Therefore, the dismissal came as no surprise when court resumed on Wednesday, August 21. Judge Aldrich
had been informed in advance of the decision to end the suit, thus his
unusual opening query: "What's next, gentlemen?" Chandler began,
"May it please the Court, it will doubtless be a relief to the Masters
to be informed that the counsel for the 'next friends' have this day
filed with the Clerk of the Court a motion for the dismissal of the
pending suit and that they hereby withdraw their appearance before
the Masters without asking from them any finding upon the question
submitted to them by Judge Chamberlin." Chandler cited the reasons
for the decision: "[the] unprofitableness of any immediate result of a
decision in our favor . . . compared with the burdens and disadvantages
to be endured by us." Restating that the suit was "wholly altruistic

in its nature," Chandler recognized that "not a single dollar" from Eddy's large fortune could "become at this time the property of the 'next friends.'"[15]

Streeter then offered the following motion: "That the masters proceed with the hearing, to determine the question submitted, namely, Mrs. Eddy's competency to manage her business affairs March 1, 1907." Streeter spoke passionately in support of his motion. He reminded the court that Eddy had begun to arrange her affairs on February 12, including making "liberal provision for her kindred." Even before this suit had been brought, "she was dealing with those questions with sagacity, so far as her business matters were concerned, and as a noble, Christian woman, so far as her next of kin were concerned." According to Streeter, the next friends had begun "this wretched assault upon the person, property, and religious faith of a good citizen of New Hampshire." He continued, "When the charges have utterly collapsed, they run to cover." The masters had the right to dismiss the case, but Streeter was speaking to Eddy's legal rights. Streeter reminded the court that Eddy was an honored citizen of the state, "founder and head of a great religious organization," who had been "living peacefully in her home, surrounded by faithful friends of her own choice" when "a great newspaper" brought this suit, which was "primarily an attack upon the religious teachings of a great religious leader." The newspaper hired and paid an eminent counsel, and "a son and an adopted son inconsiderately loaned the use of their names as 'next friends.'" They brought a suit in her name against ten "honest men," claiming that she was incompetent and that the defendants had "wrongfully appropriated her funds." Streeter asserted, "The suit was based on false pretenses." In Streeter's view, this was a unique situation, in which Eddy was not a defendant, but, in fact, the proceedings were "being directed solely against her."[16]

Streeter continued, saying that Eddy filed petitions stating that her property interests were now fully protected by a deed of trust and that the proceedings were not "brought in good faith for her personal benefit" by the next friends." He stated, "So-called 'next friends,' her

assailants, bitterly opposed her petitions and they were denied." Eddy
then cooperated fully with the investigation into her competence by
the masters: "Nothing that your Honors thought would aid in the
ascertainment of the truth has been objected to by her or her counsel." After five days of trial, not "one word of testimony [had] been
introduced," and the "charge that she is incompetent [had] utterly
collapsed." Streeter referred to an observation made in "a Boston
newspaper published this morning," saying, "They [the next friends]
cannot succeed in demonstrating Mrs. Eddy's incompetency while she
is living, but (I quote) 'it is now proposed to await Mrs. Eddy's death'
. . . when she can no longer speak to contest her last will and testa-
ment." All the evidence of her "alleged delusions" that the plaintiffs
succeeded in entering into the record of the hearing might "be useful
in subsequent litigation," so the plaintiffs withdrew prior "to a finding
. . . that Mrs. Eddy [was] competent." Therefore, Streeter submitted
that Mary Baker Eddy had "a legal right to a finding of her competency." Streeter continued, "Any other result will bring reproach, in
the eyes of the world, upon the administration of justice here."[17]

Judge Aldrich defended the masters, stating that from the first
they had determined that it "was purely a property issue." They had
excluded "so far as possible all considerations in respect to religious
doctrines or religious faith." He noted that because the next friends
had "withdrawn from this hearing . . . there [was] nothing left to be
answered by Mrs. Eddy or decided" by the court. The masters should
not go "forward *ex parte*" to determine "the mental status of Mrs.
Eddy on the first of March." All that the masters should do was "report
to the Court what has been done, that is, report the evidence under the
commission." It would be up to Judge Chamberlin to accept the dismissal of the suit or "to direct that the trial proceed." Streeter excepted
to the decision of the masters, and the hearing was concluded.[18]

The *New York World* continued to deny the obvious in its report of
the dismissal. Claiming that "new evidence of great importance" had
been discovered by Chandler, the *World* asserted that the plaintiffs'
dismissal of the suit was only part of "a new plan of attack widely

different from the present." The *World* reported, "Students of the remarkable case predict that armed with the evidence already crystalized in legal records the 'Next Friends' are in position to execute a flank movement." Most of the press saw the result differently. The *Concord Patriot* was more accurate in its conclusion that the plaintiffs had been "beaten at every turn." In its editorial, the *Patriot* stated, "Mrs. Eddy is a greater woman today than when that suit was commenced. Her high sense of equity and justice and her clear vision of duty are more firmly and thoroughly established." The *Patriot* had long criticized the next friends and repeated its charge that the suit had been brought "to bolster the false utterances of a set of perjured reporters that the *New York World* sent to [Concord]" in order "to heap contumely upon a number of men associated with Mrs. Eddy," "to give a black eye to Christian Science," and "to secure" a share of her estate "by wrongful methods." An editorial in the *Boston Journal* stated that if the case had been brought by a New York newspaper "for the purpose of causing dissension and disaster to the Christian Science body, the outcome [was] certainly far from the original intent." The editorial continued, "The cult has been strengthened, solidified, extended by it [the case]." In fact, Eddy had gone through her examination by the masters with "flying colors." The *Journal* was insightful in questioning the format of the hearing before the masters: "The loose organization of the masters themselves and their own lack of positiveness as to what their powers were counted heavily against the efforts of Mr. Chandler and his associates to proceed along strictly legal lines."[19]

Alerted to the imminent dismissal of the suit, Alfred Farlow was prepared with a statement on behalf of Christian Science.

> For months glaring charges concerning the condition of Mrs. Eddy and the conduct of her near supporters have been blazoned forth to the public and counsel for the next friends have given out the impression that startling disclosures were to be made; that they would be able to prove that Mrs. Eddy is in a helpless state and in the hands of designing men who were not given proper

account of her income. After months of noisy boasting it now turns out that the so-called next friends and their counsel are not able to produce a scintilla of evidence in favor of their allegations, but that they have made their charges without the slightest provocation, that they never have had the slightest evidence but have manufactured their charges out of whole cloth.

Farlow concluded that the motive of the plaintiffs in bringing about "this gigantic farce" was simply "to annoy and discredit Mrs. Eddy and stigmatize the religion of which she [was] the Founder." Farlow went on at length to praise Eddy's "thoroughly competent but exceedingly alert" performance before the masters. Farlow also praised Eddy's counsel: "Great credit is due them for the calm, considerate, indulgent and judicial manner in which they conducted their case." He went on to quote at length from Dr. Allen McLane Hamilton's report of his visit with Eddy.[20]

While it would be up to Judge Chamberlin to officially accept the plaintiffs' motion for dismissal, in the public's view the case was over. Concord mayor Charles Corning viewed the dismissal as a "checkmate" of the next friends, with Chandler "& his hungry gang" crying "enough." But Corning predicted, "There will be a tremendous fight when death overtakes the old lady and her property comes within the jurisdiction of the Probate Court." According to Corning, "The 'Nexters' as Mrs. Eddy calls them may have come into possession of ampler material after death than they possess at the present time." Whatever was to happen in the future, the immediate result of the dismissal of the case was relief on all sides. Chandler reported in his diary on August 22 that he had had a "good nights sleep." Mayor Corning wrote that same day, "Mrs. Eddy rode past as usual but on this occasion she leant out of the carriage window and bowed most courteously."[21]

= 11 =

NEXT FRIENDS AWAIT EVENTS

To the press and public, the pending dismissal of the case of *Eddy v. Frye* ended legal proceedings. Even Mary Baker Eddy's closest associates, including her confidant, trustee, and close relative Henry M. Baker, expressed confidence that the church leader would be able to live out her life without the threat of legal action: "The suit brought by the alleged 'next friends' never had any justification in law or in fact, and the 'next friends' and their counsel are entitled to congratulations that they are out of a disgraceful situation." Among the counsel for the next friends, only Frederick Peabody expressed disapproval of the outcome of the case: "I cannot personally, but feel deep regret that the hearing could not proceed to its conclusion." But even Peabody acknowledged that the next friends had nothing to gain by continuing the suit, as Eddy's property was safeguarded by the deed of trust and the plaintiffs could not afford to continue the hearing, which would likely "have run along three or four weeks more." He continued to declare Eddy's "alleged religion" to be "utterly nonsensical" and repeated his long-held opinion that "so-called Christian Science could not by judicial decree, have been shown to be the creation of a disordered mind." After a meeting on August 23, Chandler, Kelley, and Howe agreed to make "no public statement but await events."[1]

After several days of rest, however, William Chandler wrote to friends, explaining the decision to dismiss the case. To Chandler, bringing the case was the right decision, but because the court placed "absurd limitations" on his team, the plaintiffs' "best testimony" was "wholly excluded," and Chandler's team "could make no money out of it," counsel decided "to withdraw and wait." But Chandler had every intention of continuing to pursue Christian Science. In his view, Eddy was "an insane woman, full of delusions," and because of her "general insanity," she was likely to disinherit her children. When that question arose, he was ready to pounce with another lawsuit, to contest her will. Chandler even had an answer for the expert alienists, Drs. Hamilton and French, who had recently examined Eddy and pronounced her sane and in control of her life. As Chandler saw it, they had declared she had no delusions, but neither of them had attempted to examine "any one of the seven delusions which possessed her." In the meantime, Chandler wrestled with what he saw as his "duty to the public to expose the evil and criminality of Eddyism" and his duty to his clients, who were poor and had gained nothing monetarily from the withdrawal of the suit. Initially, Chandler had been hired by the *New York World* because of his contempt for Christian Science and Eddy, but to his credit, he had become emotionally attached to George Glover and his daughter Mary, both of whom he viewed as practically noble savages struggling without benefit of education, George having been abandoned by his mother and forced to fend for himself in a hostile environment. Chandler even grew fonder of the supercilious Dr. Foster Eddy, particularly after he provided much documentation and assistance in preparing the case.[2]

While they were in the East, Chandler had kept George Glover away from the press, but when the case was dismissed, he and Mary headed back to South Dakota by train on August 24. It was not easy controlling the vitriolic, outgoing, and unsophisticated Glover, as Henry Hopkins acknowledged in a letter to Chandler: "Am delighted to hear that you have no longer to cheer and quiet poor Mr. Glover—it was quite a task." But Chandler felt ongoing responsibility and was concerned what Glover might say to the press upon his arrival home. The day the Glovers left, Chandler penciled a series of instructions for George, based on questions the lawyer expected the press to ask: "What have you gained by the suit? Why did you give up the suit? What are you going to do next?" Upon the Glovers' arrival in South Dakota, Judge Granville Bennett revised the talking points prepared by Chandler, and to his credit, George Glover followed the script to the letter when interviewed in Deadwood on August 31. To the first question, he responded that the suit had revealed that Mary Baker Eddy was worth over a million dollars and that he was satisfied that her property was in the hands of trustees and not Calvin Frye. To the second question, Glover responded that the masters had not given the next friends a fair chance to present their evidence and that he was pro-hibited from being present for any examination of his mother. To the final question, Glover stated, "I shall await the future developments before deciding my next step in the case, and my only bitterness is that I was not permitted to talk freely with my own mother as I wished." In a personal letter to Chandler, Mary Glover expressed her thanks: "I can realize how hard and trying the past six months have been for you, and I do hope you will get some rest now." Dr. Hopkins was even more effusive in his praise of Chandler, stating that the Eddy case was "the most momentous occasion of [Hopkins's] life." Hopkins also told Chandler, "Your exceeding kindness made the task a pleasing and altogether agreeable work."[3]

Having won a nearly compete victory, Eddy took the high road in commenting about the next friends. On August 25, she granted an interview to W. T. MacIntyre of the *New York American*, in which she stated, "Persecution cannot last forever. There is always a reaction. But I hold no enmity. Those who have attempted to injure me have gained nothing." Aware of the departure of George Glover to the West, she expressed disappointment that her sons, Glover and Foster Eddy, had not come to see her. She still appeared confused by the suit, asking, "Why would they persecute me? All that I ask in the remaining years of my life is peace and quietude. Are not gray hairs sacred? Have

I injured anyone? Am I not to be left alone to pursue that mission in which I am the appointed agent of the Divine Being to spread truth and peace and happiness throughout the world?" She did not blame her sons but did blame "those who forced the actions" against her, and she credited "the eminent sense of fairness of the Hearst newspapers." Though it had already been attested to by recent visitors, reporters, and alienists, MacIntyre reiterated, "She is a woman in full possession of her faculties." Eddy's attorney, Frank Streeter, was not happy that she granted such a lengthy interview so soon after the end of the hearing. He offered her simple advice: "Attend to your ordinary affairs, eat according to your relish and sleep peacefully, with a sense of perfect security. Don't write either to or about your 'next friends' except upon the fullest consideration and after conferring with your counsel."[4]

Upon learning of the motion to dismiss the suit, Judge Bennett wrote Chandler, "What is to become of the Trust Deed executed for the benefit of Mr. G. and his family?" The $125,000 trust fund that George had previously rejected because of the egregious conditions imposed by the trustees regarding the dispersal of the money and the education of his younger sons would become a major source of contention between Chandler and Streeter. Chandler soon prepared a bill, *Glover et al. v. Streeter et al.*, which would guarantee that the money was set aside for Glover and was under the protection of the court; otherwise, Chandler would contest Eddy's competence to have made the trust deed on February 25. In the meantime, he hoped to open negotiations with Streeter to increase the money Glover would receive in advance of Eddy's death, and was determined to include Foster Eddy in any final settlement. Chandler called Foster Eddy "one of the most amiable and best of men," who had expressed a willingness to step aside if it was best for George Glover, "although it might leave [Foster Eddy] out in the cold to make the fight against the will alone."[5]

Despite the failure of the case of *Eddy v. Frye*, Chandler remained consumed by Eddy and Christian Science. Throughout the fall, he tried to move forward on three fronts: on the renegotiation of the trust deed for George Glover and family, to relieve their financial plight;

on preparation of arguments and motions in response to the fifteen exceptions made by Chandler and company during the recent hearing before the masters and in response to Streeter's opposition to the motion to dismiss the case; and on formulation of a strategy to publicly attack Eddy and her Christian Science doctrine. He met frequently with Kelley and Howe, playfully referring to them as "young tyrants" and to himself as "the aged and meek senior counsel." In preparation for a final hearing before Judge Chamberlin, Chandler prepared two new motions, to contest any costs being "rendered against the Next Friends" and to seek an allowance for the expenses of the next friends because they had "probable cause for bringing the suit." Howe wrote back that he did not think the court would grant either motion.[6]

Chandler was somewhat duplicitous in his dealings with George Glover. The naïve Glover had joined the suit to free his mother from the control of Frye and company, whom Glover despised because they had effectively replaced him in his mother's affections or, at least, replaced him by providing for her daily needs. He also was highly motivated by his need for money and fear that he would be left out of her will. But Glover never opposed his mother's doctrine, and he did profess himself to be a Christian Scientist, if an unsophisticated one. Chandler, in turn, never criticized Eddy's teaching in Glover's presence, yet one wonders what Glover, who was experienced in legal action and was present throughout, understood of the hearing before the masters, which had presented evidence of Eddy's delusions and claimed that her religious teachings were proof of her insanity. At least in correspondence between them, Chandler never alluded to his pursuit of a public crusade against Christian Science. But with Glover in South Dakota, Chandler was free to pursue his opposition to Eddyism. He was in constant communication with Henry Hopkins, John W. Slaght, and Frederick Peabody and was trying to elicit some kind of "movement of doctors and religionists against Mrs. Eddy's healers and fakirs." To Slaght he professed, "I have a duty to perform beyond any legal duty I owe my clients," and Chandler asked Slaght to convince "Mr. McClure and his associates, Mr. Pulitzer and his associates" to join Dr. Hopkins, who was "eager to do his share." Chandler, at least, seemed to accept the fact that Christian Science could not be discredited by a judicial decision. This fact was not so clear to alienist Hopkins, who criticized Judge Aldrich for "his fool theory that one should not be called insane when this insanity has a religious phase."[7]

Chandler believed he had additional evidence not brought out during the recent hearing, but he would need to bide his time before finding an opportunity to present it. Dr. Hopkins's interview with Vincent Tomlinson revealed that his sister Mary's suicide was brought on by her disillusionment with Eddy, who had asked her to put the next friends to death by mental treatment. Hopkins proposed investigating this claim further, and Chandler asked Slaght and Peabody to look into it. Foster Eddy had been on the stand only briefly as the hearing ended, but he owned a diary of his time with Mary Baker Eddy that had not been introduced into evidence. Chandler stated, "The other side do not sufficiently understand Dr. Foster's strength against them. His writings are very strong to show her delusions. His oral testimony would be overwhelming." Hopkins expressed a concern: "What a fix we would be in should the M.A.M.'s kill him [Foster Eddy] some dark night." Hopkins asked Chandler if Foster Eddy's statement could be put "into such shape—that it could be used as evidence in the event of his death." When Dr. Foster Eddy received a letter from his mother—a letter addressed to "My Dear Benny" asking him to visit her at Pleasant View "for a chat with [him] after the old way"— Chandler advised him to stay away: "If they could get you to visit Mrs. Eddy with two or three listeners in hiding you would be done for and if afterwards you moved [against her will] you would be hooted at." Chandler may not have feared for Foster Eddy's life as Hopkins did, but the lawyer acknowledged to Slaght the "retaliatory" nature of Eddy's forgiveness: "She forgives her enemies; would even put them to death by mental argument and treatment so they may go to Heaven and happiness quickly."[8]

Since the close of the hearing with the masters, both sides had been preparing for a final hearing before Judge Robert Chamberlin.

Many matters had been left unsettled. Chandler, Kelley, and Howe had some fifteen exceptions to the rulings of the masters, particularly the decision not to go back before 1890 in presenting evidence in the case, which they intended to protest. Chandler also prepared a detailed statement of his reasons for seeking a dismissal of the case, to contest the expected argument of Streeter that Eddy was entitled to a determination from the court as to her competency. Streeter's impassioned plea that Eddy had a right to a decision about her competence had closed the hearing before the masters, and Chandler fully expected this to be the main issue to be resolved by Judge Chamberlin. But Eddy had changed her mind about insisting on this and instructed Streeter to simply end the case. Streeter agreed, and with the main issue off the table, he predicted, "I now confidently expect that this case will go off the docket, by order of Judge Chamberlin, on Monday next." Of course, Streeter did not inform Chandler of this in advance, letting Chandler work feverishly to prepare to defend his motion to dismiss. Therefore, when the hearing before Judge Chamberlin took place on September 30, Chandler opened with a statement explaining the reasons for dismissal and opposing Streeter's motion to have the case sent back to the masters for a decision. Chamberlin asked Streeter, "You now oppose this motion to dismiss?" To which Streeter responded, "No, Your Honor, and we have no motion to have this case sent back to the Masters. My friend is mistaken about that. The case here stands on his motion to dismiss, and we do not oppose it; it is assented to."[9]

Chandler, taken by surprise at Streeter's assent, rambled on that he "would have saved all the trouble" he had "put to in preparing to argue the question" if he had known Streeter would agree to dismiss the case. Judge Chamberlin then moved to the question of court costs, with Chandler offering that "no costs should be allowed against the 'next friends'"; instead, costs should be paid out of "the million dollar fund which the trustees gathered in so expeditiously on the 5th of March." He also asked that the "expenses" of the next friends be paid from Eddy's trust fund. Chandler cited several cases demonstrating that unlike "a suit at law," in which the court costs invariably follow

the decision in the case, "an equity suit" allows the judge the discretion to assign costs, and in some cases no costs are awarded to either
side. Streeter agreed about the judge's ability to assign costs, saying,
"That statute vests in Your Honor absolute discretion with reference
to costs." But Streeter objected to "any order made on Mrs. Eddy for
the payment of those fees." He did not close the door on the possibility
that the trustees of Eddy's estate might pay the court costs, but only
"by an order of the court for the protection of the trustees," and only
the court costs would be paid, not the expenses of the next friends.
The process was moving too fast for Chandler, who was prepared to
argue against continuing the case but was not adequately prepared to
argue about costs and expenses. He asked for more time, and Judge
Chamberlin granted until October 10 for Chandler to file a brief on
the question of costs. Chamberlin then closed the hearing.[10]

Immediately upon learning of the final dismissal of the case of *Eddy
v. Frye*, Mary Baker Eddy attempted a reconciliation with William E.
Chandler. Her motive was a combination of Christian forgiveness
and a preemptive strike to win over Chandler and prevent any future
litigation. She wrote a note to be published in the local Concord newspapers: "Hon. William E. Chandler should be lauded for squelching
a suit at law which he has proved to be illegal. Christian Scientists the
world over, unite with me in thanking him therefor. St. Paul declares:
'Love worketh no ill to his neighbor: therefore Love is the fulfilling
of the Law.'" In the note, she also intended to invite Chandler to visit
her at Pleasant View, but first she asked the advice of her attorney,
Frank Streeter. He advised her strongly against publishing the note
and inviting Chandler to meet her. In his response to Eddy, Streeter
correctly judged Chandler and his motives.

> I think I thoroughly know W. E. Chandler. . . . The objection
> to your plan is that he strongly disbelieves in you and in your
> system of healing and in your religion. He has convinced himself
> that the claims of yourself and your followers with reference to
> healing the sick, are arrant humbuggery. . . . The differences

between you and Chandler are fundamental. His only purpose
in going to your house would be to get some advantage over
you. He would not meet you with the same spirit with which you
would receive him. I advise you not to invite him.

Streeter did offer Eddy hope that she might someday reconcile
with her son George: "I still have hopes that he and Mary may see
that they have been wrong and ask leave to go and tell you so. I should
encourage that meeting but not the other." Streeter concluded with
further advice as to how Eddy should conduct herself in the future:
"Let me add that your policy of dignified silence with reference to
these enemies of yourself has commended itself to strong men who
have talked with me and who have not the pleasure of knowing you
personally." Eddy had learned to value Streeter's advice, as she
explained in a letter to Dr. Hamilton, saying that Streeter was "a far
superior lawyer to Mr. Chandler" and that she esteemed Streeter as
"nature's own nobleman."[11]

In November, Judge Chamberlin issued his final ruling with regard
to the costs of the case. He awarded $10,000 to the masters for their
fees but ordered that this amount be paid by the trustees of Eddy's
estate. Chamberlin also ruled, "Judgment is ordered in favor of said
MARY BAKER G. EDDY against the said Next Friends, in the sum
of Three Thousand ($3,000)." By agreement with Streeter and Hollis,
this amount was waived, with Chandler agreeing to withdraw all
"depositions taken and filed in said suit." With these final decisions of
the superior court, the case of *Eddy v. Frye* came to an end.[12]

Because Chandler had been hoping to negotiate a settlement
that would provide for Glover's financial needs, he and Kelley were
delighted when Streeter began negotiating with them in earnest in late
October. Chandler had previously warned Glover that any settlement
would require him to waive his right to contest Eddy's will in the
future and would likely also require him to state that Mary Baker Eddy
was both competent to make the trust deed and that his participation in
the lawsuit had been a mistake. Chandler advised Glover not to agree

to this for less than $200,000, which was a $75,000 increase over the original trust deed. This amount would include cash for Glover to pay his debts, and money for him to pay his attorneys for the recent lawsuit. Armed with correspondence from Judge Aldrich stating, "How important I think it is that counsel, the trustees and the parties should adjust this matter among themselves," Chandler entered the negotiations on October 28. Chandler stated his negotiating positions to Judge Granville Bennett. Chandler would declare that the next friends were preparing for future litigation and that a public movement was being organized "by doctors, ministers and others to expose and to control by legislation the healers of disease who pretend to act as religionists in trying to effect their cures." If a settlement was reached, the next friends would not participate in this movement, but Chandler refused to say that he himself would "not enter into such a movement." He would ask for the $75,000 additional sum for Glover, and for a reasonable settlement for Foster Eddy, whom Streeter had previously excluded from any negotiation. If the negotiations failed, Chandler admitted he was "doubtful" about starting "another trial of her competency" now "during Mrs. Eddy's lifetime." But he did expect to be successful in the pending suit of *Glover v. Streeter* in proving that George Glover and Mary Glover could not "be held to have forfeited their rights under the February trust deed by opposing any disposition of her [Eddy's] property."[13]

Chandler reported to Bennett that the meeting with Streeter on October 28 "was much more promising than . . . expected." Streeter indicated, however, that he was negotiating without Eddy's knowledge and that only after agreeing on amounts would he "ascertain if *she* wished as *they* wished." In fact, Streeter advised Chandler that "they must approach her carefully and only when they knew exactly what could be done." In negotiating, Chandler's advantage was "that Mrs. Eddy [dreaded] to have the fights reopened during her lifetime and after her death," but Streeter's advantage was Glover's poverty and immediate need for money, which might cause Eddy's son "to be so anxious to hurry them to a conclusion that he will agree to the best offer in addition to the $125,000." Chandler need not have worried about Glover, however, as the obstreperous frontiersman urged his attorneys to "prepare [their] case for court as rapidly as possible," because Streeter was preparing "a trap" and could not be trusted. Chandler should have been more worried about Eddy, whose unpredictability would turn out to be the major stumbling block to any settlement.[14]

As the negotiations continued, a delicate and confidential matter arose. Streeter, probably reflecting something he had once heard from Eddy, questioned the paternity of Glover's oldest son, Edward Gershom Glover, called Gershom, who was born in March 1875, and even the paternity of oldest daughter Mary, born in October 1877. It was likely that Streeter expected some controversy from Eddy if a settlement was reached and Gershom and Mary were included in it. Judge Bennett responded to Chandler's query, saying that the question was "a very delicate one" which "would be embarrassing . . . to Mr. Glover." Bennett said, "[I have] no doubt but Gershom is the son of Mr. Glover, but whether he is Mrs. Glover's son I have sometimes questioned in my own mind. I have never entertained a suspicion of Mary's legitimacy." Nevertheless, the laws of South Dakota were clear on the matter: "A child born before wedlock becomes legitimate by the subsequent marriage of its parents." Further, the law stated that if "the father of an illegitimate child" fully acknowledged the child, that child was "thereupon deemed for *all purposes* legitimate from the time of its birth." Thus the law would prevent the exclusion of Gershom and Mary from any final settlement, but this did not take into consideration Eddy's feelings on the matter. Bennett advised Chandler to be careful of Glover, however, because he was "stubborn and somewhat unreasonable" and had expressed to the judge that he would never agree to a trust deed containing the provisions regarding Irving Tomlinson's direction of the education of young George Glover. Bennett also advised Chandler not to allow much cash to go immediately to Glover.

> He would proceed at once to blow it into some chimerical mining scheme under the inspiration of his forked stick—called by

him a mineral attraction, with which he has never yet found a
mine, and at the end of a year or two he would have no money,
and in all probability no mine. I have frankly told him that in
this contemplated settlement, I would not aid him in getting one
dollar to put into mining ground.[15]

In the midst of the negotiations, newspapers in the East reported
an assassination attempt on George Glover. On the morning of
November 24, according to the reports, "An infernal machine, loaded
with slugs and dynamite, was found . . . near the home of George W.
Glover." Glover reportedly found a wire across the path from his
home, followed the wire "to a cylindrical object, and on examination
found a percussion cap and a can filled with slugs and dynamite."
According to the papers, had Glover simply kicked the wire off the
path, an explosion would have followed. The chief of police had "in
his charge the explosive, and . . . a quiet investigation [was] being
made." Interestingly, Glover denied finding "a wire or bomb" and had
"simply kicked a piece of wire off his walk." Chandler asked Bennett
for details, but the judge wrote that "this [was] the first" he "had heard
of the 'bomb' story," because it had not appeared in local newspapers. Bennett concluded that Glover was a strong believer in M.A.M.
and expected the "Concord cabal" to try to destroy him with "these
occult influences," but he had said nothing to the Bennett about any
bomb. Granville wrote, "He is an ignorant man, consequently super-
stitious and suspicious. He may have found an old oyster can in his
door yard and jumpped at the conclusion that some one was trying to
dynamite him." Judge Bennett promised to look into the matter, but
nothing more about it appears in his correspondence with Chandler.
In fact, newspaper reports of the attempted bombing mention friends
of Glover as the source, not Glover himself.[16]

Willa Cather contacted Chandler again at the end of November,
requesting permission to read Dr. Foster Eddy's diary, which she
had learned was in Chandler's possession, for use in her exposé of
Eddyism in *McClure's*. She requested that Chandler turn the diary over

to Peabody so that she could read it, but because of the ongoing negotiations with Streeter, Chandler refused to allow her to see the diary
at this time. Glover continued to give Chandler headaches, constantly
writing with suggestions and questions relating to future litigation. In
one instance, Glover obtained a pamphlet written by R. D. Kathryns,
which claimed that the next friends suit had ended because of an undisclosed secret financial settlement. George W. Baker had been quite
exercised by Kathryns's contention, but Chandler had already "convinced him of the contrary and he was content." Chandler tried to do
the same with Glover, relaying the fact that Kathryns had earlier contacted Slaght and claimed to have important information about Farlow.
On Slaght's recommendation, Chandler paid Kathryns's expenses to
travel from Kansas City to Boston to share what he knew. Chandler
stated, "He turned out to be a very wordy, rhetorical, plausible adven-
turer and as soon as I realized that he knew nothing I dismissed the
subject." Chandler told Glover that Kathryns also saw Farlow during his trip, presumably to blackmail Eddy's publicist, but Farlow
"treated him at last in the same way," and both Chandler and Farlow
concluded that Kathryns was only out "to make mischief." Chandler
tried to get Glover to calm down by stating that if negotiations with
Streeter failed, Chandler would undertake some kind of movement to
free Eddy from her captors: "Yet you know our great trouble is that
she and her jailors are rich and we are poor." He advised Glover "to
keep perfectly cool and calm on this whole subject": "You need not
be afraid that any of us will compromise you or Dr. Foster without
your and his consent."[17]

Negotiations with Streeter and Henry M. Baker, one of Eddy's
trustees, took on a serious note in early December, following a meeting in Washington, D.C. Streeter informed Chandler that Eddy had
accepted "the idea of an adjustment" but "wishe[d] it put through
immediately." Chandler informed Bennett and Glover of the progress
in the negotiations, stating to Glover, "It will be a smaller amount than
I would be willing to advise you to take if it were not for our entire lack
of funds with which to fight and to prepare to fight our opponents."

Streeter seemed to be offering to increase the trust fund to $140,000, with Glover receiving an additional $10,000 in cash to pay off his debts, but Chandler was pushing for a trust fund of $165,000 and at least $20,000 to Glover in cash. Streeter met with Eddy on December 9 and immediately telegrammed Chandler: "Have had conference and believe that if final conclusion not reached latter part of next week, further consideration of whole matter will be dismissed." In a follow-up letter to Chandler, Streeter reasserted that this deadline would "be adhered to." A question arose as to whether Glover's release or agreement with the settlement would also bar his children from contesting any will in the future. Streeter insisted, "The declarations of Mrs. Eddy's competency, which is the sole basis for making any arrangement with reference to the future, must be made by George and his daughter Mary, they both having been parties to the former litigation." This, according to Streeter, "would bind the minor grandchildren so far as practicable." It is important to remember that of Glover's four living children, George Washington Glover III and Andrew Jackson Glover were still teenagers, young George having been born in 1889 and Andrew in 1891. Chandler agreed with Streeter's legal research into the issue and promised that George and Mary were ready, once a settlement was reached, to come east immediately to reconcile with Eddy, presumably on Christmas Day. Kelley correctly assessed the sudden rush in negotiations: "The old lady is on another rampage, and in her imperious way has informed F.S. that if that thing is going to be settled it has got to be done now." Kelley continued, "You can quote me at any time as saying that I hope she can get on a rampage and refuse." Judge Bennett met with Glover and assured Chandler that George would agree to a trust fund of $165,000, with "twenty thousand to be paid in cash to Mr. Glover."[18]

To conclude the negotiations, Chandler traveled to Boston, staying at the Parker House and meeting at various times with Peabody, Kelley, and Foster Eddy, and with Frank Streeter, Henry M. Baker, and Archibald McLellan of Eddy's trustees. Chandler's diary records the hectic pace of negotiations over the next four days, back and forth, in rooms 360, 367, 501, and 236 of the hotel before a final breakdown took place late on Friday, December 20, when, Chandler recorded, "differences arose," and the meeting ended at 6:00 p.m. Over the weekend, however, a final draft was completed, but on December 23 Eddy rejected it, stating on the back of an envelope that "she would not sign it nor change the original trust deed." Chandler urged Streeter to go see Eddy in person, but "he said it would be of no use," at which point Kelley, with Streeter's approval, burned the two copies of the final draft. Chandler reported that he and Streeter then "separated pleasantly." Judge Bennett blamed the failure of the negotiations on Chandler's refusal "to accede to [the] demand that Mr. G. should sign a document admitting that Mrs. Eddy" was at the time "and at all times heretofore . . . of sound mind and competent to manage her own affairs and transact her own business." Recognizing that Glover was opposed to backing down on this issue, Bennett believed Chandler was wrong to end negotiations over it, as Glover should have had to "swallow his pride and spleen for his own sake and that of his family and creditors." Having been unable to prove her incompetence in court and having "incurred the deathless hate and enmity of the Christian Science cult," Glover was now relegated, Bennett concluded, to "a long, bitter legal battle, which he [might] not live to see concluded, after a hard and troubled life." Bennett might not have accurately understood the breakdown of negotiations, in that Eddy was as stubborn, if not more so, than her son George. In the end, it was her decision to refuse a final settlement at this time, and whatever amount was agreed to by the attorneys in December 1907 was far less than what Eddy would ultimately accept as a final settlement with her sons, George Glover and Ebenezer Foster Eddy.[19]

In the December 21 issue of the *Christian Science Sentinel,* Mary Baker Eddy announced her intention to found a Christian Science institution "for the special benefit of the poor and the general good of all mankind." She anticipated that the institution would be funded by an endowment of one million dollars. Her trustee Archibald McLellan wrote her, asking for details and pledging his "best effort in whatever way" he could "be of service in this grand undertaking." Alarmed at the prospect of Eddy looting her estate of a million dollars and thus leaving little left for George Glover and Foster Eddy to contest at her passing, Chandler protested to the trustees that Eddy's plan violated the terms of her trust deed, which clearly stated in clause three that the only money that trustees could pay out of the fund was for Eddy's personal expenses and for the upkeep of Pleasant View. Chandler reminded the trustees that Eddy's "*capacity* to transact business [had] not been affirmatively judicially determined" and that they could not dispense money from her estate for a "purpose foreign to the provisions of said trust deed, without first obtaining the consent of her sons, George W. Glover and E. J. Foster Eddy, the presumptive heirs at law of Mrs. Eddy." Kelley reminded Chandler that clause two of the trust deed did permit Eddy's money to go to "charitable purposes," but Kelley also stated that he had "no fear" that Eddy would "contribute any money to this proposition," as the money to establish the institution would likely come from the "faithful." But he also feared that the trustees "could loot this fund in a day if they thought it advantageous."[20]

Since nothing came of this effort to establish a Christian Science institution, one wonders in retrospect at Eddy's real intention. Her statement to the *Christian Science Sentinel* came at the height of negotiations between her attorneys and the next friends over a possible settlement. Having won a nearly complete victory in court and yet finding herself still being held up by her sons for money, being still under the threat of a contest over her will after her death, she may have been reacting from personal pique or even spite: by removing a million dollars from her estate, she would leave nothing for Glover and Foster Eddy to fight over. Normally, Eddy took her time in contemplating decisions regarding Christian Science and her money; once convinced of the direction she wanted to take, she then demanded quick and sudden compliance from all around her. Her statement of intent to found a charitable Christian Science institution seems to be at odds with her usual method of decision making, and one is left to speculate that she was reacting emotionally to the pressures imposed by her attorneys and by the next friends to settle with them when she saw no justification in doing so.

Kelley's letter to Chandler contained other information, which they failed to interpret accurately. A reporter for the *Boston American* informed Kelley that he, the reporter, had been rejected in his attempt to interview Eddy at Pleasant View, being told by Henry M. Baker, "Things are in such a condition up there now that she can not see anybody." When pressed to explain, Baker responded that the next friends case had caused Eddy to fall behind in her work and correspondence, and she was "so occupied" that she was unable to see the reporter. This reporter informed Kelley, "There was a mix-up up there . . . some sort of disturbance." Kelley flattered himself and the attorneys for the next friends by interpreting the anxiety at Pleasant View to be caused by Eddy and her staff's fear of further litigation, and said that the reporter, a Mr. Jackson, confirmed that Pleasant View "deplored it and said that this persecution ought to stop." Kelley reported, "They [members of Eddy's staff] told Jackson that the newspapers ought to say that the public would have no patience with any further persecution." Jackson asked Kelley if any new lawsuit was contemplated, to which Kelley confirmed that the Chandler team had "one on the docket," the case of *Glover v. Streeter*, which once again raised the issue of Mary Baker Eddy's competency. According to Kelley, Jackson "noticed, evidently, an air of some excitement in the people surrounding Mrs. Eddy, because he used the words 'bustle,' and 'confusion' and 'a feeling in the air.'" Kelley was suspicious enough to recommend getting "some young friend . . . to spend a day or two keeping track of who [went] in or out of there" and to "pay him for it." The reporter had accidentally stumbled upon something important happening at Pleasant View, but as 1907 drew to a close, no one correctly guessed at the surprise Eddy had in store for the new year. As Chandler closed his diary for 1907, he wrote at the end of the entry for December 31, "This has been an Eddy—Glover year."[21]

On Sunday, January 26, 1908, Mary Baker Eddy unexpectedly left

Pleasant View and Concord, New Hampshire, never to return. While
the move to a mansion in Chestnut Hill, outside of Boston, had been
in the works for months, it had been kept entirely secret from the outside world; only the residents of Pleasant View and church officials in
Boston knew of the pending change. At 8:00 a.m. Sunday morning,
five hacks were ordered to Pleasant View and arrived shortly after
noon. At that time, nearly a score of Eddy's attendants left the residence and entered the hacks, which were lined up on Pleasant Street.
Immediately after they departed, Eddy's carriage emerged, as if she
was going out on her daily drive. The five hacks drove down Pleasant
Street to the train depot, as Eddy's carriage detoured through town. At
the depot a special train with three cars was waiting on the west track
under the train shed. As soon as her attendants had boarded one of the
cars, Eddy's carriage arrived, and she was assisted into a different car
by her loyal attendant John Salchow, with Tomlinson, McLellan, and
Frye watching. At precisely 2:00 p.m., the special train left the station
with Mary Baker Eddy waving to the railroad employees, who were
the only citizens of Concord present to see her off. Eddy's train was
preceded by a pilot engine and protected from the rear by another
engine. A circuitous route over the tracks of three railroad systems
made it possible for Eddy to avoid having to change trains in downtown Boston, and the party was deposited at the Chestnut Hill station,
where it was but a short carriage drive to her new home, the former
Lawrence mansion on Beacon Street, which was reached at 5:20 p.m.
The press had been alerted, however, and were waiting when her carriage arrived. Unwilling to run the gauntlet of reporters and photographers, Eddy asked her husky man-of-all-work, John Salchow, "Can
you get me into the house?" He picked her up bodily and carried her
past the reporters and photographers into the house, depositing her
in an armchair as Eddy roared with laughter.[22]

The move had gone as planned, but the reasons for the change
prompted much discussion. Alfred Farlow explained it as a decision that had been contemplated for several years as a result of
Eddy's purpose "to be more convenient to the Mother Church of the

denomination, nearer to its headquarters." There is no doubt that it was increasingly inconvenient for church officials to come to Pleasant View from Boston each week and have to sleep on cots on the first floor. In fact, these same officials helped disguise the move in the weeks preceding, by carrying away a trunk following each visit to Eddy. But the next friends suit and the continuing threat of litigation also played a role. The "unhappy experience" had demonstrated to Eddy that she was not safe in Concord, that her attempt to live in solitude in the quiet New Hampshire capital had been a failure, as she was confronted by reporters and photographers camped outside her home each day as she left on her daily drive. And Pleasant View was only a few feet from a busy main street, whereas the eight-acre estate in Chestnut Hill was set further back from the road and was more easily secured. At Pleasant View, Eddy feared that her sons or her enemies, "might take her from her home and friends" by forcing their way in, this anxiety adding to her sense of insecurity and lack of privacy. Whatever the reasons for her departure from Pleasant View, Mayor Corning spoke for Concord in his official statement.

> During her long residence in this city Mrs. Eddy has contrib-
> uted largely of her means to improve and beautify Concord. Her
> interest in the welfare and attractiveness of the city has never
> waned and to her and her friends Concord is indebted for many
> things. Good streets have been built largely through her gener-
> ous contributions and influence. . . . The world may never know
> the extent of her benefactions. Moreover, the fact of her living
> in Concord has brought countless visitors to the city during her
> residence, which naturally stimulated local pride. The news that
> Mrs. Eddy has chosen another home comes with great surprise
> to our people and will carry with it widespread regret.

While Corning undoubtedly spoke for most people in Concord, William E. Chandler, learning of her move while at his home in Washington, D.C., was not so gracious.

Mrs. Eddy's conduct is very strange and must excite the appre-
hensions of her relatives and friends concerning her soundness
of mind. . . . She planned a reconciliation with her sons and then
suddenly broke it into pieces. She put her $1,000,000 of property
into the hands of trustees. . . . No sooner is this done than she
announces her purpose to give away the whole million while she
lives. Now she has left one prison-house for another. Is this the
decision of a sane person? Is she a free agent? Is she in the hands
of designing men who intend to hold her and seize all her property to their own uses, rather than any use of hers? Certainly
legal proceedings ought to be commenced to settle all of these
questions, but her sons are poor and it is doubtful whether they
can raise the money with which to prosecute immediately the
necessary legal inquiries.[23]

Mayor Corning was more forthcoming in his diary: "The supreme
surprise & sensation of the epoch in this city is the sudden & unan-
nounced departure of Mrs. Eddy for Newton, Mass where she will
hereafter make her home." The shock of her departure was intense:
"Nobody save the Pleasant View crowd had an inkling of this remarkable performance. To think that a woman 87 years old shd. change
her old home of 20 years for surroundings new amazed me. But she
has gone & Concord has sufficient reasons to regret the fact." As had
the attorneys for the next friends, Corning had missed the signs of
Eddy's move, writing later, "Mrs. E is passionately fond of flowers
among which tulips stood first and the great beds at Pleasant View
were most beautiful. Thousands were planted year after year but last
October the beds were covered with turf indicating the closing of the
custom." Corning summed up the personal and financial impact of
her departure.

Personally my regret is deep for the presence of the most distinguished woman in America gave Concord a prestige &
brought thousands here who went away with a friendly feeling

for our handsome Capital. Then again in a commercial point of view Mrs. Eddy & her visitors left many thousands every year. Dunklee says that this departure will make $1,000 difference in his livery stable receipts & the Eagle Hotel puts its loss far higher. Mrs. E. paid a city tax of nearly $4,600.[24]

= 12 =

A FAMILY SETTLEMENT

Mary Baker Eddy's departure from Concord was lamented by many people, including the members of the exclusive Wonolancet Club, of which Frank Streeter was a leading member. Conservatively, they estimated her financial impact on the city over the past twenty years at over $1.5 million. This included $1 million in contracts to local granite quarries to build Christian Science churches around the nation, and Eddy's own gift of $225,000 to the local Christian Science Church. Charitable donations, paved roads, and expenditures on Pleasant View made up the rest of the $1.5 million, and this figure did not include an estimate of the amount infused into the local economy from the many Christian Science visitors who came to Concord to see Eddy and spent money for taxi service, in local hotels, in restaurants, and so on. The money spent on train travel from Boston to Concord and back by church officials and visitors was also not calculated.[1]

William Chandler was more interested in trying to determine the reason for the failure of negotiations for the settlement between Eddy and her sons, George Glover and E. J. Foster Eddy. Chandler speculated that at the height of the negotiations, Streeter presented Eddy with a bill for legal fees, which amounted to around $90,000 (Chandler estimated $60,000 for Streeter and $25,000 for Eastman), and that the "crazy miser" balked at paying this amount along with the increase in Glover's trust to $165,000. To Frank Streeter, Chandler charged that either Eddy was insane or that she was not acting in good faith during the negotiations. Chandler believed that Eddy and Streeter were trying to "entrap" Glover by bringing him east to Boston, having Glover and Foster Eddy admit to Eddy's sanity as a condition of the settlement, and then "abruptly" terminating the conferences. Chandler complimented himself on advising Glover and his daughter Mary not to travel from South Dakota until a settlement was reached. Chandler threatened to make public all of the many meetings held about adjusting the Glover trust since the dismissal of the next friends suit. John Kelley went even farther, charging Streeter with perpetuating a "farce" and "a little comedy." Streeter responded that he had acted in good faith but had warned Chandler "not only orally but by letters and a telegram" that Eddy had set a deadline of mid-December for the completion of a settlement, and when that time passed "she declined to execute the draft submitted."[2]

Still considering how to resurrect the negotiated settlement, Chandler proposed the possibility that, in fact, a "family settlement was completed on December 21st and that the signatures were not necessary to make it valid" and binding on Eddy, assuming she was competent to do so. He asked Judge Granville Bennett if the next friends should bring a suit in equity on this basis, with the fallback position that if they failed, they would then contest her will. Bennett informed Chandler that George Glover was confined to bed following an injury caused by a kick from a horse and that he was also suffering from rheumatism and "la-grippe." In his weakened condition, Glover was discouraged and needed the settlement to be revived, but Bennett did not think Chandler's proposal was realistic, because no money or stock was ever deposited in the trust fund, and no attorney's fees were paid. Bennett concluded, "This was not a completed transaction—not a completed trust, and in my judgment a suit in equity for specific performance could not be maintained." Chandler was not content with Bennett's advice, however, and consulted the Washington, D.C., law firm of Taylor and Chambers. Hannis Taylor was a prominent legal scholar and expert in international law, former U.S. minister plenipotentiary to Spain, and special counsel to Chandler's Spanish Treaty Claims Commission. He offered an "affirmative reply" to Chandler's query, stating, "There [is] no provision in the New Hampshire statute of frauds which requires such an agreement to be in writing to establish its legal character and binding effect." Taylor and Chambers advised Chandler "that a suit should be brought by Mr. Glover . . . to have the terms of the agreement enforced," assuming again that Eddy "was competent to pray for a decree that the agreement was complete." Chandler chose not to proceed along these lines, however, writing to Bennett, "You and Mr. Glover have taken the responsibility of stopping the suggested proceeding." Chandler did insist on receiving full power of attorney from both Glover and Foster Eddy so that if any future negotiations occurred, the lawyer would be legally empowered to conclude the settlement before Eddy could change her mind. Not surprisingly, the suspicious Glover resisted signing over power of attorney to Chandler, but Judge Bennett convinced him to do it.[3]

In January 1908, the first book about the next friends case appeared and just as quickly disappeared. The story of Michael Meehan's book illustrates the fact that neither side in the original case believed that anything had been settled or that no future litigation would occur. Meehan was the editor of the *Concord Patriot*, the daily newspaper in competition with Chandler's own *Concord Monitor*, and had taken a decidedly anti-Chandler and pro-Eddy editorial position throughout the months leading up to the hearing. In January Meehan sent a copy of his book, *Mrs. Eddy and "Next Friends,"* to Mary Baker Eddy for her review. She was disappointed in the book, particularly the term "Next Friends" in the title, as she thought it a pejorative reflection on her sons, whom she did not want to further antagonize. According to Meehan, Eddy met with him at Pleasant View on January 11 or 12, 1908, and he agreed to withdraw the book and destroy all copies already in print if she would lend him $2,500 for this purpose, and he also stated his intention to revise the book and republish it to resolve

Eddy's objections. Meehan's recollection of a meeting with Eddy seems unlikely, however, as the date was only a week prior to her sudden departure for Chestnut Hill, and it seems doubtful that Meehan would not have observed something suspicious. DeWitt Howe wrote to Chandler to explain: "Meehan tells me his book has been suppressed because of 'harsh terms' applied to next friends and their counsel. 'She roared' when she saw the title, thought 'next friend' in it derogatory to her son. He is going to expurgate the objectionable matter and then publish the book." Meehan revised the text and republished the book in February under the title *Mrs. Eddy and the Late Suit in Equity,* stating in a letter to Eddy that the book was "all fixed up." In March, Eddy, still concerned about the book's impact, decided that while it was "historically accurate," it continued to place the next friends in a negative light. In fact, Meehan had previously asked Chandler to contribute to the book, but knowing Meehan's views about the case, Chandler refused to have anything to do with it, refusing to even contribute a photograph of himself or a brief biography. Eddy then asked the Christian Science Publishing Society to purchase the revised book from Meehan in order to destroy all copies. After several meetings with Meehan, the board of trustees informed Eddy that they had paid Meehan $8,832.05 for the book, and Meehan then repaid the loan with interest. All copies of the book, which was already in circulation, were repurchased, although the Chandlers—father William E. and son William D.— refused to return their copies, which eventually made their way to the New Hampshire Historical Society Library. For decades the book was nearly impossible to find, but the copyright having long expired, it can now be purchased on the Internet.[4]

Interestingly, both versions of Meehan's book were published by the Rumford Press, the local printing company once owned by Chandler and to which he still maintained a close association. In fact, Chandler considered writing his own book about the case. In the summer of 1908, he contacted Henry R. Hopkins, Frederick Peabody, John W. Slaght, reporter E. J. Park of the *Boston Globe,* and even Michael Meehan, asking them to each contribute a chapter to his work. Frank

Streeter got wind of this development and advised Meehan not to work with Chandler.[5] In the end, Chandler never completed his book, and Meehan's work remains the only contemporary and relatively accurate account of the next friends case to be published.

Having failed to negotiate a settlement for Glover, Chandler continued, like a mosquito in the ear, to annoy Christian Science officials. His next effort concerned taxes Eddy had paid or failed to pay to the city of Concord. Chandler wrote to city solicitor E. S. Cook, explaining that because the next friends suit had determined Eddy's worth and because nearly all of it was in "interest bearing taxable securities," Calvin Frye had made "undoubtedly false statements" when he declared she only had $35,000 in taxable income. Chandler concluded, "It is the duty of the city authorities to see that she pays what she ought to pay." Chandler imposed on his old friend and former Concord mayor Henry Robinson to bring further pressure on the Concord Board of Assessors by soliciting letters from Concord residents concerned about Eddy's taxes. The board did write to Streeter and Eddy's trustees, requesting "an account of the ratable estates and property in [their] hands as trustees" for the year beginning on April 1, 1907. In April 1908, they assessed Eddy with a tax bill of $11,000, which, while twice what she had been paying, was still less than Chandler believed she owed. To the disappointment of officials in Newtown, Massachusetts, where Chestnut Hill is located, Eddy never changed her legal residence from Concord, therefore disallowing Newtown from assessing and collecting on her taxable income each year.[6]

Demonstrating how much public opinion had changed in Eddy's favor, on April 24 New Hampshire Governor Charles M. Floyd presided over the annual Christian Science lecture, which took place in Manchester, New Hampshire. According to Floyd, "Christian Science has made New Hampshire known throughout the world and has done much to build up and maintain the morals of this and other states." In lamenting the loss of Mary Baker Eddy from New Hampshire, Governor Floyd quoted a hotel operator he met while traveling in the West: "I would rather deal with Christian Scientists than any others that come to my hotel." Floyd observed that Christian Scientists "build up the good in men and never tear down what is in them." Reading Floyd's remarks in the Boston press, Peabody could not help writing Chandler, "New Hampshire has a queer sort of a governor to lend himself to the C.S. outfit. If he didn't know anything about it, he was an ass to *say* what he did."[7]

From his home in South Dakota, George Glover continued to be obsessed with his mother's "imprisonment" by Frye and church officials. Glover repeatedly asked Chandler if something couldn't be done to assess Eddy's well-being. Chandler patiently replied, "There is no possibility that Mrs. Eddy will die without the fact being well ascertained." He also asserted that any movement on the part of the next friends would work against them in a future challenge of her will because a finding of her current well-being would reinforce the notion that she had been competent to make the will. Chandler noted, "If she were taken away there is no doubt we could destroy any will disinheriting you or Dr. Foster." Glover was temporarily quieted, until he received a startling letter from Robert C. Hannon. The Hannons had long been convinced that Augusta Stetson of the First Church of Christ, Scientist, of New York City, was plotting to succeed Eddy and had infiltrated Pleasant View with her staff, who were practicing malicious animal magnetism on the terrified founder of Christian Science. Chandler had visited the Hannons in East Windsor, Connecticut, the previous year and had accepted much of what they said and repeated it to the press. Now the fanciful Robert Hannon, who had not been associated with Stetson or Christian Science since around 1890, wrote Glover, "Mrs. Eddy is dead and burried. I am told that her body was taken to Concord to Pleasant View and burried in the cellar. If this is true, then it is the worst crime ever known in the History of man." Hannon went on to claim that Augusta Stetson had "made a gown of white Satin, with a very long train" covered with lace "to be worn at the *'Assention'* of Mrs. Eddy." Stetson and company would stage the "bogus *'Assention'* in order to deceive the people," and "seven young ladies" would hold Mrs. Stetson's train during the *"Assention,"* which they were all practicing daily in Stetson's "New York quarters." The ceremony would not take place until "quick lime" had destroyed "every vestage" of Eddy's body, at which time Stetson would "declair herself supream ruler of all the Christian Science affairs. . . [and] be in possession of all of Mrs. Eddy's affairs. She intends that you will never get one dollar of your mothers money but that she will get it *all*." Hannon concluded that Stetson was "a representative of *Hell*, the wife of the *Devil*," but since Hannon did not know when this extraordinary ceremony would take place, there might still be time for Glover to "take steps to see and know" if his mother was "dead or alive, and put a stop to the Stetson power."[8]

George Glover was sufficiently alarmed by Hannon's letter to send it on to Ebenezer Foster Eddy, with the instruction "to go and see mother at Boston in her new home" to "obtain the facts as quickly as possible." The usually level-headed Judge Bennett was also concerned and wrote Hannon, asking for more information, specifically "whether [Eddy was] living or dead, and if dead, when, where and the circumstances under which, she died." He admitted to Hannon, "I am strongly of the opinion that Mrs. Eddy is dead; that she died and was secretly buried, before that strange cartage wended its way from Concord to Brookline, or her body was then carried to the mansion to be laid in some private vault in that building." He admitted his concern to Chandler: "When I first read it I said to Mr. Glover that it impressed me strongly as being a 'Pipe dream' but the more I have considered it the more I have been led to the conclusion that it may be true, at least there is sufficient to justify further investigation."[9]

Cooler heads prevailed in the East, however. Foster Eddy sent Hannon's letter on to Chandler with a note: "The Hannons are serving up the Glovers and I think without real cause, and yet I have no better opinion of those people who have Mrs. Eddy in charge." Chandler tried to reassure Glover, writing, "There is nothing in it so far as it suggests that Mrs. Eddy may not now be living." Chandler had heard the ascension story before and concluded, "[It] is an extraordinary idea of theirs as I think are the notions of some others that an

ascension is to be prepared for Mrs. Eddy when she dies." To Foster
Eddy, Chandler was more direct: "Of course Hannon's notions are
crazy ones." Chandler did investigate by sending Kelley to Boston
to meet with E. J. Park, a reporter for the *Boston Globe*, who had met
Eddy previously. Park reported that "Mrs. Eddy was about the same
as last year—quite as vigorous in body and mind." Chandler then
wrote to Bennett that he had "thought it wise not to ridicule [Glover's]
notions but to investigate them" and asked Bennett to "satisfy the
doubts of the Glovers."[10]

The Hannons were correct about two things: Augusta Stetson's
power within the successful and affluent Christian Science church of
New York City and her expectation that she was the logical successor
to Mary Baker Eddy. But their continuing fantasies about Stetson's
infiltration and manipulation of church officials and the staff surrounding Eddy was pure fiction. The story of the relationship between Eddy
and Stetson is not a subject for this book, but it was a real concern
of Eddy's in the years immediately preceding her death. She spoke
out against the personalization and idolatry associated with her leadership of Christian Science and determined that there would be no
successor to her, but that only *Science and Health* and her manual of
bylaws would guide future generations of Christian Scientists. After
a twenty-five-year relationship with her "brilliant, volatile student,"
during which the church leader frequently and patiently tried to direct
and redirect Stetson, Eddy finally imposed the bylaws against Stetson's
"impious conduct." Stetson was called to Boston and examined by the
board of directors and expelled from the Mother Church. The final
trial occurred in November 1909, and there is no question that the
Stetson situation, along with the ongoing threat of litigation from the
next friends, dominated Eddy's final years.[11]

The outrageous treatment Eddy had received from the press, particularly the highly inaccurate and false claims in the *New York World*
and *McClure's Magazine* that launched the next friends case, "had
taught Mary Baker Eddy a peculiarly painful lesson about the press's
quest for sensationalism and disregard for truth." Believing herself

to be in a position to do something about it, and feeling empowered by God, on July 28, 1908, she sent the following note to her board of directors, "So soon as the Pub. House debt is paid I request the C.S. Board [of] Directors to start a daily newspaper called *Christian Science Monitor*. This must be done without fail." Eddy seemed to understand the power of the media; at least she had founded her own religious magazines, the *Christian Science Journal* and the *Christian Science Sentinel*, at important moments in the early history of her movement, to bring her teaching to the masses. The Christian Science Publishing Society had recently moved into a new, purposefully constructed building in Boston and had been flourishing for over twenty years professionally publishing and distributing her various publications. At the same time, however, Eddy had been somewhat naïve to think that she could live in relative seclusion in Concord, New Hampshire, and not attract the suspicious scrutiny of an unquenchable press determined to write sensational stories. As Christian Science grew and Eddy's fame increased, her withdrawal from public view only attracted an avaricious press, which came to understand that they could write anything, even that she was dead, and not face public ridicule because the subject of the story was not available, was working in seclusion, and spoke only through surrogates.[12]

Her directors understood the enormous task involved in starting a daily newspaper. The newly built Publishing Society building would need to be expanded, new presses purchased, a staff of reporters and columnists recruited and hired, and editorial and managerial responsibility reassigned among the staff of the society. The directors urged Eddy to reconsider or at least delay, but on August 8, 1908, she sent the following letter to the trustees of the Publishing Society: "It is my request that you start a daily newspaper at once, and call it the *Christian Science Monitor*. Let there be no delay. The Cause demands that it be issued now. You may consult with the Board of Directors, I have notified them of my intention."[13]

Archibald McLellan of the Publishing Society became the paper's editor. He promised Eddy that it would take about three months to get the paper up and running, and the first issue was printed on November 25, 1908. In the meantime, Eddy had taken a personal interest in many details, including paper and type, and inspected a sample issue. It was her insistence that the name remain the *Christian Science Monitor,* despite warnings that the name would insure the paper's failure. She stated, "God gave me this name and it remains." She also chose the motto for the editorial page: "First the blade, then the ear, then the full grain in the ear." The paper was to be free from sensationalism and constructive in emphasis, but it was intended to be a "real" newspaper covering the whole world and not simply a denominational or local publication. Eddy did insist on a religious article on Christian Science to appear each day on the Home Forum page, and she announced in an editorial in the first issue that the paper's purpose was "to injure no man, but to bless all mankind." Over the next hundred years, the paper would fulfill her ambition for it, each day taking an unbiased and truthful look at the nation and the world. Ironically, the *Christian Science Monitor* would win the Pulitzer Prize for journalism several times, a prize created by the Columbia University School of Journalism from the large bequest made by Joseph Pulitzer, the owner of the *New York World,* which had tried so hard to destroy Eddy and Christian Science. One also wonders at the coincidence of the name *Monitor* and the fact that the leading daily newspaper throughout Eddy's twenty years in Concord was the *Concord Monitor.* Eddy was known to be personally very fond of the paper's editor, George H. Moses, who had visited her many times and published her submissions regularly, though she certainly was not so fond of the paper's former owner, William E. Chandler. Always a risk taker, Eddy reportedly told her household staff, "When I established *The Christian Science Monitor,* I took the greatest step forward since I gave *Science and Health* to the world."[14]

Chandler had always stated his preference for contesting Eddy's will after she died. To him, if the will disinherited her sons, it was because she believed they were infected by M.A.M. and were out to hurt her, and this was clear evidence of her insanity and inability to make a will. He believed that this inability would be relatively easy to prove after she was dead and no longer able to speak for herself, and would result in the sons inheriting most of her estate—or that Eddy's attorneys would make a lucrative settlement to avoid a judgment against the estate. But Chandler also understood his responsibility to his clients, particularly George Glover, who was desperately poor and in need of immediate relief. Throughout the winter of 1909, Judge Bennett pushed for Chandler to do something to relieve Glover, stating, "I do not know how he and his family live. He has no visible means of support, is not able to do hard work, and has no income. He is greatly in debt." Bennett was continually holding off Glover's creditors "and preventing judgments being rendered against him." To Bennett, "it would [have been] better for him to accept the provisions of the Trust Deed," the $125,000 fund created back in February 1907, if Eddy had added "in cash enough to pay George's debts and attorneys fees, so he could [have started] clear." But Bennett knew George Glover would never touch that money so long as Irving Tomlinson remained one of the trustees and had control over the education of George's minor sons, George and Andrew.[15]

In Chandler's view, the major obstacle to a family settlement was Eddy's attorneys, Streeter and Eastman, who saw "a bitter will-contest and big fees, and [who could] see no money for them in a settlement." Chandler now learned that Streeter had been paid $50,000 and Eastman $12,000 for defending the next friends suit and anticipated a similar amount from a will contest. While Streeter was out of the country, Chandler approached Henry M. Baker, Eddy's cousin and trustee, in Washington, D.C., where they both lived. Chandler was convinced that Baker supported an immediate settlement, as did another trustee, Archibald McLellan. Chandler wrote to Judge Edgar Aldrich, asking him to see McLellan personally and urge him to see Eddy. Chandler believed a settlement could be arranged quickly if only he could meet with Eddy along with Baker and McLellan. But nothing came of the effort, and Chandler could only inform Bennett, "I haven't any considerable hope but it may come." Reports in May that Eddy was dangerously ill proved to be untrue, though the reports prompted Chandler to push Glover and Bennett to nominate Chandler to be administrator of her estate.[16] A glimpse of Chandler's view toward Christian Science is found in a letter to Henry Hopkins. To Hopkins, Christian Science was "utterly incompatible with the orthodox view of the bible." Why a so-called man of science was writing about theology is not clear, but as a Unitarian, Chandler also had an unorthodox view of the Bible, as Unitarians did not believe in the Trinity. He explained to Hopkins,

> The main ideas in my mind which I wish to exploit, are, first, the folly and wickedness of calling it a religion deduced or based upon a re-discovery of Christ's miraculous power. That, as you and I know, is almost blasphemy, as the Eddyites put it. Then I am interested in it as a delusion of Mrs. Eddy; practically insanity, which it is my duty to demonstrate, and make her incompetent to do justice to her children in her will. But the most important point of all is the fact that by means of this imposture, declaring that they make miraculous cures of disease, they profess to do it without medicine or any physical act whatever, to do it while absent, and as a climax charge solid cash as doctor's fees for making miraculous cures. This brings the business down to a money swindle and I wonder there is not an uprising of the doctors of the whole country against it;—also the ministers should rise up en masse and proclaim the atrocity of the movement.[17]

It did not seem to dawn on Chandler that if Christian Scientists were attempting to cure disease without medicine or without "any physical act whatever," they were not, in fact, practicing traditional, licensed medicine, but simply practicing their religion.

In June 1909, Howe wrote to Chandler, to inform him that the equity case of *Glover et al. v. Streeter, Tomlinson, and McLellan,* was set for trial June 7. Howe described the case as Chandler's attempt to obtain advice from the court as to whether Glover's children could accept the provisions of the trust without affecting their rights if they later contested Eddy's will. Chandler responded that he could not travel to Concord from Washington, D.C., at that time, and since Streeter had not answered Chandler's amended bill, Chandler did not believe the case could come to trial until a hearing on Streeter's demurrer had taken place. Chandler did indicate a willingness to hold a hearing later in the summer when he was at his home in Waterloo, but since Streeter never answered Chandler's amended bill, nothing more was heard about this case.[18]

Chandler met with Henry Baker on September 9, 1909, to try to revive the family settlement along the lines of the negotiated agreement of December 1907. To Baker, Chandler admitted that at his age he wished "to have the preparations" for a will contest "equally ready whether [he was] alive or dead when they [became] applicable." But he had delayed making these final preparations, in hopes that a family settlement could be arranged. He now asserted, "I can delay no longer." Though he wished to avoid future litigation, "ample moneys must be secured" to pay for "additional counsel more capable than the present ones." He appealed to Baker one last time to approach Eddy: "I have no reason to doubt that she is as competent physically and mentally to do business as she was in December, 1907." Chandler also repeated his willingness and full authority to act immediately.[19]

Again, nothing was done right away, but in October Chandler met with Streeter, who offered to pay Glover's taxes in South Dakota. Chandler asked Judge Bennett to find out what Glover owed, but Glover refused to provide the names of his creditors, stating to Chandler, "I do not care to have the cult handling my name and my creditors names through their papers." Bennett was increasingly frustrated with Glover, who feared that someone associated with Christian Science would go around "and pay his bills" if he provided a list of his creditors, which would "humiliate him" and "wound his pride." Bennett assured him that this would not happen but admitted to Chandler, "I have but little patience with a man in his deplorable financial condition talking about *humiliation* and *pride* in connection with any proposed arrangements for the payment of his debts."[20]

In the meantime, Mary Baker Eddy had changed her mind about

a settlement. Two years earlier, flush with confidence following the dismissal of the next friends suit, she had rejected, at the last minute, the settlement negotiated by Streeter and Chandler. Now, however, with constant pressure from Chandler and in the midst of the critical Stetson controversy, Eddy had a change of heart. Calvin Frye recorded in his diary that on September 25, 1909, Laura Sargent prevailed upon Eddy's newest favorite, Adam Dickey, to inform Eddy that the *New York World* was stating that the next friends suit was about to be revived. This news upset Eddy greatly, to the extent that Dickey had to assure her, "There will be no suit. All the next friends want is money." Frye recorded her response: "To compromise Mrs. Eddy told him to get a settlement with them." She then called her staff together, including Sargent, Dickey, Frye, and Tomlinson, and had each raise their right hand and promise never to leave her "till this next 'next friend' threat was met—the threat to revive the next friends suit."[21]

Unaware of Eddy's decision, Chandler finally heard back in October from Baker, who asked him to state what kind of settlement would be acceptable. Chandler informed Baker that a settlement along the lines of the former settlement "with a 'substantial addition thereto'" was what he was seeking for Glover and Foster Eddy. To Judge Bennett, Chandler reported that Eddy was willing to increase the original $125,000 trust fund by $50,000, or $10,000 over the original proposal of December 1907. Chandler was insisting on an additional $20,000 in cash, for Glover to repay his debts and start over. Chandler wrote to Glover, insisting that he sign over "specific authority" to Chandler, stating what minimum amounts would be acceptable. Glover's response was that Chandler should seek $40,000 to $45,000 additional to the original trust fund of $125,000 and "not less than $20,000 to be paid to [Glover] in cash." He also agreed that if his terms were met, he would "give to Mrs. Eddy all letters and papers signed by her or in her handwriting, or dictated by her, which were in the possession of Glover, his family, or his attorney."[22]

As a final settlement seemed likely, Glover became more open about his indebtedness, informing Chandler and Bennett that he owed almost $13,000, including doctor's bills and "drug store bills," which he admitted were "enormous" and illustrated "to a certain extent the threat of the 'cult' to destroy" Glover and his family. Bennett professed to Chandler, "I was amazed, as you will be, by the amount." But he attributed some of it to Nellie Glover's long illness and "surgical operation" at "a Chicago Hospital." But Chandler "was not wholly surprised at the amount of the indebtedness and [had] no criticisms to make." He was proud to report that a final settlement had been reached.[23]

According to Chandler's diary, the final settlement was concluded with Streeter, Baker, and McLellan on Monday, October 25, 1909, but was not signed until November 10. This time, the delay was not due to Eddy or her attorneys but rather to a local Judge Elder, who once again raised the issue of whether Glover could "make a release which [would] bind his heirs," particularly if any of those heirs later questioned the mental competency of Glover. Streeter and Baker agreed with Chandler that it was both impractical and unnecessary to provide guardians for the Glover's minor children so that they could release their father, and it would produce an interminable delay, which might cause Eddy to change her mind. Chandler labeled as "absurd" Elder's suggestion that Glover be brought to Boston to sign the papers: "I am willing to make petty concessions but I will not agree that a resident of South Dakota, a resident of Vermont and a resident attorney in New Hampshire cannot make a contract with another citizen of New Hampshire without all these parties going into Massachusetts!"[24]

In spite of Elder's concerns, all parties signed the papers in Concord on Wednesday, November 10, and at 1:00 p.m. Josiah Fernald, one of Eddy's trustees, presented Chandler with checks totaling $115,000. With the final agreement, George W. Glover and family received $245,000, and Ebenezer J. Foster Eddy received $45,000. Glover's trust fund was increased from $125,000 to $175,000. He was also presented with a cash amount of $25,000. The remaining $45,000, approximately 20 percent, was to go to his attorneys, for their work on the next friends case and the settlement negotiations. Foster Eddy's total was all in cash, with $3,000 deducted by Chandler for attorney's fees; the bulk of the attorney's fees were charged to Glover. The terms of the Glover trust had not changed, however, with Irving Tomlinson continuing as a trustee, and with Glover to receive only $1,500 per year. Streeter determined that these provisions could be changed at any time by the trustees, and he did not want to burden Eddy with too much detail, so long as she agreed to the final totals. The Glover trust would continue during the life of George W. Glover and his wife, at which time the trust would terminate and the balance be divided equally among Glover's children. The Glover trust deed stated that no beneficiaries of the trust should "directly or indirectly make any contest or opposition" to Eddy's final will "or to the disposition of other property by [Eddy]." And the family settlement was similarly limited: "The sons respectively covenant that neither they nor any one claiming under them will contest or retard the probate of any will which their mother may leave or attempt to set aside any gifts, deed or other dispositions of property which she has heretofore made or may hereafter make, or make any further claims at any time to any portion of her property or estate." As part of the family settlement, the sons returned all "letters and documents" in their possession written by or from Eddy. Chandler gathered up some seventy letters, dating from 1881 to June 1907, from Glover and Foster Eddy.[25]

At first, Glover expressed his confusion over the terms of the settlement. His wishes as to the trust deed had not been fulfilled, nor had his annual income been increased from the $1,500 prescribed from the original $125,000 trust. He wrote Chandler, "We may be very much misled and perhaps have made a mistake or charged into some snare that will be a very serious one. For my part I am entirely at sea." But as usual, Judge Bennett managed to calm George, particularly with the presentation of two checks, one for $12,000 and the other for $13,000, to pay his debts, which he and Mary proceeded to do immediately. Bennett was relieved: "I think we are all to be congratulated on getting through with this troublesom affair." Eventually, Glover was completed placated about the settlement and sent Chandler a solid gold ring as a Christmas gift; Chandler, in turn, sent a lovely bracelet and other jewelry to Mary and to Nellie Glover.[26]

As soon as the press reported the terms of the settlement, creditors of Chandler and company began lining up for payment. William G. Nixon, who had once been Eddy's publisher and had presented the next friends with many letters of Eddy's, begged Chandler for more money and for the return of Nixon's letters, which were in the possession of Frederick Peabody. The clerk who had taken depositions in Boston asked if he could finally be paid after two years. Granville Bennett thanked Chandler for his check of $2,500, but Frederick Peabody rejected his check for the same amount, stating that he expected to be paid the same amount as Kelley and Howe. Peabody believed that the two New Hampshire attorneys each received $7,000 from Chandler, who was paid $10,000. A heated exchange of letters ensued, in which Chandler stated that no such agreement had ever taken place, and, in fact, all of the other attorneys had accepted whatever amount Chandler paid them without complaint, even though no specific amounts had ever been promised to anyone. Chandler reminded Peabody that he had already been sent $700 for past services prior to the check for $2,500 and that Chandler had never at any time valued Peabody's "services by comparing them with Mr. Kelley's or Mr. Howe's." In fact, Chandler did not think these services were worth the sum Peabody had already been paid and accused him of an "ungovernable temper" that "made a *failure* of the life of a man who has many good traits." Ultimately, Peabody offered to accept $3,500, and Chandler agreed to pay that amount "as soon" as Nixon confirmed that he had "received his letters," which Peabody appears to have been holding for ransom.[27]

In contrast, John W. Kelley professed delight at a $774.17 check sent to him by Chandler in December. How much Kelley and Howe had been paid before this point is not clear, but Kelley wrote, "I had really no expectation of seeing as much as I did then. The matter of compensation never troubled me any. You know the Irish are proverbially careless about money."[28]

Now that the settlement had been completed, Chandler wrote

to Mary Glover in his usually flirtatious manner, suggesting "a wicked conspiracy" between them to get George Glover to write to his mother. Chandler enclosed a draft of what Glover might write, reminding Mary that even though her father had "released all claim to Mrs. Eddy's estate . . . there [was] nothing to prevent her from giving more in a future will." Glover complied with the request but without much confidence that his mother would ever see the letter. Following closely the draft sent to him by Chandler, Glover started, "I am very glad that any money differences between us are ended and I hope your feelings toward me are kind." He went on to explain, once again, why he had initiated a suit two years earlier: because "rumors" were circulating about her and because "it was so difficult to get access to [her]." The issue of the return of Eddy's letters also played a role, Glover writing, "The way that Mr. Farlow and Mr. Tomlinson followed me up when I was in Washington was very disturbing." He also mentioned the letter from Eddy, owned by Nixon, which charged that her sons were out to do her harm through malicious animal magnetism. George concluded, "This is now all in the past and I trust you will hereafter have nothing to complain about against me or my children. I assure you that Mary and the boys are worthy of your kindness and affection, and I do not think there ought longer to be any cloud between you and me and my family." He signed the letter "Affectionately your son, George W. Glover."[29]

Several days later George received the following reply,

> My Dear George:—
> I thank you for your kind letter. I am too busy to entertain company, but I do not forget you or any of my grandchildren.
> As ever,
> Sincerely yours,
> Mary Baker Eddy

The letter was typewritten and signed with Eddy's signature.[30] George was upset by this letter, complaining to Chandler that his mother did not even spell her own name correctly, since she left out "Glover," which had generally been included in her signature. She also wrote that she could not "entertain company" even though Glover had not suggested a visit to her. Left unsaid by Glover was the lack of warmth in Eddy's letter, particularly in the complimentary closing, "Sincerely yours." Chandler responded that in recent years Eddy had dropped "Glover" from her signature.[31] Regardless of the lack of affection between her and her son, Mary Baker Eddy could feel comforted by the fact that as 1909 drew to a close, she had secured her son's financial future and his promise to never contest her will. Augusta Stetson had been excommunicated from the church, and the issue of a successor to Eddy was resolved. She could look with renewed confidence to her final days.

= 13 =

MENTALLY MURDERED?

As anticipated by Judge Granville Bennett, George Glover quickly spent all the cash sent to him as a result of the family settlement. He did pay all of his debts with the $13,000 check, and then with the additional $12,000, he purchased 526 acres of land for the mineral rights, invested in a real estate company offering lots, and purchased a business on the main street of Lead, South Dakota—an ice cream parlor, which his son George ran on a daily basis. Convinced that the rent on the store was exorbitant, he had asked Chandler to have the trustees advance him an additional $12,000 so that Glover could purchase the building. At a meeting of the Glover trustees in Boston in June 1910, the trustees decided to begin paying George $1,500 a year, and his older children, Mary and Gershom, would each be paid $500 a year. The trustees also agreed to pay for repairs to Glover's home in Lead, which amounted to $2,800. The family settlement also called for the trust fund to pay for the education of the younger children, George and Andrew, who were, respectively, twenty-one and nineteen years old. Not knowing what type of future the boys aspired to, the trustees asked them to come east to meet with the board. Chandler then invited young George and Andrew to spend the summer of 1910 with him at Waterloo. The trustees rejected the senior Glover's request for an annual income of $3,000, claiming the income from the trust fund would not support this amount, and they also rejected his request for $12,000 to buy the building in Lead.[1]

The rapid disposal of all the cash Glover received from the family settlement undoubtedly frustrated his longtime attorney, Granville G. Bennett, who filed suit against Glover for attorney fees. Bennett had accepted the $2,500 sent him by Chandler as final payment for all work on the next friends case, but Bennett was owed more than that for all the other legal work he had done for the litigious George Glover. Bennett was not well at the time and probably thought this was his last opportunity to get some money from Glover for past work. Bennett died on June 30, 1910, at age seventy-six. George Glover wrote to Chandler, "He was my attorney for 25 years and we never lost a suit." Glover even excused Bennett's filing suit against him, stating, "I then was satisfied that he was failing very fast."[2]

Young George and Andrew Glover arrived at Waterloo on Sunday, July 10. Two days later, Chandler took the boys on a tour around Concord, showing them the vacant Pleasant View and meeting with DeWitt Howe. Still suspecting that his mother might be dead, George senior requested that the boys visit Eddy at Chestnut Hill and stated that young George would likely recognize whether it was really her, as he had met her as a young child.[3] The boys met with the trustees at the Parker House in Boston on July 16 and were then taken to Chestnut Hill for a meeting with their grandmother. It was Mary Baker Eddy's eighty-ninth birthday. The boys presented Eddy with a gift from her son: a pin made of gold from the Glover gold mine, which she seemed genuinely pleased to receive. In turn, she gave each boy a copy of *Science and Health*, inscribed "Lovingly Grandmother Mary Baker Eddy." During the brief meeting, Andrew did most of the talking, and George "just sat there and smiled at her." The boys had been photographed outside the mansion, and Eddy was given a copy of the photo, which she kept prominently displayed for the remaining days of her life. On the back of the photo of the boys, she wrote, "My Grandsons Mary Baker Eddy." The rest of the visit was not as pleasant for the boys, as Chandler put them to work around his property at Waterloo, particularly to repair his boats. Andrew reportedly got a girl pregnant during the summer, which Chandler learned about after the boys had gone home.[4]

In November, with the completion of the family settlement and evidence that the trustees were managing the trust fund in the best interest of the Glovers, Chandler decided it was time to end all activity related to the next friends. He wrote to Kelley and Howe, asking each to sign off that they had been fully compensated for their services and did not expect any future fees. He added, "You have been faithful, able and pleasant associates in very important and successful litigation." Although Chandler was pleased by what they had achieved for the Glover family, the real purpose of the litigation was revealed in one of his statements: "The fraudulent cult, however, still remains in existence. It does not seem to be our business to further fight it." Howe wrote of his satisfaction with "the financial remuneration" and added, "Personally I look back upon that case with much pleasure and it is due in no small measure to being associated with you and Brother Kelley. . . . I feel that I have received very much from the case in the way of experience and reputation which will be helpful to me in the future. I feel deeply indebted to you and to Brother Kelley for the opportunity to participate in the case."[5]

Mary Baker Glover Eddy died peacefully at Chestnut Hill at age eighty-nine on December 3, 1910, nearly three and a half years after the dismissal of the next friends suit. At one time, she had expected to "demonstrate the way over old age," but in her last years she blamed the continuing hostility toward her for "literally impelling her into the grave." She once asked Adam Dickey that if she died, whether he would say that she "was mentally murdered." A week or so prior to her death, she asked Calvin Frye to tell her students that "it was malicious animal magnetism" that had overcome her and not the natural results of old age. Frye wrote in his diary, "The malice and hate which poured in upon her thought . . . through the next friends suit in the New Hampshire courts . . . I believe was largely a burden which seemed to undermine her vitality."[6]

In Washington, D.C., Chandler issued the following statement: "Mrs. Eddy was certainly a very remarkable character, whatever may be the ultimate judgment of mankind concerning Christian Science. Her intense correctness, her capacity for influencing a new Christian sect, have been all powerful and make her one of the notable women of the time." He went on to explain, "Her difficulties with her son, George W. Glover, and his family, and with her adopted son, Dr. E. J. Foster (Eddy), were, under my   direction as counsel for them, adjusted in a family settlement in 1909 and doubtless all her large estate of nearly $2,000,000 has been given to promote Christian Science and also the perpetual use as a religious ritual of her book, 'Science and Health and the Key to the Scriptures.'"[7]

Frank Streeter spoke even more directly about the next friends suit in his remarks upon learning of Eddy's death.

> I desire to express my profound admiration for Mrs. Eddy as a woman and as a leader of a religious movement which has deeply impressed itself upon the world. My professional and friendly relations with her covered many years, and were especially intimate during 1907, when she was compelled to submit to a most vexatious and harrassing litigation, the purpose of which was not only to establish her mental unsoundness but to overturn the religious faith of which she was the acknowledged founder and revered head.

Streeter went on to describe his relationship with Eddy during the next friends suit, noting that he conferred with her "almost daily," and concluded that "she met the charge of mental infirmity with brilliant sanity and reasonableness." Referring to "these most troubled months of her life," Streeter said, "[Mrs. Eddy] inspired me with the highest regard for her character and personality."[8]

Dr. E. J. Foster Eddy was also gracious in his statement: "Mrs. Eddy was the most wonderful and lovable woman that the world has ever known, and I believe that her teachings rightly understood and

demonstrated, will benefit mankind more than any other on record."
He did criticize those who surrounded her in the last years for "a lack
of mental or spiritual support" and concluded, "This is the severest
blow that Christian Science has ever received." He also noted, "The
ranks are so strongly fortified that the work will be carried on without
disintegration."[9]

Glover was informed of his mother's passing by a telegram from
Calvin Frye. Glover left immediately by train, accompanied by
daughter Mary and son George, to attend the funeral. Within days,
a controversy arose over Eddy's place of burial. George Glover, as
next of kin, believed interment should be at Tilton, New Hampshire
(formerly Sanbornton Bridge), where Eddy's mother and father were
buried, and Foster Eddy agreed with Glover. Church officials wanted
the burial to be at Mount Auburn Cemetery, near Boston, where a suitable mausoleum would be constructed. Others, including Chandler's
son, William D. Chandler, and George W. Baker, one of Eddy's relatives, believed she should be buried at Pleasant View in Concord.
Newspapers speculated that George Glover's wishes would "likely
prevail." Amid this latest controversy, the simple funeral took place
at Eddy's home at Chestnut Hill at 11:00 a.m. on December 8, 1910,
followed by a procession to Mount Auburn Cemetery, where the body
was placed in a receiving vault until a final decision could be reached
as to a permanent resting place. William E. Chandler, nearly seventy-
five years of age, did not make the trip from his home in Washington,
D.C., but was represented by his son William, who also reported the
event for the *Concord Monitor*. John W. Kelley also attended the funeral
from his home in Portsmouth, New Hampshire, as did Frank Streeter
and his wife, a personal friend of Eddy.[10]

Chandler fully expected the bulk of Eddy's estate to go to promoting Christian Science. In a letter to Dr. Henry R. Hopkins on December
10, Chandler indicated that there was nothing for George Glover "to
quarrel about (probably) except as to the place of burial." Chandler
did credit the next friends lawsuit for causing the Christian Scientists
"in earnest to get rid of their M.A.M. business." To Chandler, the

controversy about Augusta Stetson, which led to her ultimate expulsion, was a way of expunging malicious animal magnetism from the creed, as she was charged with being "the sole believer in it." Within twenty-four hours after writing to Hopkins, Chandler had changed his mind about Eddy's will. Somehow, details of the wording of the will had produced a serious reaction in Boston from Frederick Peabody, the Glovers, and John W. Kelley. Glover was scheduled to meet with Streeter and the trustees on December 13, but Chandler, on learning of their concerns about the will, wired Kelley, "Glover postpone meeting Trustees and come here. We must see the will before saying one word. Peabody dangerous. I cannot visit Boston now. . . . Danger in haste." Kelley wrote that after receiving Chandler's telegram, "a family conference was held" at Kelley's home. After that, the Glovers and Foster Eddy departed for Washington to meet with Chandler. Kelley then had William D. Chandler phone Streeter and postpone the meeting with the trustees. Kelley disconnected his own phone, knowing that Streeter would want to know why the meeting was postponed, where the Glovers had gone, and why. Kelley wrote to Chandler, "I didn't want to lie to him." Kelley also stated, "The newspapers are still in ignorance as to the whereabouts of the Glovers." Kelley admitted that the people he called "our clients," the Glovers, were becoming "unsettled": "[They] are being pestered to death by outsiders, some of them lawyers, who keep telling them they have a chance to make a will contest, and can't help but win it."[11]

Eddy's will was filed in Concord on December 14, 1910, and contained the excuse for future litigation. The original will was written in 1901, reexecuted in 1903, with various codicils and the Glover trust deed among the many additions made after that date. Henry M. Baker was designated sole executor of Eddy's will. The will gave $10,000 each to George Glover and his four children. It bequeathed to the Mother Church $50,000. The amount of $100,000 was given to the Christian Science Board of Directors. The controversy arose over the eighth clause of the will, known as the residuary clause: it bequeathed "all the rest, residue, and remainder of [Eddy's] estate, of every kind and description, to the Mother Church—The First Church of Christ, Scientist, in Boston, Massachusetts, in trust," for the purpose of keeping the church building in repair and "for the purpose of more effectually promoting and extending the religion of Christian Science as taught by me." The remainder of the estate, after all of the designated amounts, was estimated in excess of $2 million. This was all to go to one church in Boston. The problem was that the laws of both Massachusetts and New Hampshire stated that no church could receive more than $5,000 a year in income from a gift. The income from Eddy's estate would far exceed the limit of the states' laws. The original intent of the laws was somewhat obscure in that it dated back to England, but it had to do with the possibility that large gifts to a single church might impede religious freedom in a particular community. Since Eddy's will seemed to give the bulk of her estate to the Mother Church in Boston and not to Christian Science in general, it would be left to the courts to determine if the bequest violated the law. If the Mother Church could not receive this legacy, another issue to be determined was who should receive it, the state or Eddy's next of kin, who had agreed in the family settlement never to challenge her will.[12]

Frederick Peabody had met with Glover and Foster Eddy prior to their departure for Washington and had tried to impress upon them that "Mrs. Eddy's crazy rules and by laws . . left the door wide open in other respects." Chandler wasn't willing to accept Peabody's word for anything, however, after the conflict they had previously over Peabody's fee from the next friends suit. From December 12 through December 16, Chandler met daily with the Glovers and Foster Eddy before they departed for South Dakota and Vermont, respectively. Chandler also called in Washington attorney Hannis Taylor and his partner, William L. Chambers, for advice. Chandler "refused to give any opinion" about the will. Through the family settlement, Glover and Foster Eddy had agreed that Eddy could give away her remaining property "as she pleased." Now, however, Chandler explained, "The will must be a lawful will and the legatees must be competent to take it." He concluded that if the First Church of Christ, Scientist, in

Boston, could not "lawfully take the one and one-half million dollars it would certainly go to the two sons."[13]

Chandler shared a "tentative" plan with Kelley and Howe. The will was scheduled to be probated in Concord on January 17, and Chandler proposed not challenging the proving of the will. Both Massachusetts and New Hampshire had similar laws: no church could receive more than $5,000 a year in income in New Hampshire, or more than $2,000 a year in Massachusetts. But since Eddy's legal residence was New Hampshire, he concluded, "If the property is seized by any state it must be taken by New Hampshire!" To Glover, Chandler explained further, "It is my decided impression that you had better not undertake to destroy the will on any contention that Mrs. Eddy was incompetent, deluded or controlled by undue influence. You agreed in the settlement that you would not do this." He went on, "Besides, if you were to attack the will the Trustees would stop paying you money under the trust and would claim that you had forfeited $175,000." Chandler had met in Washington with Henry M. Baker, who seemed unconcerned about "the bequest to the church being defeated" because "such bequests [had] been made in Massachusetts for 100 years." Chandler did advise, "After the will is approved, [you should take] the position that all the residuary bequest of personal property to the mother church over $5,000 per year is void and that [the money and property] goes to the heirs and not to the State of Massachusetts or of New Hampshire." To Chandler, "the chance of getting a million dollars [was] worth something" and might produce a settlement. He further advised George that as soon as the will was probated in January, he should agree to "have the interment at Mt. Auburn" in return for receiving immediately the $40,000 in legacies left to the four Glover children.[14]

As promised, Chandler kept the *New York World* informed in advance of any potential activity regarding Eddy and the next friends. John Slaght's article on December 25, 1910, was the first to report the possibility of a lawsuit to determine if Eddy's will was in violation of Massachusetts and New Hampshire state laws. But Chandler waited until he received a report from Hannis Taylor and William L. Chambers. They advised Chandler that the bequest of $2 million to the First Church of Christ, Scientist, of Boston, was in fact forbidden by the laws of both Massachusetts and New Hampshire. Therefore, according to this opinion, Eddy died intestate, and her money and property passed to her next of kin under New Hampshire statutes of distribution. The legal opinion quoted the laws for each state. The Revised Law of Massachusetts for the year 1902, chapter 37, section 9, reads, "The income of the gifts, grants, bequests and devises made to or for the use of any one church shall not exceed $2,000 a year, exclusive of the income of any parsonage land granted to or for the use of the ministry." The New Hampshire law stated, "The income of any grant or donation made to or for the use of a church shall not exceed $5,000 a year exclusive of the income of any parsonage land granted to or for the use of the ministry."[15]

With this opinion in hand, Chandler filed two bills on January 13, 1911. The first bill in equity, filed in George Glover's name, was in the Merrimack County Superior Court, while the second bill, in Foster Eddy's name, was filed in the United States Court for the District of New England. Chandler explained to the *World* that the next friends were not opposed to the proving of the will to take place in Concord on January 17, because in the family settlement in 1909, they promised "not to oppose the vesting of title under any lawful bequest or deed that Mrs. Eddy might have made," but if her estate was to be given away in violation of "statute law it [would] be void," so the property would go to Eddy's sons, "the same as if no will had been found in existence after her death." According to Chandler, this was another "friendly" suit, in that the Mother Church would want to know if it was "exempt from the laws to which other churches must submit." Chandler asserted, "[If] any one local Christian Science church can have a two million dollar fund, Christian Science can count upon a future growth and expansion beyond all the other religions in the world, and will rejoice at receiving a judicial decision so strengthening its power, already marvelous." In contrast, if the court ruled that the law could not be disregarded, it would require even religious societies to respect and obey "hereafter . . . the paramount law of America."[16]

Because John W. Kelley was preoccupied with representing the Boston and Maine Railroad, the burden of conducting the New Hampshire lawsuit fell on young DeWitt Howe. He and Chandler had a minor disagreement over the best approach to take in arguing the case. As DeWitt had argued in the next friends case, he did not believe that Christian Science was a religion but rather a medical practice that was against public policy, because this practice accepted money for false claims to cure disease. Chandler did not want to argue the case in this way. He explained his reasons to Howe: "We have started our suit on the theory that the First Church is a religious society and limited in its property by the very law under which it is organized. To now turn around and declare it not to be a religious society, but a public nuisance, might be unwise." Desiring to make light of the disagreement, Chandler sent Howe a humorous poem, which Howe "hanged" in the chandelier above his desk. Howe, to get "even with" Chandler, wrote that a local dentist had "one of Mrs. Eddy's teeth" and that Howe planned to acquire the tooth "and present it to the New Hampshire Historical Society" in Chandler's name. According to Howe, the tooth would be preserved in the vault of the new Historical Society building as evidence that Christian Science "prevented the decaying of teeth and rendered their extraction unnecessary."[17]

In Massachusetts the Christian Science Board of Directors initiated a law suit, *Dickey v. Dickey*, to resolve whether the Mother Church could receive the bequest of real estate valued at more than $250,000, which was left by Eddy in that state. Because bequests to charities were not restricted, the directors argued that the Mother Church was, in fact, a charitable organization. Howe and Chandler disagreed as to whether the next friends should appear in that suit. Howe believed that if the Massachusetts Supreme Court ruled in favor of the church, that decision would determine the fate of Eddy's bequest in New Hampshire. Chandler believed there was no way that New Hampshire would allow the bulk of Eddy's estate, valued at more than $2 million, to leave

New Hampshire if that state ruled the bequest was illegal, regardless of what Massachusetts decided. Chandler retained his longtime friend and political colleague, seventy-two-year-old John Davis Long, to argue the case in New Hampshire. Besides serving as Massachusetts governor, Long had also spent six years in Congress and served as secretary of the navy in the McKinley administration. In the months leading up to the Spanish-American War, he clashed with Assistant Secretary Theodore Roosevelt over expansion of the U.S. Navy. Long resigned from the cabinet soon after Roosevelt succeeded McKinley as president; Long's reasons are unclear but certainly were related to his belief that Roosevelt intended to interfere with Long's running of the Navy Department. Long shared Chandler's personal animosity toward the former president, and as a strong advocate for women's suffrage, Long was considered a progressive. Chandler clarified that Long's purpose was "to argue the proposition that a church-religion is not a charity" and that Long would "not . . . be charged with any responsibility for the incidental goings on in the case." Chandler frequently quoted Judge Joseph Story: "Anything expressly forbidden by law cannot be treated as a charity."[18]

To further complicate matters, a petition was filed in the Merrimack County Superior Court in the name of George W. Baker, who was asking for permission to intervene in the suit brought by George W. Glover. Baker's petition argued that in the family settlement, Glover and Foster Eddy had forfeited their rights to any of Eddy's estate; therefore, if the courts ruled that her bequest was a violation of law, Baker, as Eddy's next closest relative, would inherit the estate. In fact, the *World* speculated that Chandler was behind this petition, since Baker's attorney was Sherman E. Burroughs, a close friend to Chandler and his choice for the Republican nomination for governor in the hotly contested election of 1910. But Burroughs was also a distant relative of Mary Baker Eddy and was related to Henry M. Baker and George W. Baker, so Burroughs's involvement may have been more of a family matter. In fact, Burroughs had served as Henry M. Baker's personal secretary for several years and had been mentored by the wealthy former congressman. It is unlikely that Burroughs would have done anything to cross his former employer, mentor, and relative. Since George W. Baker had no part in the family settlement, presumably if he was successful in replacing Glover and Foster Eddy, Burroughs could argue not only that the bequest was against state law but that Eddy had been incompetent to make any will, a position that the sons had signed off on as part of the family settlement. But whether Burroughs, considering his family connections, had any intention of doing so seems unlikely. Originally living in Bangor, Maine, at the time of the next friends suit, Baker had moved back to Concord after his wife's death and worked as a journeyman printer. Since the *World* received most of its information directly from Chandler, it seems likely that he did encourage the Burroughs-Baker petition, although Chandler stated to Glover that the "Baker performance" would not do any harm: "It is only a little amusement."[19]

While Chandler claimed that the sons had a "duty" to challenge Eddy's bequest, editorial reaction to the lawsuits was not favorable. The *Boston Republican* predicted that the courts would "sustain the will of Mary Baker Eddy," given that "very few wills [were] broken" in New Hampshire and that she had disposed of her property in accordance with her forty-year effort "for the propagation of the faith which she founded." The newspaper asserted, "The fact that the heirs have already signed off in consideration of a sum agreed upon would seem to be an almost insuperable bar against their contentions now." The *Providence Evening Bulletin* was even more direct in its hostility to the sons.

> Even those citizens that are opposed to Christian Science on principle but are actuated by the spirit of fair play, will not approve of the attempt of the attorneys for Mrs. Eddy's son and adopted son to break her will after they had accepted a settlement of the estate during her lifetime. It is only natural that she should wish to leave the bulk of her fortune to the institution that she established as the result of many years of struggle.

The editorial went on to proclaim that if Eddy's wishes were denied by the courts, positive public sympathy for the "new" religion would be aroused, as "under persecution or unfair treatment of any kind even irrational religions must flourish."[20]

Following the death of Judge Granville Bennett, George Glover had attained new counsel, the law firm of Hodgson and Stewart in Deadwood, South Dakota. In March, Chandler met J. M. Hodgson in Washington, D.C., where he was arguing a case before the U.S. Supreme Court. Chandler was impressed with Hodgson and "arranged with him to render such assistance in South Dakota, in [the] Eastern litigation, as he [might] be asked to do." Hearing Chandler's explanation of the case, but being unaware of the disagreement between Chandler and Howe, Hodgson offered, "New Hampshire would not allow that money to go out of State to a religious institution."[21]

Ever ready to try the case in the press, Chandler stated to Kelley, "This is a great national question and public sentiment will have something to do with it." In March, Chandler found an opportunity for publicity. He had been composing an article to counteract paid advertisements that Christian Scientists cured disease. His article asked why it was that Mary E. Tomlinson had committed suicide. He sent a copy of his article to Frank Streeter, suggesting that he sue Chandler for libel if he didn't like the article. Streeter wrote back, in an entirely humorous manner, that Chandler "deserved chastisement" but not a libel suit and that Chandler would "be most effectively treated by the ever ready workers of the Christian Science body." This reference to malicious animal magnetism, prompted Chandler to write an open letter "To the Citizens of Concord, New Hampshire."

> To hear that Mr. Streeter has adopted such methods as a part of his machinery, in a law suit wherein the one church is fighting for two and one half millions of dollars, when the laws forbid it to take more than $100,000, and wherein the 5,000 practitioners, with an annual income from bogus healing work, of five millions of dollars, and all the other crazy victims of the believers

in M.A.M., are directed by the dominating counsel in the law
suit to destroy me as counsel for the sons, as they were directed
in 1907 to destroy George W. Glover himself so as to stop the
law suit then pending—is not a wholly pleasant notification to
receive from a Unitarian Deacon.

But Chandler pledged not to be deterred from speaking out "freely
and plainly in court and out of court in [his] usual way." Reaction
to Chandler's letter was mixed. On one hand, the *New York World*
editorialized that Chandler showed the same courage that could be
expected from someone who had challenged the powerful Boston
and Maine Railroad and Theodore Roosevelt and who was "undis-
mayed" by the threat of malicious animal magnetism. The *Concord
Patriot*, on the other hand, editorialized about this "violent outbreak":
"[That Streeter] as counsel for the Christian Science church, has lately
threatened [Chandler] with death through the mysterious destroyer
of humanity known as 'Malicious Animal Magnetism' is conclusive
evidence of the ex-senator's dotage, and for public protection his next
friends ought to summon alienists."[22]

On March 25, 1911, Chandler and company filed an amended bill
in superior court in Merrimack County, New Hampshire, in the case
of *Glover v. Henry M. Baker, Executor, et al.* The original bill asserted
that Eddy's bequest was illegal under the laws of both New Hampshire
and Massachusetts and that Eddy had been ignorant of this fact. The
amended bill added several new allegations, including that George
Glover was deceived into the family settlement not to contest Eddy's
will and that the deception, by Eddy's representatives, was willful. The
amended bill also attacked the religion for falsely claiming it cured disease and for Christian Scientists' acceptance of the idea of malicious
animal magnetism. Finally, the bill asserted that the bequests in the will
were "contrary to public policy," because "said purposes if effectuated
[were] destructive of the policy of said state as to hygiene, sanitation, medicine and surgery." The bequest, if allowed, would result in
"negligence toward" Glover's "children and other dependents." Howe

had succeeded in convincing Chandler to attack the religion directly. In fact, the amended bill was now to be argued so broadly as to be a repetition of the charges made four years earlier in the next friends suit. As Chandler had promised, the *World* was given the scoop a day in advance of the filing of the amended bill, after a lengthy conference in New York City of Chandler, Kelley, Howe, and Hannis Taylor. Chandler was on his way to Concord to contest Streeter's attempt to have the suit thrown out of court by contending that the sons had waived their right to bring suit. The Merrimack County Superior Court postponed a decision on the matter until the summer.[23]

Glover's family in South Dakota was fully behind the lawsuits. Chandler needed money to carry on the litigation, and George Glover's four children each pledged $1,500 from their $10,000 legacies to help pay the expenses. Chandler asked for only $1,000 from each, however; but he was pleased by the commitment of all the Glovers. The political ramifications of the lawsuits engaged Chandler in the spring of 1911. Because the laws of both New Hampshire and Massachusetts seemed to prevent gifts of this size going to one church, Chandler expected the attorneys general of both states to intervene, either to oppose the ratification of the gifts and urge the courts to enforce the laws or, at least, to refuse to aid in ratifying the bequest. Attorney General James M. Swift of Massachusetts was amenable to intervening, but in New Hampshire the attorney general was Edwin Eastman, who had been part of Streeter's legal team during the next friends suit. He refused to become engaged in any way in the lawsuits in New Hampshire, claiming that Christian Science fit the definition of a charity and that the state should be happy to receive the inheritance tax on the $2 million. That left Chandler with no choice but to approach Governor Robert Perkins Bass for help. Bass and Chandler should have been political allies, as they were both progressives, but Bass was a Roosevelt Republican who had divided the state Republican Party when he ran for governor in 1910. Chandler wrote to Long in Massachusetts, "As I am differing with Governor Bass, I cannot ask him to do it. I am a radical progressive and he is rapidly becoming a

moderate progressive." Chandler did ultimately meet with Governor
Bass on the Eddy matter, but inevitably the conversation turned to
Theodore Roosevelt, although Bass did later urge his new attorney
general to seek enforcement of the law.[24]

To cover all bases, Chandler encouraged Concord attorney James
W. Remick to file suit on behalf of George W. Glover III (Chandler
and the courts referred to him as George W. Glover Jr.) and Andrew
Glover. Remick claimed that "if Mrs. Eddy's residuary bequest to the
First Church of Christ Scientist in Boston" was void, and if the sons by
their family settlement had lost their right to take the property, it would
"descend" to the grandchildren, in that George Glover II ("Senior,"
according to Chandler) could not waive their rights without their
approval. Chandler then invited Remick to join his team of attorneys,
to provide whatever legal assistance he could in the "principal contest"
of "the illegality of the bequest." Glover was very ill again in South
Dakota, eventually traveling to Hot Springs, Arkansas, for treatment.
There he spoke with a reporter, who referred to him as a "man of many
peculiarities." Glover professed faith in Christian Science but was following a doctor's advice and was seen regularly in "the tub" taking the
mineral bath treatment. The reporter commented on Glover's "voice
of great carrying power" and stated that on a visit to Chicago several
years earlier, Glover had been arrested for disturbing the peace while
simply standing on a street corner talking with an acquaintance about
his mining properties. Chandler was back in New Hampshire in June
for more conferences with his legal team, now including James Remick
along with DeWitt Howe, John W. Kelley, Hannis Taylor, William L.
Chambers, and John D. Long, with J. M. Hodgson standing by in South
Dakota. Chandler took the visitors from out of state on a walking tour
of Concord's State House and other buildings, including the newly
constructed home of the New Hampshire Historical Society. Chandler
also commented in his diary on the immense crowds in Concord who
had come to see Buffalo Bill's Wild West Show, which, apparently,
Chandler and company did not attend.[25]

In July, Merrimack County Superior Court Chief Justice Robert

M. Wallace denied Streeter's motion that George W. Glover had no standing in court as a result of the family settlement of 1909. At the same time, Judge Wallace transferred the case to the New Hampshire Supreme Court without first trying it in superior court, a most unusual decision but one that he undertook so that the supreme court would rule on all the questions of law relating to the case prior to trial. Chandler appealed Wallace's decision to transfer the case, believing that the facts in the case must be tried first before the supreme court ruled on the questions of law.[26]

In September, Chandler was deposed in Concord in the equity case of *Glover v. Baker*. His deposition made headlines because of the magistrate's decision to allow representatives of the press and the public to be present for the questioning. Streeter objected strenuously to the presence of the press, who included John W. Slaght, who was on leave from the *World* and serving as an aide to Chandler; Chester A. Clark of the *Boston Herald;* Fred Leighton of the *Concord Monitor;* Keeler of the *Boston Globe*, Sexton of the *Concord Patriot;* and Chandler's old friend and former Concord mayor Henry Robinson. This was the first time in New Hampshire history that newspaper men were admitted during the taking of a deposition, but Chandler was always seeking ways to try the case in the press. The lengthy deposition, later published in book form, revealed for the first time the *World's* early involvement in the next friends case, the way Chandler became the next friends' attorney, and the recruitment of George W. Glover to become a plaintiff in the case. In terms of more recent events, the negotiations to produce a family settlement were revealed, with Streeter questioning Chandler about the agreement by which Glover and Foster Eddy waived their right to contest Eddy's will and admitted that their mother had been competent to make it. Another revelation covered in the press was Chandler's statement that Mary Baker Eddy had never been a part of the negotiations for the family settlement and that he could not swear that it was really her signature on the document.[27]

The state supreme court met on November 14 to hear arguments on Chandler's motion to remand the case of *Glover v. Baker* back to the superior court for trial before the case was finally sent up to the supreme court. Chandler was present, along with Hannis Taylor, Howe, and Kelley, while Streeter and his associate Fred C. Demond appeared for Baker. Chandler objected to Associate Justice Reuben E. Walker's sitting on the case, because Walker had once been an attorney for Eddy. The associate justice withdrew, but not before an angry exchange with Chandler in private, in which Walker objected to Chandler's not coming to him in person. Chandler apologized to Chief Justice Parsons in a letter, explaining that Chandler thought he had acted "in a proper way" in the matter. Taylor and Kelley argued the case for the plaintiffs, stating that Chief Justice Wallace had no right to transfer the case without the consent of counsel before the facts had been determined by trial. Taylor and Kelley also argued that since all of the evidence in the case was in possession of the defense, it was of the utmost importance that a trial take place to determine the facts prior to the case being sent to the supreme court for a final determination on the question of law. Streeter did not speak but submitted his opposition to Chandler's motion in a brief.[28]

On December 5, 1911, the New Hampshire Supreme Court denied Chandler's motion to remand the case back to the superior court, ruling, "Against the objection of either party, questions of law arising in the superior court may be transferred to and determined by the supreme court, without a ruling by the former tribunal and exception thereto." In the unanimous decision of the four judges, minus Walker, Chief Justice Parsons wrote, "It has been the practice here, as far back as the memory of any member of the bar can go, when important questions of law were involved in a controversy the decision of which might shorten the trial of the facts, to settle such questions first." The decision went on to state that the trial judge never decides questions of law, that the plaintiff had not been deprived of any rights, and that determining questions of law in advance of a trial "may prevent a useless prolonged struggle over evidence . . . [and] may greatly simplify or remove all controverted questions of law." The ruling concluded,

"In this case the law should be determined before proceeding to a trial of the facts."[29]

To further confuse things, on December 10 Judge Edgar Aldrich in the Federal Circuit Court denied Streeter's general demurrer to Chandler's bill on behalf of Foster Eddy, a bill that broadly stated that the residuary clause in Eddy's will was illegal, that the family settlement was the result of fraud, that Eddy was under delusions against her sons when she made her will, and that Christian Science was against public policy in that its medical practices violated the laws regarding sanitation and protection of health. Streeter's general demurrer claimed that the residuary clause was not a violation of law, because Christian Science was a charitable organization able to accept the large bequest, that the facts alleged did not constitute fraud, and that the question of public policy should be determined as a matter of law based on Eddy's writings and teaching, not on proofs offered by individual witnesses. The denial of Streeter's demurrer meant that a full hearing on all of the charges in Chandler's bill must go to trial, and was viewed as "a preliminary victory for the plaintiff."[30]

During the winter of 1912, both Chandler and Taylor were ill in Washington. Howe took on the burden of preparing the case before the New Hampshire Supreme Court. He summarized his position in a letter to Chandler: "If the bequest is a charity we lose; if it is not a charity they lose; therefore we must attack its character. It is not a charity, because It is prohibited by the Religious Societies Acts; It is too indefinite; It is for the promotion of a money making business; and, It is for a purpose which is contrary to public policy." But prior to the New Hampshire Supreme Court hearing, the Massachusetts Supreme Court held an equity session before Supreme Court Justice Braley. The principal question in Massachusetts was whether two parcels of land, one in Boston and one in Newton, could be legally transferred to the directors of the church, given the statute limiting the size of gifts to churches. Streeter and Howe were present in court, but the arguments were made by former Massachusetts attorney general Herbert

Parker, who was another attorney working for the next friends, as assistant to former governor Long, and by Charles F. S. Choate, as part of Streeter's team. Parker argued that Glover and Foster Eddy should be joined in the suit, in case the court decided against the will. Choate claimed that because of the family settlement, the rights of the sons to participate in the suit were "completely extinguished as if they were civilly dead." Braley ruled that all points of contention involving Eddy's estate would go before the entire Massachusetts Supreme Court, which would be asked to decide four points.

> First, whether a certain conveyance from Mrs. Eddy's trustees for the directors of the church is prohibited by the so-called 'church' statute of the state; second, whether her son, George W. Glover, and her adopted son, Dr. E. J. Foster Eddy, are entitled to intervene in the case in this state after relinquishing their rights four years ago; third, whether the trust created by Mrs. Eddy by her will in favor of the church is a charitable trust; and fourth, in case the property in the hands of the trustees cannot be legally transferred because of the statute . . . what shall be done with the estate, the estimated value of which is about $2,000,000.[31]

In a letter to Chandler, Parker stated that he felt "very strongly" about limiting the case to the residuary clause and its enforcement. He explained, "There is no evidence known to me upon which we have any right to expect that the Court would hold the releases [of the sons] to have been procured by any fraud and I think the presentation of the evidence upon this ground, or insistence upon this issue before our Court here, would avail us nothing, and further prejudice our real case and its presentation before the Court." But Chandler disagreed and insisted upon including the fraud allegation as part of the case: "I do not wish to narrow the issue and leave out part of the case. If we thereby lose I shall never forgive myself. If we make the broad fight and lose I shall bear it without self reproach." Still suffering from a bronchial infection and acting against the advice of his doctor, Chandler traveled to Boston in February, to meet with all of the attorneys for the next friends and with Judge Braley. Chandler wrote Parker, "[I am] satisfied and gratified . . . by your presentation . . . yesterday to Judge Braley against the adroit and eloquent pleading of Brothers [Samuel J.] Elder and Choate." Braley scheduled the hearing before the Massachusetts Supreme Court for its March term.[32]

Chandler then moved on to Concord, where he met again with Governor Bass, this time securing from him a commitment to intervene on behalf of the state in the case before the New Hampshire Supreme Court. Bass appointed a special counsel, Robert L. Manning of Manchester, to represent the state. Manning pledged to have the residuary clause of Eddy's will declared void and the estate "escheated" to the state. In a letter to Manning, Chandler summarized the state's position: "You agree with the plaintiffs and disagree with the defendants, on one point, that the residuary bequest is void and disagree with the plaintiffs concerning their claim to take the property notwithstanding the releases; and you agree with the defendants on the one point that the heirs cannot take the property, and disagree with the defendants on the other point, the validity of the bequest to the church." Chandler regretted but understood "that [Manning] should take position with the defendants concerning the effect of the releases."[33]

Arguments in the case before the New Hampshire Supreme Court took place on March 13 and 14, 1912. Hannis Taylor opened for the plaintiffs, followed by DeWitt Howe, Herbert Parker, and John D. Long. Among them, they covered every phase of the plaintiffs' case. The next day, Streeter opened for the defense, followed by Samuel J. Elder. Howe presented the case for fraud in securing the releases of the sons to contest Eddy's will. Parker challenged the defense's claim that Eddy's bequest to the Christian Science church in Boston could be considered a gift to a charity. Then Long explained the purpose of the law limiting gifts to churches as "a law based upon the desire of the fathers to keep separate the state and the church." He stated, "It is a dangerous thing to put a million dollars into the hands of a church eager to promulgate its tenets; a million dollars with which it can affect popular elections, reach the legislature and influence the election of judges in commonwealths where judges are elected by popular vote." Long went on to challenge Eddy's claim to divine intervention and her ability to work miracles and said that she had instituted a system that "violated every principle of good medical treatment." Long professed that Eddy's delusions did not constitute a public charity. In fact, she had accumulated her fortune "by the printing press and by the business she established." Long said, "There isn't the slightest element of a charity in it." The court was being asked to turn over $2 million "to the promotion and extension of that commercialism." In a biblical reference, Long stated, "If the Christian Scientist encountered the unfortunate traveler upon the highway to Jericho he would pour no oil in his wounds or give him wine, but he would give him a prayer and charge him $5 for the service." Chandler recorded in his diary that Parker and Long "*made glorious speeches.*"[34]

Streeter then opened for the defense, stating that the whole case should be thrown out of court, based on the releases of the sons in the family settlement of 1909. Chief Justice Parson interrupted to ask Streeter why it mattered who got the estate if the residuary clause was declared void. The judge admitted that the action of the sons was "immoral and unsportsmanlike," and Streeter agreed that the main issue was the validity of the bequest. Elder spoke next for the defense, declaring it "monstrous" that the court should consider the heirs in this case. He asserted that Eddy wanted to protect the religion of Christian Science and had been "pathetically persecuted" by the assault on her and her religion by the next friends. To Elder, the bequest did not come within the prohibitions of the New Hampshire and Massachusetts laws. Elder went on to defend Christian Science on the question of public policy, contending that Eddy advised in *Science and Health* that surgeons could be employed when necessary. One decision made during the hearing was that Dr. Ebenezer J. Foster Eddy was ordered to become a party to the action so that all "heirs at law and next of kin" might "be bound by any finding or order that the court" might "make in the case."[35]

Both sides now awaited the decisions of the courts. As he waited, Chandler, back in Washington, was shocked by news of the sinking of the *Titanic,* recording several times in his diary, *"Depression about Titanic."*[36]

= 14 =

A CHARITABLE TRUST

On May 7, 1912, the New Hampshire Supreme Court ruled against the plaintiffs in the case of *Glover v. Baker,* declaring that the residuary clause of the will "create[d] a valid trust." According to the twelve-thousand-word unanimous opinion written by Chief Justice Parsons, "The residuary clause is not a gift to a church but a gift for religious purposes sustainable as a charitable trust." Answering each of the plaintiffs' charges, the court ruled that the charitable trust was "not invalid for indefiniteness or ambiguity" and that it was not invalid "merely because that religion include[d] a system of faith-cure for disease" and was "in some sense a business . . . carried on for pecuniary profit." On this last point, the justices compared Christian Science to Dartmouth College, in that the college, though a charitable organization, was also a business that charged tuition, paid its staff, and contracted for work done. The court also interpreted the purpose of the New Hampshire statute limiting gifts to churches differently than the plaintiffs had. On behalf of the plaintiffs, former governor Long had contended that the law was meant to help preserve freedom of religion by keeping one church from becoming too powerful in a particular community. The court had an entirely different interpretation of the law, claiming that its purpose, as plainly stated in the preamble, was to promote and preserve "gifts to or for

churches," because the law "was a general incorporation act as well as
an act of religious toleration." The court asserted, "The income limitation is easily understood as a limitation upon the corporate power
created by the act." The court concluded, "The plaintiff's construction cannot be read into it."[1]

The court declared that it had no concern about the truth of religious theories. Even if, as some believed, Mary Baker Eddy was "'a
foolish, ignorant woman,' and her teachings absurd and illogical delusions," she "had the constitutional right to entertain such opinions as
she chose, and to make a religion of them, and to teach them to others." The court asserted, "Her legal right to teach was not ended with
her death." The court also said, "Whether her opinions are theologically true 'the court are not competent to decide.'" The court explored
the plaintiffs' charge that Christian Science was against public policy
because of the institution's claim "to cure physical ills without drugs
or surgery." The court's opinion recognized the "close association
between mental health and physical ills" and acknowledged that "hun-
dreds of thousands of patients to Christian Science . . . were for the
most part benefited, and greatly benefited, by Christian Science after
having received no benefit, often injury, from the [medical] profession." The court concluded, "No person could be convicted of crime
upon an indictment charging the practice of Christian Science healing,
because there is no law which forbids it." The devastating opinion
for the plaintiffs, or next friends, left open only one small window of
opportunity, in that the opinion did not deal with "the issues of fraud
and undue influence in securing the will," because that was something
only a trial in superior court could determine.[2]

But William E. Chandler and company recognized the court's
decision as "practically a complete victory for the Church." While
the decision in New Hampshire did "not affect or determine any
question pending in Massachusetts," Chandler wrote to Hodgson
in South Dakota, "We have no great hopes in our favor." Chandler
asked Hodgson to explain all this carefully to George Glover, to
prepare the family "for defeat" and to help him understand that

while Massachusetts and the U.S. court had yet to rule, "practically" Chandler did "not expect the U.S. court to overcome the two state courts." Chandler continued, "It might overcome one of them if the other decided that the statute or public policy destroyed the bequest." To Glover, Chandler wrote, "I am very much disappointed but so I was when we withdrew our suit in 1907." He asserted, "Let us be hopeful to the last."[3]

While waiting for the Massachusetts Supreme Court to rule on its case, both sides were "shocked" by the death of Henry M. Baker in Washington, D.C., on May 30, 1912. Baker was the executor of Eddy's estate, her cousin, former trustee, and loyal defender. But to Chandler, Baker was also an "upright and honorable" man, whose sincere interest in the well-being of Glover and family had prompted the negotiations that resulted in the family settlement of 1909. A former congressman, the seventy-one-year-old Baker saw Chandler frequently in Washington, as they both attended the same Unitarian Church. Frank Streeter advised Chandler that Baker's successor as executor would be Concord banker Josiah E. Fernald, longtime financial advisor to Mary Baker Eddy. Chandler wrote, "I anticipated Mr. Fernald's appointment and know of no better one that could be made."[4]

Throughout the summer and fall of 1912, Chandler worked tirelessly for William Howard Taft's reelection. Chandler's hatred of Theodore Roosevelt, who was running as the third-party Bull Moose candidate, and rejection of any Democrat pushed the "radical progressive" Chandler back into the mainstream of the Republican Party and into closer association with Frank Streeter. It was not easy for Chandler to swallow the candidacy of Taft, whom Chandler had previously opposed, but his loyalty to the Republican Party and hostility to Roosevelt overcame his doubts about Taft's leadership. Chandler was pleased that Roosevelt failed to win but was appalled by the election of the Democrat candidate, Woodrow Wilson. While engaged politically, Chandler also kept in touch with the Glovers and was particularly concerned with George's deteriorating health resulting from Bright's disease, a kidney ailment.[5]

On October 9, 1912, the Massachusetts Supreme Court finally issued its ruling. Initially, the case of *Dickey v. Dickey* was a friendly suit brought by the directors of the Mother Church against the trustees of the will, to determine the legality of the trust. Adam Dickey was a member of both boards, and thus his name appears twice in the original lawsuit. But the friendly suit was joined by the Massachusetts attorney general, who urged the court to enforce the statute limiting the amount one church could receive each year to $2,000. And the next friends also joined the plaintiffs, charging that Christian Science medical practice was against the state's public policy; therefore, if the court ruled the statute must be enforced, then the next of kin would inherit the estate. At first glance, the court's ruling appears to be a split decision, as it determined the trust to the Mother Church was void and the statute prohibiting it was enforceable, but at the same time, the court determined that Christian Science was a religion, that a charitable trust had been created, but that new trustees must be appointed by the state to administer the trust. The court dismissed the bill brought by the next friends, which asserted that the teachings of Christian Science were against public policy, but the court allowed the next friends thirty days to bring additional evidence to support their claim and to try it before a single judge of the court.[6]

The court's decision stated, "It is plain that a gift directly to a church for its own benefit is within the prohibition [of the statute]." The residuary clause of Eddy's will stated that the gift was to be used to repair the church buildings and to promote the religion of Christian Science "as taught by [Eddy]." The decision continued,

> This latter purpose in substance is not a gift to a particular ecclesiastical organization for its special needs. It manifests a broader design, and authorizes the use of the gift for spreading the tenets of faith taught by the testatrix over an area more extensive than could possibly be gathered in one congregation. It includes the most Catholic missionary effect, both as to territory, peoples and times. It is the founding of a trust of comprehensive scope for

the up-building of the sect which the testatrix made the object
of her bounty.

The court went on to declare that the directors of the church, "as a
body corporate under the laws when objection [was] made by the commonwealth," were "restrained from taking and holding the property
described in the bill." But, since a charitable trust had been created by
the will, new trustees could be appointed to manage the trust.[7]

At the invitation of the *Concord Patriot*, Henry Robinson attempted
to explain the "effect" of the decision. Robinson's equally confusing
analysis states, "The court says that it has not sufficient facts before
it to enable it to determine whether 'the religion of Christian Science
as taught' by Mrs. Eddy is a proper subject for charity." According
to Robinson, the court invited the next friends to amend their bill
with additional facts, which would be considered by a single justice
of the state supreme court. In a telegram to the press, Chandler was
more succinct, writing, "The Massachusetts Supreme Court says that
Christian Science with its healers is a religion and a charity and must
be aided by the court as a trust, but the Mother Church cannot be
the trustee." A spokesman for the Christian Science Committee on
Publication gave the most accurate pronouncement: "The decision is
of course a victory for the church in that the estate is to go to the charitable uses designated by Mrs. Eddy. . . . Right minded people everywhere will rejoice with Christian Scientists." To Parker and Long in
Massachusetts, Chandler summed up the effect of the decision: "The
two courts [New Hampshire and Massachusetts] seem to have agreed
to take the responsibility of giving the two millions to the religion
but not to the church. The difference does not help the sons much."[8]

As in New Hampshire, the state supreme court in Massachusetts
did leave one window of opportunity open to the next friends, which
was that the bequest would be void if the sons could prove that the religion was contrary to public policy. Chandler met with Long, Parker,
Remick, Howe, and Kelley in Boston on October 21 to decide how
to proceed. Chandler then wrote to Long and Parker, asking them to

withdraw all suits for Glover and Foster Eddy dealing with the residuary clause of Eddy's will. Chandler explained,

> I have become convinced that the sons had better discontinue
> their suits and not attempt to prove, for their pecuniary benefit,
> as the sole issue now made that the religion of C.S. with its heal-
> ing arts is a religion forbidden by the public policy of the land.
> Not to attempt that (with substantially all the facts concerning
> the religion of C.S. known to the sons at the time of the making
> of the family settlement) now seems to me to be fairly required
> by the settlement made in 1909. Therefore without any arrange-
> ment with our opponents I request you to dismiss all proceedings
> on our part.

In the end, Chandler understood that to challenge the religion on the basis of public policy would jeopardize the family settlement, as the trustees could revoke the trust based on the violation of the agreement made by the sons declaring that Eddy was competent at the time of the settlement and that they would not challenge her will. The risk to the future of the Glovers was simply too great to proceed, despite Chandler's desire to strike a blow against Christian Science.[9]

Chandler was able to explain this decision directly to young Andrew Glover, who traveled east that fall to get married. It is not known if the now twenty-one-year-old Andrew married the same girl he had impregnated in the summer of 1910, but the fact that the wedding took place in New Hampshire and that Andrew met three times with Chandler that fall would lead one to that conclusion. Before long, the couple would have two children, one named William, whom Chandler referred to as "an angel," and young Mrs. Glover would correspond occasionally with Chandler, keeping him informed of the growing family, further indication that Chandler knew the bride prior to the wedding. He tried to explain to George Glover the decision to drop all suits, in what reads as a valedictory, concluding, "During the events of the last six years I have become very much attached to you and your family and any misfortune which may touch you distresses me deeply. . . . Yet I believe I love Mary Baker Glover best of all." Chandler admitted that his health was poor ("I am not strong"), that his wife was an invalid, and that he was now seventy-seven years old, and, worst of all, that "the Democrats [were] coming into power!!"[10]

Before dismissing all the law suits, Chandler discovered he had one more card to play. Eddy's copyrights were coming due for renewal, and while they were worth nothing to the sons, he had Parker negotiate with Streeter for a payment of $5,000 to George Glover in exchange for releasing any claim to the copyrights. The final settlement also acknowledged the right of Glover to the $175,000 trust fund and to all arrears due Glover since Streeter had stopped all payments during the litigation over Eddy's will. With the lawsuits finally dismissed and Glover's trust fund assured, it was finally time for Chandler to attempt to settle up with all the lawyers who had worked on the unsuccessful litigations. He had Long and Parker keep $4,000 of the copyright money for themselves, to be divided equally. Streeter, one of the trustees of Glover's trust fund, approved of Chandler's asking Glover for $11,000 from the principal of the fund to pay the other attorneys and to reimburse the four Glover children for advancing $1,000 each to pay for the litigation. Foster Eddy had also advanced $1,000 to Chandler, which he would not recover. Chandler then paid $1,000 each to Hannis Taylor, James W. Remick, James M. Hodgson, and DeWitt Howe. Kelley and Chambers each received $500, though Kelley claimed he had done so little work on the will litigations, as he was heavily engaged working for the Boston and Maine Railroad, that he was willing to give his share to Howe. Chandler stated that he would pay himself only $1,000 as senior attorney. What he paid to Slaght is not clear, but the reporter for the *World* expressed his friendship for Chandler: "My tribute to you—the biggest and best man I ever met. I am never going to part with your letter." Feeling "bitterly disappointed" by the dropping of the lawsuits, Slaght pledged, "I shall keep fighting the blasphemous crooks of the Mother Church all the days of my life."[11]

Howe refused to accept only $1,000, insisting that "the great bulk of the labor and responsibility of these cases [had] fallen" on him. He asked Chandler to inform him how much each of the other attorneys had been paid. Chandler agreed that Howe had done much of the work, but Chandler didn't have any more money to pay him. Their correspondence became highly contentious until Howe finally offered to accept $2,500 plus expenses amounting to around $250. Kelley tried to intervene, meeting in Concord with Howe, who was threatening a lawsuit to recover the money. Kelley reported, "He feels grieved because Remick got a thousand, equalling his own compensation, and that the Boston men [Long and Parker] got more and did less." But Kelley informed Howe that "a petty suit for compensation" wouldn't look good: "What a spectacle it would be! Howe having been paid ten or eleven thousand dollars by his clients sues them and trustees their income because he says he is entitled to five hundred dollars more," particularly since "when employed no figure was made for his compensation." Kelley concluded, "We all got paid more than we earned before [for the next friends case and family settlement], and we all got paid less than we earned now." And he stated, "[Howe] does not need the money. He is rich, as things go in New Hampshire, only he is stuffy." But Howe "flatly refused to compromise" and even contacted Glover directly, informing him that he had wanted to pursue the case on the issue of public policy, only to be overruled by Chandler. In the end, Howe got his $2,500 plus expenses but drew the enmity of Chandler, who urged Glover to pay him: "It would be unwise to have a lawsuit with the   . You may fill the blank."[12]

Attempting to calm Howe proved to be Kelley's last service to Chandler and the next friends. Kelley died on September 20, 1913, in a Portsmouth hospital at age forty-seven. He had served as a practical antidote to the more fanatically anti–Christian Science attorneys for the next friends. Besides trying to negotiate with Howe over a final fee, Kelley also urged Howe to accept defeat in the will litigation cases, as pursuing the public policy question that Howe advocated would likely fail and result in the forfeiture of the Glover trust fund.[13]

The election of Wilson as president also swept in the Democrats in New Hampshire over a divided Republican Party. The election of the first Democratic governor and legislature in nearly fifty years worked to Chandler's advantage in one important way. Chandler had long advocated the erection of a statue to the only president ever from New Hampshire, Chandler's first employer, Franklin Pierce. But since Pierce was a Democrat and an opponent of the Civil War, the Republican legislature and administrations had always blocked Chandler's efforts. Chandler did not support all of Pierce's policies but acknowledged his innate kindness to the young Chandler and Pierce's unique status as the only president from the Granite State. The new Democratic legislature allocated $15,000 for the statue to be placed on Main Street in front of the State House, and Chandler was invited to give the keynote address at the dedication ceremony in 1914. Hodgson, in South Dakota, acknowledged Chandler's effort: "You must be gratified at the success of your efforts to obtain a memorial for President Pierce. . . . I sincerely hope you may live to make the dedicatory address when this memorial to a worthy but much misunderstood president is unveiled in New Hampshire."[14]

Chandler kept in touch with the Glovers and Hodgson while trying to get George's annual allotment increased from $1,500 to $3,000 per year. As Glover's health deteriorated, Chandler tried to shame Streeter into increasing the annual income, but Streeter steadfastly refused until Glover had signed all papers related to the dismissal of the lawsuits. Glover stubbornly refused to do this until he had received all arrears from the trustees, who had withheld his income during the will litigations. Finally, Glover agreed, through Hodgson, sending Chandler the following telegram: "Dismiss my suit for legacy upon Streeter and associates making specific agreement as to payment of amounts due from Trust Fund and $1500.00 a year extra and fixing specific dates when payments will be made and amounts. When this is done I will sign and send copyright papers." Glover's distrust and hatred of Streeter is evident in what he wrote to Chandler: "I am tired of being harassed by Streeter and his associates by their withholding the pittance that is to be paid to me under the strict letter of the trust deed whenever they see fit or whenever their malevolence dictates such course to them. I have signed every paper they have asked to date and they are still as bitter and vindictive against me as they ever were and my business seems to be entirely unsettled." Chandler passed Glover's letter along to Streeter, adding, "I am afraid that Glover will not long survive; having realized for two or three years that he was in failing condition. I wish you would send him some money unconditionally and without delay. Two millions and a half for the Directors and $136,000 besides your $50,000 as fees, with Glover in his present needs upon the point of death makes a sad picture. Who is responsible for it? I am sure I know." Chandler was referring to the final settlement of Eddy's estate by her executor, Josiah Fernald, which took place on March 26, 1914. After expenses, Fernald passed along to Eddy's trustees $2,590,632.18, the largest estate ever settled in a New Hampshire court. This amount was given after the paying of $135,500 to Streeter's law firm and of $118,582.45 in estate taxes to New Hampshire. Chandler was correct; Streeter had profited greatly as lead attorney for Mary Baker Eddy. While Chandler was passing out small fees to each of the attorneys for the next friends, Streeter had raked in at least $50,000 from Eddy for the original next friends case, and an additional $136,000 for everything that followed. This amounted to between $3 million and $4 million in today's money, compared with a maximum of $10,000 (worth maybe as much as $200,000 today) to any of the attorneys for the next friends, but, of course, Streeter was successful whereas Chandler and company had failed in every lawsuit, and the directors of Christian Science likely believed the investment in Streeter was worth every penny.[15]

Glover finally received his $3,000 annual income but had little time to enjoy the extra money. He died at age seventy-one of peritonitis in Lead, South Dakota, on December 26, 1915. It is easy to dismiss George W. Glover as a naïve primitive duped into the next friends suit by the manipulative *New York World* and its henchman, William E. Chandler, but that would be an insufficient explanation of more than six years of continuous litigation. A more complete understanding of Glover requires analysis of the distance, physical and emotional, that existed between mother and son. Glover had been taken away from his mother as a young child, and they did not see each other between 1856 and 1879. By that time, Glover had a wife and children in South Dakota. When he visited Eddy in Boston, she was appalled at his rough ways and lack of education. One can only imagine what Glover thought of her life in the East, but the term "fish out of water" best describes him during this visit. Both mother and son attempted to establish a more normal relationship, with Glover adopting Christian Science, although in a rudimentary manner. At one point, he invited his mother to move in with his family in South Dakota. In turn, Eddy asked her son to come east, to comfort her following the death of her third husband, Asa Gilbert Eddy. George declined because of the needs of his family in South Dakota. Her adoption of E. J. Foster Eddy can only be explained as an attempt to establish a familial relationship with someone who resembled the son she knew Glover could never be. Like his mother, Glover was a gambler; only in his case, he hoped to strike it rich through his mining endeavors. Mary Baker Eddy gambled everything on the establishment of her religion. Each had created a life for themselves thousands of miles apart, yet both knew that convention required them at least to express their love for one another and to attempt to support each other in spite of the emotional and physical distance between them. A sense of obligation accompanied by some level of affection motivated their actions over the years.[16]

That physical distance added to George's growing suspicion and antipathy toward the people who surrounded his mother, seemingly replaced him in her life, and prevented him from easy access to her. Even Foster Eddy was ultimately dismissed from Eddy's affections as Glover had been, and Glover believed a conspiracy of her followers was responsible. It was only after this dismissal that Glover and his adopted brother became close. In South Dakota, Glover was known to be an expert at the law. His attorneys, Judge Granville Bennett and J. M. Hodgson, marveled at his litigious nature and many lawsuits.

They informed Chandler that Glover was "a very hard man to handle" because he was so stubborn and had "a holy horror of settling a case." Glover was never duped by Chandler in the next friends suit. Glover's long experience with the law and frequent interactions with attorneys in South Dakota made him a knowledgeable and willing partner in all the legal actions that took place. In fact, it was Glover and his family who manipulated Chandler, who became so fond of his western clients that after the next friends suit was dismissed, he always placed the family's financial needs above his own obsession of striking a blow against Christian Science. In the end, Glover gambled that success in the next friends case would secure his family's financial future; whether it damaged his mother's religion was never a serious concern to him. While Chandler did not always reveal his utter contempt for the tenets of Christian Science to Glover, Eddy's son was so involved in every aspect of the case, and was clever enough and knowledgeable enough about the law, that he must have understood that the attorneys in the next friends case were not motivated by a desire to protect his mother but, like Glover himself, had other priorities.[17]

Chandler's wife died in October 1915, and his own health deteriorated significantly as he passed his eightieth birthday. In fact, it took him nearly a year to acknowledge all of the condolences he received following Lucy Chandler's death. He did, finally, write back to several participants in the original next friends suit. To Foster Eddy, he wrote, "About half the time I have been prostrate. At other times I rally and try to do something. . . . You always were kind and gracious to me, and always responded to any advice from me." Chandler was far more informative to Dr. Henry Hopkins in Buffalo: "George Glover is dead, Mrs. Eddy is dead, and the children are married [Mary had recently become Mrs. Billings] and all your and my experience in connection with Mrs. Eddy has passed into the beyond." But Chandler never regretted pursuing Christian Science and took credit for what he saw as changes in the religion. He told Hopkins,

> The Christian Science Church is being handled on a new basis.
> The Directors have come to realize that the humbugs must be

discarded, and they have been trying to do it. In the last pleadings of the law suit before the family dropped every contention,
the Directors deliberately filed a pleading which disclaimed the
use of any other agency in healing except that of prayer, and
made one or two other averments that I could not help thinking were made in order to be able to prove, if necessary, the
abandonment of any of the absurd claims Mrs. Eddy had kept
up. But they have never decided to refuse to receive money as
Doctors' fees, and I see they have recently in your State managed to evade the statute against practising medicine without a
license. I wish I could continue my condemnation of Christian
Science as a healing art, but my physical and mental faculties do
not permit, and I have not felt that the family ought to do so.
The ministers and doctors should do that, and you and a few
other people, can't do it.

Chandler gave himself too much credit for modifying the teachings
of the church. Mary Baker Eddy had never allowed anything other than
prayer as treatment of disease and, in fact, had broken with Richard
Kennedy many years earlier because of his use of touch in the practice
of healing. And Eddy had been rethinking the concept of M.A.M. for
years prior to the next friends case. It was not unusual for a new religion to change as it grew in order to attract more converts and take its
place within the mainstream of society. The Mormons had done that
when discarding the practice of polygamy to make Mormonism more
acceptable and to allow Utah to be admitted as a state.[18]

An important clue to what motivated Chandler in his crusade
against Eddy's teachings is found in a letter he wrote to the astrono-
mer E. C. Pickering of Harvard in 1906.

As you know, my faith in immortality is derived principally from
the teachings of astronomy. If I could see nothing but the earth
and the sun and the moon I should not know where we could
live after the body dies and the approaching gloom would be
terrifying indeed. The immortality which I have faith in is to be

a physical life. We are not to make the transition suddenly from
material existence into an ethereal realm to live entirely without
contact with matter. We are to have bodies as well as souls and
are to go to the stars as our future homes. . . . In our father's
house are many mansions—in the stars.[19]

To Chandler, the physical world was the only reality, and he believed
as strongly in it as revealed by modern science as Eddy believed in the
spirit world and relegated the physical world to the realm of "mortal
mind." Therefore, Chandler believed Eddy's teachings threatened scientific progress and was a return to primitive superstition.

It is worth noting how many of the attorneys involved in the next
friends litigations were Unitarians: William E. Chandler, former governor John Davis Long, and Herbert Parker for the plaintiffs, and
Frank Streeter and Henry M. Baker for the defense. In denying the
Trinity, Unitarians were free to interpret the Bible as they chose. Long
expressed this freedom in his journal.

It is a denomination whose fold is not close & the range of which
is large & free. It permits all shades of opinion. I say "opinion,"
for I doubt if one can say "belief" in any denomination. Belief,
in an intelligent mind, is inconsistent with conventional theological views—in the absolute sense. Agnosticism is the necessity of
our human limitations. We hope, we make induction, we trust,
but we cannot know. If we could, we should be omniscient & so,
not human. This is true to some extent even in material things,
in science, in ordinary life. By the way, I see that somebody says
that life may yet be produced by chemical forces. This is an old
surmise of mine—at least the probability of it. I have looked for
some such possible development from electricity. Is life only an
electric spark?[20]

To Long, the explanation of life itself was a matter of science or
electricity. Eddy's teaching was an absolute denial of every one of

Long's "opinions," as she not only believed, but her beliefs set "conventional theological views" on their head. Unitarians like Chandler and Long were able to find refuge for their own unconventional agnostic beliefs within the respectable confines of Unitarianism.

That freedom to think and interpret may help explain why Unitarians Streeter and Baker defended Mary Baker Eddy so strongly and consistently. The advantage of these two men over their opponents is that they knew her, visited frequently, and understood that while her ideas may have been unconventional, she was at least not a danger and had every right to interpret man and the universe as she chose. One wonders if Chandler would have been so harsh and determined in his attacks on Eddy and Christian Science if he had actually sat down and discussed things with her.

But Chandler referred to himself as a "radical progressive" and accepted and practiced the methods of change that characterize Progressivism. Chandler believed that when a problem was exposed to public scrutiny through the press and the courts, public opinion would rally around a solution, and corrective measures would result. This had been the result of the works of muckrakers, like Upton Sinclair and Ida Tarbell, who had exposed the evils of the meat-packing industry and Standard Oil Company to public scrutiny, bringing about new legislation to protect the health of consumers and the safety of workers, and to break up too-powerful trusts. This is why Chandler always fought "Eddyism" in the press as well as in the courts. But Christian Science did not fit this model of change. Chandler expected the public to be scandalized by Eddy's belief in M.A.M. and by the dangers of her alternative form of healing, and he was always frustrated that ministers and medical professionals did not take up his cause. The problem for Chandler was that, unlike the meat-packing industry, Christian Science did not affect most people. For those who believed in it, Chandler's efforts had no effect, while to the vast majority of Americans, it was irrelevant that some people had such different beliefs. Thus progressive methods did not work to combat Christian Science, and the efforts of the next friends only tends to verify the

interpretation of some historians that Progressivism was really a
movement of conventional, intolerant Protestants out to reclaim
their prominence in a changing society. As a "radical" progressive,
Chandler had broader goals. Just as Prohibition demonstrates how
progressives had overreached in trying to legislate peoples' behavior, Chandler overreached in attempting to change people's thinking
about and behavior toward religion and the universe. The public drew
the line at the attempt of progressives like Chandler to transform all
Americans into his model of a right-thinking, utopian middle class.
Even the New Deal was not so ambitious, and Franklin D. Roosevelt,
who learned something from the overreach of the progressive era,
stated this in 1932: "We know that the old 'rights of personal competency,' the right to read, to think, to speak, to choose and live a mode
of life, must be respected at all hazards."[21]

A final word belongs to Frank S. Streeter, who was the consistent
winner in every confrontation with Chandler. The two were constantly
thrown together in the small world of Concord, New Hampshire, as
attorneys, politicians, and Republicans. When not in court, Streeter
had always shown respect and kindness toward Chandler, whose usual
response was personal animosity toward anyone who disagreed with
him, in politics or in the practice of law. But in one of the last acts
of his life, Chandler sent Streeter a copy of a book about the fall of
the Roman Empire, along with an admonishment to not be "so arbitrary and violent" in court while defending a client. Streeter thanked
Chandler for the present, remarking, "As you advance in years you are
growing into the habit of doing nice things." But in what can only be
viewed as a justification of his defense of Mary Baker Eddy, Streeter
attempted to defend the harsh words he had used in court recently in
defending a "mother against whom . . . nothing was found to impair
her good name." Her relatives "had conspired to wreck the reputation of the mother and drive her as a discredited woman out into the
world." They had investigated her fully, sworn "falsely," "cheated" in
court, but the woman had been "left standing with an honorable reputation before the world." Streeter wondered what Chandler would do

in defending such a woman: "What kind of language would you use?" Streeter asked, "Please advise me what to say?"[22]

While Streeter gained immensely in reputation and in wealth from his defense of Mary Baker Eddy, to him it was also a chivalrous act to protect a woman from abuse. Chandler had hoped the press and the public would rally to his side to bring an end to the dangers of Christian Science, but instead, while news about the case was being fully reported, editorial after editorial condemned the next friends for attacking freedom of religion and for forcing a helpless old lady to defend herself in court. Eddy was anything but helpless as she dominated her followers and expertly managed Christian Science right up until the end of her life. But at that time, a woman being such an innovator in religion and in healing was extraordinary, and she asserted, "If I had been a man they would not have treated me so." Nevertheless, she benefited in the end from the generally accepted view that a woman, particularly one of a certain age, was entitled to protection from a male-dominated society. And the editorials proved that on the question of women, the pro-Eddy press was just as antiquated as those who attacked Eddy and Christian Science. In the end, the next friends cases demonstrated one thing only: that the vast majority of Americans accepted the right of each individual to find his or her own truth regarding the relationship between God and man.[23]

A NOTE ON SOURCES

The letters and papers of participants in the next friends case and Eddy will litigation were used extensively throughout the narrative. Most of these are part of the William Eaton Chandler Papers at the New Hampshire Historical Society Library in Concord. The Chandler Papers amount to twenty-two linear feet of material, which includes forty-four archival boxes and forty pocket diaries. Ten boxes of papers relate solely to Eddy matters, and the small pocket diaries help to track the comings and goings of the next friends and some of the private thoughts of the lead attorney in the case. In addition, all of the letters to and from Mary Baker Eddy that were owned by her son, George Washington Glover II, and her adopted son, Dr. Ebenezer J. Foster Eddy, were once in Chandler's possession. One condition of the family settlement was that Chandler return all of the originals of these letters to the Mary Baker Eddy Library. He did so, but only after having transcriptions made of all the letters. These copies are also kept in a box in the vault of the New Hampshire Historical Society Library and are still cataloged as part of the Chandler Papers. Because Chandler had such a close relationship with the *New York World*, many of these letters appeared in print at the time. Most of these were submitted as evidence in the case of *Eddy v. Frye*, and some appear in the testimony of the case and are, thus, public records.

The Mary Baker Eddy Collection at the Mary Baker Eddy Library in Boston is the repository of all of Eddy's correspondence, the reminiscences of some of her staff, and many other records relating to the next friends case and the Eddy will litigation. Whenever a catalog number appears in an endnote (L16209, for example), it means that the letter was first discovered by the author at the Mary Baker Eddy Library. The staff was very helpful in attaining permission for the author to use this material in the book, as much of it is copyrighted by The Mary Baker Eddy Collection. Other letters to and from Eddy and her son or adopted son were published at the time in the newspapers or were part of the trial transcript. In these cases, the transcription copy at the New Hampshire Historical Society was used by the author, but the endnote states that the original is at the Mary Baker Eddy Library in Boston.

The author read many of Eddy's writings, including *Science and Health with Key to the Scriptures, Retrospection and Introspection, Miscellany,* and *Christ and Christmas.* While these are helpful, a fuller understanding of Mary Baker Eddy's life and teachings are found in several good biographies that were used throughout the narrative. The best of these are the three-volume work of Robert Peel published in the 1960s and 1970s (*Mary Baker Eddy: The Years of Discovery,* 1966; *Mary Baker Eddy: The Years of Trial,* 1971; and *Mary Baker Eddy: The Years of Authority,* 1977) and the biography of Eddy by Gillian Gill published in 1998 (*Mary Baker Eddy*). Peel was a Christian Scientist who had full access to all materials relating to Eddy but who did not shy away from exploring the many controversies in her life. Gill is a feminist historian who attempted to place Eddy within the framework of the feminist movement, and her work is very reliable and balanced in exploring all of the events in Eddy's life. Stephen Gottschalk, a religious scholar, wrote of Eddy's later life in *Rolling Away the Stone,* published in 2006. All of these works helped the author to understand the teachings of Eddy and the tenets of Christian Science. Each also covers the next friends case and will litigation from the perspective of Mary Baker Eddy and Christian Science.

Published at the time of the next friends case are the books by Mark Twain (*Christian Science,* 1907) and by Georgine Milmine, also credited to Willa Cather and published serially in *McClure's Magazine* (*The Life of Mary Baker G. Eddy and The History of Christian Science,* 1909). While less reliable factually than the above-mentioned biographies, these works express well the tone of hostility toward Eddy and Christian Science that was prominent in 1907. By demonstrating how much interest and controversy surrounded Eddy and her church, the Twain and Milmine books provided the author with much material and a better understanding of the actions of Chandler and the next friends.

The yellow press played a pivotal role in Eddy-related matters throughout the litigation. The *New York World* first reported the accusations that Mary Baker Eddy was either dead or incapacitated and then hired former senator William E. Chandler to investigate and litigate the case. *McClure's Magazine* put the same emphasis on investigating Eddy and Christian Science as it had recently put on its muckraking exposé of the Standard Oil Company, and published its distorted findings each month during 1907. Therefore, newspapers were a major source of information for this book, both in reporting the facts about Eddy and Christian Science and in charting editorial comment and public opinion. Fortunately for the author, Eddy's chief attorney, Frank Sherwin Streeter, kept thirty-two albums of clippings about the case from newspapers around the nation. These albums reside at the New Hampshire Historical Society Library and contain articles from newspapers across the nation, including the *Toledo Blade, Philadelphia Press, Minneapolis Tribune,* and many others. Boston newspapers, particularly the *Globe* and the *Herald,* and local New Hampshire newspapers, the *Concord Monitor, Concord Patriot,* and *Manchester Union,* were also searched extensively for material. It was the media's persistence that kept Mary Baker Eddy and Christian Science before the public, and it was the same newspapers that reported the facts as they emerged during the testimony at the hearings and trial.

Whenever possible, the actual transcript of trial testimony was used. Much of this was printed at the time and is found today in the Streeter Papers at the New Hampshire Historical Society Library and among the Eddy Collection at the Mary Baker Eddy Library. While the daily newspapers covered all the legal proceedings with relish, the official transcripts were used, whenever available, for all quotations taken from the hearings or trial. To meet daily deadlines, the press employed its own stenographer, who made a verbatim copy of all the hearings and the trial, a copy that appeared in many of the newspapers, particularly the *Concord Monitor, Concord Patriot, Manchester Union,* some of the Boston papers, and the *New York World.* However, the press version differs in minor ways from the official transcript kept by the court stenographer, who passed his draft along to the attorneys for both sides for editing before a final official transcript was published. Newspapers around the nation tended to all publish identical stories about the case, indicating that some type of wire service was operating, though no specific attribution for the stories was ever provided. When identical articles and quotes appeared in several newspapers all are cited in the endnote.

The best book published at the time about the case, Michael Meehan's *Mrs. Eddy and the Late Suit in Equity,* 1908, is largely a collection of official documents, bills, motions, affidavits, and rulings, and contains very little narrative by the author. But it was very helpful to find so many official documents together in one place. For the later will litigation, online sources were utilized.

NOTES

NOTES TO INTRODUCTION

1. *New York World*, October 28, 1906.

2. Ibid. At the time it was accepted that a "galvanic battery" producing an electrical charge could reenergize a person suffering from a serious ailment. Slaght's first name is John. No first name for Lithchild could be found

3. Ibid.

4. Ibid.

5. James McGrath Morris, *Pulitzer: A Life in Politics, Print, and Power* (New York: HarperCollins, 2010), p. 415; Robert Peel, *Mary Baker Eddy: The Years of Authority* (New York: Holt, Rinehart and Winston, 1977), p. 262; Steven J. Diner, *A Very Different Age: Americans of the Progressive Era* (New York: Hill and Wang, 1998), p. 204.

6. Charles H. Corning, diary, Sunday, October 28 [1906], New Hampshire Historical Society, Concord (hereafter, NHHS).

7. Ibid.

8. Ibid.

9. Ibid.

10. Ibid.

11. Ibid.

12. *New York World*, October 29, 1906; *Concord Evening Monitor*, October 29, 1906.

13. "Mrs. Eddy and Frye Invisible; Denials Galore," *New York World*, October 29, 1906.

14. Calvin A. Frye to *Concord Monitor*, October 29, 1906, Mary Baker Eddy Letters, Mary Baker Eddy Library (hereafter, the MBE Library), Boston; Pamelia J. Leonard, statement, October 29, 1906, Mary Baker Eddy Letters, MBE Library, Boston: Both letters © The Mary Baker Eddy Collection. Used by permission. Both letters are notarized by Josiah E. Fernald.

15. Lewis Strang to Alfred Farlow, October 15, 1906, accession #L16078, Mary

Baker Eddy Letters, MBE Library, © The Mary Baker Eddy Collection. Used by permission. "Statement Regarding the Visits of Messrs. Slaght and Lithchild of the New York World at Pleasant View," Lewis Strang, October 15, 1906, accession #L16215, Mary Baker Eddy Letters, MBE Library, © The Mary Baker Eddy Collection. Used by permission.

16. Michael Meehan to Joseph Pulitzer, October 26, 1906, quoted in Michael Meehan, *Mrs. Eddy and the Late Suit in Equity* (Concord, NH: Michael Meehan, 1908), pp. 4–5.

17. H. Cornell Wilson to Mary Baker Eddy, October 30, 1906, Mary Baker Eddy Letters, accession #L09802, MBE Library. © The Mary Baker Eddy Collection. Used by permission.

18. Robert Peel, *Mary Baker Eddy: The Years of Authority* (New York: Holt, Rinehart and Winston, 1977), p. 268; Gillian Gill, *Mary Baker Eddy*, Radcliffe Biography Series (Reading, MA: Perseus Books, 1998), pp. 479–480.

19. Fleta Campbell Spring, *According to the Flesh* (New York: Coward-McCann, 1930), pp. 413–414, quoted in Peel, *The Years of Authority*, p. 269, and Gill, *Mary Baker Eddy*, p. 480. The *Boston Herald* headline read "Eyes Bright But Seemed Feeble," October 30, 1906; *Boston Globe* headlines read "Pitiful Spectacle" and "Mrs. Eddy Weak and Decrepit," October 30, 1906.

20. *Concord Monitor*, October 30, 1906. Pearson was also New Hampshire's secretary of state (1899–1915).

21. Lewis C. Strang to Alfred Farlow, October 31, 1906, Mary Baker Eddy Letters, accession #L16209, MBE Library, © The Mary Baker Eddy Collection. Used by permission.

22. Charles H. Corning, diary, October 30, 1906, NHHS.

23. *New York World*, October 28, 1906.

24. Corning, diary, October 30, 1906, NHHS.

NOTES TO CHAPTER 2
MARY BAKER EDDY AND CHRISTIAN SCIENCE

1. Mark Twain, *Christian Science* (New York: Harper and Brothers, 1907), p. 63.

2. Mary Baker Eddy to George Glover, April 27, 1898, Mary Baker Eddy Letters, accession #L02127, Mary Baker Eddy Library, Boston (hereafter, MBE Library), © The Mary Baker Eddy Collection. Used by permission.

3. Gillian Gill, *Mary Baker Eddy*, Radcliffe Biography Series (Reading, MA: Perseus Books, 1998), pp. 450, 468–470.

4. Mary Baker Eddy, *The First Church of Christ, Scientist and Miscellany* (Boston: Christian Science Board of Directors, 1913), p. 70.

5. Twain, *Christian Science*, p. 61.

6. Robert Peel, *Mary Baker Eddy: The Years of Discovery* (New York: Holt, Rinehart and Winston, 1966), p. 4.

7. Georgine Milmine, *The Life of Mary Baker Eddy and the History of Christian Science* (New York: Doubleday, Page, 1909), pp. 5–7. In the introduction to a later edition of this book, David Strouck, a professor at the University of Nebraska, conclusively demonstrated that future novelist Willa Cather, at that time an editor for *McClure's Magazine*, was the actual author of the book credited to Milmine, who had done the research but was not able to put the book into final form. See Milmine, *The Life of Mary Baker Eddy and the History of Christian Science* (N.p., University of Nebraska, 1993), pp. xv–xxviii.

8. Peel, *The Years of Discovery*, p. 6.

9. Milmine, *The Life of Mary Baker Eddy*, p. 12.

10. Gill, *Mary Baker Eddy*, pp. 45–48.

11. Mary Baker Eddy, *Retrospection and Introspection* (Boston: Allison V. Stewart, 1916), p. 10.

12. Gill, *Mary Baker Eddy*, pp. 19–21; Peter A. Wallner, *Franklin Pierce: New Hampshire's Favorite Son* (Concord, NH: Plaidswede Publishing, 2004), pp. 56, 79, 81, 86, 94.

13. Peel, *The Years of Discovery*, pp. 23–24, 50.

14. Gill, *Mary Baker Eddy*, p. 57–63; Peel, *The Years of Discovery*, pp. 68–78.

15. Gill, *Mary Baker Eddy*, pp. 72–76.

16. Milmine, *The Life of Mary Baker Eddy*, pp. 27–32; Gill, *Mary Baker Eddy*, pp. 100–101.

17. Gill, *Mary Baker Eddy*, pp. 87–90; Peel, *The Years of Discovery*, pp. 80, 99.

18. Eddy, *Retrospection and Introspection*, pp. 26–27; Gill, *Mary Baker Eddy*, pp. 90–94 (quotation, p. 94).

19. Gill, *Mary Baker Eddy*, pp. 96–105 (quotation, p. 97); Peel, *The Years of Discovery*, pp. 109–116.

20. Gill, *Mary Baker Eddy*, p. 105. Mary's older sister Abigail married Alexander Tilton, owner of the thriving Tilton mills in Sanbornton Bridge (now Tilton), New Hampshire.

21. Jewel Spangler Smaus, "Family: From New England to the Black Hills, Part IV," *Quarterly News, Mary Baker Eddy Museum and Historic Sites* (Longyear Historical Society) 20, no. 3 (Autumn 1983): 314–315; Eddy, *Retrospection and Introspection*, pp. 20–21.

22. Gill, *Mary Baker Eddy*, pp. 107, 114–115.

23. Peel, *The Years of Discovery*, p. 132, 146, 152, 167, 178, 181; Milmine, *The Life of Mary Baker Eddy*, pp. 42–53; Gill, *Mary Baker Eddy*, pp. 129–139.

24. Gill, *Mary Baker Eddy*, pp. 134–136 (quotation, p. 135), 148; Ernest Sutherland Bates and John V. Dittemore, *Mary Baker Eddy: The Truth and the Tradition* (New York: Knopf, 1932), p. 95.

25. Peel, *The Years of Discovery*, p. 144.

26. Jewel Spangler Smaus, "Family: From New England to the Black Hills, Part III," *Quarterly News, Mary Baker Eddy Museum and Historic Sites* (Longyear Historical Society) 20, no. 1 (Spring 1983): 306–308; Gill, *Mary Baker Eddy*, p. 155.

27. Gill, *Mary Baker Eddy*, pp. 161–162, 167; Peel, *The Years of Discovery*, pp. 195–197.

28. Gill, *Mary Baker Eddy*, pp. 163–166; Milmine, *The Life of Mary Baker Eddy*, pp. 69–70, 82–87; Peel, *The Years of Discovery*, pp. 197–199.

29. Peel, *The Years of Discovery*, p. 197; Gill, *Mary Baker Eddy*, pp. 167–168.

30. Peel, *The Years of Discovery*, pp. 233–235.

31. Gill, *Mary Baker Eddy*, pp. 221–228; Mary Baker Eddy, *Science and Health*, 1st ed. (Boston: Christian Science Publishing, 1875), pp. 35–37, 236–238, 284–290; Stephen Gottschalk, *Rolling Away the Stone: Mary Baker Eddy's Challenge to Materialism* (Bloomington: Indiana University Press, 2006), p. 26.

32. Gill, *Mary Baker Eddy*, p. 221; Gottschalk, *Rolling Away the Stone*, pp. 26–27.

33. Milmine, *The Life of Mary Baker Eddy*, pp. 109–119; Gill, *Mary Baker Eddy*, pp. 172–183.

34. Gill, *Mary Baker Eddy*, pp. 189–195, 202–207; Milmine, *The Life of Mary Baker Eddy*, pp. 135–140; Peel, *The Years of Discovery*, pp. 247–268.

35. Robert Peel, *Mary Baker Eddy: The Years of Trial* (New York: Holt, Rinehart and Winston, 1971), pp. 14–18, 25–28 (quotation on "unique spiritual mission," p. 27); Gill, *Mary Baker Eddy*, pp. 234–256; Milmine, *The Life of Mary Baker Eddy*, pp. 232–233.

36. Peel, *The Years of Trial*, pp. 5–7, 18–23; Gill, *Mary Baker Eddy*, pp. 243–248 (quotation, p. 244); Milmine, *The Life of Mary Baker Eddy*, pp. 169–172.

37. Gill, *Mary Baker Eddy*, pp. 251–255; Milmine, *The Life of Mary Baker Eddy*, pp. 245–246; Peel, *The Years of Trial*, pp. 39–40.

38. "Commonwealth of Massachusetts, Lucretia L. S. Brown, Plaintiff, v. Daniel H. Spofford, Defendant," filed May 17, 1878, Subject Files, box 63, folder 2, MBE Library, © The Mary Baker Eddy Collection. Used by permission. Gill, *Mary Baker Eddy*, pp. 253–256; Milmine, *The Life of Mary Baker Eddy*, pp. 234–247; Peel, *The Years of Trial*, pp. 42–44.

39. Gill, *Mary Baker Eddy*, pp. 257–270; Milmine, *The Life of Mary Baker Eddy*, pp. 247–267; Peel, *The Years of Trial*, pp. 50–58.

40. Jewel Spangler Smaus, "Family: From New England to the Black Hills,

Part V," *Quarterly News, Mary Baker Eddy Museum and Historic Sites* (Longyear Historical Society) 20, no. 4 (Winter 1983–1984): 319–320; Gill, *Mary Baker Eddy*, pp. 275–279.

41. Peel, *The Years of Trial*, pp. 96–98; Milmine, *The Life of Mary Baker Eddy*, p. 276; Gill, *Mary Baker Eddy*, pp. 282–284. All of these sources cite the quotations in text.

42. Gill, *Mary Baker Eddy*, pp. 287–291; Peel, *The Years of Trial*, pp. 113–116; Milmine, *The Life of Mary Baker Eddy*, pp. 283–289.

43. Gill, *Mary Baker Eddy*, pp. 305, 319; Peel, *The Years of Trial*, p.124; Milmine, *The Life of Mary Baker Eddy*, p. 312.

44. Gill, *Mary Baker Eddy*, pp. 318–319, 332–337 (quotations, 318, 332); Peel, *The Years of Trial*, pp. 186–187.

45. Ernest Sutherland Bates and John V. Dittemore, *Mary Baker Eddy: The Truth and the Tradition* (New York: Knopf, 1932), pp. 267–268; Gill, *Mary Baker Eddy*, p. 333; Twain, *Christian Science* (New York: Harper and Brothers, 1907), pp. 69, 86.

46. Milmine, *The Life of a Mary Baker Eddy*, pp. 331–338; Gill, *Mary Baker Eddy*, p. 338.

47. Gill, *Mary Baker Eddy*, pp. 344–348 ("demonstration" cited on p. 347); Peel, *The Years of Trial*, pp. 243–244; Milmine, *The Life of Mary Baker Eddy*, pp. 353–360.

48. Jewel Spangler Smaus, "Family: From New England to the Black Hills, Part VI," *Quarterly News, Mary Baker Eddy Museum and Historic Sites* (Longyear Historical Society) 21, no. 1 (Spring 1984): 321–323; Gill, *Mary Baker Eddy*, pp. 371–375; Peel, *The Years of Trial*, pp. 216–218.

49. Peel, *The Years of Trial*, pp. 221–222; Robert Peel, *Mary Baker Eddy: The Years of Authority* (New York: Holt, Rinehart and Winston, 1977), pp. 24–29, 78–87, 113–114; Gill, *Mary Baker Eddy*, pp. 376–382, 663 n16; Milmine, *The Life of Mary Baker Eddy*, pp. 419–425.

50. Gill, *Mary Baker Eddy*, pp. 347–349, 369–379, 458; Peel, *The Years of Trial*, pp. 251–254; Twain, *Christian Science*, pp. 103–106, 114; Sue S. Dunlap, "Visiting Mary Baker Eddy—Welcome to Pleasant View and Concord, New Hampshire, Part I," *Quarterly News, Longyear Museum and Historical Society* (Longyear Museum and Historical Society) 33, no. 3 (1996): 538.

51. Cheryl P. Moneyhum, "Pleasant View—a Home for Mary Baker Eddy," *Quarterly News, Longyear Museum and Historical Society* (Longyear Museum and Historical Society) 29, no. 1 (Spring 1992): 434–435; Peel, *The Years of Authority*, pp. 9–13; "Spring Tide at Pleasant View," *Concord Daily Patriot*, May 9, 1904, also available online at http://marybakereddylibrary.org.

52. Kathleen Wagner Starrett, "Calvin A. Frye," *Quarterly News, Longyear Museum and Historical Society* 27, no. 3, (Autumn 1990): 413–416; Gill, *Mary*

Baker Eddy, pp. 302–305 (quoted descriptions of Frye, p. 303); Milmine, *The Life of Mary Baker Eddy*, pp. 293–297; Mary Baker Eddy to George Glover, April 27, 1898, Mary Baker Eddy Letters, accession #L02127, MBE Library, © The Mary Baker Eddy Collection. Used by permission. All these sources include the quotation about Frye being "disagreeable."

53. Sue S. Dunlap, "Visiting Mary Baker Eddy—Welcome to Pleasant View and Concord, New Hampshire, Part 1 & 2," *Quarterly News, Longyear Museum and Historical Society* 33, nos. 3 & 4 (1996): 537–544, and 34, nos. 1 & 2 (1997): 545–552; Anne Holliday Webb, "Pleasant View Years," *Quarterly News, Mary Baker Eddy Museum and Historic Sites* (Longyear Historical Society) 7, no. 4 (Winter 1970–1971): 109–112; *Concord Monitor*, September 7, 1900; *Manchester (NH) Union*, June 30, 1903.

54. Peel, *The Years of Authority*, pp. 143–146; Gill, *Mary Baker Eddy*, pp. 418–428 (quotations about mothers and husbands, p. 421); Milmine, *The Life of Mary Baker Eddy*, pp. 428–433.

55. Gill, *Mary Baker Eddy*, pp.431 (Woodbury's depiction of Eddy as "tyrant"), 433–436; Peel, *The Years of Authority*, pp. 151–156; Milmine, *The Life of Mary Baker Eddy*, pp. 436–439. The "Babylonish woman" cited in both Peel, p. 154, and Gill, p. 435.

56. Gill, *Mary Baker Eddy*, pp. 436–439; Peel, *The Years of Authority*, pp. 155–156.

57. Gill, *Mary Baker Eddy*, pp. 441–446; Peel, *The Years of Authority*, pp. 170–171.

58. Peel, *The Years of Authority*, pp. 194–197 (quotations, p. 195); Gill, *Mary Baker Eddy*, pp. 445–449.

59. Gill, *Mary Baker Eddy*, p. 447.

60. Gill, *Mary Baker Eddy*, pp. xvii, xv.

NOTES TO CHAPTER 3
CHANDLER AND STREETER

1. George W. Glover to Prof. Hermann Hering, October 29, 1906, Mary Baker Eddy Letters, Mary Baker Eddy Library, Boston (hereafter, MBE Library) (the letter is in Mary Glover's handwriting), © The Mary Baker Eddy Collection. Used by permission. Hermann Hering to George W. Glover, November 5, 1906, copy found in William E. Chandler Papers (hereafter, Chandler Papers), New Hampshire Historical Society, Concord (hereafter, NHHS).

2. "Eddy Will Litigation, Deposition of William E. Chandler, Taken in Concord, N.H.; begun September 7, 1911; completed January 1, 1912," filed January 3, 1912, in Merrimack County, N.H., Superior Court, equity no. 5382, George W. Glover v. Henry M. Baker, Executor, et al., pp. 36, 88; Samuel Blythe to William E. Chandler, November [?], 1906; William E. Chandler to John W. Kelley, November 20, 1906, both in Chandler Papers, NHHS.

3. William Chandler, diary, November 21 and 22, 1906, Chandler Papers, NHHS; William E. Chandler to John W. Kelley, November 20, 1906, Chandler Papers, NHHS; William E. Chandler to John W. Kelley, November 22, 1906, Chandler Papers, NHHS.

4. Leon Burr Richardson, *William E. Chandler, Republican* (New York: Dodd, Mead, 1940), p. 18.

5. Ibid., pp. 37–49.

6. Ibid., pp. 57, 73, 119, 121, 141, 164.

7. Ibid., pp. 187–199 (quotations, pp. 193, 199).

8. H. Wayne Morgan, *From Hayes to McKinley: National Party Politics, 1877–1896* (Syracuse, NY: Syracuse University Press, 1969), pp. 219, 358.

9. Ibid., pp. 341.

10. Richardson, *Chandler*, pp. 526–527; Paula Baker, *Curbing Campaign Cash: Henry Ford, Truman Newberry and the Politics of Progressive Reform* (Lawrence: University Press of Kansas, 2012), p. 59.

11. *Concord Monitor*, July 20, 1900, October 8, 1900, and November 19, 1900. *Boston Herald* cited in *Concord Monitor*, July 20, 1900; *Boston Post* cited in *Concord Monitor*, October 8, 1900; and *Washington Post* cited in *Concord Monitor*, November 19, 1900.

12. *Washington Post* cited in *Concord Monitor*, December 24, 1900, and January 16, 1901.

13. Richardson, *Chandler*, pp. 641–662.

14. William E. Chandler to John W. Slaght, November 22, 1906, Chandler Papers, NHHS.

15. William E. Chandler to George W. Glover, November 22, 1906, Chandler Papers, NHHS.

16. George W. Glover to William E. Chandler, November 30, 1906, Chandler Papers, NHHS.

17. Slaght was wrong, in that Glover and his daughter Mary had met with Eddy as recently as 1903.

18. John W. Slaght to William E. Chandler, December 5, 1906, Chandler Papers, NHHS.

19. Jewel Spangler Smaus, "Family: From New England to the Black Hills, Part VI," *Quarterly News, Mary Baker Eddy Museum and Historic Sites* (Longyear

Historical Society) 21, no. 1 (Spring 1984): 321–324; Eddy quoted in Robert Peel, *Mary Baker Eddy: The Years of Trial* (New York: Holt, Rinehart and Winston, 1971), p. 70.

20. John W. Kelley to William E. Chandler, December 4, 1906, Chandler Papers, NHHS.

21. Charles A. Hazlett, *History of Rockingham County, New Hampshire, and Representative Citizens* (Chicago: Richmond-Arnold Publishing, 1915), pp. 779–780.

22. William E. Chandler to Bradford Merrill, December 10, 1906, Chandler Papers, NHHS.

23. Bradford Merrill to William E. Chandler, December 12, 1906, Chandler Papers, NHHS; David Brian, *Pulitzer: A Life* (New York: John Wiley and Sons, 2001), pp. 276, 368.

24. Bradford Merrill to William E. Chandler, December 12, 1906, Chandler Papers, NHHS.

25. Chandler, diary, December 9, 1906, Chandler Papers, NHHS; William E. Chandler to George W. Glover, December 10, 1906, Chandler Papers, NHHS; William E. Chandler to George W. Glover, December 13, 1906, Chandler Papers, NHHS.

26. Robert Peel, *Mary Baker Eddy: The Years of Authority* (New York: Holt, Rinehart and Winston, 1977), pp. 260–261 (Farlow on assurances from *McClure's*, p. 261); Alfred Farlow to Mary Baker Eddy, December 22, 1906, Mary Baker Eddy Letters, accession #L16383, MBE Library. © The Mary Baker Eddy Collection. Used by permission.

27. Cornell Wilson to Alfred Farlow, July 18, 1906, Mary Baker Eddy Letters, MBE Library; Peel, *The Years of Authority*, pp. 261–162; Augusta B. Bensley to John B. Willis, July 10, 1906, Mary Baker Eddy Letters, MBE Library, quoted in Peel, *Mary Baker Eddy: The Years of Authority*, p.261.

28. Charles H. Corning, diary, October 31, 1906, NHHS.

29. Lewis Strang to William B. Johnson, August 20, 1906, Mary Baker Eddy Letters, accession #L15993, MBE Library; David Strouck, "Introduction," *The Life of Mary Baker G. Eddy and the History of Christian Science* (Lincoln: University of Nebraska Press, 1993), pp. xv–xxviii.

30. Calvin Frye to Alfred Farlow, November 26, 1906, Mary Baker Eddy Letters, accession #L18331, MBE Library; Alfred Farlow to Calvin Frye, November 29, 1906, Mary Baker Eddy Letters, accession #L16089, MBE Library. All letters © The Mary Baker Eddy Collection. Used by permission.

31. Alfred Farlow to Mary Baker Eddy, December 22, 1906, Mary Baker Eddy Letters, accession #L16383, MBE Library, © The Mary Baker Eddy Collection. Used by permission. Peel, *The Years of Authority*, p. 495 n49.

32. William E. Chandler to John W. Slaght, December 12, 1906, Chandler Papers, NHHS; John W. Slaght to William E. Chandler, December 26, 1906, Chandler Papers, NHHS.

33. George W. Glover to William E. Chandler, December 21, 1906; Chandler, diary, December 26, 27, 28, 1906, Chandler Papers, NHHS.

34. William E. Chandler to John W. Kelley, December 28, 1906, and December 31, 1906, Chandler Papers, NHHS (Chandler quoted from December 31 letter); William E. Chandler to John W. Slaght, December 12, 1906, Chandler Papers, NHHS.

35. William E. Chandler to John W. Kelley, December 28, 1906, Chandler Papers, NHHS.

36. Joan Latady, "Frank Sherwin Streeter," *Quarterly News, Mary Baker Eddy Museum and Historic Sites* (Longyear Museum) 19, no. 1 (Spring 1982): 291–292; Henry Harrison Metcalf, ed., *One Thousand New Hampshire Notables* (Concord, NH: Rumford Printing, 1919), p. 45.

37. Alec MacGillis, "General Frank Streeter," in *The New Hampshire Century*, ed. Felice Belman and Mike Pride (Hanover, NH: University Press of New England, 2001), pp. 87–88.

38. Metcalf, *One Thousand New Hampshire Notables*, p. 45; *Concord Monitor*, November 14, 1906; Mark Sullivan to William E. Chandler, November 16, 1906, Chandler Papers, NHHS; William E. Chandler to Mark Sullivan, November 21, 1906, Chandler Papers, NHHS.

NOTES TO CHAPTER 4
BOTH SIDES PREPARE FOR BATTLE

1. *Crosscurrents of Change: Concord, New Hampshire in the 20th Century* (Concord, NH: Concord Historical Society, 2011), pp. 79–84.

2. Signed affidavit of George W. Glover, January 2, 1907, William E. Chandler Papers (hereafter, Chandler Papers), New Hampshire Historical Society (hereafter, NHHS). The report is signed by George W. Glover and Mary Baker Glover, and notarized by F. E. Sturdevant.

3. Ibid.

4. Ibid.

5. Ibid.

6. Ibid.

7. John W. Kelley to William E. Chandler, January 5, 1906, Chandler Papers, NHHS.

8. Mary Baker Eddy to Alfred Farlow, December 22, 1906, Mary Baker Eddy Letters, accession #01707, Mary Baker Eddy Library (hereafter, MBE Library), Boston, © The Mary Baker Eddy Collection. Used by permission.

9. Mary Baker Eddy and Calvin Frye, January, 1907, Mary Baker Eddy Letters, accession #A11078, MBE Library, © The Mary Baker Eddy Collection. Used by permission. The library credits Calvin Frye with this "typewritten" draft, which, it was claimed, contained "corrections in Mrs. Eddy's handwriting." The final version as it appeared in the newspapers is found in Michael Meehan, *Mrs. Eddy and the Late Suit in Equity* (Concord, NH: Michael Meehan, 1908), pp. 65–72.

10. James P. Wilson to Mary Baker Eddy, January 7, 1907, quoted in Robert Peel, *Mary Baker Eddy: The Years of Authority* (New York: Holt, Rinehart and Winston, 1977), pp. 278–279.

11. Mary Baker Eddy to George W. Glover, January 11, 1906[7], and January 12, 1907, William Chandler Papers, NHHS.

12. George W. Glover to Mary Baker Eddy, January 14, 1907, Chandler Papers, NHHS. Glover did have some fifty letters written by his mother since 1880.

13. Mary Baker Eddy to George W. Glover, January 19, 1907, Chandler Papers, NHHS.

14. Telegram, Mrs. [Nellie] Glover to Miss [Mary] Glover, January 21, 1907, Chandler Papers, NHHS; George W. Glover to Mrs. George W. Glover, January 21, 1907, Chandler Papers, NHHS; also, William E. Chandler, diary, January 22, 1907, Chandler Papers, NHHS.

15. Mary Baker G. Eddy to George W. Glover, January 26, 1907, Chandler Papers, NHHS; Mary B. G. Eddy to son and granddaughter, January 26, 1907, Chandler Papers, NHHS.

16. *Biographical Dictionary of the American Congress* (Washington, DC: United States Government Printing Office, 1928), p. 693; Thadd Turner, *Wild Bill Hickok: Deadwood City—End of the Trail* (N.p.: Universal Publishers, 2001), pp. 187–188.

17. Copies of telegrams, George W. Glover to G. G. Bennett, January 26, 1907, Granville G. Bennett to George W. Glover, January 27, 1907, George W. Glover to Mrs. George W. Glover, January 28, 1907, William Chandler to Granville G. Bennett, January 28, 1907, Ellen [Nellie] Glover to George W. Glover, January 28, 1907, George W. Glover to Mrs. George W. Glover, January 28, 1907, William E. Chandler to Granville G. Bennett, January 30, 1907: all in Chandler Papers, NHHS; Chandler, diary, January 27, 28, 29, 1907, Chandler Papers, NHHS; Alfred Farlow to Mr. [George W.] Glover, January 28, 29, 30, 1907, Chandler Papers, NHHS; George W. Glover to Mr. [Alfred] Farlow, January 30, 1907, Chandler Papers, NHHS.

18. Granville G. Bennett to William E. Chandler, January 31, 1907, Chandler Papers, NHHS.

19. Mary Baker Eddy to George Glover, July 18, 1892, copy in Chandler Papers, NHHS.

20. Frederick Peabody to William E. Chandler, January 3, 19, 20, 1907, Chandler Papers, NHHS.

21. John W. Kelley to William E. Chandler, January 25, 1907, Chandler Papers, NHHS.

22. George W. Baker to William E. Chandler and John W. Kelley, Attorneys-at-Law, January 8, 1907, Chandler Papers, NHHS; George W. Baker to Mary Baker G. Eddy, November 17, 1905, copy in Chandler Papers, NHHS; William E. Chandler to John W. Slaght, December 31, 1906, Chandler Papers, NHHS.

23. Chandler, diary, February 3, 1907, Chandler Papers, NHHS.

24. Ralph Pulitzer to William E. Chandler, February 6, 1907, Chandler Papers, NHHS.

25. William E. Chandler to Ralph Pulitzer, February 7, 1907, Chandler Papers, NHHS.

26. Ralph Pulitzer to William E. Chandler, February 18, 1907, Chandler Papers, NHHS.

27. William E. Chandler to Joseph Pulitzer, February 27, 1907, Chandler Papers, NHHS.

28. Mary B. G. Eddy to [Warren] Schell, February 8, 1907, copy forwarded to William E. Chandler by George W. Glover and included in letter from Glover of March 1, 1907, Chandler Papers, NHHS.

29. Warren S. Schell to "Dear Grandma" [Mary Baker Eddy], February 14, 1907, copy in Chandler Papers, NHHS; M.G.B. [Mary Glover Baker] Eddy to George Glover, June 26, 1889, copy in Chandler Papers, NHHS; Mary Baker G. Eddy to George Glover, August 16, 1893, Mary Baker Eddy Letters, accession #L02109, MBE Library; Mary Baker G. Eddy to George Glover, August 12, 1892, copy in Chandler Papers, NHHS; George Glover to Mary Baker G. Eddy, July 20, 1900, and M.B.G. [Mary Baker] Eddy to George Glover, July 28, 1907, copies in Chandler Papers, NHHS. All letters © The Mary Baker Eddy Collection. Used by permission.

30. Telegrams, Mary Baker Eddy to George W. Glover, February 9, 11, 1907, copies in Chandler Papers, NHHS; J. E. Fernald, President, National State Bank, February 12, 1907, copy in Chandler Papers, NHHS; R. H. Driscoll, Cashier, First National Bank of Lead, February 14, 19, 1907, copy in Chandler Papers, NHHS; George W. Glover to J. E. Fernald, February 15, 1907, copy in Chandler Papers, NHHS; George W. Glover to R. D. Driscoll, February 16, 1907, copy in Chandler Papers, NHHS; R. H. Driscoll to George W. Glover, February 18 and 19, 1907, copies in Chandler Papers, NHHS.

31. Chandler, diary, January and February 1907, particularly February 25, 1907, Chandler Papers, NHHS; William E. Chandler to G. G. Bennett, February 22, 1907, Chandler Papers, NHHS.

32. Mark Twain, *Christian Science* (New York: Harper and Brothers, 1907), pp. 28, 37.

33. Ibid., pp. 52, 77; see also Robert Peel, *The Years of Authority*, pp. 199–206.

34. Gillian Gill, *Mary Baker Eddy*, Radcliffe Biography Series (Reading, MA: Perseus Books, 1998), pp. 453–463; Ron Powers, *Mark Twain: A Life* (New York: Free Press, 2005), pp. 570, 614–615.

35. William E. Chandler to John W. Kelley, February 25, 1907, and John W. Kelley to William E. Chandler, February 28, 1907, both in Chandler Papers, NHHS.

36. George W. Glover to Mary B. G. Eddy, February 25, 1907, Chandler Papers, NHHS. A copy of the letter in which Eddy accuses her son of M.A.M. is found in the Chandler Papers: M.B.G. Eddy to "Dear Student," September 22, 1890.

37. Affidavit of Henry M. Baker, in Meehan, *Mrs. Eddy and the Late Suit*, pp. 88–89.

NOTES TO CHAPTER 5
THE BATTLE IS JOINED

1. Bill and Order, Mary Baker Glover Eddy v. Calvin A. Frye & A., Merrimack SS, Superior Court, April Term, 1907; Concord *Monitor*, March 2, 1907; *Philadelphia Press*, March 2, 1907.

2. Bill and Order, Mary Baker Glover Eddy v. Calvin A. Frye & A.

3. John W. Kelley to William E. Chandler, March 1, 1907, William E. Chandler Papers (hereafter, Chandler Papers), New Hampshire Historical Society (hereafter, NHHS), Concord. Nathaniel E. Martin, who specialized in tort law, was also a former mayor of Concord. In 1918, he was the unsuccessful Democratic candidate for governor of the state.

4. *Concord Monitor*, March 2, 1907; *Philadelphia Press*, March 2, 1907; *Minneapolis Tribune*, March 2 and March 3, 1907.

5. "A sympathizer" to George Glover, March 3, 1907, Chandler Papers, NHHS.

6. William. E. Chandler to George W. Glover, March 14, 1907, Chandler Papers, NHHS.

7. Telegrams, William Chandler to George Glover, March 4, 1907; William Chandler to Granville Bennett, March 4, 1907; George Glover to William Chandler, March 9, 1907; Granville Bennett to William Chandler, March 11, 1907; William Chandler to George Glover, March 14, 1907; George Glover to William Chandler, March 15, 1907: all in Chandler Papers, NHHS.

8. *Denver Post*, March 13 and 14, 1907; Granville G. Bennett, "Mr. Glover's Statement," March 16, 1907, Chandler Papers, NHHS. Although Chandler agreed with Glover that Wilson was motivated by money, Chandler corrected Glover on one fact: Tomlinson did not arrive in South Dakota until January 24, and Wilson's letter to Eddy was written on January 7, 1907 (William E. Chandler to George Glover, March 19, 1907, Chandler Papers, NHHS).

9. E. J. Foster Eddy to Laura Sargent, March 4, 1907; William E. Chandler, diary, March 6, 8, 11, 1907; E. J. Foster Eddy to J. W. Slaght, March 8, 1907; E. J. Foster Eddy to William E. Chandler, March 11, 1907; William E. Chandler to E. J. Foster, March 15, 1907: William E. Chandler to E. J. Foster Eddy, April 4, 1907 ("a half heir"): all in Chandler Papers, NHHS. Though Ebenezer J. Foster preferred to drop "Eddy" from his name after 1897, court records, documents, newspaper accounts of the case, and correspondence between the attorneys consistently referred to him as Foster Eddy. Only Chandler addressed him as Foster. Therefore, Foster Eddy is used throughout this book to avoid confusion.

10. Fred W. Baker to William E. Chandler, March 7, 1907, Chandler Papers, NHHS; Chandler, diary, March 9 and 11, 1907, Chandler Papers, NHHS; *Boston Globe*, March 12, 1907.

11. *New York World*, March 12, 1907; *Boston Globe*, March 12, 1907; *Boston American*, March 12, 1907. All three sources contain Foster Eddy's description of this story.

12. Henry Robinson, *A Biographical Sketch of Reverent Mary Baker G. Eddy* (Concord, NH: People and Patriot, 1903).

13. Henry Robinson to William E. Chandler, March 20, 1907, March 23, 1907, Chandler Papers, NHHS.

14. Henry Robinson to William E. Chandler, March 20, 23, 28, 1907, Chandler Papers, NHHS.

15. George Glover to William E. Chandler, March 9, 1907; Emily Hannon to William E. Chandler, April 17, 1907; R. C. Hannon to William E. Chandler, May 14, 1907: all found in Chandler Papers, NHHS; *New York World*, May 8, 1907.

16. H. R. Hopkins to William E. Chandler, March 7, March 17, March 28, March 31, April 6, 1907; William E. Chandler to H. R. Hopkins, March 22, 1907: all found in Chandler Papers, NHHS.

17. H. R. Hopkins to William E. Chandler, April 9, April 10, April 12, April 17, 1907, Chandler Papers, NHHS; *Boston Herald*, April 25 and May 1, 1907.

18. William E. Chandler to Granville G. Bennett, March 14, 1907, William E. Chandler to John W. Kelley, Martin and Howe, and Frederick Peabody, March 25, 1907; William E. Chandler to Granville G. Bennett, April 7, 1907: all in Chandler Papers, NHHS.

19. S. S. McClure to William G. Nixon, March 25, 1907, Chandler Papers, NHHS; A. M. Cushing to Frederick Peabody, March 27, 1907, Chandler Papers, NHHS; Luther M. Marston to Frederick Peabody, May, 1907, Mary Baker Eddy Letters, box 67, folder 6, Mary Baker Eddy Library (hereafter, MBE Library), Boston; George A. Quimby to William E. Chandler, May 6, 1907, Chandler Papers, NHHS.

20. Edward N. Pearson to William E. Chandler, March 28, 1907, Chandler Papers, NHHS.

21. Coca-Cola once contained cocaine from coca leaves, but active cocaine leaves were removed from the formula in 1903; after that only "spent" leaves were used. According to experts, by 1907 only 1/400 of a gram of cocaine, a trace amount, was found in one ounce of syrup. One website states that this was "not enough to give a fly a buzz." See Frederick Allen, *Secret Formula* (New York: HarperCollins, 1994), pp. 35–36, 41–42; "Cocaine-Cola," Snopes.com, www.snopes.com/cokelore/cocaine.asp, last accessed February 6, 2014.

22. Chandler, diary, March 24, 27, 28, 29, 1907; William E. Chandler to J. W. Kelley, April 6, 1907; William E. Chandler to Granville Bennett, April 7 1907: all in Chandler Papers, NHHS.

23. Mary Baker G. Eddy to John C. Lathrop, March, 1907, Eddy Letter, accession #L04295, MBE Library, © The Mary Baker Eddy Collection. Used by permission.

NOTES TO CHAPTER 6
THE DEFENSE ANSWERS THE CHARGES

1. "Deed of Trust," in Michael Meehan, *Mrs. Eddy and the Late Suit in Equity* (Concord, NH: Michael Meehan, 1908), pp. 36–39; *Concord Monitor*, April 2, 1907.

2. "Deed of Trust," in Meehan, *Mrs. Eddy and the Late Suit*, pp. 36–39. For biographical information on Henry Moore Baker, see Ezra S. Stearns, ed., *Genealogical and Family History of the State of New Hampshire* (New York: Lewis Publishing, 1908), vol. 1, pp. 116–117.

3. *Boston Mirror*, April 2, 1907.

4. Charles A. Hazlett, *History of Rockingham County, New Hampshire, and Representative Citizens* (Chicago: Richmond-Arnold Publisher, 1915), pp. 1107–1110.

5. John W. Kelley to William E. Chandler, March 1, 1907, William E. Chandler Papers (hereafter, Chandler Papers), New Hampshire Historical Society (hereafter, NHHS), Concord; Gillian Gill, *Mary Baker Eddy*, Radcliffe Biography Series (Reading, MA: Perseus Books, 1998), pp. 509–510.

6. *Boston Post*, April 3, 1907; *Boston American*, April 3, 1907.

7. William E. Chandler, Martin and Howe, and John W. Kelley to Frank S. Streeter, March 28, 1907, Chandler Papers, NHHS; Frank S. Streeter to William E. Chandler, John W. Kelley, Martin and Howe, April 5, 1907, Chandler Papers, NHHS.

8. George W. Glover, by M.B.G [Mary Glover], to William E. Chandler, April 3, 1907, and Granville G. Bennett to William E. Chandler, April 5, 1907, both in Chandler Papers, NHHS; *Concord Monitor*, April 6, 1907; *Boston Herald*, April 6, 1907; Meehan, *Mrs. Eddy and the Late Suit*, p. 50.

9. William E. Chandler to Granville G. Bennett, April 7, 1907, Chandler Papers, NHHS.

10. *Concord Patriot*, April 1 and April 8, 1907; *Concord Monitor*, April 6, 1907.

11. "Answer of Trustees to Supplemental Bill, Filed April 15, 1907," in Meehan, *Mrs. Eddy and the Late Suit*, pp. 51–53.

12. Meehan, *Mrs. Eddy and the Late Suit*, pp. 55–64; *Concord Monitor*, April 17, 1907; *Concord Patriot*, April 17, 1907; *Toledo Blade*, April 17, 1907; *Saginaw (MI) News*, April 18, 1907.

13. *Boston Globe*, April 20, 1907; William E. Chandler to Frederick Peabody, April 19, 1907, Chandler Papers, NHHS.

14. *Boston Globe*, April 20, 1907; *Concord Monitor*, April 19, 1907; Frederick Peabody to William E. Chandler, April 20 and April 22, 1907, Chandler Papers, NHHS.

15. William E. Chandler to George W. Glover, May 5, 1907, Chandler Papers, NHHS.

16. William E. Chandler, diary, April 21–28, 1907, Chandler Papers, NHHS; Meehan, *Mrs. Eddy and the Late Suit*, pp. 331–332; William E. Chandler to George W. Glover, April 15, 1907; William E. Chandler to Granville G. Bennett, April 24, 1907; William E. Chandler to Mary B. Glover, April 1, 1907: all in Chandler Papers, NHHS.

17. *Boston Herald*, April 26, 1907; *New York World*, April 29, 1907; *Boston Post*, May 7, 1907; *Boston American*, May 7, 1907.

18. Meehan, *Mrs. Eddy and the Late Suit*, pp. 73–79; *Concord Monitor*, May 18,

1907; *New York World,* May 18, 1907. Chase is quoted in both the *Concord Monitor* and the *New York World.*

19. *Concord Monitor,* May 20, 1907; Charles H. Corning, diary, May 20, 1907, NHHS; Mary Baker Eddy on forgiving her enemies, quoted in Reminiscences of Laura Sargent, "Black Leather Notebook Kept While in Mrs. Eddy's Home," May 22, 1907, Mary Baker Eddy Library (hereafter, MBE Library), Boston, © The Mary Baker Eddy Collection. Used by permission. Mary Baker Eddy to coachman and comment on "leaden weight" quoted in Stephen Gottschalk, *Rolling Away the Stone: Mary Baker Eddy's Challenge to Materialism* (Bloomington: Indiana University Press, 2006), pp. 10, 22.

20. Typed notes, "Hearing Before Judge Chamberlin at Concord, N.H., May 23, 1907," Streeter testimony, pp. 4, 21, 45, Frank Streeter Papers (hereafter, Streeter Papers), NHHS. See also *Concord Monitor,* May 23, 1907; *Concord Patriot,* May 23, 1907; *Boston Herald,* May 23, 1907.

21. Typed notes, "Hearing Before Judge Chamberlin at Concord, N.H., May 23, 1907," Streeter testimony, pp. 36, 48, Streeter Papers, NHHS.

22. Typed notes, "Hearing Before Judge Chamberlin at Concord, N.H., May 24, 1907," Howe testimony, pp. 14, 15, 61, 74, Streeter Papers, NHHS. See also *Concord Monitor,* May 24, 1907; *Concord Patriot,* May 24, 1907.

23. Corning, diary, May 24, 1907, NHHS.

24. Typed notes, "Hearing Before Judge Chamberlin at Concord, N.H., May 24, 1907," Chandler testimony, pp. 1–5, Streeter Papers, NHHS; *Boston Globe,* May 25, 1907 (quotation about "sensations" in Chandler's argument); *Concord Monitor,* May 25, 1907; *New York World,* May 25, 1907.

25. Typed notes, "Hearing Before Judge Chamberlin at Concord, N.H., May 24, 1907," Chandler testimony, pp. 3, 5, 7, 22, Streeter Papers, NHHS; *Concord Monitor,* May 25, 1907; *Boston Globe,* May 25, 1907; *New York World,* May 25, 1907. The following dialogue between Chandler and Streeter in text is also from these sources.

26. Typed notes, "Hearing Before Judge Chamberlin at Concord, N.H., May 24, 1907," Chandler testimony, pp. 3, 5, 7, 22, Streeter Papers, NHHS; *Concord Monitor,* May 25, 1907; *Boston Globe,* May 25, 1907 (headline reads "Streeter Passes Lie to Chandler"); *New York World,* May 25, 1907.

27. Typed notes, "Hearing Before Judge Chamberlin at Concord, N.H., May 24, 1907," Chandler testimony, pp. 3, 5, 7, 22, Streeter Papers, NHHS; *Concord Monitor,* May 25, 1907; *Boston Globe,* May 25, 1907 (quoted headline); *New York World,* May 25, 1907.

28. Typed notes, "Hearing Before Judge Chamberlin at Concord, N.H., May 24, 1907," Streeter testimony, p. 26, Streeter Papers, NHHS; *Boston Globe,* June 5,

1907; *Concord Monitor,* June 5, 1907; Michael Meehan, *Mrs. Eddy and the Late Suit in Equity* (Concord: Michael Meehan, 1908), pp. 125–126.

29. Mary Baker Eddy to Frank Streeter, June 6[?], 1907, copy and postscript to "N.B.," Mary Baker Eddy Letters, accession #L02632, MBE Library. © The Mary Baker Eddy Collection. Used by permission.

30. Frank Streeter to Mary Baker Eddy, June 6, 1907, Mary Baker Eddy Letters, accession #L16437, MBE Library; Archibald McLellan to Mary Baker Eddy, June 6, 1907, Mary Baker Eddy Letters, accession #L16437, MBE Library. © The Mary Baker Eddy Collection. Used courtesy of The Mary Baker Eddy Collection and The Mary Baker Eddy Library.

31. DeWitt Howe to William E. Chandler, June 5, 1907, Chandler Papers, NHHS.

32. William E. Chandler to John W. Kelley, June 6, 1907, and June 7, 1907; William E. Chandler to DeWitt Howe, June 7, 1907; Telegram, William E. Chandler to DeWitt Howe, June 9, 1907: all in Chandler Papers, NHHS.

33. *Concord Monitor,* June 10, 1907; Telegram, DeWitt Howe to William E. Chandler, June 10, 1907, Chandler Papers, NHHS; John W. Kelley to William E. Chandler, June 11, 1907, Chandler Papers, NHHS.

34. Frederick Peabody to Martin and Howe, June 13, 1907, Chandler Papers, NHHS.

35. William E. Chandler, diary, May 25, 1907; DeWitt Howe to William E. Chandler, June 11, 1907 (Howe recited to Chandler the situation about Baker in this letter); William E. Chandler to DeWitt Howe, June 12, 1907; William E. Chandler to Fred W. Baker, June 15, 1907; Fred W. Baker to William E. Chandler, June 24, 1907: all in Chandler Papers, NHHS; *Concord Patriot,* June 24, 1907.

36. Calvin Frye to Frank Streeter, June 8, 1907, Mary Baker Eddy Letters, accession #L14080, MBE Library, © The Mary Baker Eddy Collection. Used by permission.

37. Statement of William R. Brown to Alfred Farlow, June 12, 1907 (quotations describing Chamberlin's conversations at the table), and Statement of J. V. Dittemore to Alfred Farlow, June 12, 1907 (Howe's comment about "puff ball"), Mary Baker Eddy, Lawsuits, Next Friends, Alfred Farlow Research, pp. 47–51, MBE Library, © The Mary Baker Eddy Collection. Used by permission.

38. Brisbane had a long career as a journalist and editor. William Randolph Hearst once called him "the greatest journalist of his day" ("The Press: Death of Brisbane," January 4, 1937, *Time,* www.time.com/time/magazine/article/0,9171,762350,00.html, last accessed April 2, 2014). *Boston Globe,* June 10, 190; John J. Spurgeon to William E. Chandler, June 10, 1907, and William E. Chandler to John J. Spurgeon, June 11, 1907, Chandler Papers, NHHS; Rufus

Steele, *What Mrs. Eddy Said to Arthur Brisbane*, pamphlet (Boston: Christian Science Publishing Society, 1930); Meehan, *Mrs. Eddy and the Late Suit*, pp. 263–274.

39. *Boston Globe*, June 16, 1907; Meehan, *Mrs. Eddy and the Late Suit*, pp. 248–258; William E. Chandler to John W. Kelley, June 17, 1907, Chandler Papers, NHHS.

40. "William E. Curtis Interviews Mrs. Eddy," in Meehan, *Mrs. Eddy and the Late Suit*, pp. 259–263; Chandler, diary, memoranda section, June 29, 1907, Chandler Papers, NHHS; Leigh Mitchell Hodges, interview with Mary Baker Eddy, *Philadelphia North American*, July 14, 1907.

41. Frank Streeter to George W. Glover, June 19, 1907, and George W. Glover to William E. Chandler, June 25, 1907, Chandler Papers, NHHS; "Trust Deed for the Benefit of George W. Glover and Family," in Meehan, *Mrs. Eddy and the Late Suit*, pp. 41–43; Telegram, William E. Chandler to George W. Glover, June 27, 1907, Chandler Papers, NHHS.

42. Mary B. G. Eddy to "My dear George" [George W. Glover], June 17, 1907, copy in Chandler Papers, NHHS; Thompson reminiscences in Robert Peel, *The Years of Authority* (New York: Holt, Rinehart and Winston, 1977), p. 486 n115; George W. Glover to William E. Chandler, June 25, 1907, Chandler Papers, NHHS.

43. George W. Glover to William E. Chandler, July 5 and July 18, 1907; William E. Chandler to Frank Streeter, July 22, 1907; Frank Streeter to William E. Chandler, July 24, 1907: all in Chandler Papers, NHHS.

NOTES TO CHAPTER 7
A MASTER TAKES CHARGE OF THE CASE

1. *Concord Monitor*, June 29, 1907; *Boston Globe*, June 29, 1907.

2. Edgar Aldrich (1848–1916) biography in Henry Harrison Metcalf, ed., *One Thousand New Hampshire Notables* (Concord, NH: Rumford Press, 1919), p. 503; James Robert Jackson, ed., *History of Littleton, New Hampshire, in Three Volumes*, vol. 1, *Annals* (Cambridge, MA: University Press, 1905), pp. 571–573 (quotation about "enormous growth of the trust evil," p. 572); George Higgins Moses, ed., *New Hampshire Men* (Concord, NH: n.p., 1893), p. 211; John W. Kelley to Granville G. Bennett, July 3, 1907, William E. Chandler Papers (hereafter, Chandler Papers), New Hampshire Historical Society (hereafter, NHHS),

Concord; Frank Streeter to Edgar Aldrich, June 29, 1907, Chandler Papers,
NHHS; Frank Streeter to H. Cornell Wilson, July 1, 1907, Mary Baker Eddy
Letters, accession #L16442, Mary Baker Eddy Library (hereafter, MBE Library),
Boston, © The Mary Baker Eddy Collection. Used by permission. A Pierce
monument would have to wait until the Democrats attained the governorship
and a majority in the state legislature, which occurred in 1912 and at which
point a Pierce memorial was approved. Chandler was the keynote speaker at the
dedication ceremony in 1914.

3. Edgar Aldrich to Robert N. Chamberlin, July 4, 1907, and Robert N.
Chamberlin to Edgar Aldrich,

July 5, 1907, copies in Chandler Papers, NHHS; *Concord Monitor*, July 9 and
15, 1907; *Boston Globe*, July 17, 1907.

4. "Mrs. Eddy Excepts to Appointment of Masters and Co-Masters," in
Michael Meehan, *Mrs. Eddy and the Late Suit in Equity* (Concord, NH: Michael
Meehan, 1908), pp. 129–130; Robert N. Chamberlin to Brothers Streeter and
Hollis, July 12, 1907, Chandler Papers, NHHS; William E. Chandler to John W.
Kelley and Martin and Howe, July 12, 1907, Chandler Papers, NHHS; Streeter
and Hollis to Robert N. Chamberlin, July 13, 1907, Chandler Papers, NHHS;
Concord Monitor, July 15, 1907.

5. William E. Chandler to John Slaght, July 10, 1907; William E. Chandler
to N. E. Martin, July 10, 1907; William E. Chandler to Henry R. Hopkins, July
10, 1907; Henry R. Hopkins to William E. Chandler, July 11, 1907; William E.
Chandler to Granville Bennett, July 15, 1907; William E. Chandler to Frank
Streeter, July 20, 1907: all in Chandler Papers, NHHS.

6. Willa Cather to William E. Chandler, July 16, 1907, Chandler Papers,
NHHS.

7. William E. Chandler to Henry R. Hopkins, July 15, 1907, Chandler Papers,
NHHS.

8. *Boston Globe*, July 20, 1907.

9. *Chicago Record–Herald*, July 14–15, 1907; *Concord Monitor*, July 23, 1907.

10. DeWitt Howe to Edgar Aldrich, July 20, 1907; Edgar Aldrich to Streeter
and Hollis, July 21, 1907: both in Chandler Papers, NHHS.

11. *Concord Monitor*, July 25, 1907; William E. Chandler, diary, July 25, 1907,
Chandler Papers, NHHS; *Chicago Tribune*, July 26, 1907.

12. *Concord Monitor*, July 26 and 27, 1907.

13. *Concord Patriot*, July 30, 1907; *Concord Monitor*, July 30, 1907.

14. Transcript, "Telephone Conversation with Judge Aldrich," July 30, 1907,
Chandler Papers, NHHS.

15. *New York World*, July 31, 1907; *Concord Patriot*, July 31, 1907; *Concord
Monitor*, July 31, 1907; *Pittsburgh Post*, July 31, 1907; *Baltimore Sun*, July 31, 1907;

Edmund S. Cook to William E. Chandler, July 31, 1907, and William E. Chandler to Edmund S. Cook, July 31, 1907, Chandler Papers, NHHS. The interchange that follows in the text is also from these sources.

16. *New York World*, July 31, 1907; *Concord Patriot*, July 31, 1907; *Concord Monitor*, July 31, 1907; *Pittsburgh Post*, July 31, 1907; *Baltimore Sun*, July 31, 1907; Edmund S. Cook to William E. Chandler, July 31, 1907, and William E. Chandler to Edmund S. Cook, July 31, 1907, both in Chandler Papers, NHHS.

17. Charles H. Corning, diary, July 30, 1907, NHHS; Chandler, diary, July 29 and 30, 1907, Chandler Papers, NHHS.

18. Frederick Peabody to William E. Chandler, August 1, 3, and 8, 1907 ("amazingly decent" in August 1 letter); Willa Cather to William E. Chandler, August 1, 1907; Ralph Pulitzer to William E. Chandler, August 11, 1907; Florence White, financial manager, *New York World*, to William E. Chandler, August 13, 1907; Henry R. Stedman and George T. Tuttle to William E. Chandler, August 13, 1907; William E. Chandler to Frederick Peabody, August 12, 1907 (quotation about "mutilated" edition): all in Chandler Papers, NHHS.

19. Edmund S. Cook to Robert N. Chamberlin, August 1, 1907 (Chamberlin's undated response to "Bro. Cook" is affixed to Cook's original letter), copy in Chandler Papers, NHHS; *Concord Monitor*, August 9, 1907.

20. Mary Baker Eddy to Frank Streeter, August 8, 1907, Mary Baker Eddy Letters, accession #L13524, MBE Library, © The Mary Baker Eddy Collection. Used by permission.

21. Granville G. Bennett to William E. Chandler, July 22 and July 28, 1907, Chandler Papers, NHHS.

22. Chandler, diary, August 5, 1907, Chandler Papers, NHHS (quotation about boarding house); *Concord Monitor*, August 5, 1907; *New York World*, August 5, 1907; *Boston Post*, August 6, 1907.

23. Chandler, diary, August 3–12, 1907; George W. Baker to William E. Chandler, August 7, 1907; William E. Chandler to George W. Baker, August 10, 1907; John W. Kelley to William E. Chandler, August 10, 1907: all in Chandler Papers, NHHS.

24. "Dr. Edward French's Report," in Meehan, *Mrs. Eddy and the Late Suit*, p. 247.

25. "Dr. Allan McLane Hamilton's Report," Meehan, *Mrs. Eddy and the Late Suit*, pp. 233–240.

26. Hamilton comment to *Times* cited in Gillian Gill, *Mary Baker Eddy*, Radcliff Biography Series (Reading, MA: Perseus Books, 1998), p. 515 (also cited in Michael Meehan, *Mrs. Eddy and the Late Suit*, pp. 241–246).

27. Gill, *Mary Baker Eddy*, p. 397 (quotation on "mental malpractice" for "wicked purpose"; "anything that pulls" and "taking up"); Robert Peel, *Mary*

Baker Eddy: The Years of Authority (New York: Holt, Rinehart and Winston, 1977), p. 393 n50; Stephen Gottschalk, *Rolling Away the Stone: Mary Baker Eddy's Challenge to Materialism* (Bloomington: Indiana University Press, 2006), p. 36.

NOTES TO CHAPTER 8
THE TRIAL BEGINS

1. *New York World*, August 17, 1907; *Concord Monitor*, August 13, 1907.

2. Quotes from transcript cited from *Concord Monitor*, August 13, 1907. See also *In the Suit Entitled Mary Baker G. Eddy, By her Next Friends, George W. Glover et als. vs. Calvin A. Frye et als., Record, Comprising Papers and Documents on Clerk's Files* (Concord, NH: Rumford Printing, 1907), Streeter Papers, New Hampshire Historical Society (hereafter, NHHS), which contains all motions, briefs, and affidavits made prior to the opening of the trial.

3. *Concord Monitor*, August 13, 1907.

4. Ibid.

5. *Concord Monitor*, August 13 and 14, 1907.

6. *Concord Monitor*, August 14, 1907.

7. Draft of Official Transcript, Eddy et al. v. Frye et al., pp. 79–82, Frank Streeter Papers, NHHS.

8. Draft of Official Transcript, pp. 83–84, Frank Streeter Papers, NHHS.

9. Ibid., pp. 85–88.

10. Ibid.

11. Ibid., pp. 90–95, Frank Streeter Papers, NHHS.

12. *Concord Monitor*, August 14, 1907.

13. Draft of Official Transcript, pp. 96–97, Frank Streeter Papers, NHHS. The long conversation between Aldrich and Eddy that follows in the text is also taken from pp. 96–97. For another verbatim account of the hearing, see *Concord Monitor*, August 15, 1907.

14. Ibid., p. 97.

15. Ibid., 98–99.

16. Ibid., pp. 99–101.

17. Ibid., pp. 102–103.

18. Ibid., pp. 103–106.

19. Ibid., pp. 106–109.

20. Ibid., pp. 109–110.

21. Ibid., pp. 110–112.

22. *Concord Monitor*, August 15, 1907; *Boston American*, August 15, 1907; *Boston Herald*, August 21, 1907; *New York World*, August 15, 1907; "steel trap" comment cited in Robert Peel, *Mary Baker Eddy: The Years of Authority* (New York: Holt, Rinehart and Winston, 1977), p.289, and Gillian Gill, *Mary Baker Eddy*, Radcliffe Biography Series (Reading, MA: Perseus Books, 1998), p. 519.

23.A transcript of the hearing can be found in both the *Concord Monitor*, August 15, 1907, and Draft of Official Transcript, pp. 113–117.

24. Draft of Official Transcript, pp. 117–120.

25. Ibid., pp. 120–123.

26. Ibid., pp. 123–124.

NOTES TO CHAPTER 9
THE TRIAL: DAYS THREE AND FOUR

1. *Concord Patriot*, August 15, 1907; *Buffalo Sunday Courier*, August 18, 1907.

2. *Concord Monitor*, August 15, 1907.

3. Ibid.

4. Ibid. The conversation that follows in the text is also from this source.

5. Ibid.

6. *Concord Monitor*, August 16, 1907; *New York World*, August 16, 1907; *Concord Patriot*, August 16, 1907.

7. *Concord Monitor*, August 16, 1907.

8. Quotation from John Salchow's wife cited in "Reminiscences of John Salchow," p. 78, Mary Baker Eddy Library (hereafter, MBE Library), Boston, © The Mary Baker Eddy Collection. Used by permission. "Official Transcript," pp. 225–238, Frank Streeter Papers (hereafter, Streeter Papers), New Hampshire Historical Society (hereafter, NHHS) Concord.

9. Draft of Official Transcript, *Eddy et al. v. Frye et al.*, pp. 225–230, Streeter Papers, NHHS.

10. Ibid., pp. 231–237.

11. Ibid., pp. 238–244.

12. Ibid., pp. 245–250.

13. Ibid., pp. 251–259.

14. Ibid., pp. 264–273. The transcript also appears in *Concord Monitor,* August 17, 1907, and *New York World*, August 17, 1907.

15. Draft of Official Transcript, pp. 273–276.

16. Ibid., pp. 276–277.

17. Ibid., pp. 277–283.

18. Ibid., pp. 283–286

19. Ibid., pp. 287–288.

20. Alfred Farlow to Mary Baker G. Eddy, August 16, 1907, Mary Baker Eddy Letters, accession #L19000, Mary Baker Eddy Library, Boston, © The Mary Baker Eddy Collection. Used by permission.

21. *New York World,* August 17, 1907; *Concord Monitor,* August 17, 1907; *Concord Patriot,* August 17, 1907; *Boston American,* August 17, 1907.

NOTES TO CHAPTER 10
CASE DISMISSED

1. William E. Chandler, diary, August 17, 1907; William E. Chandler to Dewitt Howe, August 17, 1907; William E. Chandler to John W. Kelley, August 17, 1907: all in , William E. Chandler Papers (hereafter, Chandler Papers), New Hampshire Historical Society (hereafter, NHHS), Concord.

2. William E. Chandler to Ralph Pulitzer, August 17, 1907, Chandler Papers, NHHS.

3. Henry R. Hopkins to William E. Chandler, August 18, 1907; Henry R. Hopkins to William E. Chandler, August 19, 1907: both in Chandler Papers, NHHS.

4. Vincent E. Tomlinson to William E. Chandler, August 20, 1907, Chandler Papers, NHHS.

5. William E. Chandler to Henry R. Stedman, August 18, 1907; Henry R. Stedman to William E. Chandler, August 19, 1907: both in Chandler Papers, NHHS.

6. Chandler, diary, August 17–19, 1907, Chandler Papers, NHHS; *New York Journal* editorial, reprinted in the *Concord Patriot,* August 19, 1907.

7. Chandler, diary, August 19–20, 1907; Memo, Streeter and Hollis to William E. Chandler, September 30, 1907: both in Chandler Papers, NHHS.

8. Mary Baker Eddy to Frank Streeter, August 20, 1907, Mary Baker Eddy Letters, accession #L13525, Mary Baker Eddy Library, Boston, © The Mary Baker

Eddy Collection. Used by permission. This letter is in Frye's handwriting but is signed by Eddy.

9. Draft of Official Transcript, Eddy et al. vs. Frye et al., pp. 289–307, Streeter Papers, NHHS.

10. Ibid., pp. 308–313.

11. Ibid., pp. 314–329.

12. Ibid., pp. 330–340.

13. Ibid., pp. 340–341; Chandler, diary, August 20, 1907, Chandler Papers, NHHS; *Concord Monitor,* August 20, 1907.

14. *Boston Globe,* August 20, 1907.

15. Motion to Dismiss, filed in the Superior Court, Merrimack SS, Eddy v. Frye, et al., Chandler Papers, NHHS; "Draft of Official Transcript, p. 342.

16. Draft of Official Transcript, pp. 342–345.

17. Ibid., pp. 345–347; *Boston Globe,* August 21, 1907; *Boston Herald,* August 21, 1907; *New York World,* August 21, 1907; *New York Times,* August 22, 1907.

18. Draft of Official Transcript, pp. 348–349.

19. *New York World,* August 21, 1907; *Concord Patriot,* August 21, 1907; *Boston Journal,* August 21, 1907.

20. Quotations cited in *Concord Monitor,* August 21, 1907; *Concord Patriot,* August 21, 1907; *Boston Herald,* August 21, 1907; *Boston Globe,* August 21, 1907; see also *New York Times,* August 22, 1907.

21. Charles H. Corning, diary, August 21 and 22, 1907, NHHS; Chandler, diary, August 22, 1907, Chandler Papers, NHHS.

NOTES TO CHAPTER 11
NEXT FRIENDS AWAIT EVENTS

1. Baker cited in *Boston Globe,* August 22, 1907; William E. Chandler, diary, August 23, 1907, William E. Chandler Papers (hereafter, Chandler Papers), New Hampshire Historical Society (hereafter, NHHS), Concord.

2. William E. Chandler to Senator Burrows, August 28, 1907; William E. Chandler to A. Coolidge, August 28, 1907; William E. Chandler to H. R. Storer, August 28, 1907; William E. Chandler to W. L. Chambers, August 28, 1907; William E. Chandler to Henry R. Stedman, August 28, 1907; William E. Chandler to George W. Baker, August 28, 1907; William E. Chandler to Bradford Merrill, September 7, 1907: all in Chandler Papers, NHHS.

3. "Questions which will be asked," August 24, 1907, Chandler Papers, NHHS; Granville G. Bennett to William E. Chandler, August 31, 1907, Chandler Papers, NHHS; *Des Moines Register and Leader*, September 1, 1907; *New York Times*, September 1, 1907; Mary B. Glover to William E. Chandler, August 31, 1907, Chandler Papers, NHHS; H. R. Hopkins to Chandler, August 23, 1907, Chandler Papers, NHHS.

4. *New York Journal*, August 26, 1907; Frank Streeter to Mary Baker Eddy, September 2, 1907, Mary Baker Eddy Letters, accession #L16447, Mary Baker Eddy Library (hereafter, MBE Library), Boston, © The Mary Baker Eddy Collection. Used by permission.

5. Granville G. Bennett to William E. Chandler, August 28, 1907, and William E. Chandler to Granville G. Bennett, September 7, 1907: both in Chandler Papers, NHHS.

6. To [John W.] Kelley and [DeWitt] Howe from W.E.C. [William E. Chandler], August 30, 1907, Chandler Papers, NHHS. Howe's response is handwritten at the bottom of the memo.

7. William E. Chandler to George Glover, September 7, 1907; William E. Chandler to J. W. Slaght, August 30, 1907; William E. Chandler to F. W. Peabody, September 13, 1907; Henry Hopkins to William E. Chandler, September 5, 1907: all in Chandler Papers, NHHS.

8. Henry Hopkins to William E. Chandler, September 1, 1907; William E. Chandler to Granville Bennett, September 7, 1907; Mary B. G. Eddy to "My Dear Benny" [Ebenezer Foster Eddy], August 30, 1907, quoted in *Concord Patriot*, November 11, 1909; William E. Chandler to Ebenezer Foster [Eddy], September[?], 1907; William E. Chandler to Frank W. Peabody, September 13, 1907; William E. Chandler to John W. Slaght, August 30, 1907; John W. Slaght to William E. Chandler, August 22, 1907: all in Chandler Papers, NHHS.

9. Memo to Streeter & Hollis, September 18, 1907, Chandler Papers, NHHS; Frank S. Streeter to Mary Baker Eddy, September 26, 1907, Eddy Letters, accession #L16449, MBE Library, © The Mary Baker Eddy Collection. Used by permission. Official Transcript, Hearing of Eddy v. Frye, September 30, 1907, before Judge Chamberlin, pp. 1–4, Streeter Papers, NHHS.

10. Official Transcript, pp. 5–17.

11. Mary Baker Eddy, card, September 30, 1907, Eddy Letters, accession #L09479, MBE Library; Frank S. Streeter to Mary Baker Eddy, September 30, 1907, Eddy Letters, accession #L17994, MBE Library; Mary Baker G. Eddy to Allen McLane Hamilton, November 15, 1907, Eddy Letters, accession #L08098, MBE Library. All letters © The Mary Baker Eddy Collection. Used by permission.

12. Mary Baker G. Eddy (by her Next Friends) v. Calvin A. Frye, et als.

Decree Relating to Costs in the Above Action, Superior Court, Merrimack, ss.,
October Term, 1907, November 12, 1907, Streeter Papers, NHHS; "Stipulation
for Dismissal, Waiver of Costs and with Reference to Depositions on File, signed
by William E. Chandler, Counsel for the Next Friends, Streeter & Hollis, Counsel
for Mary Baker Eddy, Streeter Papers, NHHS; *Concord Monitor*, November 12,
1907; *Concord Patriot*, November 12, 1907.

13. William E. Chandler to George Glover, September 17, 1907; William E.
Chandler to John Kelley, September 26, 1907; William E. Chandler to Edgar
Aldrich, October 26, 1907; Edgar Aldrich to William E. Chandler, October 29,
1907; William E. Chandler to Granville G. Bennett, October 28, 1907: all in
Chandler Papers, NHHS.

14. William E. Chandler to Granville G. Bennett, October 30, 1907; William
E. Chandler to George Glover, October 30, 1907; George Glover to William E.
Chandler, November 4, 1907: all in Chandler Papers, NHHS.

15. Granville G. Bennett to William E. Chandler, November 9, 1907, Chandler
Papers, NHHS; Gillian Gill, *Mary Baker Eddy*, Radcliff Biography Series
(Reading, MA: Perseus Books, 1998), pp. 276, 645n9; Granville G. Bennett to
William E. Chandler, November 13, 1907, Chandler Papers, NHHS.

16. *Boston Post*, November 25, 1907; *Boston Globe*, November 25, 1907
(includes denial by Glover); *Boston Journal*, November 25, 1907; *Boston American*,
November 25, 1907; *New York World*, November 25, 1907 (all reports of the story
were out of Sioux City, Iowa); Granville G. Bennett to William E. Chandler,
November 29, 1907, Chandler Papers, NHHS.

17. Willa Cather to William E. Chandler, November 29, 1907; William E.
Chandler to Willa Cather, December 3, 1907; William E. Chandler to George W.
Glover, December 3, 1907: all in Chandler Papers, NHHS.

18. William E. Chandler to John Kelley and DeWitt Howe, December 8,
1907; William E. Chandler to Granville G. Bennett, December 8, 1907; William
E. Chandler to George W. Glover, December 8, 1907; Frank Streeter to William
E. Chandler, December 10, 1907 (the telegram is quoted in this letter); William
E. Chandler to Frank Streeter, December 11, 1907; John Kelley to William E.
Chandler, December 13, 1907; Granville G. Bennett to William E. Chandler,
December 15, 1907: all in Chandler Papers, NHHS.

19. Granville G. Bennett to William E. Chandler, December 17, 1907;
Chandler, diary, December 17–20, 1907; Chandler, diary, entry at end of book
dated December 23; Granville Bennett to William E. Chandler, December 25,
1907; Granville Bennett to William E. Chandler, December 26, 1907: all in
Chandler Papers, NHHS.

20. John W. Kelley, Martin and Howe, William E. Chandler, attorneys for
George W. Glover and E. J. Foster Eddy, to Henry M. Baker, Archibald McLellan,

and Josiah Fernald, trustees of the estate of Mary Baker G. Eddy, December 26, 1907 (McLellan's letter is quoted in full in this document); John W. Kelley to Hon. W. E. C., M. & H. [William E. Chandler, Martin and Howe], December 28, 1907: all in Chandler Papers, NHHS.

21. John W. Kelley to William E. Chandler, December 28, 1907; Chandler, diary, December 31, 1907: both in Chandler Papers, NHHS.

22. *Boston Herald*, January 27, 1908; *Concord Monitor*, January 27, 1908; *Boston Mirror*, January 27, 1908; *New York World*, January 27, 1908; Gill, *Mary Baker Eddy*, pp. 522–525 (Eddy asking Salchow to carry her is quoted from this source, p. 525).

23. Reminiscences of Adelaide Still, chap. 3, pp. 21–26, MBE Library (Farlow's explanation and "unhappy experience" are quoted from this document); Reminiscences of John Salchow, pp. 78–80, MBE Library, © The Mary Baker Eddy Collection. Used by permission. Gill, *Mary Baker Eddy*, p. 524 ("might take her from her home and friends"). Corning's official statement and Chandler's statement cited in *Concord Monitor*, January 27, 1908; Chandler's statement also cited in *New York World*, January 27, 1908;.

24. Charles H. Corning, diary, January 26, 1908, NHHS.

NOTES TO CHAPTER I2
A FAMILY SETTLEMENT

1. The figures estimated by the Wonolancet Club are as follows: Concord Christian Science Church gift, $225,000; charitable donations, $25,000; money donated for good roads, $25,000; miscellaneous gifts and contributions, $25,000; money spent on Pleasant View estate, $40,000; household expenditures, $100,000; income from special privileges granted to Concord manufacturers and businessmen, $40,000; granite contracts for Christian Science churches obtained because of Eddy's residence and Eddy's influence, $1 million; other known expenditures, $90,000. Total: $1,570,000. In *Quarterly News, Mary Baker Eddy Museum and Historic Sites* (Longyear Historical Society) 7, no. 4 (Winter 1970–1971): 109–112.

2. John W. Kelley, Martin and Howe, and William E. Chandler to Frank Streeter, January 4, 1908; William E. Chandler to John W. Kelley, January, 1908; John W. Kelley to Frank Streeter, January 9, 1908; Frank Streeter to William E. Chandler, John W. Kelley, Martin and Howe, January 23, 1908: all in William E.

Chandler Papers (hereafter, Chandler Papers), New Hampshire Historical Society (hereafter, NHHS), Concord.

3. William E. Chandler to Granville G. Bennett, February 2, 1908; Granville G. Bennett to William E. Chandler, February 14, 1908; Granville G. Bennett to William E. Chandler, February 21, 1908; Hannis Taylor and W. L. Chambers to William E. Chandler, February 26, 1908 all in Chandler Papers, NHHS; Hannis Taylor biography, Genealogy Trails, http://genealogytrails.com/ala/baldwin/bios/hannis_taylor.html, accessed January 4, 2012; William E. Chandler to Granville G. Bennett, February 26, 1908, Chandler Papers, NHHS. For more on Hannis Taylor, see Tennant S. McWilliams, *Hannis Taylor: The New Southerner as an American* (N.p.: University of Alabama Press, 1978).

4. A summary of all events involving Michael Meehan's book is found under "Church History: Mrs. Eddy and the Late Suit in Equity, Datelist," box 67, folder 8 (titled "Lawsuits—Next Friends—Miscellaneous Papers"), Mary Baker Eddy Library (hereafter, MBE Library), Boston. The summary contains reference to Eddy's letters, accession nos. L13508, F00488, L13509, L14053, written by her to Michael Meehan, and L00566, L12493, written by Eddy to the Christian Science Board of Trustees or to Archibald McLellan. I have checked several of these letters but relied largely on the summary account. The story is verified by a letter written by William D. Chandler and deposited inside the cover of his copy of the book *Mrs. Eddy and the Late Suit in Equity*, which is in the vault at the New Hampshire Historical Society Library in Concord; DeWitt Howe to William E. Chandler, February ,1908, Chandler Papers, NHHS.

5. William E. Chandler to Michael Meehan, August 10, 1908; Michael Meehan to William E. Chandler, August 11, 1908; Henry R. Hopkins to William E. Chandler, September 1, 1908; William E. Chandler to E. J. Parks, September 5, 1908: all in Chandler Papers, NHHS.

6. William E. Chandler to E. S. Cook, February 18, 1908; Henry Robinson to William E. Chandler, January 30, April 1, and April 1, 1908; Charles J. French to Charles R. Corning, February 1, 1908; Assessors of the City of Concord, NH, to Frank S. Streeter, Archibald McLellan, and Irving C. Tomlinson, March 16, 1908: all in Chandler Papers, NHHS; *Boston Herald*, April 25, 1908; *Boston Journal*, August 31, 1908.

7. *Boston Herald*, April 25, 1908; Frederick Peabody to William E. Chandler, April 25, 1908, Chandler Papers, NHHS.

8. William E. Chandler to George W. Glover, March 20, 1908; Robert C. Hannon to George W. Glover, July 14, 1908: both in Chandler Papers, NHH

9. George W. Glover to E. J. Foster [Eddy], July 19, 1908; Granville G. Bennett to Robert C. Hannon, July 20, 1908; Granville G. Bennett to William E. Chandler, July 20, 1908: all in Chandler Papers, NHHS.

10. William E. Chandler to George W. Glover, July 22, 1908; William E. Chandler to E. J. Foster [Eddy], July 22, 1908; William E. Chandler to Granville G. Bennett, August 8, 1908 (Kelley's comments to Chandler about Park's visit to Eddy are included in this letter); Robert C. Hannon to George Glover, July 20, 1908 (Foster Eddy wrote his note to Chandler at the top of this letter when passing it on to Chandler): all in Chandler Papers, NHHS.

11. For a more complete account of Eddy's relationship with Augusta Stetson, see Robert Peel, *Mary Baker Eddy: The Years of Authority* (Holt, Rinehart and Winston, 1971), pp. 329–343; Gillian Gill, *Mary Baker Eddy*, Radcliffe Biography Series (Reading, MA: Perseus Books, 1998), pp. 534–544; and Stephen Gottschalk, *Rolling Away the Stone: Mary Baker Eddy's Challenge to Materialism* (Bloomington: Indiana University Press, 2006), pp. 365–379.

12. Gill, *Mary Baker Eddy*, pp. 532–533 ("painful lesson," p. 532); Eddy's note to board of directors cited in Peel, *The Years of Authority*, p. 310.

13. Gill, *Mary Baker Eddy*, p. 533; Eddy's letter to Publishing Society cited in Peel, *The Years of Authority*, p. 311.

14. Gill, *Mary Baker Eddy*, pp. 532–533; Peel, *The Years of Authority*, pp. 311–312; Irving C. Tomlinson, *Twelve Years with Mary Baker Eddy: Recollections and Experiences* (Boston: Christian Science Publishing Society), pp. 105–107. For more on the life of George H. Moses, see "Names, Dates, and Places, That Part of the Life of George Higgins Moses, Minister to Greece and Senator from New Hampshire, Which He Is Willing to Reveal," unpublished biography by George H. Moses, ca. 1942. Two copies of this unpublished manuscript are at the New Hampshire Historical Society Library and were given in May 1993 by George H. Moses II.

15. William E. Chandler to George W. Glover, January 23, 1909; Granville G. Bennett to William E. Chandler, March 23, 1909: both in Chandler Papers, NHHS.

16. William E. Chandler to George W. Glover, January 23, 1909; William Chandler to Edgar Aldrich, April 1, 1909; William E. Chandler to Granville G. Bennett, April 1, 1909; Granville G. Bennett to William E. Chandler, April 8, 1909; William E. Chandler to Granville G. Bennett, May 4, 1909; William E. Chandler to Granville G. Bennett, May 5, 1909: all in Chandler Papers, NHHS.

17. William E. Chandler to H. R. Hopkins, April 26, 1909, Chandler Papers, NHHS.

18. DeWitt Howe to William E. Chandler and John W. Kelley, June 1, 1909; William E. Chandler to DeWitt Howe, June 2, 1909: both in Chandler Papers, NHHS.

19. Draft of letter from William E. Chandler to Henry M. Baker, September 10, 1909, Chandler Papers, NHHS.

20. Draft of letter from William E. Chandler to Granville G. Bennett, October 4, 1909; George W. Glover to William E. Chandler, October 12, 1909; Granville G. Bennett to William E. Chandler, October 18, 1909: all in Chandler Papers, NHHS.

21. Calvin Frye, diary, September 25, 1909, MBE Library.

22. William E. Chandler to John W. Kelley and DeWitt Howe, October 19, 1909; William E. Chandler to Granville G. Bennett, October 21, 1909; William E. Chandler to George W. Glover, October 22, 1909; George W. Glover, affidavit to William E. Chandler, copy not signed or dated: all in Chandler Papers, NHHS.

23. George W. Glover to William E. Chandler, October 28, 1909; Granville G. Bennett to William E. Chandler, October 28, 1909; William E. Chandler to Granville G. Bennett, November 1, 1909: all in Chandler Papers, NHHS.

24. Chandler, diary, October 25, 1909; William E. Chandler to Granville G. Bennett, November 3, 1909, and November 6, 1909 (all quotations are cited from this November 6 letter): all in Chandler Papers, NHHS.

25. William E. Chandler, diary, November 10, 1909; "Glover Trust" document in New Hampshire Historical Society Library; "A family settlement," including a list of all "Letters and Documents delivered to the Trustees," document in Chandler Papers, NHHS.

26. George W. Glover to William E. Chandler, November 20, 1909; Granville G. Bennett to William E. Chandler, November 20, 1909; William E. Chandler to Mary B. Glover, December 5, 1909; Mary B. Glover to William E. Chandler, December 11, 1909; Mary B. Glover and Mother [Nellie Glover] to William E. Chandler, December 26, 1909: all in Chandler Papers, NHHS.

27. *Concord Patriot*, November 11, 1909; Granville G. Bennett to William E. Chandler, November 20, 1909; William G. Nixon to William E. Chandler, November 11, 1909; Fred A. Fernald to William E. Chandler, November 12, 1909; William E. Chandler to Frederick Peabody, November 15, November 24, November 26, December 3, December 6, December 9, December 11, and December 14, 1909; Frederick Peabody to William E. Chandler, November 12 and November 30, 1909; William Nixon to William E. Chandler, December 17, 1909: all in Chandler Papers, NHHS.

28. John W. Kelley to William E. Chandler, December 3, 1909, Chandler Papers, NHHS.

29. George W. Glover to William E. Chandler, December 11, 1909; copy of letter to Mary B. G. Eddy from George W. Glover, December 11, 1909: both in Chandler Papers, NHHS.

30. Copy of letter, Mary Baker Eddy to "My Dear George" [George W. Glover], December 17, 1909, Chandler Papers, NHHS.

31. George W. Glover to William E. Chandler, December 23, 1909, Chandler Papers, NHHS.

NOTES TO CHAPTER 13
MENTALLY MURDERED?

1. George W. Glover to William E. Chandler, March 13, 1910; Minutes of "Meeting of Glover Trustees," Union Club, Boston, June 14, 1910: both in William E. Chandler Papers (hereafter, Chandler Papers), New Hampshire Historical Society (hereafter, NHHS), Concord.

2. *Lead Call*, April 21, 1910; William E. Chandler to George W. Glover, April 19, 1910; George W. Glover to William E. Chandler, June 30, 1910: all in Chandler Papers, NHHS.

3. Eddy's son, George Washington Glover, was actually Glover II, and his son George Washington Glover was Glover III, but Chandler and company generally referred to them as Glover senior and junior.

4. George W. Glover to William E. Chandler, July 10, 1910; William E. Chandler, diary, July 10 and 12, 1910; George W. Glover to William E. Chandler, July 19, 1910; Archibald McLellan to William E. Chandler, July 14, 1910: all in Chandler Papers, NHHS; Jewel Spangler Smaus, "'Family': From New England to the Black Hills, Part VIII," *Quarterly News, Mary Baker Eddy Museum and Historic Sites* (Longyear Historical Society) 21, no. 3 (Autumn 1984): 329–332 (quoted inscription in *Science and Health*, "just sat there and smiled," and inscription on the back of photo from this source); Adelaide Still, Reminiscences, Mary Baker Eddy Library (hereafter, MBE Library), Boston; Gillian Gill, *Mary Baker Eddy*, Radcliffe Biography Series (Reading, MA: Perseus Books, 1998), p. 696n40 ("just sat there and smiled").

5. William E. Chandler to John W. Kelley and DeWitt Howe, November 9, 1910; DeWitt Howe to William E. Chandler, November 12, 1910: both in Chandler Papers, NHHS.

6. William E. Chandler, diary, December 4, 1910, Chandler Papers, NHHS; Gill, *Mary Baker Eddy*, p. 532 ("demonstrate the way over old age," "literally impelling her," "mentally murdered"); Calvin Frye, diary, MBE Library ("it was malicious animal magnetism").

7. *Manchester Union*, December 5, 1910.

8. Chandler and Streeter quoted in both Ibid. and *Boston Globe*, December 5, 1910.

9. *Concord Monitor*, December 5, 1910.

10. *Boston Globe*, December 8 and 9, 1910; Telegrams, George W. Baker to William E. Chandler, December 5, 1910, and William D. Chandler to William E. Chandler: both in Chandler Papers, NHHS.

11. William E. Chandler to H. R. Hopkins, December 10, 1910; Draft of telegram, William E. Chandler to John Kelley, December 11, 1910; John Kelley to William E. Chandler, December 12, 1910: all in Chandler Papers, NHHS.

12. Mary Baker G. Eddy, Copy of Wills and Codicils and Settlement Deeds, Powers of Attorney and Receipts of George W. Glover and Ebenezer J. Foster-Eddy, Probate Proceedings, Concord, New Hampshire, December 14, 1910, Henry M. Baker, Executor.

13. Frederick W. Peabody to William E. Chandler, December 15, 1910; Chandler, diary, December 12–20, 1910; William E. Chandler to John W. Kelley, December 16, 1910; William E. Chandler to DeWitt Howe, December 17, 1910: all in Chandler Papers, NHHS.

14. William E. Chandler to John W. Kelley and DeWitt Howe, December 19, 1910; William E. Chandler to George Glover, December 19, 21, and 23, 1910; William E. Chandler to Mary Glover, December 22, 1910: all in Chandler Papers, NHHS.

15. *New York World*, December 25, 1910; *Concord Monitor*, January 12, 1911; *New York World*, January 13, 1911; *New York Times*, January 13, 1911; William E. Chandler to DeWitt C. Howe, January 6, 1911. Chandler Papers, NHHS. Chandler's letters to and from Taylor are also quoted, in full, in the January 12, 1911, issue of the *Concord Monitor*. The quotations from laws of Massachusetts and New Hampshire appeared in the newspapers cited above.

16. William E. Chandler to George Glover, January 8 and January 14, 1911, in Chandler Papers, NHHS; *New York World*, January 13, 1911; *Concord Monitor*, January 12 and 13, 1911; *Concord Monitor*, January 16, 1911.

17. William E. Chandler to DeWitt Howe, January 19, 1911; DeWitt Howe to William E. Chandler, January 20, 1911: both in Chandler Papers, NHHS.

18. Chandler, diary, February 1, 1911, Chandler Papers, NHHS; Margaret Long, ed., *The Journal of John D. Long* (Rindge, NH: Richard R. Smith, 1956), pp.vi-ix; William E. Chandler to John D. Long, February 23, 1911; William E. Chandler to DeWitt Howe, March 1, 1911; William E. Chandler to John D. Long, March 3, 1911: all in Chandler Papers, NHHS.

19.*New York World*, February 12, 1911; *Watertown (NY) Daily Standard*, February 11, 1911; William E. Chandler to George Glover, February 17, 1911, Chandler Papers, NHHS.

20. *Boston Republican*, February 4, 1911; *Providence Evening Bulletin*, February 20, 1911.

21. William E. Chandler to John W. Kelley, March 1, 1911; William E. Chandler to George W. Glover, March 7, 1911: both in Chandler Papers, NHHS.

22. William E. Chandler to John W. Kelley, March 1, 1911; William E. Chandler, "To the Citizens of Concord," March 17, 1911, Chandler Papers, NHHS; *New York World*, March 20, 1911; *Concord Patriot*, March 21, 1911; *New York Tribune*, March 19, 1911. Chandler's open letter was published in all of the newspapers cited here.

23. The *Concord Monitor*, March 25, 1911, contains the full amended bill, in "State of New Hampshire, Merrimack County, Superior Court, In Equity, No. 5382. George M. Glover v. Henry M. Baker, Executor, et al. Amendment of the Plaintiff's Bill. (By Leave of the Court Filed March 25, 1911)"; *New York World*, March 24, 1911; William E. Chandler to John W. Kelley and DeWitt Howe, March 15, 1911.

24. George Glover to William E. Chandler, March 21, 1911; J. M. Hodgson to William E. Chandler, April 7, 1911; William E. Chandler to Andrew J. Glover, March 27, 1911; William E. Chandler to John D. Long, March 28 and 31, 1911; Robert P. Bass to William E. Chandler, April 21, 1911; Chandler, diary, November 4 and 5, 1911: all in Chandler Papers, NHHS.

25. William E. Chandler to James W. Remick, April 21, 1911; J. M. Hodgson to William E. Chandler, April 20, 1911: both in Chandler Papers, NHHS; reporter quoted in *Denver Post*, April 29, 1911; Chandler, diary, June 12, 1911, Chandler Papers, NHHS.

26. Remick cited in *Concord Monitor*, July 3 and September 8, 1911; William E. Chandler, "Memorandum for Mr. Howe to send to Chief Justice Wallace," n.d., Chandler Papers, NHHS.

27. *Concord Monitor*, September 8, 1911; *Boston Herald*, September 9, 1911; William E. Chandler to J. J. Spurgeon, Managing Editor, *New York World*, September 11, 1911; Florence D. White, Financial Manager, *New York World*, to William E. Chandler, September 20, 1911: both in Chandler Papers, NHHS; Eddy Will Litigation, Deposition of William E. Chandler, filed January 3, 1912, in Merrimack County Superior Court, Equity No. 5382, George W. Glover v. Henry M. Baker, Executor, et. al. Chandler's deposition began on September 7 and continued on September 8, 11, 15, 21, and 29 and on October 5, 1911.

28. *Concord Monitor*, November 14, 1911; Chandler, diary, November 11 through 17, 1911; William Chandler to Chief Justice Parsons, November 14, 1911, Chandler Papers, NHHS.

29. *Concord Monitor*, December 5, 1911; Glover v. Baker, Ex'r, & a., Supreme Court of New Hampshire, 76 N.H. 261, 81 A. 1081, 1911 N. H. Lexis 201, Lexis Nexis.

30. *Boston Globe,* December 11, 1911; *Concord Monitor,* December 11, 1911.

31. DeWitt Howe to William E. Chandler, January 23, 1912, Chandler Papers, NHHS; *Concord Monitor,* January 30, 1912 (Choate and Braley quoted in this source); *Portland (ME) Evening Express,* January 31, 1912; *Lawrence (MA) Telegram,* January 31, 1912.

32. Herbert Parker to William E. Chandler, February 6, 1912; William E. Chandler to Herbert Parker, February 1, 1912; William E. Chandler to John Slaght, February 9, 1912; Chandler, diary, February 16–19, 1912; William E. Chandler to Herbert Parker, February 17, 1912: all in Chandler Papers, NHHS; *Concord Monitor,* February 19, 1912.

33. Chandler, diary, January 10 and February 28, 1912; Memorandum, William E. Chandler to Robert P. Bass, February 29, 1912; William E. Chandler to John Slaght, March 2,1912; William E. Chandler to Robert L. Manning, March 7, 1912: all in Chandler Papers, NHHS; *Concord Monitor,* March 5 and 6, 1912.

34. *Concord Monitor,* March 13 and 14, 1912; Chandler, diary, March 14, 1912, Chandler Papers, NHHS.

35. *Concord Monitor,* March 14, 1912.

36. Chandler, diary, April 14–18, 1912, Chandler Papers, NHHS.

NOTES TO CHAPTER 14
A CHARITABLE TRUST

1. Glover v. Baker, Ex'r, & a., Supreme Court of New Hampshire, 76 N.H. 393, 83 A. 916, 1912 N.H. LEXIS 62, Lexis Nexis; *Concord Monitor,* May 7, 1912; *Concord Patriot,* May 7, 1912; *Boston Herald,* May 8, 1912.

2. Glover v. Baker, Ex'r, & a., Supreme Court of New Hampshire, 76 N.H. 393, 83 A. 916, 1912 N.H. LEXIS 62, pp. 16, 17, Nexis Lexis; *Concord Monitor,* May 7, 1912 ("issues of fraud and undue influence").

3. Herbert Parker to William E. Chandler, May 8, 1912; William E. Chandler to J. M. Hodgson, May 17, 1912; William E. Chandler to George Glover, May 10, 1912: all in William E. Chandler Papers (hereafter, Chandler Papers), New Hampshire Historical Society (hereafter, NHHS), Concord.

4. Frank Streeter to William E. Chandler, June 5, 1912; William E. Chandler to Frank Streeter, June 6, 1912: both in Chandler Papers, NHHS.

5. J. M. Hodgson to William E. Chandler, August 31, 1912; William E. Chandler, diary, October and November, 1912: both in Chandler Papers, NHHS.

6. *Manchester Union,* October 10, 1912.

7. Ibid.

8. *Concord Patriot*, October 10, 1912 (Chandler's telegram and Christian Science spokesman quoted in this source); William E. Chandler to John D. Long and Herbert Parker, October 9, 1912, Chandler Papers, NHHS.

9. J. M. Hodgson to William E. Chandler, October 17, 1912; William E. Chandler to John D. Long and Herbert Parker, November 18, 1912: both in Chandler Papers, NHHS.

10. Chandler, diary, October 19–22, 1912; Chandler to Mrs. Andrew J. Glover, September 7, 1914, and January 21, 1915; William E. Chandler to George W. Glover, December 18, 1912: all in Chandler Papers, NHHS.

11. William E. Chandler to Herbert Parker, January 20, 1913; William E. Chandler to J. M. Hodgson, January 20, 1913; William E. Chandler to James W. Remick, February 5, 1913; William E. Chandler to John Kelley, February 5, 1913; William E. Chandler to DeWitt Howe, February 5, 1913; John Slaght to William E. Chandler, February 1, 1913; William E. Chandler to George W. Glover, May 2, 1913: all in Chandler Papers, NHHS. *Manchester Union*, February 8, 1913, contains the full text of "Memo, January 16, 1913. Method Disposing of Litigation Relating to Mary Baker G. Eddy's Will and Estate," this being the agreement worked out between Parker and Streeter.

12. DeWitt Howe to William E. Chandler, February 7, 1913; DeWitt Howe to William E. Chandler, February 21, 1913; John W. Kelley to William E. Chandler, February 24, 1913; John Kelley to William E. Chandler, May 16, 1913; William E. Chandler to George W. Glover, May 2, 1913: all in Chandler Papers, NHHS. Howe soon ended his partnership with Nathaniel Martin, moved to Manchester, New Hampshire, and became one of the state's leading trial lawyers before dying at a young age in the 1920s.

13. Albert R. Hatch to William E. Chandler, December 2, 1913, Chandler Papers, NHHS.

14. Russell Bastedo, *The Portrait Gallery: Governors and Early Leaders of New Hampshire* (Concord, NH: Plaidswede Publishing, 2012), pp. 122–123; Henry Harrison Metcalf, ed., *Dedication of a Statue of General Franklin Pierce, Fourteenth President of the United States* (Concord: State of New Hampshire, 1914), p. 36; J. M. Hodgson to William E. Chandler, February 18, 1914, Chandler Papers, NHHS.

15. J. M. Hodgson to William E. Chandler, February 18, 1914; George W. Glover to William E. Chandler, March 26, 1914; William E. Chandler to Frank Streeter, March 28, 1914: all in Chandler Papers, NHHS; *New York World*, March 16, 1914; *Concord Monitor*, March 16, 1914; *Manchester Union*, March 27, 1914.

16. *Concord Patriot*, December 28, 1915.

17. J. M. Hodgson to William E. Chandler, December 18, 1911, Chandler Papers, NHHS.

18. J. M. Hodgson to William E. Chandler, February 16, 1916; William E. Chandler to E. J. Foster [Eddy], December 13, 1916; William E. Chandler to Henry R. Hopkins, December 13, 1916: all in Chandler Papers, NHHS.

19. William E. Chandler to E. C. Pickering, May 3, 1906, Chandler Papers, NHHS.

20. Margaret Long, ed., *The Journal of John D. Long* (Rindge, NH: Richard R. Smith, 1956), p. 286.

21. Revisionist historians in the 1960s tended to see the progressives as conservative. See Gabriel Kolko, *The Triumph of Conservatism* (New York: Free Press of Glencoe, 1963), and Robert Wiebe, *The Search for Order, 1877–1920* (New York: Hill and Wang, 1966). More recently, historians have viewed the progressive era as an extremely radical attempt to transform all of America into the progressives' image of a "middle class paradise." Still, this latter interpretation owes much to the recognition that progressives were largely conservative in their goals for society, desiring a return to a more disciplined, orderly, uniform nation. See Michael McGerr, *A Fierce Discontent: The Rise and Fall of the Progressive Movement in America* Oxford University Press, 2003), pp. 317–319 ("We know the old 'rights of personal competency,'" cited from this source).

22. Frank Streeter to William E. Chandler, January 9, 1917, Chandler Papers, NHHS.

23. William E. Chandler died on November 30, 1917, one month shy of his eighty-second birthday. During World War I, Frank Streeter was appalled at the rate of illiteracy among New Hampshire's young men and the fact that many were rejected for military service. He became a leading advocate of what became known as the Great School Law of 1919, which established statewide minimum educational standards, and he was named chairman of the first state board of education. Streeter died in December, 1922, at age sixty-nine. See Alec MacGillis, "General Frank Streeter," in *New Hampshire Century*, ed. Felice Belman and Mike Pride (Hanover, NH: University Press of New England), pp. 87, 89; Michael Meehan, ed., *Mrs. Eddy and the Late Suit in Equity* (Concord, NH: Michael Meehan, 1908), p. 319; Stephen Gottschalk, *Rolling Away the Stone: Mary Baker Eddy's Challenge to Materialism* (Bloomington: Indiana University Press, 2006), p. 41 ("If I had been a man").

PHOTO CREDITS

INDEX